A Virtuous Church

Catholic Theology, Ethics, and Liturgy for the 21st Century

R. KEVIN SEASOLTZ, O.S.B.

ORBIS BOOKS

Maryknoll, New York 10545

Copyright © 2012 by R. Kevin Seasoltz.

Published by Orbis Books, Maryknoll, New York 10545–0302.
Manufactured in the United States of America.
Manuscript editing and typesetting by Joan Weber Laflamme.

Translations of conciliar documents are taken from *Vatican II: The Conciliar and Post-conciliar Documents,* ed. Austin Flannery (Northport, NY: Costello 1992).

Queries regarding rights and permissions should be addressed to: Orbis Books, P.O. Box 302, Maryknoll, New York 10545–0302.

Library of Congress Cataloging-in-Publication Data

Seasoltz, R. Kevin.
   A virtuous church : Catholic theology, ethics, and liturgy for the 21st century / R. Kevin Seasoltz.
      p. cm.
   Includes bibliographical references (p.   ) and index.
   ISBN 978–1–57075–973–4
1. Church renewal—Catholic Church. 2. Christianity and culture. I. Title.
BX1746.S38 2012
261—dc23

2012003722

Contents

Introduction   **1**

1. Cultures and the Contemporary World   **5**
Primal Culture   9
African American Culture   11
Hispanic American Culture   14
Asian American Culture   15
Classical Culture   16
Modern or Scientific Culture   22
Postmodernism/Postmodernity   26

2. Current Trends and the Church   **35**
Globalization   35
Migration   44
Ecology   48
Migration and Relations with Other World Religions   51
    Confucianism   52
    Hinduism   53
    Buddhism   53
    Islam   54
Shift in the Center of Christianity from North to South   56
Christianity in the Twenty-First Century   59

3. The Bible and Christian Moral Life   **63**
The Old Testament and Morality   66
The New Testament and Morality   71

4. Moral Theology and Ethics: A Historical Survey   **85**
Patristic Period   85
The High Middle Ages   88
Origins of Modern Moral Theology   93
Catholic Moral Theology and Protestant Ethics: Early
    Distinctions   98
Moral Theology in the Seventeenth and Eighteenth Centuries   100
Moral Theology in the Nineteenth and Twentieth Centuries   101
Initiating Reform   104

5. A Virtuous Church   **113**
   Virtue Ethics   113
   Ecclesiology: Historical Background   114
      The Parish   138
      The Diocese   142
      Episcopal Conferences   145
      The Universal Church   145
   Some Tentative Conclusions   148

6. A Virtuous Liturgy and Sacramental Practice   **151**
   Models of the Church and Sacramental Implications   152
   Christology and Liturgy   153
   Trinitarian Communion Ecclesiology   156
   Worship in Spirit and Truth   157
   The Paschal Foundation of All Christian Life   160
   A Virtuous Life and the Sacraments   167
      Christian Initiation   168
      Confirmation   174
      Eucharist   177
      Ordained Priesthood   182
      Marriage   186
      Reconciliation   188
      Pastoral Care of the Sick: Rites of Anointing and Viaticum   191
   Other Liturgical and Worship Issues   193
   Ecclesial and Liturgical Impasse and the Response of Lament   195

Conclusion   **199**

Notes   **203**

Reference List   **231**

Index   **243**

Introduction

In 1988 Pope John Paul II sent a letter to the participants of a conference in Rome that was studying the relationship between evolution and religion. He asked this intriguing question: "Does an evolutionary perspective bring any light to bear upon theological anthropology, the meaning of the human person as the *imago Dei*, the problem of Christology—and even upon the development of doctrine itself?"[1] The pope went on to comment that such an exploration was badly needed to help people "struggling to integrate the worlds of science and religion in their own intellectual and spiritual lives." He acknowledged, however, that on the whole such dialogue had not been taken up by most theologians. Since that time serious Christian theologians have been involved in exploring the major challenges that evolution places on the traditional interpretation of church dogmas, especially those concerned with original sin, the image of God, God's purpose in creation, the incarnation, the church, and the church's worship, especially the Eucharist.[2] Nevertheless our various religious traditions have either not yet begun or are just beginning to take cognizance of the new cosmology and its implications for ecclesiology and liturgical studies.

The present book does not attempt to treat the complex doctrinal issues that have recently been raised by the dialogue with evolution. It is primarily concerned with some of the implications that contemporary understandings of the workings of the world have for cultural sensibilities, especially for the Christian churches, and in particular for the Roman Catholic Church. It concentrates on morality and its implications for ecclesiology and the practice of worship.

The first two chapters are foundational; they provide the context in which virtue morality, a virtuous church, and virtuous worship are understood and experienced today. Chapter 1 discusses the prevalent world cultures today. It has become clear that there is no such thing as a pure culture, because cultures today are hybrid, interacting with one another, constantly mixing and changing. The Christian churches today are generally multilingual and multicultural communities with the present center of vitality not in the northern hemisphere but in the South—in Latin America, Africa, and Asia, not in Europe and North America. For purposes of analysis, human cultures in the West are analyzed in terms of four broad categories: primal, classical, modern or scientific, and postmodern. These forms are constantly impinging upon and modifying one another. In the United States at the present time primal culture finds an important expression among African Americans, Latin Americans, and to a limited extent Asian American peoples. However, we need to remember that the term *primal* in no way should be equated with *primitive*, for these people are often quite sophisticated in terms of their life styles, their thought patterns, and their contributions to society in general.

Chapter 2 reflects on current trends and the life of the Christian churches. Various broad-ranging developments affect one another and at the same time elicit complex responses on the part of the Christian churches, including ethical and moral responses. They affect the identity of the churches and consequently deserve serious consideration in an ecclesiological context. These major trends include globalization; the migration of countless peoples throughout the world; the ecological crisis, which affects the whole planet; and the geographical shift in the center of Christianity from the North to the South. Attention is drawn to the economic, political, and cultural dimensions of globalization as well as the globalization of languages. The discussion concludes with a summary of the Roman Catholic contemporary teaching on globalization.

Certainly the majority of people on the planet today are quite mobile; they move from place to place, often from country to country. Much of this mobility is not voluntary but is forced upon people by poverty, by a search for better living and professional opportunities, and by trafficking for prostitution and forced labor. Immigration has raised very complex and serious problems for the Christian churches, since many of the people who migrate belong to other major world religions, including Confucianism, Hinduism, Buddhism, and Islam.

There is an enormous literature on the topic of ecology. Our planet's ecosystems are continuously assaulted by widespread and wasteful lifestyles; they are also seriously affected by the enormous growth in the planet's population and lavish consumption habits, above all those of the people living in the global North. The churches have often sought to address the concept of stewardship and the right of all people to a safe and healthy natural environment. These issues certainly have implications for our understanding of morality and our responsibility for one another on this planet.

The Christian churches generally espouse the teachings of the Bible as constituting basic norms for Christian living in the world and for confronting the complex cultural and social issues that affect the churches. Hence Chapter 3 seeks to summarize the basic teaching of both the Old and the New Testaments. It seeks to draw out the summary moral teaching in the Genesis accounts of creation, in the Exodus, and in the wisdom and the prophetic literature. It is significant that although the churches often have paid much attention to the Ten Commandments and the moral responsibility of people to observe them, it is the practice of the virtues that lies at the basis of Old Testament morality. We have a covenant relationship with God, not one that is primarily legal. In the New Testament it is the Letters of St. Paul and the Beatitudes as set out in the Gospels of Matthew and Luke that provide us with the basic moral teaching of Jesus and his early disciples. At the foundation of Christian morality is the person of Jesus, not a legal system.

Chapter 4 sets out the ups and downs of moral theology and ethics throughout history. In the patristic period the moral teaching of the church fathers is found in their homilies and commentaries on scripture, as well as their treatises dealing with specific issues, such as virginity. In the Middle Ages, extending from Gregory the Great to Bernard of Clairvaux, writers generally confined their teaching to the doctrines set out by the patristic writers. Hence, it was not a creative period in moral theology. A significant development in theological method occurred, however, with the development of the Scholastic method, which used dialectic as the principal tool in reflecting on and teaching theology. As a result there was a fruitful link between faith and reason.

The twelfth century was a period of significant moral awakening, for canon lawyers began to codify personal rights and procedures through ecclesiastical legislation. Writers were fascinated with the human person as the image of God. Theology became the work of faith relying on scripture and the church fathers, but also analyzing the material offered by philosophy and other sciences. Theology, however, became an almost exclusively academic pursuit.

In the thirteenth century the scientific character of morality was advanced by outstanding theologians, including Albert the Great and Thomas Aquinas. The virtues were at the center of Thomas's moral teaching. His theology was widely accepted because it responded effectively to pastoral needs, especially those of the mendicant orders of friars. A contrasting approach was taken by the Franciscan School, especially by Alexander Hales and Bonaventure. Thomas had stressed the primacy of the intellect; the Franciscans emphasized the primacy of charity and will over intellect.

In the fourteenth century the Thomistic tradition was challenged above all by William of Ockham, who denied the existence of universal concepts such as goodness and evil and affirmed the existence only of particulars, such as individual acts. William emphasized obligations rather than virtues.

In the fourteenth century moral theology was more and more carefully distinguished from the literature on spirituality and mysticism; it carefully developed a scientific and specialized vocabulary and generally abstracted from the concerns of daily life in the world. Francis de Sales attempted to achieve a balance among theology, pastoral concerns, and spirituality. He also emphasized that a deep spiritual life was available to all Christians, not simply to priests and religious.

The Protestant Reformers in the sixteenth century emphasized the Ten Commandments and sought to integrate the teachings of scripture. The Council of Trent sought to improve the quality of priestly training and encouraged the development of seminary courses in moral theology. Above all, the Society of Jesus took on pastoral responsibilities and sought to respond to contemporary issues, especially in the confessional. In the seventeenth century manuals of moral theology proliferated; special attention was given to the administration of the sacrament of penance.

In the seventeenth and eighteenth centuries moral theology tended to focus on the responsibility of conscience to make sound moral judgments. Alphonsus Liguori sought to develop a balanced moral theology equally removed from rigorism and laxism; he also tried to take into account the concrete circumstances of moral actions. In the nineteenth century moral theology began to undergo a positive renewal, especially through the efforts of theologians at Tübingen. In English-speaking countries manuals proliferated in the early twentieth century, especially for the use of confessors. A genuine reform, however, was initiated by the writings of Odo Lottin, Franz Tillman, and Gérard Gilleman; it reached a climax in the important work of Bernard Häring and the publication of *The*

Law of Christ in 1984. In a way his work stimulated the development of what has been called virtue morality, which systematically emphasizes the Christian virtues. Häring related the virtues to both church life and worship.

Chapter 5 initially seeks to clarify the meaning of virtue morality and then explores the implications of that approach for ecclesiology and the various structures that constitute the life and function of the Roman Catholic Church today. Special attention is given to the role of the parish, the diocese, episcopal conferences, the papacy, and the Roman curia, as well as to the tensions between the local and the universal churches. The final chapter, Chapter 6, discusses the celebration of the church's liturgy and the practice of the virtues that should characterize those celebrations. The book concludes with a short summary, a select bibliography, and an index.

1

Cultures and the Contemporary World

No matter where we live these days, it seems we live in a multicultural world in which various cultures impinge on one another, thus making it difficult for individuals and groups to internalize a secure sense of identity. Culture is one of the most complex concepts in the human language. Recent decades have witnessed a cosmic shift in the understanding of culture. Until the 1980s most anthropologists accepted the modern description of cultures as specific entities, frozen in time, and unreceptive to outside factors. It has become clear now that there is no such thing as a pure culture because cultures are hybrid, interacting with one another, constantly mixing, and changing. The static, classical understanding of *culture* has often been mirrored in the writings of theologians and ecclesiastical documents; they have applied the term to the intellectual, artistic, and spiritual achievements of a distinct people, implying that culture is a homogeneous and integrated whole. Among theologians and church leaders there is often little or no understanding of the fact that the institutional Catholic Church is itself predominantly Eurocentric. In fact, the church today is a multilingual and multicultural community with its present center of vitality and growth in the southern hemisphere—in Latin America, Africa, and Asia, not in Europe and North America.[1]

Culture has been defined in many other ways, however. A definition in the nineteenth century that was popular with anthropologists and is still held by non-specialists maintains that culture is a visible, comprehensible entity created by rational minds. Culture was thought of as a separate, impenetrable unit, passing from one generation to the next without change, resistant to outside influences, and accepted without internal dissent. That definition stressed observable phenomena, for example, food, dances, literature, and music. In a sense it froze culture and implicitly emphasized the normative role of European civilization and at the same time degraded non-European peoples. This claim to European superiority is implicit in Pope Benedict's efforts to restore the use of Latin, Gregorian chant, and European polyphony in Roman Catholic liturgy, an effort also implied in Vatican II's *Constitution on the Sacred Liturgy* (chap. VI). A simple definition set out by Bernard Lonergan in the 1970s asserts that *culture* is basically "a set of meanings and values informing a common way of life."[2]

A similar short definition was included in the *Constitution on the Church in the Modern World* by the Second Vatican Council in 1965: Culture consists of "all those things which go to the refining and developing of humanity's diverse mental and physical endowments" (no. 53). An empirical approach to understanding culture was evident in the work of various cultural anthropologists in the 1960s and 1970s. Culture was understood as a system of adaptation to the environment, as a cognitive system, a structural system, a symbolic system. This approach was reflected in the important work of Clifford Geertz, who defined culture as "an historically transmitted pattern of meanings embodied in symbols, a system of inherited conceptions expressed in symbolic forms by means of which men communicate, perpetuate, and develop their knowledge about and attitudes toward life."[3] Geertz insisted not only on the role of anthropologists in interpreting symbols, but on the right and need of people themselves to decipher the meaning of their symbols and rites. Geertz stressed that religion is an especially important symbol system.

In a critique of the symbolic anthropology reflected in the work of classic anthropologists, Roger Keesing maintained that the older approach must be enlarged. He held that "views of cultures as collective phenomena, of symbols and meaning as public and shared, need to be qualified by a view of knowledge as distributed and controlled." He notes that symbolic anthropologists have sometimes looked upon cultures as texts, but then he stresses that texts are usually differently read and differently constructed by diverse people.[4] When Keesing revisited the subject of various theories of culture in the 1980s and 1990s, he concluded that most theories seemed to present cultures as self-contained units. By contrast, he advocated a more theoretical approach in which the concept of culture as a bounded unit should give way to one that is more complex, involving "interpenetration, superimposition, and pastiche."[5] Keesing emphasized the permeability of cultural boundaries. What has become clear is that since the 1970s new directions have developed in the study of culture; they have critiqued and displaced earlier static notions and stress the fact that cultural boundaries are not merely territorial, that many people experience multiple belongings, and that there exists today a significant amount of cultural hybridity.[6] Kathryn Tanner has stressed that contemporary studies of culture have critiqued and displaced earlier static notions and have stressed the importance of cultural processes as dynamic, often fragmented, and at times conflictual.[7] Culture is not a specific entity but rather a process of becoming. Certainly cultural boundaries have been opened and made much more porous by the phenomena of migration and globalization. As a result, people often live in several cultures—one which is perhaps expressed primarily in domestic and religious relations, another in work, business, education, and economics.

In a sense cultures are webs of symbols and myths. Arbuckle defines a symbol as "any reality that by its very dynamism or power leads to . . . another deeper . . . reality through a sharing in the dynamism that the symbol itself offers."[8] Unlike mere signs, which are concerned with visible and quantifiable experience, symbols seek to draw us beyond what is observable to a transcendent level of knowing. It should be clear that symbols always possess meaning that words alone cannot capture. There is always a significant degree of subjectivity in our understanding and interpretations, implying the possibility of misinterpretation and ambiguity.

Myths are story symbols; mythologies are interconnected myths. A myth is a story or tradition that seeks to reveal in a symbolic or imaginative way a fundamental truth about human life in the world. The meaning cannot be contained in technical or rational statements; hence it is closer to poetry than to any other speech patterns.[9] Myths are stories that seek to make human lives in the past intelligible here and now, but the retelling of those stories with the hope of shedding light on the present is usually called narrative. In narratives, myths from the past are applied to what is significant for people today; in the process of retelling the myths are often enlarged, or altered, and if proved unhelpful, they are simply discarded. They are meant to provide people with a sense of order, identity, and meaning in the present. They are usually interesting because they enlighten or validate human life and people's struggles to find meaning.[10]

For communication to occur in religion, theology, and liturgy, the structure of symbols, myths, and rituals must express something that is meaningful to the culture of the people for whom they are intended; otherwise what is communicated is meaningless. For example, the typically western symbols of Jesus as king or judge make little or no sense in an Asian context, where symbols such as teacher of wisdom, healer, liberator, and obedient one would be much more appropriate.[11]

Catherine Bell's analysis of the polyphonic structure of ritual is also helpful in understanding the polyphonic character of most cultures today. Certainly most cultures involve the exercise of diverse bodily rituals, for the human body is the medium by which people construct and experience culture. Bell insists that neither bodies nor cultures are finished products whose identities are fixed. Both bodies and cultures are involved in processes; they are fluid, porous, subject to regular variation and change. They are complex networks of communication necessitating constant adaptation and fine tuning.[12] Many years ago the French phenomenologist Maurice Merleau-Ponty stressed the fact that human beings not only *have* bodies but *are* bodies; they not only *create* cultures but *inhabit* cultures that in turn *inhabit* human beings.[13]

Culture is in many ways a window through which persons and communities internalize meanings that are embodied in images and other symbols that enable people to relate cognitively, emotionally, and behaviorally to the world, and to communicate that appreciation and understanding to others. There is, however, usually enormous ambiguity in diverse cultural systems. The point that contemporary cultural anthropologists are making is that what is communicated is often not very clear to the communicator because of the complexity of what has been internalized. In other words, the cultural content is often derived from various cultural systems that impinge upon and affect one another. Nevertheless, culture tends to be a prism through which communities and individuals view the whole of their experience—domestic, political, social, and economic.[14] It is preserved and transmitted by institutions that are themselves in the process of change. A specific culture is often analyzed in terms of space and time, for those categories are often the fundamental perceptions in which people tend to cast their understanding of reality. In terms of space, culture provides people with a structure in which to live and function; in terms of time, it manifests an internal dynamic, a historical movement, and various stages of development.

Religion is certainly one of the primary cultural institutions for many people in the contemporary world, if by religion we mean that institution which seeks to disclose the deepest meaning of human experience or what is ultimate in life. Religion itself is generally communicated, shared, and transmitted through symbols, rituals, myths, stories, and metaphors rather than through doctrinal statements and creeds. Doctrinal statements are the result of reflection on the meaning of the symbols, myths, and rituals by those who have the background to engage in theological reflection. Theologians speak, then, of symbols, myths, metaphors, and rituals as constituting *theologia prima*. Doctrinal creeds and theological statements are usually the result of conscious reflection on the interpretation of the former; hence, they constitute what theologians describe as *theologia secunda*.[15]

It might be noted here that liturgical language, like all ritual language, is performative. Ritual language is not meant to be a bearer of dogmatic statements of our faith. The only dogmatic formula in the Roman Catholic Eucharist is the Nicene Creed, which was not composed originally for liturgical proclamation. The liturgy communicates to the gathered assembly the faith of the church, but it does so not in the language of systematic theology or speculative philosophy but in the language used for acclamations and narratives. The liturgy is not exposition but persuasion. As Ansgar Chupungco has noted, "In the prayers we, as it were, remind God about his divine deeds (anamnesis) in order to persuade God to renew them in our day (epiclesis). Even the homily is not meant to be a doctrinal treatise, but a persuasive speech addressed to the assembly to regard people, events, and things in the light of God's proclaimed word."[16]

In spite of some vociferous objections on the part of those who seek to maintain a strict separation between church and state, experience has clearly demonstrated that religion is usually not divorced from social, political, and economic aspects of human life; rather, it seeks to expose the deepest meaning of all those aspects of human existence.[17] In theological terms, it is through creation, through human bodiliness, language, texts, and other material institutions that divine revelation takes place. All meaning is personal, but meaning that has cultural implications is above all social. Interpreted at its deepest level, meaning is religious.

Cultures are mediated through institutions that have the task of sustaining and cultivating meaning and naming it so people can own it. More specifically, culture is mediated through both verbal and nonverbal symbols, including myths, rituals, stories, and metaphors. Unless the symbols are cultivated and sustained, social structures are apt to collapse; they enable the social system to produce and reproduce. Without them chaos results because meaning becomes exclusively personal and privatized.[18] Some cultural systems are obviously much stronger than others. Hence, they tend to overpower other cultures that might impinge upon them, so that eventually the weaker cultural system is partially assimilated or simply disappears.

One of the complex aspects of human life in the western world today is that we have not one dominant culture but rather many different cultures that are regularly impinging on one another. As Christopher Dawson noted in his various studies of western culture, the major reason that western culture was so creative in the past was that it regularly interacted with other cultures. Because it had a sure sense of its own identity, it was able to assimilate certain aspects of other cultures to itself, which resulted in an eventual enrichment rather than impoverishment of western culture.[19] At the present time migrating peoples rarely want to be assimilated into the culture of the receiving country; the image of the "melting pot" no longer prevails. They want to maintain as much of their native culture as possible while making only necessary adjustments to live peacefully and successfully in their new country. At the present time so-called western culture is itself so pluriform that diffusion rather than enrichment is often the case.

When cultural institutions interact with one another and try to relate and respond to historical changes in society, three things can happen: new symbols can be created; old symbols can be preserved and protected from contamination; or extant symbols can be transformed through inculturation. One of the major questions facing the Christian religion in the West today is whether it is the proper time to create new symbols, simply preserve the old, or transform those that already exist. What has become increasingly clear is that religious symbols cannot easily be isolated from the rest of human life. When political, social, educational, and economic institutions change, culture changes too. Since religion involves the interpretation of those institutions on the deepest level, religion and its symbolic expressions will be affected too. In the midst of such developments, it is imperative to discern which changes are creative and which are destructive of human life, and ultimately to discern which changes foster idolatry and which promote true love and worship of God and love of one another.[20]

For purposes of analysis, human culture in the West might be analyzed in terms of four broad cultural categories that are somewhat useful for understanding various cultural experiences and interpretations of life today: (1) primal culture; (2) classical culture; (3) modern or scientific culture; (4) postmodernism/postmodernity.[21] It is important to realize that all four categories of culture are to be found in the West today, sometimes existing side by side within Christian churches. It is especially important to acknowledge that they are continually impinging upon and modifying one another.

PRIMAL CULTURE

What can be described as the primal form of culture began perhaps one and a half million years ago when Homo sapiens developed. It continued to be the dominant form until perhaps 2000 BCE, but it is still found in various forms throughout the world today. The dominant culture of the Amerindian tribes in the United States and the Aborigines in Australia and Canada as well as the culture of many of the people of Africa and Central and South America would be described as predominantly primal, but there are variations among both the Amerindian tribes and the Aborigines. Certainly numerous aspects of primal culture are being brought to many countries in the western world today through widespread immigration, especially by those coming from countries in the southern hemisphere.

In primal culture the social form is tribal and the religious form is shamanistic. People coming out of primal culture tend to view space in terms of a circular web; everything in life is thought to be part of a single circular communion, but the web is vital rather than restrictive. It is permeated with religious mystery. It provides the context in which the divine is revealed; in fact, the divine is known primarily in and through creation. In primal culture the spiritual energy is animistic, so that the divine is revealed immanently, that is, in and through the regenerative cycles of nature. The divine then tends to be transparent in nature.[22]

This natural spirituality of immanence continues to exist in the western world as a powerful substratum carried by the folk traditions of many peasant people, including those coming from the Celtic tradition.[23] In Africa it is reflected in many of the dance steps that tend to thrust the body downward into the ground rather than upward, as is common in many dance steps in the West. The African steps symbolize the desire to be rooted in the earth, in creation, for the divine is believed to be not only transcendent in the heavens but immanent in all of creation.[24]

Primal culture tends to experience time in terms of a moving arrow, driving forward yet in the form of a circle or spiral. Time is rhythmic; it is circular and cyclical. Great emphasis is placed on the natural seasons, months, weeks, and days of the year.

Primal culture has tended to be polytheistic because spiritual energy surfaces in many places, resulting in a belief in many gods, although there is usually a hierarchy among the gods. Hence, primal culture has stressed the sky father, symbolic of divine transcendence, but above all the earth mother, symbolic of divine immanence. She has been linked especially to rivers, wells, caves, and fruit-bearing plants.

Early European evangelizers, following the Christian principle that grace builds on nature, carefully grounded the Christian faith in that primal spirituality. In the early years of Christianity there was considerable contact between Roman Christianity and the various mystery cults popular at the time. Christian rituals incorporated many of those cultural elements but reinterpreted them for Christian usage. As a result there were similarities between early Roman Christianity and the mystery religions manifested in common vocabulary and in initiation rites. British evangelizers, for example, were encouraged by the pope to retain the Druid shrines and to transform them into Christian centers.[25] Similarly, in Ireland the shrine of the goddess Brigit of Kildare was supposedly converted into a Christian monastery, though there is no direct contemporary evidence for this.[26]

Closer to our own day, the manifestation of the mother of God in Mexico known as Our Lady of Guadalupe took place at the site of a former shrine dedicated to an Indian earth goddess named Tonantsin, which means Beloved Earth Mother. In the apparition Mary wore the robes of Tonantsin. Thus, while not herself divine, Mary was a symbol of the feminine face of God. Until that mystical communication of the earth-mother symbol, many of the native Mexicans were not able to accept the gospel from their cruel Spanish oppressors, but with the apparition of Mary as Tonantsin, the earth mother who consoled her defeated children, Mexico was dramatically evangelized.[27]

The same phenomenon happened in Europe much earlier. Time and time again, the image of Mary and Jesus as mother and child was transposed from the pagan worship of the earth mother and her young child. The famous black madonnas of Europe suggest an African origin for this primal mother-goddess image.

In primal culture the dominant forms of communication are nonverbal gestures and rituals as well as speech. The development of speech, possibly discovered by women in the context of the mother-child relationship, represented a major stage in the development of primal culture, for it certainly facilitated communication and the sharing of nuanced meanings.

Aboriginal art is especially expressive of the religious character of primal culture.[28] Aboriginal religion, in its diverse forms, yields a rich reservoir of symbols that are deeply rooted in the consciousness of the people; the symbols are closely associated with myths that tell the story of people who have never lost contact with their ancestor spirits in the land and who see divine power living in and energizing every plant, animal, and human being. Their religion is vitalistic in that it is centered in the life force that circulates through everything. In the same way that their religious rites both express certain realities and actually bring them about or make them real for the practitioners, so their works of art are not merely objects to be looked at but have an active religious role in the lives of the people.

There are three contemporary cultures that are in many ways expressions of primal culture and that find important places in the United States at the present time: African American, Latin American, and Asian American cultures. They deserve some comment.

AFRICAN AMERICAN CULTURE

In the second half of the twentieth century, African American communities made considerable efforts to retrieve their roots and to rediscover the ritual and art forms characteristic of their rich traditions.[29] In terms of cosmology they discovered that they held some tenets in common with Native Americans. African peoples tend to perceive reality as one related whole rather than as separate compartments. There is no clear distinction between the sacred and the secular, for the divine always seems to penetrate all of creation. The rhythm of life is bound up in the cosmos—a harmonious world created and ordered by God. While many postmodern trains of thought are now reflecting the interrelatedness of disciplines in theology, black people have continuously reflected this method of theologizing. The African heritage is not a monolithic heritage, and some branches of that heritage were involved in the origins of Christian worship and played a major role in the development of worship patterns and their theological underpinnings. Certainly a number of the most important church fathers came from or ministered in Africa, including Clement of Alexandria, Origen, Tertullian, Cyprian, Dionysius, Athanasius, Augustine, and Cyril. Hence African primal worldviews that shaped foundational belief systems also often undergird African American forms of church life and worship. Worldviews usually determine and affect cultural symbols through which beliefs are expressed and transmitted.[30]

While there are variations in the understanding of the presence and activity of God in the world, creation is looked upon as the work of God. The cosmos is understood as a unit or body that is vibrant and sacred; it is at the foundation of religious values. Modalities of the sacred and of being are revealed above all through the natural world and cosmic rhythms. The harmonious structure of the cosmos is a means by which God's transcendence is remembered. The link with the divine is activated through symbols. For example, water symbolizes the origin and sustenance of life as well as death and rebirth. Contact with water signifies a reincorporation into creation and pre-creation.

African peoples respond to God's presence in various ways. Worship is generally expressed vocally and physically rather than silently through meditation or contemplation. Beliefs as well as ritual actions are related to the lived experience of the community. Hence, biblical readings are apt to speak directly to the concrete realities of ordinary people. Worship is more experiential rather than rationalistic. Its focus is on the communal sharing of reality rather than simply on the transmission of information. Since the stress is primarily on experience, common symbols, shaped by the community itself, are the major means of communication. Through nonverbal symbols the community expresses what might be difficult or impossible to verbalize. Symbols help free the mind of clutter so that clarity can be given to phenomena that might otherwise be incomprehensible. Music, movement, physical gestures, colors, shapes, and the gifts of nature common to the community are all very important symbols.

A composite of fundamental beliefs based on primal worldviews has emerged as African Americans make deliberate efforts to theologize from within the African American experience. Unlike western-oriented Christians, whose theology is regularly rooted in Greco-Roman concepts and culture, African and African American people tend to seek to know God personally rather than to know about God through doctrines and creeds. Everybody, including children, knows that God is, as if by instinct. Christian faith, for traditional Africans, does not mean that one has to assent to or recite written doctrines or creeds to prove that one knows about God. What matters is that one seeks to know God through God's revelational activity in one's own life and in the life of the community. Black spirituals are often expressed in the first person, but the individual person never exists apart from the community.

African peoples in America have expressed in a number of ways the importance of experiencing and knowing God in Jesus Christ. In gospel songs African Americans continue to document the importance of knowing God. The language of these songs reflects a reaching out through space and time as singers identity with the lived experience of others, so that characters, scenes, and events in the Bible become present and provide evidence of hope.[31]

One of the strongest forces in traditional African life that continues among African Americans is a deep sense of kinship or relatedness. From the perspective of primal worldviews God is the continuing source and sustenance of all that is good. Since God called forth the cosmos as an orderly, complete, and perfect entity, all creatures and the inhabited universe are sacred to God. Humanity is part of the created order, thus human beings are to exist in unity with one another and with all of creation. To be a human being is to be defined by a sense of belonging, for it is not enough to be a human being; one must participate in and demonstrate a sense of belonging to the community. Religion, understood as one with life, is not an isolated part of the community's life but permeates every facet of the community's existence. The sense of kinship is not limited to human relations. It involves all of nature, including animal and plant life. Kinship is the basis for an understanding of the community, including the living, the living-dead (the deceased who are alive in the memories of the family), and those yet unborn who are still in the loins of the living. The anticipated arrival of future generations yet unborn provides hope in the continuation of God's ongoing family. The deeply ingrained urge for expression is represented in art and art forms that evolved as functional adjuncts to African religious rites. The blending of music and rhythmical movements is a universal expression of the interrelatedness of living in community.[32]

The circle plays an important role in African life. For example, the daily meal is taken in a circle, signifying unity and equality. Once in the circle, age, social status, and gender are unimportant. Everyone shares in what is available in the circle. People dance in the form of a circle, expressing their common joys and concerns. Family, clan, and public meetings are also held in the form of a circle. The participants stand or sit in a circle to listen to stories. The chief gathers his advisers in a circle to listen to their advice. The ground plan of many traditional houses is also a circle; so is the basic design for Christian churches. Worshipers sit in a circle. Naturally, Protestant and evangelical churches tend to emphasize the pulpit; Catholic churches stress the importance of the altar, which is often circular. Churches are adorned with African artifacts. Especially prominent are images of the African Christ. The people have a special interest in the principal events in the life of Jesus, such as his birth, death, and resurrection, and have hope for the resurrection of those who have been incorporated into the body of Christ through baptism. Hence, Jesus is often viewed as the victor, the one who triumphs over the powers of evil, disease, fear, and even death itself. Africans and African American Christians are often quite aware of the various powers of evil in their lives and their environment. Jesus, as the perfect human being, suffered and died in order to complete his identification with human beings. The cross then is not a sign of shame and humiliation. What happened before Easter happens to all people; what happens after Easter happens only to the God-man and constitutes the uniqueness of the Christian gospel.[33]

It should be clear that as Africans have migrated to various countries in the northern hemisphere, their religious traditions have almost always been at least somewhat affected by the dominant secular cultures of the countries to which they migrate. Furthermore, in recent times many Muslims have migrated to the North, especially when they have come from war-torn countries such as Somalia. In their new countries they make very strong efforts to maintain their own distinctive religious identity and customs, such as scarfs for women and regular times for prayer and fasting.

HISPANIC AMERICAN CULTURE

People living in the United States whose native language is Spanish do not constitute a completely homogeneous population; however, they do tend to share many cultural elements, including a more or less common language, similar values, and some form of the Christian religion. Although the majority of these people were probably baptized as Catholics, many Protestant groups, especially storefront, evangelical, and Pentecostal sects, have in recent years made deep inroads into Latin-American Catholicism.

One of the most cherished values among all of these people is family life. Flowing out of that value are an appreciation for and love of children, keen devotion to the mother of the family, and deep reverence and compassion for the elderly. Children are shaped by the values of their elders, who are looked to as the transmitters of wisdom. Parents and godparents play an important role in the life of the children; in fact, godparents are often viewed as co-parents. Hospitality is also a distinctive characteristic of Hispanic people, manifested in a genuine concern not only for visitors but even for strangers. They look upon death as an awakening to real life; hence, they consider themselves as pilgrim people.

A basic and a more or less constant aspect of these Christians is a sense of the presence of God, who is found above all in the arms of the Virgin Mary. Strong emphasis is placed on the humanity of Jesus, particularly as a weak infant, as a suffering servant dying on the cross, or as an understanding person whose symbol is the image of the Sacred Heart. Mary is at the heart of Hispanic spirituality, though each Hispanic community tends to have its own particular devotion to Mary. Spirituality is expressed above all in popular devotion and in the use of symbols, gestures, and rituals.[34] It is also expressed in behavior and human attitudes. Prayer and hospitality, endurance and hope, commitment and forgiveness tend to be prominent characteristic traits. Christian faith is kept alive at home through religious practices in daily life, particularly during the principal seasons of the liturgical year, such as Advent and Lent. All celebrations are looked upon as communal events; most of them include prayer and sharing of food, as well as singing, processions, dancing, and reciting poetry or telling stories. The people rarely pray for themselves but pray regularly for others.[35]

Many Hispanic peoples in the United States have inherited their spirituality from indigenous people. Hence, they often cultivate the seeds of their religion as found in pre-Hispanic customs and ideas that sometimes seem to be less than Christian. Many of their practices, especially those belonging to Mexican

Americans, were brought to North America by sixteenth-century missionaries from Spain.

In the United States, Hispanic people have generally inherited church structures built in the baroque tradition. Altar screens are placed not only above the main altar but also at the side altars throughout the nave. Sculptures regularly dominate these altar screens, with the iconography of Mary and the saints set out to elicit a very direct, emotional response. Mary and the saints are not looked upon as transcendental beings but rather as intimate friends. The statues are often carefully dressed for special occasions. During Advent, processions are held in preparation for Christmas. Elaborate nativity scenes are given prominence during the Christmas season. During Lent, statues of the various saints associated with the passion of Christ, especially the Mother of Sorrows, Mary Magdalen, Veronica, and the apostles, are given special places of honor in the churches.[36]

ASIAN AMERICAN CULTURE

The cultures associated with Asian people have traditionally been very sophisticated. Although they do not have many of the characteristics associated with primal culture, it must be noted that neither do they have the characteristics usually associated with classical culture in the West. Like those in primal cultures, Asians tend to think of the world as a circle and think of time cyclically, whereas Westerners think of it linearly. Asians generally believe in constant change but believe things move back to some earlier state. They attend to a wide range of events and search for relationships among things. They likewise think they cannot understand the part without the whole, in contrast to Westerners who tend to live in a simpler, more deterministic world and who focus on salient objects or people instead of the larger picture.[37]

Asian spirituality is generally rooted in an experience of the sacred based on the vedic scriptures (1800–500 BCE) and encompasses several religious traditions—Hinduism, Buddhism, Confucianism, and Taoism. Many Christians today have incorporated into their own spirituality elements of Asian spirituality, for example, the practice of yoga.[38]

There is little doubt that Asians and Westerners are culturally quite different in many ways. Since the Second World War, but above all during the latter part of the twentieth century, numerous Asians and Pacific Islanders migrated to various western countries. They brought with them distinctively Asian resources both for the way they live and how they reflect religiously on their experiences. These resources include memories of suffering and joy, despair and hope, hatred and love, oppression and freedom. These accounts are not found in official books but are simply kept alive in the dangerous memories of Asian people.[39] If they happen to be Christian, their faith is kept alive by their deep trust in God despite their countless struggles against oppression, especially in recent decades by Communist regimes.

Another source of their distinctive culture is the account of the lives that women have lived. Asian societies are predominantly patriarchal; as a result, women often experience oppression and poverty. Hence, women's stories currently have a dominant place in Asian theology; they provide a hermeneutical tool for interpreting the stories in the Bible.[40] The sacred texts and ethical and spiritual practices of Asian religions that have shaped the spirituality of Asian people thousands of years before the advent of Christianity to their lands continue in many ways to nourish the spirituality and practice of Asian immigrants today. Likewise they find a rich resource for their religious lives in Asian philosophy, understood as a whole way of life and being in the world. For example, the metaphysics of *yin* and *yang* have been pressed into service in an effort to explain the Christian understanding of Christology and trinitarian theology.[41]

Asian monastic traditions with their distinctive rituals, ascetic practices, and ethical commitments have likewise affected the cultural ambiance of many Asians who have migrated to western countries. Like the monks themselves, Asians do not sense any incongruity between a commitment to a deep spiritual life and involvement in social and political struggles.[42] Wherever they go, Asians tend to take with them an immense storehouse of symbols, rituals, stories, myths, songs, and dances. These images have regularly been expressed in sacred art and architecture and have been incorporated in Shinto and Buddhist temples. Shinto temples are often found in places of natural beauty or places with an atmosphere of mystery or grandeur about them. Most are found within a garden or in the midst of trees. A clear boundary separates the shrine from the secular environment. When they have migrated to western countries, Asian devotees of the Shinto religion regularly have incorporated images of their traditional gods into their homes. Buddhist temples are found throughout India and Asia. The temple is the primary Buddhist sanctuary and is often attached to a monastery where monks meditate and pursue self-enlightenment. When economically possible, Asian Buddhists who migrate to the West often build a temple that in turn attracts Westerners who have converted to Buddhism. Where there are large numbers of Asians who are Christian, they have often tried to incorporate into their worship spaces and their homes Christian art executed in an Asian style.[43]

CLASSICAL CULTURE

From about 3000 BCE and the development of the ancient Greco-Roman world, the classical form of human culture emerged and developed.[44] Identified with "civilization," this classical form began to gather people into the large structures of empires.[45] This imperial form began probably first in Africa, then in Asia, later in Europe, and still later in the Americas. Monotheism began to displace polytheism. In stressing that God is one, classical culture should have stressed at the same time the unity of life; however, it tended to emphasize the transcendence of the divine, symbolized by the primal sky father, and to neglect the immanence of God, symbolized by the primal earth mother. In fact, the latter image was frequently suppressed in classical culture. It likewise emphasized the primal image of the divine as light but suppressed the image of the divine as nurturing darkness. Darkness, like woman, became a symbol of evil. The end result was often the exaltation of the divine and the denigration of the human.

In classical culture the innovative means of communication was writing, invented by people after the metalurgical revolution that created tools and weapons necessary for imperial civilization based on tribal conquest and large-scale production. The use of writing instruments enabled treaties to be enacted across wider tribal confederations, censuses to be taken of large populations, and records to be kept of sacred traditions. With these records organizational structures became possible on an imperial scale.

Enormous religious organizational structures also became possible, generating what we know today as world religions of the book. With handwritten texts, religious traditions and teachings could be standardized over vast geographical areas, even gathering large numbers of tribes into monotheistic belief systems. Leadership in religion belonged no longer to nature-based shamans but rather to temple-based priests and later to cloister-based monks, who carefully copied and interpreted the written word and adorned the pages with beautiful illuminations. These priests and monks were often the only educated people who had the skills of writing and reading. To some extent Judaism and to a great extent Christianity, both religions of the Bible, a holy book, were historically rooted in classical culture, though they were also influenced by various aspects of primal culture. In fact, both have deeper origins in oral traditions of speech and both emerged in many ways as prophetic, marginal, countercultural forces to the imperial civilization.

Classical culture maintained that there is but one normative culture whose values and meanings are universal in claim and scope. It affirmed an abstract ideal that is unchanging; it was preoccupied with universals rather than particulars. As it developed in the West, it was rooted in a dualistic philosophy structured especially according to Aristotelian logic. Likewise, it issued laws that were thought to be universally applicable and truths that were considered eternal. The circumstances of time and space, so important in primal culture, were merely accidental in a classical framework. Human nature itself was thought to be a universal concept denoting an unchanging reality.

Although classical culture destroyed the circle and the web, it did introduce a sense of creative responsibility into the human race. In the biblical tradition men and women were to cultivate the earth and make it productive. In primal culture human beings were simply expected to commune with and stand in awe of the divine mystery in creation. Classical culture allowed human beings to become involved in the ongoing process of creation or in its transformation. The overall goal, however, was to rise above the cycle of nature and the web of human life, to break out of the horizontal circle of time and to rise above the normal structures of society. Historically, the result was the replacement of the web with a pyramid. Those at the top of the pyramid were thought to be freed from temporal and spatial concerns so they could transcend the material world. Classical spirituality stressed transcendence, but the experience was generally reserved to an elite group of people who contemplated and communed with the divine mystery beyond the material world. Historically, the result was the development of two classes in society, the aristocracy or higher class, and the peasantry or lower class.

Christianity developed against this background of early Roman and Greek classical culture, but it developed its own distinctive interpretation of reality. Early Christian theologians simply discoursed on what they thought was the given character of reality, and once Aristotelian philosophy was available in Latin translation theologians articulated their reflections as clearly as possible in what became known as the Scholastic method. Eventually liturgy came to be looked upon as the uniform worship of God; it reflected the unchanging character of both God and creatures. As a complex of symbols and rituals, the liturgy was in a special way a cultural expression of the life of the church; it also manifested an understanding of the church as a pyramidally structured society. Increasingly it reflected an institutional model of the church and a descending model of Christology whereby the divine Logos came down from on high to take on a human nature; he redeemed humanity from its sinfulness by his death on the cross and then rose from the dead to take his place with the Father at the right hand of God on high. The permanence and uniformity of the liturgy were eventually expressed by Latin as a common language;[46] its unchanging character was ensured by well-defined, universally applicable rubrics that became increasingly uniform as cultural controls, such as a strong, authoritarian papacy and the accessibility of printed books, became available.

As Christianity aligned itself to the classical model of Roman imperial culture, monasticism in its eremitic and cenobitic forms emerged as prophetic counter-points. As the Roman imperialist structure collapsed, patriarchal monasticism developed and preserved the classical tradition. Indeed, in the post-imperial period monasteries became the central institutions for producing written documents. Monasticism thus carried the classical tradition after the imperial structure collapsed. Later in the thirteenth century religious life took on a mendicant form, especially among the Dominicans and Franciscans. The friars constituted a transitional stage between the classical handwritten forms and the modern print-based apostolic forms of religious life and spirituality.

Classical culture did not succeed in entirely repressing primal culture in the church. It continued to find some expression in the sacramental rites, especially the rites of initiation and passage, in the liturgical year, and in the liturgy of the hours, which relied on symbols rooted in creation and in the human life cycle. Furthermore, monasticism, particularly in its Benedictine and Cistercian forms, continued to stay close to the earth and to maintain a sense of stewardship over creation. Although the classical tradition more or less suppressed the image of darkness as a bearer of the divine by unambiguously asserting that God is light, mystics surfaced within the classical tradition who retrieved the image of darkness as a path to the divine that cannot be captured or confined in any way.

A critical turning point in the history of western culture occurred in the thirteenth century, sometimes referred to as the greatest of centuries. There is no doubt that extraordinary achievements were accomplished in that era, especially in the areas of architecture, sculpture, and stained glass. The university might be cited as a condensed symbol of major changes that took place in that century. As a cultural institution the university had no counterpart in the ancient world or in the earlier Middle Ages. The central intellectual problems of the thirteenth century began to be debated within the faculty of theology, where Greek philosophy, especially in its Aristotelian form, confronted the Bible. In other words, the confrontation was between reason and divine revelation, or the achievements of human culture and transcendence. Another cultural development that affected the theological faculty was the ongoing movement in the western world from an oral to a literate culture. The thirteenth century probably witnessed the most significant advances in that direction.

In the thirteenth century theology moved out of the monasteries and cathedrals into the classrooms. Until the development of the universities it had existed primarily in a liturgical context. In the university it became professedly academic and scientific. The Bible shifted from being a book of prayer and holy reading to a data base, a source of concrete information about the sacred with which one could confront the natural theology of the Greek philosophers, especially Aristotle. One has only to read the sermons of Augustine in the fifth century or those of Bernard, the twelfth-century Cistercian, to grasp the difference in style and content from thirteenth-century treatises. Both Augustine and Bernard were theologians, but they practiced their discipline quite differently from the Scholastics of the thirteenth and following centuries. Both were influenced by the power of the spoken word. They usually began their sermons by quoting a text from scripture, but as they developed their reflections on the biblical texts, their discourse is distinguished by the use of mnemonic devices and other traits characteristic of oral cultures. Their sentences are marked by a conscious use of rhythm; their style is closely related to music and consequently appeals to human emotions. Their sermons speak not only to the mind but also and above all to the heart.[47]

Nothing was more characteristic of the Scholastics, the university professors of the thirteenth century, than their penchant for definition, argumentation, and precise conclusions. They usually opted for a literal interpretation of the Bible rather than an allegorical or poetic interpretation. Likewise, under their direction, doctrine underwent a significant redefinition; it came to be abstract propositions to which one was obliged to give intellectual assent. As a result, the affective dimension of theology, so characteristic of the church fathers, was undercut.[48]

The Scholastics were responsible for what might be called the doctrinalization of Christianity. Faith, instead of involving the Christian in a whole way of life, became more or less equated with intellectual assent to propositions. Grace, instead of being the presence and power of God in human hearts and communities through the power of the Holy Spirit, became an abstract power that enlightened one's intellect and fortified one's will so that a person believed the right doctrines, worshiped the correct way, and lived a moral life in accord with prescribed laws. This resulted in a subtle shift in Christian priorities as proofs marginalized affections, as analysis displaced poetry, as mind took precedence over heart, and as religious language changed from communication charged with affective and aesthetic overtones to a language dominated by critical analysis and rigorous argumentation. These significant developments led the institutional church in many areas to assign secondary importance to the emotional life of Christians and consequently to the role of art and architecture in developing the faith life of individuals and communities. In a sense, the artistic and affective dimensions of Christianity were left to those humble lay folk who could not get seriously engaged in the pursuits of intellectual Christianity. Nevertheless, classical culture was expressed in extraordinary achievements in architecture, sculpture, and painting, all analyzed, appreciated, and promoted down to the present time in what came to be described as Romanesque and Gothic. Scattered throughout Europe these works manifested the power and majesty of God revealed above all as a transcendent reality.[49]

In Christianity, the dualistic structure of classical culture (spirit and matter and the superiority of spirit over matter) was expressed by clear distinctions between clerics and religious, who constituted the higher class of spiritual beings, and lay men and women, who constituted the lower class. Class consciousness was given a strong theological foundation in the late Middle Ages with the development of the so-called state of perfection, which consisted of a formal commitment to a life of chaste celibacy, poverty, and obedience. Through celibacy, professed religious and clerics were thought to be freed from the biological aspects of the life cycle; through a commitment to simplicity of life, they were thought to be freed from material concerns; and through obedience they were thought to be freed from self-will and immersion in secular affairs. By removing themselves from the secular cares of life, those in the state of perfection were thought to be free to contemplate the divine. This all gave rise to the development of an elitist spirituality available to clergy and religious but usually not available to lay people. Obviously what was considered ideal in regard to these commitments was certainly not always achieved in practice.

The lower class of lay men and women was forced to live according to the biological cycles of the secular world. They were expected to marry and beget children, attend to material cares, and fulfill their personal needs and desires. Lay men and women were immersed in the lower cycles of life here below from which they could be liberated only by death. For many, life was simply one long, painful endurance test. Sanctity was identified with the transcendent experience of the higher class; the lives of the lower class were often spent in a valley of tears to be endured until death brought them the reward of eternal life.

In the Middle Ages the church began to think of itself as a perfect society, as a social and political entity superior to all other institutions but accountable to no one but God. This understanding of the church among Roman Catholics prevailed during the Council of Trent (1545–63) but came under pressure to redefine itself during the Enlightenment in the early eighteenth century and the various revolutions of the eighteenth and nineteenth centuries when powerful secular institutions refused to submit to the authority of the church. With the loss of the Papal States by 1870, the Catholic Church in fact had lost almost all of its civil authority but refused to share any of its spiritual power. It centralized its authority in the papacy and the Roman curia so that all major decisions and important activities were controlled by the pope and members of the Roman curia, with very limited authority delegated to local bishops. In a sense local bishops became mere "messenger boys" delivering Roman directives to the people in their dioceses; they usually exercised little initiative of their own, at least in important matters. The laity became mere clients of the various institutions governed and maintained by the pope, bishops, and other ordained clergy.

The Catholic Church adopted several major characteristics from classical culture, especially its monarchical and patriarchal structures of government. In the church's distinctive culture there has long been a fundamental tension between papal Rome and the local churches. Rome became increasingly the dominant partner in the relationship, so that local churches were often seen by Roman authorities as threats to Rome's survival; consequently, the powers of local churches were severely limited or removed. A local church was considered, not as a province of the universal church, but rather as the universal church in a particular place. Over time the church at Rome claimed that it was the universal church and other local churches were simply dependent on it. Rome increasingly dominated other local churches and prevented them from developing their legitimate autonomy. Rome often acted both theologically and administratively in an intimidating manner to the detriment of episcopal collegiality. Since the Protestant Reformation, Rome has increasingly sought to strengthen its supremacy over local churches.[50]

The Catholic Church has consistently adopted monarchical customs. Since the peace of Constantine in 313 CE, bishops have used the power symbols of royalty, for example, in dress and titles, and priests assumed power over lay people and downplayed their role as servants within the community of the baptized. Worship ceased to be centered in the home and moved into the basilicas and other church buildings. Aspects of the Roman legal system were emphasized, so that sin, instead of being a fracture of one's relationship with Christ, was looked upon as breaking a divine or ecclesiastical law. As Yves Congar has noted, "There existed an imperialism which tended to confuse unity and uniformity, to impose everywhere the Roman customs and rites, in a word, considering the universal church as a simple extension of the Church of Rome."[51]

Throughout the Middle Ages the subordination of episcopal government to papal control increased as a way to prevent lay involvement in church affairs; papal legates became more and more common in the European courts.[52] The title Vicar of Christ was applied exclusively to the pope, though earlier it had been used for abbots, kings, and bishops. The idea was that the pope alone represented Christ; the bishops were simply vicars of the apostles. Firm control was also extended to the liturgy. In the eleventh century Gregory VII demanded that dioceses in the West adopt the liturgical usages of Rome and strictly follow Roman liturgical laws.[53] After the Reformation, the Council of Trent gave the Roman curia exclusive jurisdiction over liturgical matters.[54]

In many ways the culture that was adopted by the church before the modern period was a culture of intimidation and control, though it would probably not have been perceived as such because that way of governing was simply taken for granted within the church. Prophetic people, for example, St. Bernard of

Clairvaux (d. 1153) and St. Francis of Assisi (d. 1226), challenged the church's imitation of the secular feudal and monarchical governmental structures and values but with very limited success. With the Enlightenment and the development of democratic governments throughout the western world, the church withdrew from dialogue with the world and developed a strong culture of protection. Its reaction to the rise of modernity was largely negative and defensive. The result was a divorce of secular culture from the church.[55] Its contempt for much in the world was reflected in the development of a non-historical orthodoxy and the assertion that we have not here a lasting city.[56] An alternative understanding of the church was proposed in the various documents of the Second Vatican Council, but that vision has yet to be implemented in most aspects of the church's life.

MODERN OR SCIENTIFIC CULTURE

The dualistic understanding of the universe—spirit and matter—began to collapse in the fourteenth century under the impetus of several cultural revolutions.[57] The first was the development of nominalism, a theory of knowledge that denied the reality of universal concepts and affirmed the existence only of particulars. Associated above all with William of Ockham (ca. 1298–1347), the theory challenged the contempt for matter that seemed to be implied in Platonic and Aristotelian philosophy and emphasized a return to rootedness in the earth.[58]

The second revolution was the Protestant Reformation with Martin Luther (1483–1546) as the focus. Above all, Luther undermined the pyramidal structure of both church and state. He emphasized the basic dignity and equality of all Christians through baptism and the freedom of human conscience.[59]

The third and most powerful revolution was the scientific discovery symbolized by the demonstration made by Galileo Galilei (1564–1642) that the earth moved around the sun. His experimentally rigorous and verifiable method of investigation lay at the heart of the seventeenth-century conflict between religion and science; it was science that was thought to put one in touch with what was real.[60] The development of empirical investigation dislodged the place of religion in the lives of many people. The Roman Catholic Inquisition's condemnation of Galileo and the church's efforts to curtail the scientific revolution only served to isolate the Roman Catholic Church from the dominant intellectual currents of the time.

What was in the seventeenth century primarily a movement among scientists developed in the eighteenth century into a broad cultural outlook that eventually affected either directly or indirectly much of western society. The scientific revolution begun by Galileo induced the industrial revolution in the middle of the eighteenth century and also spawned the economic revolution of laissez-faire capitalism inaugurated by Adam Smith in 1776.

In a sense modern culture eliminated the natural cycles as well as transcendence. The direction of human life was simply linear; the goals were production and progress. Compulsive work and competition tended to take over so that there was little or no time for human beings to renew themselves socially. The result was individualism, fragmentation, specialization, differentiation, and a loss of the sense of the whole of reality. Modern science has so stressed the parts of reality that people have lost a comprehensive sense of the whole. Religion is naturally dislodged because its focus is on the meaning of the whole of life at its deepest level.

The expression of modern culture was due in many ways to the development of printing, which revolutionized Europe. It enabled power to be taken from the landed aristocracy, who used handwriting as their means of communication. Power was assumed by the expanding urban bourgeoisie, who enthusiastically embraced print as truly congenial to their fragmented and individualistic cultural consciousness. Print supports individualism, both in religion and in society at large, because printed books are normally read alone. Handwritten documents usually required collective assemblies in which the texts were read aloud. When handwritten documents were the rule, people went to church or to monasteries to hear the Bible read aloud, but with the beginning of printing, individuals acquired their own bibles and devotional books. The Protestant Reformation was successful partly because of the print revolution, since Luther's Bible, which was printed in the vernacular, followed quickly on the heels of Gutenberg (b. ca. 1394–99; d. 1468).[61] Gutenberg invented movable type, thus facilitating the mass printing of books in a quick and efficient manner. As a result, scholarship became more and more an individual enterprise, for individual scholars were able to collect their own books and establish their own libraries. Individual scholarship also meant lay bourgeois scholarship, which eventually broke the aristocratic, clerical, and religious control of scientific information.[62]

Various cultural trends that developed in the sixteenth and seventeenth centuries flowered in the eighteenth century under the banner of the Enlightenment. In many ways it was a continuation of the scientific spirit initiated by Galileo. Its adherents distrusted all authority and tradition in matters of intellectual inquiry and believed that truth could be achieved only by reason, observation, and experiment. On the whole, however, they were more socially committed than many of their predecessors and sought to use their knowledge in the service of the humanitarian ideals of justice, tolerance, and the moral and material welfare of humanity. It is not surprising that the thinkers of the Enlightenment often came into conflict with the church. Some were atheists; the majority were probably deists.[63]

It is important to realize that as a result of the scientific revolution the scope of reality was increasingly circumscribed. The only things that were thought to be real were those that were natural; science alone could expose and analyze that reality. As a result, what previous generations had considered sacred and mysterious was reduced to fundamental instincts for power, pleasure, and survival. Human life, instead of being appreciated in terms of the varied and profound meanings that it has in the Bible, became mere biological life expressed by the beating of the heart and the urge for sexual pleasure, food, and drink.

Science certainly provided the tools for acquiring amazing insights into the structure of reality and for improving the living conditions for many people, but it was elevated by the rationalists into the tool for knowing all the truth worth knowing. The world was no longer open to the transcendent God. It was an enclosed web in which humanity was confined. The application of the scientific method to the natural sciences progressed rapidly in the nineteenth century; before long the same method was applied to other fields of human endeavor, including the new disciplines of anthropology, sociology, economics, and psychology. For many, science became the new religion. Human persons became objects determined by natural laws to be studied by scientists using the scientific method. They were not essentially different from animals and plants, simply more complex. It was in that context that Charles Darwin (1809–82) could set out his evolutionary vision of what human beings really are and could become through the mechanics of natural selection. It was logical then, in Herbert Marcuse's terms, to speak of "one-dimensional man."[64]

In spite of its efforts to protect itself from the modern world, the church became deeply affected by modernity's stress on rationality. The church encouraged a theology that was condensed into logical theological manuals used in seminaries and was far removed from the experience and feeling of ordinary people. Much of it was aimed at responding to the rational arguments of Protestants. Scripture was used in these texts to support and prove clear theological propositions. It was, however, a theology that did not equip seminarians and priests to confront the pastoral issues and problems in the modern world.[65]

Much of the contemporary western world still operates on the principles of the Enlightenment. The overriding interest is still in the scientific method, which is looked upon by many as the only way in which to make a better world. In the nineteenth century, however, Søren Kierkegaard posed significant questions about the human condition; so did the German romanticists. In the twentieth century the existentialists pondered the absurdity of life in a world turned in on itself. Worldwide catastrophes have convinced many people that the idols of science and technology have clay feet. It is significant that the two countries that were the most scientifically advanced, namely, Germany and the United States, perpetrated the most horrendous crimes that humanity has ever known—the attempted annihilation of the Jews and the dropping of the atomic bomb on innocent Japanese civilians. As a result of these developments a crisis of meaning developed in the modern world because the dream of liberation at the heart of the Enlightenment turned into the threat of the destruction of humanity as well as the whole world. In religious language the Enlightenment vision of the modern world implicitly rejected the divine in human life, but at times it ended up extolling the demonic. From an artistic point of view it should be noted that much modern music, literature, and art forms have celebrated the satanic in modern life. These art forms simply mirror back to humanity what much of western civilization has become.

Art following the Enlightenment degenerated in many instances into art simply for art's sake, and interest in art often functioned as a kind of irreligious religion for people living in a world where religion itself was a nebulous phenomenon exercising no clearly defined role. Because art often became so esoteric, people had to be initiated into its mysteries through lectures, catalogues, and courses in so-called art appreciation. But what appeared on the surface to be a crisis in the world of the arts was in fact a cultural crisis in western society, a spiritual crisis affecting all aspects of human society, including morality, economics, and technology. Alienation, loneliness, despair, and isolation have characterized many segments of the western world for quite a few decades. Since the Enlightenment, western culture has focused above all on the relationship of humankind to the natural world in order to master that world and to take advantage of the benefits it can offer. However, the constantly increasing ability of many people to control their environment and shape the conditions in which they live has been an important cause of change in both the outlook and the lifestyles of many in the western world. This confidence in wealth and material goods has been seriously curtailed because of the economic crises that have characterized life in most countries in the western world during the twenty-first century.

The extraordinary success of modern technology and the scientific method in the western world has induced people to concentrate on the satisfaction of their material needs and wants. This preoccupation with the material world, combined with the ruthlessness and impersonalism of modern industrial societies, has resulted in a vacuum of meaning in the lives of many individuals. They have not been able to find satisfaction for their deepest longings in the worldviews that are set out by the communications media, nor have they often been able to find the meaning they are searching for in traditional, organized religion. That might well account for the fact that thousands of people in the western world attend so-called seeker service churches.[66]

The Roman Catholic Church has sought to resist various aspects of the modern world with the claim that it is basically a secular world whose values are incompatible with the values of the church. To counteract those secular values the Roman Catholic Church has developed highly centralized structures that have in many ways isolated the church from the modern world. For example, the structure of the Roman curia dates from the sixteenth century and undoubtedly reflects the centralizing efforts of popes following the Reformation. It simply developed many of the predictable weaknesses of modern bureaucracies, such as resistance to change, lack of accountability to anyone but the pope, membership limited to those who thought and acted like others in the curia, and a tendency to think of its administrative decisions as somehow sharing in papal infallibility. This all had a most unfortunate effect on local church leadership. Bishops became simple servants of the papacy and the curia, so that their ability to lead the people in their dioceses creatively, especially in times of political and social crises, was severely limited. Apart from the papal ability to write encyclicals dealing with social issues, the bishops were paralyzed, unable to respond effectively to social challenges. Consequently, the remarkable principles that were set out in the social encyclicals of Pope Leo XIII and Pope Pius XI in the late nineteenth and early twentieth centuries remained much too broad and theoretical to shed much light on what was happening locally in the church. Local churches were ill prepared to deal with serious social developments, such as industrialization; secularism; the rise of

Nazism, Communism, and Fascism; and the various independence movements in colonial territories.[67]

It should be noted that the Roman Catholic Church consists of twenty-three churches *sui iuris*, which roughly means "autonomous" churches. The Latin Church and the twenty-two Eastern Catholic Churches each have their own hierarchy in communion with the bishop of Rome. The Eastern Catholic Churches have a common code of law that affects only the Eastern churches unless it is expressly stated otherwise.[68]

The leaders of the Eastern Catholic Churches regularly complain that they are subject to a sort of Roman imperialism that results in the imposition of Roman customs and laws in the East. For example, they maintain that Eastern churches in Europe, North America, and elsewhere should be permitted to ordain married priests, not only in the "historical" territories of those churches. Since the 1930s there has been a ban on the ordination of and the exercise of ministry by married priests outside the territories of the patriarchates and the "historically" Eastern regions. They also claim that the six patriarchs of the Eastern churches should have authority over their communities all around the world, not just in their "historical" territories. They hold firmly that Eastern patriarchs should automatically vote in papal elections and should take precedence over cardinals. They claim that these reforms and others are required if the identity, authority, and heritage of the twenty-two Eastern churches in communion with Rome are to be preserved.

POSTMODERNISM/POSTMODERNITY

Since the Enlightenment, especially in the second half of the twentieth century and above all in the northern hemisphere, rapid scientific advances concerning our understanding and manipulation of the natural world induced a pragmatic mentality in no way oriented toward supernatural causes. An increase in the standard of living of many people was coupled with an increase in the number of people in the world living in destitution. Hand in hand with these developments went the possibility of mass extermination of both the human race and the material world because of the production of nuclear weapons. Democracy emerged as the preferred form of government in many parts of the world; it was thought to give people an increase in personal freedom and the ability to run their own lives, but often they were disillusioned. Furthermore, the widespread increase in the level of education available to both men and women helped them to make independent judgments about the way they lived. This was accompanied by developments in technology and mass communication—radio, television, mobile phone, the Internet—all of which greatly increased the amount of information available to ordinary people. Often, however, the poor were deprived of or limited in their access to these advantages.

In recent decades intellectuals have questioned belief in the traditional understanding of God. The challenges of atheism have had major effects on the cultural landscape, especially in Europe.[69] For centuries Christianity had been a major cultural force so that in many ways a unified worldview prevailed; most individuals and their families were at least nominally Christian both by birth and by custom. The firmness of their religious convictions was rarely put to the test. In the past century, however, Christianity became a minor player on the world stage. With the awareness of other world religions, Christians realized they were in many ways a cultural minority. Today, the Christian churches have very limited influence in the public life of Europe and often in other parts of the northern hemisphere. Further, in recent years a virulent form of atheism has developed that coexists with an agnostic outlook which maintains a studied neutrality concerning the existence of a divine being. God is no longer needed by many people to fill the gaps in their understanding of life on this planet.

The twentieth century and the early years of this century saw the development of various phenomena that are generally subsumed under the headings of *postmodernity* and *postmodernism*. Any discussion of postmodern culture must grapple with the obscure terminology and various distinctions that appear in the literature, since there is no precise meaning attached to either of those terms.[70] Postmodernity is frequently understood as a distinct culture, often as one fashioned out of late capitalism and characterized by mass media, eclecticism, and the exaltation of the popular and the occasional. If one speaks simply of postmodern culture, one inevitably includes under that name a great variety of reactions and responses to the crisis of the modern western world. Modern culture, at least at its peak development, emphasized individual subjectivity, interiority, and personal autonomy. Postmodern culture, however, is more fully aware that the human person is a relational being existing with an orientation toward others and within a complex of traditions. In general, postmodern culture refers to a current philosophical, political, theological, and artistic climate that contrasts markedly with both classical and modern culture. It is usually associated with and reflected in diverse movements, such as those associated with feminism, racial equality, gay rights, ecological concerns, and even the peace movement. In general it refers to the cultural and social shifts that have developed since the 1930s and have gradually spread from the West to other parts of the world because of globalization.[71] It is said that Arnold Toynbee was one of the first to use the term *postmodern* in 1939 as he sought to describe the complex crisis that had begun to develop in Europe throughout the nineteenth century and had manifested itself more clearly after World War I.

Scholars sometimes distinguish between "hard" and "soft" postmodernism. Hard postmodernity affirms the demise of metaphysics and the end of all grand narratives as well as the reduction of all knowledge claims to various manifestations of power. Obviously, hard postmodernity is deadly for the Christian religion because it attacks all Christian truths as ideologies that simply control and oppress both people and other ideas. On the other hand, soft postmodernity recognizes that purely objective and completely accurate expressions of reality are impossible; that the realities of power, gender, and force cannot be ignored; that all ideas have a history; and that truths that are proclaimed must be put in their cultural and historical context. Properly understood, soft postmodernism obstructs the pretensions that proceed from absolutism as well as relativism. It must be noted, however, that the human grasp of truth is in a sense always relative to the absolute truth found in God.[72] In the 1960s post-modernism made its influence felt in the arts, especially architecture, and then began to influence literature, philosophy, and theology, so that by the 1980s it became a widespread characteristic of popular culture. In its early stages it was especially associated with the radical developments in architectural design that occurred in the second half of the twentieth century and continue in our own time. Architects such as Robert Venturi and Frank Gehry have used the term *postmodernism* to refer to a cultural style that posits itself against whatever might be considered simply modern. It is very self-consciously a counter movement. The international style of architecture that was manifested in much twentieth-century architecture came under severe criticism because it was characterized by an emphasis on functionalism, organic unity, and an absence of ornamentation; buildings appeared to be starkly rational and were often characterized as glass-and-steel boxes. There was often little concern for beauty and the human need for comfort.[73]

Robert Venturi was at the forefront of the movement away from modernism. His book, *Complexity and Contradiction in Architecture,* published in 1966, was fiercely critical of functional modernism.[74] He adapted Mies van der Rohe's widely known maxim "less is more" to "less is a bore." He was one of the most active campaigners against modern architecture and advocated a style that became known as postmodern. Above all, postmodernity in architecture posits itself against the abstract, purist characteristics of what has traditionally been called modern.[75] It celebrates multivalence by incorporating various historical styles, forms, techniques, and materials. The technical changes, however, have not been so much in the basic materials used in modern architecture, such as steel, glass, and concrete, as in the greater use of plastics for components as well as structures, resulting in sophisticated geometric forms and warped surfaces. By emphasizing pluriformity, postmodern architects have sought to show that behind the principle of organic unity and practical functionality, characteristic of modern architecture, buildings were in fact dehumanizing.[76] Widely recognized architects designing in the postmodern style include John Burgee, Michael Graves, Philip Johnson, Frank Gehry, Charles Moore, James Stirling, and Cesar Pelli.[77]

Postmodernism has also played an important role in the development of contemporary literature, music, and art. The making of any art form, however, is complex, perhaps especially in these times when there is no dominant philosophical foundation for what the contemporary world is all about. Likewise, creative people often do not have any clear philosophical or academic understanding of what they are actually about in their work; they tend to get their inspiration from conversation with other artists or from the media. Jean-François Lyotard envisioned the task of contemporary artists to be to challenge the role of the meta-narratives that were used to legitimate the work of modern artists. Hence, the function of postmodern art has been to criticize the bourgeois art establishment. It rejects the stylistic integrity and so-called purity of modernity and espouses multivalence and heterogeneity. It favors the technique of juxtaposition, which employs contradictory styles. Two especially popular techniques are collage, which brings together incompatible source materials, and bricolage, which reconfigures various traditional objects. The result is pastiche, which manifests itself in an eclectic mixture of disjointed elements, questioning the modern claim to objective reality and meaning.[78] Postmodern art rejects all master narratives and the authority of all styles of art, especially the modern style, which prevailed in the past. In many ways postmodern artists have allied themselves with popular culture viewed as anti-elitist, anti-hierarchical, and dissenting. Their goal has been to prevent people from feeling at home in the contemporary world, which is looked upon as conservative and disturbing.[79]

In reaction to the development of postmodern art, the 1980s saw the emergence of "critical postmodern" art, which concentrated on the dark side of the postmodern world.[80] That art has often been well crafted and seeks to communicate on a broad level. It takes a clear stand on the subjects that are portrayed, especially the cultural values that are so widely accepted but which are often both unjust and unhealthy. It takes ethical stands and implies that people should take action on social issues. It is not detached but seeks to communicate effectively to viewers.[81]

In theater there also has been a drive toward diversity and pluralism. Following Antonin Artaud's protest against the reign of classical art and his development of the "theater of cruelty," the postmodern theater presents transience rather than temporal permanence. Artaud advocated the abandonment of the distinction between actors and audience and called for free performance based on improvisation in light, color, movement, gesture, and space.[82] Underlying postmodern theater is the belief that life is simply an eclectic assemblage of disconnected and impermanent events and narratives.

In postmodern fiction, juxtaposition blurs the distinction between real and fictitious characters, the author and the fiction itself, and the author's voice and the fictional story; as a result, the distinction between reality and unreality is also blurred. The power of postmodernism to blur the distinction between the real and the fantastic or the historical and the fictional is probably best epitomized by what appears on the screen. For example, on television serious news is regularly interrupted by commercials that blur the boundaries between truth and fiction, between what is important and what is insignificant. Reality readily becomes virtual reality.[83]

Although the terms *postmodernity* and *postmodernism* were prominent in the literature on architecture and art, they also came to be used in philosophy, the social sciences, and theology, especially in the final third of the twentieth century. The accent was placed on the complexity of the contemporary world, due above all to the radical effects of the Enlightenment. Pluralism rather than sameness came to characterize much of life on this planet. Stanley Grenz notes that the postmodern ethos is characterized above all by pessimism, holism, communitarianism, and relativistic pluralism. It is pessimistic because it abandons the Enlightenment claim of inevitable progress and emphasizes the fragility of human existence. It is holistic because it rejects the modern stress on rationality and emphasizes the emotions and intuition. It is communitarian because it rejects modernity's stress on individualism and the search for the universal, the supra-cultural and timeless truth, and emphasizes the role of community in creating truth. It is relativistic and pluralistic because it claims that there are necessarily many different truths resulting from the existence of many different human communities.[84]

The "grand narratives" that brought social cohesion and identity to many people in various parts of the world have not only disappeared from the scene but have in fact been rejected by numerous scholars. Jean-François Lyotard maintained that grand narratives, such as Marxism and capitalism, which claimed to give an all-embracing explanation of existence, are no longer important because they simply failed to achieve what they proclaimed. There is not a real world about which one can construct a true view; there is only an ever-shifting social creation. Likewise, there is no absolute truth available to people but only a pluralistic view of knowledge. In place of meta-narratives are little narratives celebrating variety and differences; they make no claim to universal knowledge or understanding of the whole of existence. Lyotard asserted that people should entertain these little narratives as a way to live peacefully and as a protest against the authoritarianism of the grand narratives, often associated with religions of the world. His assertions about the grand narratives have ceased to be credible since there have been dramatic developments of new grand narratives, especially by religious fundamentalists and market fundamentalists. Nevertheless, little narratives have continued to rise, especially those developed by feminists and those who seek to emphasize ethnic consciousness and difference.[85]

Postmodernity and postmodernism stand for a very critical evaluation of the Enlightenment, accusing it of being a simplistic or naive confidence in the ability of human reason, a presumption of an ordered and uniform view of the world, and confidence in the inevitability of human progress. Of course, this negative criticism must be complemented by an assertion that the Enlightenment, and above all developments in science and technology, greatly improved the human condition in many ways and stimulated the development of many positive characteristics of life on this planet.

Postmodern scholars claim that metaphysics, foundations, and grand meta-narratives are groundless. French authors have often been at the center of postmodern reflection. The pre-1960s writing against the modern approach to philosophy by Georges Bataille and Jacques Lacan was further developed by Emmanuel Levinas, Jacques Derrida, and Julia Kristeva. Jacques Derrida coined the term *deconstruction* in the 1960s and, as we have noted, Jean-François Lyotard wrote extensively on the spirit of postmodernism and its impact on the human situation. Others who made significant contributions to this train of thought include Derrida's former students Jean-Luc Marion and Michel Foucault.[86]

Some contemporary philosophers have attempted to go back to the pre-Enlightenment era rather than simply engage in deconstruction. Alasdair MacIntyre's writings have emphasized the importance of a virtue approach to morality that prevailed before the Enlightenment, and Stanley Hauerwas engaged in an effort to retrieve the perennial truths of classical wisdom. Still others, such as Jürgen Habermas, rejected the pessimism of so many postmoderns and argued for a renewed effort to correct the Enlightenment project rather than reject it wholeheartedly. Paul Ricoeur, while acknowledging the contemporary need for a hermeneutics of suspicion, argued also for a complementary hermeneutics of recovery.[87]

It is paradoxical that while traditional western religious commitments and practices have been declining, there appears to be an ever-increasing hunger for spirituality in which individuals travel on their own distinctive journeys to find meaning. In other words, a religious commitment to a specific set of beliefs, code of behavior, and specific rituals, usually associated with particular religions, is no longer presumed to be either necessary or helpful. Many people feel that they can dispense with a coherent set of beliefs about God, themselves, and their world. This breakdown in religious certainties has usually been accompanied by a fragmentation of social consciousness. Spiritual individualism dominates the contemporary scene. There is no longer a spirit of optimism about the human ability to solve all the serious problems that confront people today.[88]

There seems little doubt that we live in a multicultural world and in fact live in multicultural countries. The term *subculture* has been introduced to refer to cultural patterns that characterize some segments of society, and it is often applied widely to such social groups as immigrant, ethnic, gender, and sexual groups. In such subcultures there seems to be a strong element of protest against the dominant culture. For example, in the United States prior to Vatican Council II the Catholic Church was well organized and so was a powerful subculture. The more Catholics were discriminated against, the more they developed their own symbols of identity, such as their own schools and hospitals as well as their own distinctive behavioral patterns. There are certainly ethnic groups that are clearly delineated in many countries today. They usually claim a common ancestry, shared history, and various social markers, such as skin color, language, and religion. In recent years the term *ethnic* has sometimes replaced the word *race*.[89] Multiculturalism has replaced the "melting pot" and programs of assimilation. It seeks to recognize personal rights and cultural identities of various minority groups and to endorse publicly the value of cultural diversity.[90]

A very hard question surfaces for the Catholic Church: Does the church respect and foster the qualities and talents of various races and nations, or does it seek to impose its traditional Eurocentric culture on the rest of the world? St. Paul strongly defended ethnic rights and the need for people to act for the common good at the Council of Jerusalem. In his visit to England and Scotland in September 2010, Pope Benedict affirmed the rights of conscience, the rights of religions, and the responsibility of politicians and governments to respect and foster those God-given rights. Unless there is dialogue on a wide scale about these basic human rights in the church, ecclesial government is apt to be looked upon and experienced as totalitarian. In theory, Rome has claimed to be open to the theological and cultural implications of inculturation, but in practice it has given in to restorationist tendencies. It has shown itself unwilling to critique its own Eurocentric and patriarchal culture. It does not seem to understand the practical and pastoral implications of a global and multicultural world in which the majority of Catholics are no longer of European origin and are increasingly a minority in most countries of the northern hemisphere.[91]

Philip Sheldrake posits five developments that have had a major effect on our life on this planet. First, he notes that our understanding of the universe has changed because of developments in cosmology and quantum physics. Science has gone beyond the Cartesian-Newtonian-Darwinian paradigm, but unlike Aristotelian physics, which dominated classical culture, postmodern physics, at least in some of its expressions, maintains that the universe is a creative unity; it is a mystical communion that continues to unfold creatively. The changes in the universe are thought to be not the result of shifting forces but are sometimes thought by religious people to be the result of a divine mind immanent in the universe. Human beings are thought to get in touch with that mind not primarily by going beyond or outside the universe but by going deeper and deeper within it. In postmodern culture the thrust is toward convergence. The great challenge facing both science and religion is not only to tap into the creative energies inherent in the world but also to address the need for redemption and deliverance from evil. Life must be seen as both a creative and redemptive process. It has become quite clear that the human race is no longer at the center of the universe.[92]

The second major development is that evolutionary theory is accepted by the majority of people in the West, but they sense that the evolution of the human race cannot be separated from the evolution of the rest of the universe. The third development is that psychology has become a highly respected science revealing a very complex inner world that often goes beyond simple comprehension by both individuals and their therapists. Fourth, major developments in economics, political science, sociology, and cultural anthropology have exposed the constantly fluctuating character of society as well as its fragility. Finally, major political events, such as wars, genocide, and revelations of torture have disillusioned many people in the West. An overall sense of insecurity, skepticism, and doubt characterizes much of the contemporary world.

There are, both in Rome and throughout the church, carefully orchestrated efforts to restore the negative attitude toward the world that prevailed in pre-Vatican II times. It is sometimes said that we live in a culture of death. Restorationism is an undefined but powerful movement within the church that seeks an uncritical reaffirmation and restoration of pre-Vatican II structures and attitudes in reaction to the theological and cultural upheavals resulting from the changes effected by Vatican II and in the postmodern world at large. Some forms of restorationism are fanatically aggressive, especially those pursued by Catholic fundamentalists. They are usually deeply concerned about the dangers of so-called secular humanism, which they think is undermining the religious heritage and purity of both the church and the various countries in the western hemisphere through liberals, media, government, and the leftists among theologians and ecclesiastical administrators. They often assume an elitist stance and presume a kind of supernatural authority and the right to pursue and intolerantly condemn all those who disagree with them, even bishops and especially theologians. They usually take a highly selective approach to the church's teaching.

Gerald Arbuckle has called for the development of "paramodern culture," which he sees as tentatively and hesitantly emerging, especially under the leadership of prophetic leaders. It is rooted in the life and writings of people like Joan Chittister, Gustavo Gutiérrez, Elisabeth Schüssler Fiorenza, Rosemary Radford Ruether, Mohandas Gandhi, Martin Luther King Jr., Nelson Mandela, Lech Walesa, Oscar Romero, Cory Aquino, Cesar Chavez, Mircea Eliade, and Raimon Panikkar. These prophets have taught respect for each person and his or her cultural identity, interdependence, collaboration, holistic health, imagination, spirituality, gender equality, accountability, reconciliation, and nonviolence. These qualities are all signals of transcendence in a world where violence is often presumed to be the normal means of change. Paramodern culture offers the church rich opportunities for inculturation but affirms its need to purify and transform its traditional mythology into a "new creation" (2 Cor 5:17). It must make serious efforts to shed all forms of triumphalism and incorporate patterns of simplicity of life that might edify the countless people in the world who struggle with intense poverty and marginalization. This should begin with the papal liturgies and the lifestyle of the members of the Roman curia and bishops throughout the world. In many parts of the world the church needs to come to grips with its patterns of evangelization; it must learn how to proclaim Jesus Christ and the power of the Holy Sprit in ways that are attractive to people without becoming a star that draws attention simply to itself. In pursuing nonviolence it must not simply be passive, submissive, or cowardly in opposing social, economic, and political forces that are in fact dehumanizing, but it must never adopt language that is injurious to any person's sense of self-worth and dignity. Various forms of violence might in fact produce some change in the world, but ultimately they will simply make the world more violent.[93]

2

Current Trends and the Church

Within a postmodern context there are significant, broad-ranging trends that affect one another and at the same time elicit a variety of complex responses, including responses of an ethical or moral nature. These major trends include globalization, the migration of countless people, the ecological crisis affecting the whole planet, and the major shift in the center of Christianity from the northern to the southern hemisphere. These trends certainly affect the identity and life of the church so they merit serious consideration in an ecclesiological context.

GLOBALIZATION

The complex phenomenon known as globalization is probably best considered as a multidimensional set of social processes involving economic, political, technological, cultural, religious, and ecological dimensions. It has elicited strong positive and negative reactions. In the contemporary literature it is often distinguished from globality, which signifies a social condition characterized by global economic, political, cultural, and environmental connections that flow beyond determined borders and boundaries.[1] Globalization itself suggests a dynamic process of change that results in either positive or negative developments. Scholars have discarded the former geographical categories that distinguished among local, national, regional, and global developments because all of these references tend to overlap and interpenetrate one another today. In fact, the most interesting place to study the global is often at the local level in cities such as New York, London, Tokyo, and Shanghai. Scholars often use the expression "global imaginary" to refer to the growing consciousness that people actually belong to a global community. In other words, it is important to recognize that this consciousness often surfaces on the national and local level. The parameters within which people imagine their lives are often very porous and unstable, because globalization is a quite uneven process, affecting various parts of the world to diverse degrees. Some scholars maintain that economic processes are at the core of globalization, while others privilege political, cultural, religious, or ideological developments. At any rate, it seems to be a mistake to reduce the cause of globalization to a single process.[2]

Despite different emphases among scholars, there is general agreement that globalization regularly leads to the creation of something new; it involves the multiplication of social connections and various activities that transgress traditional political, economic, cultural, and geographical lines. Hence, the phenomenon stretches and expands the experience of interdependence and intensifies social communication and mutual activity. These changes not only occur on an objective level but often have profound effects on human consciousness. Manfred Steger compresses these observations into a very short definition of globalization: "Globalization refers to the expansion and intensification of social relations and consciousness across world-time and world-space."[3]

The economic dimension of globalization. Economic globalization refers to the extensive development of economic relations across the globe as a result of technology and the enormous flow of capital that has stimulated trade in both services and goods. Huge transnational corporations, international economic institutions, and amazing trading systems have surfaced as major players in the current century's global economic order. These transnational corporations include General Motors, Walmart, Exxon-Mobil, and Mitsubishi; the international economic institutions include the International Monetary Fund, the World Bank, and the World Trade Organization. As a result of these powerful forces, the gap between the rich and poor countries has widened considerably. Those who promote free trade have been severely criticized by labor unions and environmental groups who maintain that the absence of social control mechanisms has resulted in a lowering of labor standards, severe ecological problems, and the growing indebtedness of the global South to the North.[4]

The political dimensions of globalization. Political globalization refers to an enlargement and strengthening of political interrelations across the globe.[5] These processes surface important political issues concerning the principle of state sovereignty, the increasing impact of various intergovernmental organizations, and the future shape of regional and global governance.

Modern nation-states have existed since the seventeenth century. These sovereign territorial states have been subject to no superior authority; hence, legislative rights, the settlement of disputes, and law enforcement have been in the hands of individual states. All recognized states have been considered equal before the law. Differences among states have usually been settled by force. However, as globalization progressed rapidly in the 1970s, the international conglomeration of separate states gave way to a global web of political interdependencies that challenged the claims of nation-states. The globalization process rendered almost powerless any political efforts to introduce restrictive policies affecting individual states, with the result that the world in many ways turned into a borderless world. Nevertheless governments have usually exercised strict immigration regulations as well as registration of peoples living within a certain boundary. Governments often seek to restrict the migration of peoples, especially those coming from the poor countries in the global South.[6]

Political globalization is perhaps most obvious in the development of supra-national structures and associations held together by common concerns and mutually agreed upon norms. These often informal structures, which are considered binding on the part of involved parties, bring together world power centers because of common interests. For example, global cities like New York, London, Tokyo, and Singapore appear to be more closely connected with one another than they are to various cities in their own countries. The European Union might be considered such an association. Others include the United

Nations, NATO, and the World Trade Organization. Some scholars predict that political globalization might well facilitate the development of democratic structures that will take over the rights and responsibilities of territorial units. Others, however, predict opposition to such a development because of intense cultural, political, and economic forces on territorial levels.[7]

The cultural dimension of globalization. Cultural globalization refers to the increase in the amount of cultural flow across the globe. As we have already seen, *culture* itself is a very broad term, often used to describe the sum total of the human experiences of a distinctive community. Because cultural interconnections have exploded in the last few decades, some commentators suggest that cultural interconnections are at the foundation of contemporary globalization. Stimulated by the Internet and other technological devices, the dominant cultural characteristics of our age, such as individualism, consumerism, and the drive for economic success, circulate much more easily than they did in earlier periods. Since images, ideas, and values circulate so rapidly from one place to another, they are often readily and uncritically accepted and consequently have an impact on the way people experience their everyday lives. Certainly transnational media corporations play a major role in the dissemination of popular culture. As a result there is a sharp rise in what might be called a homogenized popular culture that is underwritten by the western cultural moguls. This is perhaps reflected especially in the process whereby the principles of the fast-food restaurant dominate more and more aspects of life not only in the United States but also throughout the world. This phenomenon raises a number of serious problems. The generally low nutritional value of fast foods and their high fat content have been targeted as causes of serious health problems, such as diabetes, heart disease, cancer, and juvenile obesity. The impersonal and efficient operations of various food chains tend to eclipse culinary creativity and, above all, dehumanize the lives of those who work in such environments. The young and the poor are often targeted by such restaurants.[8]

Some commentators maintain that cultural diversity is not always suppressed by flow but often results in a constructive interaction between global and local characteristics. This process, called hybridization, is often visible not only in food but also in music, dance, film, fashion, and language. As a result there is scarcely any society in the world that expresses itself in its own self-contained and authentic culture.[9]

Needless to say, the extensive flow of culture is intensely generated and directed by media empires, such as Yahoo, Google, AOL/Time Warner, Microsoft, and Disney, with the result that cultural innovators of an earlier time, such as small radio stations, movie theaters, newspapers, and book publishers, have often disappeared because they have been incapable of competing with the media moguls. Even very poor people in impoverished countries of the world somehow often manage to have a television set. In Africa it is estimated that more than one-third of the people own a mobile phone, a device that has had a major effect on relations within families, businesses, and even governance.[10] Advertisement certainly plays an important role in this cultural flow by featuring various American celebrities. Much of this advertising makes its way into private homes through television. Even newscasts have been transformed at least partially into entertainment shows.[11]

The globalization of languages. In recent decades there has been a major shift in the patterns of language use. Some languages have increased in use while others have decreased or even disappeared. This is the result of homogenizing cultural forces. A few languages, especially English, Chinese, and Spanish, have grown in significance. It is estimated that more than 80 percent of the information posted on the Internet is in English. Likewise, almost half of the foreign students attending institutions of higher education are located in Anglo-American countries. These developments have resulted in a marked decrease in the number of spoken languages in the world.[12]

Ideologies of globalization: Market globalism. Market globalization wants to put in place free-market norms and neoliberal meanings. This is undoubtedly the dominant ideology today. In recent decades it has been disseminated across the globe by power elites that include corporate executives, managers of major transnational corporations, lobbyists working for large corporations, journalists writing for business newspapers and magazines, and intellectuals who are in favor of globalization regardless of the cost and the risks involved. Serving as the primary advocates of market globalization, these individuals saturate the media with idealized images of a consumerist, free-market planet. Naturally they portray globalization in a very positive light and see it as an indispensable mechanism for the realization of public good throughout the world. The popularization of their view is itself an important commodity that is advertised and promoted by numerous magazines, newspapers, and electronic media, such as *Business Week, The Economist, Forbes, The Wall Street Journal*, and the *Financial Times*.[13]

Justice globalism. Toward the end of the twentieth century negative criticism of market globalism began to attract more attention in the public domain as people became aware of the global disparities in wealth and well-being between the rich and the poor. Appeal was made for a more equitable relationship between the wealthy North and the poor South and for better protection of the environment and human rights, especially those of women and minorities. Justice globalists believe that a very different world is possible, but it must be based on a redistribution of wealth and power; hence, they emphasize the link between globalization and local welfare. They accuse the market globalists of global inequality, environmental catastrophes, high unemployment rates, and serious decline in the quality of life for many people. Above all, they seek to protect ordinary people from the ravages of injustice.[14]

After the collapse of the Soviet system in the 1990s, globalization has increasingly brought the various economies of the world into a single system. As a result the transnational companies regularly look to global markets for expansion that is impossible to achieve in the more independent markets of the West; they invariably lower the cost of their products by outsourcing the manufacture of their goods to countries that are poor but politically stable, especially those where there is a dictatorial regime. This means that increasingly people throughout the world use identical products, such as toiletries and fast food.

But in some countries people are beginning to realize that perhaps their own native products are better, tastier, and more healthful. Fair-trade organizations have sought to provide an alternative outlet for local products. The Fairtrade Foundation has been established to ensure a more just deal for marginalized and economically disadvantaged producers in the Third World.[15]

For a variety of reasons many people outside the world of economics and business do not look upon globalization as a positive development; organizations that are thought to promote the process are looked upon with contempt, especially the World Bank, the International Monetary Fund, and the World Trade Organization. For example, critics object to the operations of the World Bank because they claim that it makes strict conditions that promote its understanding of what is economically desirable, not the ideas of the country itself. The local people are never involved in the process.[16]

There are throughout the world numerous agencies that promote the concept of justice globalism. In recent times they have been able to gather considerable political strength. Women's groups especially are becoming well organized and are beginning to affect policy changes on both local and national levels and are forming transnational networks. Given the fact that women and children, especially those in the global South, suffer most from poverty and injustice, these groups are gaining political clout by developing concrete programs that affect political elections and challenge unjust structures, such as those that support unfair labor environments and unjust wages. They are challenging the global North where manufacturers, especially in the textile industry, secure products from the South that are produced in sweat shops and then transported to the North at excessively low prices.[17]

At least some of the poverty in the South and the suffering that accompanies it result from actions or lack of action on the part of national governments. For example, in Zimbabwe President Mugabe took a very long time to act in relation to land distribution and finally did so simply to enhance his popularity in the country; this actually precipitated a famine in southern Africa. Historians and economists have given serious attention to the history of famine and the extent to which it has often been the result of human action or lack of action or been in fact exacerbated by government or colonial rulers. They have generally concluded that most modern famines are due not simply to natural causes but to human irresponsibility.[18]

In India people starve to death not because there is no food in the country but because they have no legal right to the food that is available. Today the country produces all the food it needs; in fact, government stockpiles of wheat and rice compose about one-quarter of the entire world food stocks. But because of governmental corruption and bureaucratic inefficiency in making the food available to the poor, many people starve to death. In the meantime India exports one-third of the total rice exports in the world. At the same time the country spends millions of dollars on a space program while more than half of its people suffer from serious malnutrition.[19]

Poverty and starvation are often the result not of a lack of resources but of failure to distribute the resources efficiently. Distribution is not only a transport issue but is also bound up with the lack of infrastructure to facilitate proper distribution.[20]

Jihadist globalism. The ideology of jihadist globalism is exemplified by the tragic events of 9/11, when hijacked commercial airliners hit the World Trade Center in New York and the Pentagon Building in Washington DC, killing almost three thousand innocent people. The operation was planned and executed by al-Qaeda terrorists. This religiously based organization maintained that the western world not only failed to eliminate world poverty but also encouraged political instability. Jihadist globalism is a religious response to the materialist assault by the ungodly West on the rest of the world. Coming out of what they consider a pure form of Islam, its disciples seek to destroy all those alien influences that have been imposed on Muslim people.[21]

Jihadist globalism applies above all to those extremely violent strains of religion that convert the global imaginary into very concrete political agendas and terrorist tactics. The term also applies to those violent fundamentalists in the West who seek to transform the world into a Christian empire. Bin Laden understood the term *umma* as a single community of believers professing faith in the one and only God, but at the same time committed to destroying not only alien invaders but also corrupt Islamic elites in order to return power to the Muslim masses. His followers believe that the whole process of transformation must begin with a small group of dedicated volunteers willing to sacrifice their lives as martyrs to the holy cause of inspiring people to return to their basic religious responsibilities, not only in traditionally Islamic countries but wherever members of the *umma* long for the establishment of the reign of God on earth. Since at least one-third of the world's Muslim population lives in non-Islamic countries, the restoration of God's proper reign must be a global event. Hence, al-Qaeda established jihadist cells in various parts of the world. Its ideology has especially inspired Muslim youths to sacrifice their lives, above all those who have lived in the secularized environments of the West.[22]

Bin Laden's disciples know they are fighting an uphill battle against market globalism. Their focus is on the United States, which they accuse of trying to impose a western-style democracy and an Americanized form of culture on the whole world. In spite of its violent and chilling ideology, they see their vision as an alternative to both market globalism and justice globalism. In fact, they claim that they are unambiguously committed to the establishment of community in global terms.[23] However, others believe that they certainly have an idiosyncratic view of community.

It should be noted that there is also a mystical strain in Islam associated with the Sufis, who are usually dedicated to poverty, contemplation, and the renunciation of desires. They have asserted that Islam is the way to Allah, not a religion that is primarily committed to the conquest of infidel nations or to any forms of violence. They have taught the submission of the whole self to the will of Allah, and have sought to act in conformity with Allah who is compassionate and merciful. Their basic beliefs have been captured in the powerful poetry of Julaladdin Rumi, whose thirteenth-century writings are still very popular among spiritual searchers throughout the world.[24]

Roman Catholic teaching on globalization. Although the Catholic Church has not produced a comprehensive study on globalization, it does have a well-developed social teaching that provides fundamental principles on the topic. In *Globalization and Catholic Social Thought*, John A. Coleman, a Jesuit sociologist, offers eight principles that he maintains summarize the Roman Catholic teaching.[25] The first is a commitment to universal human rights. Created in the image of God, each person is unique and unrepeatable and can reveal something about God that no other person can. Human persons carry an inherent dignity regardless of social standing, ethnic background, or personal talents and characteristics. Governments and social systems have a responsibility to see that human rights are both respected and fulfilled. The Catholic Church has regularly supported international charters of human rights, including the United Nations Declaration on Human Rights.[26]

The second commitment is to the social nature of the human person. The Catholic Church's understanding is that human beings are by nature both personal and social. They are often described these days not as rational animals but rather as networks of relationships, since they achieve their full potential only in relation to others. This implies respect for families, communities, civic associations, cultures, and diverse religious institutes that uphold the dignity of both the human person and the social nature of persons.[27]

The third and one of the most important commitments is to the common good. The right to private property is a basic human right, but it is not unlimited, for behind the right to private property is the understanding that it must always be held in trust for those in need. The goods of the earth are destined for all human beings. Pope John Paul II emphasized this principle in his 1981 encyclical *Laborem Exercens* and again in 1987 in his encyclical *Sollicitudo Rei Socialis*. Personally this principle encourages people to fulfill their responsibility for charity and generosity with the goods they possess. Socially this principle supports efforts by governments and other agencies to work for a more equitable distribution of wealth and other goods of the world. This principle must be translated into action depending on local and cultural conditions. The universal destination of goods must be enforced by law so that greedy people will not simply take what they want to the detriment of others.[28]

The fourth principle is solidarity. Pope Paul VI used the term in his 1967 encyclical *Populorum progressio,* in which he appealed for a world founded on universal solidarity. Pope John Paul II called for solidarity involving a moral commitment to concern for the welfare of others that extends beyond what might be required by strict justice. In other words, the principle of solidarity affirms that membership in the human family means that all bear responsibility for one another. It requires a conversion of the heart before a reform of the social order can effectively take place. In his 2005 encyclical *Deus caritas est*, Pope Benedict used the term in that sense. However, as a principle, solidarity must also guide relationships among states, corporations, and other large-scale social organizations. The wealthy nations of the world need to feel an honest sense of responsibility for the poor nations and the strong nations for the weaker ones.

Coleman's fifth principle concerns a preferential option for the poor. This option has been a dominant theme in the social teaching of the Catholic Church since the late 1960s. The expression was used by Father Pedro Arrupe, the superior general of the Jesuits, in a letter to the Jesuits in Latin America in 1968; it was developed extensively by Father Gustavo Gutiérrez, O.P., in his very important publication, *A Theology of Liberation*, in 1973.[29] The meaning of the expression was articulated by the Catholic Bishops of Latin America at their meetings in Medellín and Pueblo and has been used frequently in magisterial statements by the Catholic Church. Pope Benedict in 2007 emphasized the fact that this option is implicit in the theology of the Incarnation which affirms that in Christ God became poor for us so as to enrich us by his poverty. There is no doubt that the poor in the world are especially susceptible to the effects of environmental irresponsibility because they often live in countries where cheap building materials and cheap labor are readily available. They regularly work in farming, fishing, and forestry, areas which frequently suffer environmental damage. The option for the poor implies wariness about proposed easy solutions to environmental issues because they can readily consolidate western privilege while consigning the poor to deeper levels of poverty.

Coleman's sixth principle deals with subsidiarity. The Catholic Church does not advocate the creation of heavy-handed bureaucracies, but teaches that decisions should be made at the lowest level in order to achieve the common good; higher authorities should get involved only when the lower levels cannot achieve their proper objectives. This means that national and international bodies should respect the legitimate autonomy of mediating institutions such as churches and voluntary associations; above all, subsidiarity means respect for the rights of families, especially the right to educate their children in accord with their religious convictions. The principle of subsidiarity opposes excessive centralization and any unjust involvement of the state in public affairs.[30]

Coleman's seventh principle involves the distinctively Catholic concept of justice, which is usually divided into three broad categories: commutative justice, which implies fulfilling the terms of contracts and other promises, on both a personal and social level; distributive justice, which ensures a basic equity in how both the burdens and the goods of society are distributed, and which also ensures that every person enjoys a basically equal moral and legal standing apart from differences in wealth, privilege, talent, and achievements; and social justice, which refers to the creation of the conditions in which the first two categories of justice can be realized and the common good identified and defended. According to Catholic teaching a just society is one in which these forms of justice are assured because they are required by human dignity.[31]

Coleman's eighth principle involves integral humanism. Catholic doctrine seeks to foster both material and spiritual freedom. In other words, it is concerned with the whole person. Economic concerns are simply part of a larger concern for social life, which necessarily includes culture, politics, the arts, and the environment. The whole cosmos is the stage on which the drama of human life is enacted. In his 2009 encyclical *Caritas in veritate*, Pope Benedict said that one of the church's most important contributions to human and cosmic development is its promotion of Christian humanism.[32]

Although Catholics might agree on Coleman's eight principles, they are often interpreted in conflicting ways. For example, there is a wide range of opinions about the pros and cons of global capitalism. Some authors favor extreme laissez-faire operations, while others justify extensive government intervention in human affairs. Nevertheless, few Catholics dispute that the church has a serious moral responsibility to address the causes of human suffering, such as war, disease, poverty, and social prejudice and exclusion. Probably the most common criticism of globalization is that it seriously widens the gap between the rich and poor in the world. There is also agreement in strong criticism of the common attempt to settle national differences through war, especially since most of those killed or wounded are noncombatants. These conflicts are regularly stoked by widespread commerce in weapons. It is estimated that about one trillion dollars is spent every year on weaponry, and the United States is responsible for almost half of these expenditures. The United States is the world's largest supplier of arms, many of which are sold to developing nations. Catholic leaders have been very vocal in their criticism of the global arms trade. In his 1995 encyclical *Evangelium vitae*, Pope John Paul refers to the practice as scandalous. In 2005 Pope Benedict expressed dismay at the continuing growth in military spending and the flourishing arms trade while political and judicial processes get bogged down in discussions and achieve no practical results.

Human trafficking is a pernicious violation of human rights, one that has increased as a result of globalization. Thousands of people are victims of trafficking each year. The great majority are women and most of them are involved in the sex trade. Others are kidnapped for manual labor or involuntarily used as couriers for the drug trade.

Affluent nations often seek to transfer wealth to the poor nations, but often the money ends up in the hands of corrupt politicians and business elites. Although corruption is primarily a problem for law enforcement and judicial officials, there is a basic need on the part of churches and other social institutions to form the consciences of the people.

The Internet, which is practically ubiquitous today, is both a primary symbol of globalization and one of its principal drivers, but it should be noted that there is a significant shift from personal computers as the means of accessing Internet content to multiple devices such as smartphones, tablets, and so forth. In spite of these developments there are still many poor areas in the world where there is no access to the Internet. However, it is suspected that low-cost computers will follow the path that has been set by the cell phone in many of these areas.

The Catholic Church is seriously engaged in the political and social debates about globalization and is aware of both its benefits and its problems. The major concern of the church is to see that globalization is at the service of human persons and communities. Catholicism is one of the oldest globalized institutions in the world; its own life is seriously affected by the developments of the interconnected culture produced by globalization.[33] As a result, there are tensions between the local churches and the universal church. There seems little doubt that the Catholic Church, beginning with the pope and the Roman curia, has placed its primary emphasis on the universal rather than the local. It is often asserted that the church has never been so centralized as it is at the present time. There is little sympathy for liturgical inculturation, and there is a strong effort to restore the use of Latin and Gregorian chant.

MIGRATION

The extent of migration in the contemporary world is inextricably connected with other global issues, especially poverty, human rights, and development.[34] One theory of migration distinguishes between push factors and pull factors. The former refer primarily to the motives for emigrating from one's country of origin; the latter refer to those factors that encourage migrants to move to a new country. Migrants are often entrepreneurial and dynamic members of society, but they are also often exploited and abused. Integration in their new country can be very difficult, and at the same time migration can deprive the country of origin of important skills.[35]

Scholars identify international migrants as those who remain outside their usual country for at least one year. At the present time it is estimated that there are about two hundred million international migrants worldwide. Obviously this has major social, economic, and political impact on countries throughout the world. The proportion of women among migrants has increased significantly in recent years due to the demand for foreign labor by women, especially in more developed countries. Women are wanted for work in healthcare, entertainment, and domestic services. Furthermore, in recent years various countries have extended the right of family reunion to immigrants; most often this involves women and children. In some countries large sections of the economy, for example agriculture, have become so dependent on migrant workers that the enterprise would collapse if the migrant workers were withdrawn. But migrants do not simply contribute to economic growth; their impact is keenly felt in the cultural and social aspects of their new country. At the present time the largest concentration of migrants exist in so-called global cities, such as London, New York, and Hong Kong.[36] Migration is sometimes mandatory in a contract of employment. Religious missionaries, employees of transnational corporations, and diplomats and other employees of state departments are by definition expected to work "overseas." They are usually referred to as expatriates; their employment and living conditions are typically equal to or better than those existing in the host country.

International migration creates complex problems. There is a close link between migration and security, especially after 9/11 and the attacks on Madrid and London. In destination countries there is fear about the presence of migrant individuals and communities, especially those with unfamiliar cultures from those parts of the world that have a reputation for violence and radicalism. Certainly these are legitimate concerns.[37]

Many migrants leave their native countries because of persecution or death threats. Some perish on their journey. Once they arrive in their country of destination, they may be exploited and abused. The victims of human trafficking are often enslaved, frequently in the sex industry. Domestic workers may suffer abuse at the hands of their employers. Many migrants and their families suffer discrimination and prejudice, often for many years after they have settled in their new country.[38]

Certainly international migration is an important aspect of globalization and has affected economic and social structures. Widespread unemployment affects many parts of the world, so many people migrate to find jobs. The communications revolution means that people easily become aware of employment opportunities as well as information about transportation. The desire to escape from destitution is undoubtedly the major cause of migration.

Another phenomenon referred to in the globalization literature is the major change in transportation, its availability, and its costs. Although transportation has made migration feasible for many people, it is still prohibitively expensive for the majority of the world's population; arrangements for illegal travel make it even more expensive. Many who seek to migrate face complex administrative obstacles in obtaining passports and visas.

In many cases migrants send home money as well as other commodities. For example, if and when they return home, they often bring with them important skills, experiences, and contacts developed in their country of destination. Nevertheless, there are serious difficulties with separation from families at home, sometimes for very extended periods of time. Sending money to one's loved ones cannot compensate for separation from spouse, children, or parents.

When there are high levels of unemployment in one's country of origin, migration can reduce the amount of competition for a limited number of jobs. However, it can also rob countries of their most entrepreneurial, best educated, brightest, and most skilled residents. The "brain drain" is reflected in the fact that some of the best scientists and scholars in various parts of Europe have migrated to the United States to work in universities where salaries are higher, research grants more readily available, and equipment more advanced. Perhaps especially troubling is the migration of health personnel—physicians and nurses—from sub-Saharan African countries. However, the migration of ordained Roman Catholic priests from Africa and other countries in the South has been welcomed and supported by the Roman Catholic Church in the United States and Europe because of the serious shortage of native clergy. This practice is paradoxical because often there is a more serious shortage of priests in the countries where these African priests originate.

A multi-billion dollar industry in human trafficking and smuggling has developed in response to the desire of people to migrate despite legal restrictions. Irregular migrants include people who enter a country without the proper authority, perhaps without going through a border control, by obtaining fraudulent documents, or being transported by migrant smugglers or human traffickers, and those who enter a country legally but then remain beyond proper limits, for example, by staying after their visa or work permit has expired, by engaging in a sham marriage or fake adoption process, or by posing fraudulently as students or self-employed workers.[39]

Human trafficking and migrant smuggling probably account for a relatively small number of irregular migrants throughout the world. Trafficking involves the recruitment, transportation, transfer, harboring, or reception of persons through threat, force, or other forms of coercion in order to elicit the consent of a person for the purpose of exploitation. The trafficking of women and sometimes children to work or in the sex trade is especially pernicious. Migrant smuggling involves potential migrants or members of their families who pay a smuggler to transport them illegally to a new country.

Human trafficking has very negative effects for those involved because the traffickers ruthlessly exploit the migrants, who are often paid low wages, live insecure lives, and often engage in degrading work from which they find it impossible to escape. Smugglers can charge the migrant thousands of dollars for transport that may be unsafe. At times the migrants are abandoned, even though they have paid the money; it is not uncommon for them to be abused in transit.

Eliciting much more sympathy than irregular migrants are refugees and asylum seekers. A refugee is a person who, based on a well-founded fear of being personally persecuted for reasons of race, religion, nationality, membership in a particular social group, or a particular political opinion, is living outside his or her country of nationality. Refugees also include people who are persecuted because of their sex or sexual orientation; women and homosexuals, for example, have regularly been persecuted under Taliban regimes. Some people flee their country of origin because of environmental threats such as tsunamis or earthquakes. However, there are more people who have fled from their homes but have been unable to leave their native countries; these people are usually referred to as internally displaced persons. In the past refugees sought shelter in both developed and developing countries. More recently, however, refugees are more likely to seek asylum in developed countries.

There are certainly some predatory political regimes in the world today that actively persecute parts of their native population. Examples are North Korea and China. Most refugees from these countries try to escape conflict rather than direct persecution. Most conflicts today are fought within states because of ethnic or religious differences. In these countries warfare is usually privatized in the sense that it is carried out not by professional armies but by militias. The victims are usually not combatants but innocent civilians. Many of these modern conflicts tend to simmer and recur. In some countries the unemployed, especially young men who are bored and aggressive, incite conflict and often perpetrate violence. These conflicts are often carried out with modern weapons, which can kill or terrorize people very quickly. Likewise, planting land mines leaves people with no choice but to seek escape.

Refugees are often located in camps that seek to protect the inhabitants and to provide assistance as well as education, especially for children. However, both physical and sexual abuse can easily occur in these camps. These establishments can have a deleterious effect on the local environment and can have a deep psychological impact on refugees who have to live in them for long periods.

Three solutions have been proposed for refugees. First is voluntary repatriation; in other words, refugees simply return home. However, people who have been mobile for many years do not necessarily know what to call "home." The second solution is local integration, or remaining permanently in the host country. However, host countries are often hostile to refugee populations because their sheer numbers mean competition for land and jobs and sometimes degrade the environment. The third solution is permanent resettlement in a third country. The United States, Canada, and Australia resettle most refugees.

An asylum seeker is a person who has asked for international protection, usually after arriving in the country of destination. There is increasing hesitation on the part of governments to welcome asylum seekers because of the negative comments by the media. They are threatening because they arrive without official authorization; they simply arrive at borders, often from very distant countries. In various countries policies have been introduced to reduce the number of asylum seekers and to ensure that those who do arrive have a legitimate claim for asylum. Restrictive visas have been introduced in many countries; airlines and other carriers check passports and visas carefully; body searches and scans are used. Access to welfare benefits and healthcare for asylum seekers has often been restricted. Many of those seeking asylum are rejected and sent back to their country of origin, while many others hide and remain in the country illegally. Restrictive policies have been challenged by asylum advocates and human rights organizations, especially by the Catholic Church in the United States, because many asylum seekers are honestly fleeing for their life and essential freedoms and are honestly seeking protection.[40]

A major concern in many destination countries is the impact that immigrants will have. They often arrive in advanced industrial societies at the same time that these societies are undergoing immense economic, demographic, and technological changes. The economic impact especially causes concern. Some authorities maintain that migrants have a positive impact because they take low-paying jobs and are eager to work. They claim that immigrants generate more in taxes than they cost in the various services they receive. Furthermore, the destination country has not borne the cost of rearing, educating, and training migrants. Since they often return home when they reach retirement age, they are not a burden in their old age. Others, however, highlight the fact that there is often much unemployment among the foreign born; they often have large families that tax the welfare system; and they are often in competition with already-established minorities in a country.

There is no doubt that the first generation of migrants often fares badly. Their qualifications, acquired in their native country, are not recognized in the country of destination, and they usually lack language fluency. The second and third generations, however, are usually able to compete with "natives" on an equal footing. Nevertheless, there are often disproportionate unemployment rates caused by education and housing problems. Muslim immigrants at this time often raise fears because of incidents of violence and threats of violence by Muslim fundamentalists. As a result anti-immigrant political movements have developed in the western world. On the other hand, there has been the development of ethnic voting blocks among citizens of immigrant origin, which is threatening to many native residents.[41]

Despite these threats and fears, migration has affected societies and enriched native cultures. Music, literature, and the other arts have been positively influenced by the introduction of diverse and eclectic contributions on the part of immigrants. Nevertheless, cultural and religious symbols can present a challenge. When societies have responded positively to the cultural challenges, they have often benefited immensely. Global cities like New York, London, and Vancouver have especially felt both the positive and negative impacts of diversity. These cities need specialists in finance, legal services, insurance, and advertising. They also need migrants to accept lower-status jobs in waste disposal, catering, construction, and housekeeping. As a result, migrants in recent years have become concentrated in global and other large cities throughout the world. They often live in particular districts where they form community with others who speak their language and profess the same religion. Migrant districts are usually in the poorest parts of a city, where there may be much crime and unrest because of unemployment. There is no doubt that migration has intersected with globalization to bring about significant social, economic, and cultural changes that appear to be irreversible. It is obvious that today's migration of people in very large numbers raises enormous pastoral problems for the Christian churches because many of the migrants are baptized Christians.

ECOLOGY

There is an extensive literature on this complex topic.[42] In general the term *ecology* refers to the interdisciplinary and scientific study of the interaction between diverse organisms and their environment. This involves the study of ecosystems understood as the web or network of relations among organisms at various stages of organization. In a sense ecology is a subdivision of biology, which is simply the study of life.

In recent years research institutes, the media, politicians, economists, and religious bodies have given extended attention to the ecological impact of globalization with the result that the topic is widely recognized as the most significant and potentially life-threatening issue for the whole world. Attention, above all, is given to how people look upon their natural environment. World cultures that have their roots in Buddhist, Taoist, and other animist religions have for generations stressed the interdependence of all living beings and have emphasized the need for a delicate balance between human wants and ecological needs. In contrast, the Jewish-Christian tradition has usually placed human beings at the center of the universe with the result that the natural world has often been looked at simply as a resource to be used to satisfy human desires.

The dominant U.S. culture has in many ways tried to convince the rest of the world that the primary meaning and value of life is found in an unlimited accumulation of material possessions, an attitude that naturally seeks to justify the satisfaction of human desires without any concern for the effect that might have on life on this planet. It has become increasingly clear that populations on this planet are inextricably linked to one another through the air they breathe, the climate they live in, the food they consume, and the water they use. In spite of their interdependence, our planet's ecosystems are continuously assaulted by widespread wasteful lifestyles. As a result the speed, scale, and extent of our planet's environmental decline have been unprecedented in history. Two of the major factors related to this tragedy are the enormous growth in the planet's population and lavish consumption habits, above all, those of the people living in the global North. There have been vastly increased demands for food, timber, and fiber throughout the world. It has been noted that the United States comprises only 6 percent of the planet's population, but it regularly consumes between 30 and 40 percent of the planet's natural resources. By contrast, hunger characterizes many of the people living in countries such as Haiti, Indonesia, China, and various parts of Africa. Clearly the media popularize and promote overconsumption, which results in environmental degradation. The planet is now in the midst of the mass extinction of many living species. About half of the world's wetlands have already perished, and the bio-diversity of fresh-water ecosystems is seriously threatened.[43]

Pollution across national boundaries constitutes another threat to our survival on this planet. The irresponsible release of vast amounts of deadly chemicals into the air and water sources has created disastrous conditions for both human and animal life that have never been experienced before. For example, the release of chlorofluorocarbons into the air seems to be responsible for depleting the earth's protective ozone layer. Other polluting agents include sulfur and nitrogen oxides. These substances return to the ground in the form of acid rain, which damages forests, soils, and fresh-water ecosystems.[44] Because of the extensive pollution of the environment, there have been major climate changes that have caused governments on both the international and national level to attempt some sort of legal control. This phenomenon has activated much grassroots activism and has resulted in the development of Green Parties in various countries. Many scientists are pleading for immediate action by governments to curb greenhouse gas emissions.[45]

Pollution across national boundaries, global warming, climate change, and the extinction of a great variety of species are issues that simply cannot be controlled by national or regional authorities. They are all major global problems and have serious and complicated economic implications. Poor countries in the world do not usually have the necessary infrastructures or monetary resources to adapt to the various climate changes that occur because of carbon emissions. So-called developing areas are already warmer on average than many of the more developed countries. The poorer countries of the world usually depend on agriculture for the majority of their income. However, agriculture is especially sensitive to climate changes; therefore developing countries will be more adversely affected by climate changes than the more developed countries in the world. This will mean an increase in the cost of living for poor people, resulting in less money for proper healthcare and the development of necessary infrastructures in their countries.[46]

The global South will need considerable financial assistance from the wealthier countries of the world if it is to survive and prosper in the midst of severe climate changes. Clearly there are complex economic, political, cultural, and above all ethical and religious issues that require serious attention in response to the various ecological issues. Although various treaties have been adopted as a result of international discussions, very few coordinated measures have actually been put into practice because there are no effective enforcement mechanisms. Political commitment in favor of change has been very weak and limited. China and the United States, the world's most serious polluters, have regularly failed to ratify agreements because they see that such agreements pose threats to their economic development. Fortunately, however, at least in the United States, public opinion about the need to support changing policies has been developing quite rapidly, so that the majority of U.S. citizens rank climate change and global warming as a major concern for the future of the planet.[47]

The response on the part of various religious bodies—in particular the statements issued by the Roman Catholic magisterium—has been clear and strong in promoting a responsible approach to the very diverse ecological issues that have surfaced in recent decades. In the 1960s and 1970s it was fashionable to accuse the Jewish-Christian tradition of savage indifference to the planet. In a frequently cited article Lynn White Jr. blamed the Bible for making Westerners feel that they were superior to nature and hence free to use it according to their whims.[48] Although there were contrary currents in the history of Christianity, beginning with the Benedictine and Cistercian commitment to stewardship and St. Francis of Assisi's profound reverence for all of creation, it has only been in the last quarter of the past century that religious leaders have surfaced as clear spokespersons for a responsible approach to the major ecological problems of our age. Pope John Paul II fostered a sense of humility and restraint in curbing humanity's irresponsible and savage pillaging of the environment. Pope Benedict XVI has issued strong statements on the environment as part of his teaching on social justice.[49] Women religious in the United States have taken a very active role in supporting the Green movement in the country. As a result ecology has surfaced as a major concern in Catholicism. In addition to making an option for the poor, an emphasis has been placed on four other key issues.

Stewardship. This concept emphasizes that human beings are stewards and caretakers of creation, not masters. They do not own the natural world but rather have it in their care on behalf of the real owner, who is God. Creation is a free gift given to human beings by a loving God. This understanding is seen as part of the Christian commitment to the common good, a commitment that applies not only to individuals but also to society as a whole.[50]

Right to safe and healthy natural environment. Catholic social teaching affirms that the right to live and work in a safe and healthy environment is a basic human right, along with the right to healthcare, education, and a proper standard of living. It affirms the need for public authorities on a planetary scale with clear authority to protect the common good.

The precautionary principle. This principle maintains that in evaluating proposed interventions in the environment, if individuals or groups cannot be reasonably sure that the good effects will outweigh the bad, it is best to be cautious. The danger, however, is that the end result might be mere paralysis because it is almost impossible to establish with certainty all of the consequences of a given plan of action. The Catholic Church has in general endorsed the precautionary principle and has encouraged prudent policies in which risks and benefits are carefully evaluated, especially when scientific data is in a preliminary state.

Lifestyle changes. Human problems can never be resolved simply through legal and political solutions. A change of heart is necessary; so is the internalization of Christian virtues and values. Changed behavior should emerge from authentic Christian conversion. This implies a disciplined acknowledgment of others on the planet and their legitimate rights. At the root of such change is an awareness that each and every person and community is responsible ultimately to God, who is the judge of all human actions. Implied in all of this is the urgent need for very large numbers of people in affluent nations radically to change their lives, especially their patterns of consumption and waste, in order to promote global sustainability. However, it is not immediately clear that lowered consumption levels in affluent nations will benefit the world's poor because the developing nations seek greater access to Western markets since those markets are in fact so immense. Anti-poverty experts favor growing developing economies, thereby creating employment opportunities for the poor, thus helping to lift them out of their poverty. Likewise, it is important, from a Christian perspective, that living a life of voluntary simplicity does not mean living in self-made squalor or in a puritanical kind of abstemiousness that is really the opposite of the Christian understanding of simplicity of heart.

MIGRATION AND RELATIONS
WITH OTHER WORLD RELIGIONS

As a result of globalization, especially worldwide migration, Christianity has been widely exposed to other world religions but often without any informed understanding of the basic history and principles of those religions. Frequently serious tensions have developed between Christians and those who are Muslims, Buddhists, and Hindus, as well as those who have been influenced by the teachings of Confucius. A brief statement of the basic principles of those religions or philosophical systems and how the similarities and dissimilarities that exist between them and Christianity might be useful before discussing the contemporary shift in the center of Christianity from the global North to the global South.

Confucianism

Confucianism is more a philosophical system or a spirituality than an organized religion, but it seems to have had some significant influence on other world religions. It developed from the teachings of the Chinese philosopher Confucius (551–479 BCE).[51] It is a complex system of moral, social, political, philosophical, and quasi-religious thought that has had tremendous influence on the history and culture of much of East Asia. It continues in some ways to influence the lives of those who convert to Christianity, for they often bring with them a keen sense of authority and obedience that they have inherited from their Confucian tradition. The countries that have been significantly influenced by that tradition include mainland China, Korea, Taiwan, and Vietnam, as well as those territories that have been settled by Chinese people, such as Singapore, Hong Kong, Indonesia, and Malaysia. To flourish it seems to presuppose an autocratic ruler who is exhorted to refrain from acting inhumanly toward his subjects. Obedience to such a ruler is expected.

Confucius's sayings have been collected in *The Analects*. They complain about the loss of two components necessary for the development of a cultivated society: the virtue of humaneness, and the practice of rituals expressive of propriety. The meaning of humaneness is learning through proper relations in a family, above all parents loving their children and children loving their parents. The proper form of ritual behavior is learned in social relations manifesting civilized and humane behavior with other people. These patterns involve gestures of correct eye contact, respectful language, conventional greetings, following the rules of precedence, and observing the standard family and court rituals. Confucius felt that these well-practiced rituals made happy family life possible and fostered economic prosperity. He was convinced that when social anarchy took over, civilization did not exist any longer. Throughout its long history Confucianism developed various strains. With the Marxist revolution in China at the middle of the twentieth century, many of its leaders fled from China to Taiwan, Hong Kong, and the United States.

Contemporary Confucians are apt to emphasize filial piety, which implies that children have taken into their hearts the virtues of their parents, who in turn have the obligation to make their children virtuous. There is the sense that virtues are always passed down through generations; they are not achieved by individuals on their own. Likewise, contemporary Confucians have a deep devotion to heaven or God. In order to become a sage, they think they must return to God and see God's presence in self and in all things; hence their life comes into harmony with what Confucians call the Heavenly Principle. God, however, is not a personal God but rather an abstract principle. Another important characteristic of Confucianism is the stress on the humaneness of love. Selfishness inhibits love; the remedy lies in education or training undertaken as a personal search for wisdom. Unlike Christianity, which counsels conversion and transformation, the basic thrust of Confucianism is increased harmony. It should be noted that this harmony is not simply something that pertains to the individual but also affects the community, for the rituals that are observed are essentially communal.

Hinduism

Hinduism is the predominant religion of South Asia, especially India and Nepal.[52] It is made up of diverse traditions and has no single founder. Among its roots is the historical Vedic religion from Iron Age India; thus it is often described as the oldest living religion. Demographically, Hinduism is the world's third largest religion, after Christianity and Islam, with approximately one billion adherents, of whom the majority live in India. Its large body of texts discuss theology, philosophy, and mythology, and provide information about the practice of *dharma* (religious living). Among these texts the Vedas carry the most authority; other basic scriptures include the Upanishads and the Bhagavadad Gita. Hinduism is often looked at as the most complex of all surviving historical world religions. The concept of God is not only complex but takes various forms. Although Hindus may regard God as supreme, they do not deny the existence of other deities.

Karma describes an action or deed, but the term is also used to describe the moral law of cause and effect. Effects are carried over into the next life, reflecting belief in reincarnation—a cycle of events, such as action, reaction, birth, death, and rebirth, which ends only when one is perfectly united with God. Achieving one's final goal is facilitated by several forms of yoga. Hindus also practice various rituals on a daily basis, including purification rites with water. Some Hindus choose to live in a monastic context and commit themselves to a life of simplicity, celibacy, detachment from worldly pursuits, and the contemplation of the divine.

Hindus have long aimed at drawing out the implications of their beliefs and rituals for their practical approach to the world, to life, to death, and to their social relationships. Christians are in sympathy with their emphasis on an ultimate reality underlying and pervading the complexities of life in the world. Some widely known figures, such as Henri Le Saux (Swami Abhishiktananda), Bede Griffiths, Raimon Panikkar, and Anthony de Mello, have made many of the Hindu teachings known to western readers and have popularized various Hindu spiritual practices, above all the practice of meditation. Other Hindu practices that have been adopted by Christians in the West include yoga as a helpful discipline and whole way of life with both psychological and spiritual benefits.

Buddhism

Buddhism, which encompasses various traditions, beliefs, and practices, is largely rooted in teachings attributed to Siddhartha Gautama, the Buddha.[53] He lived and taught in northeastern India sometime between the sixth and fourth centuries BCE. Before his death he formulated his doctrine and rules for monks and nuns. He taught that pain could be overcome by the knowledge and practice of Four Noble Truths: (1) Human existence is suffering, which

(2) is caused by desire, and (3) can be conquered by one's victory over desire (4) by means of the Noble Eightfold Path. That path consists in (1) correct knowledge of the Four Noble Truths; (2) a proper resolve to curb evil; (3) kind and truthful speech; (4) correct action, by refraining from killing, sexual misconduct, and stealing; (5) right livelihood, which means that one cannot earn one's livelihood by working in a trade or occupation that brings harm to others, such as business in poisons, weapons or in slavery; (6) right effort; (7) right mindfulness, which implies keeping one's mind always on the present moment; and (8) proper meditation, which consists in four steps: isolation, resulting in joy; isolation, resulting in inner peace; concentration, bringing bodily happiness; and contemplation that brings indifference to happiness and misery. The Buddha departed from the prevailing thought of his day by affirming the reality of rebirth but at the same time denying that there is a self that travels from body to body and life to life. He taught that it was better not to think of the human person as an ongoing entity but rather as an ever-changing process whose relations to a previous life were of continuity rather than identity. The Buddha's disciples follow his teachings in order to end their suffering and to reach nirvana, which implies the end of suffering.

There is a strong monastic tradition in Buddhism. Any male who is not sick, disabled, a criminal, or in debt can enter a monastery. A minor with parental consent also can enter. The initiation ceremony initially consisted of renunciation, arrival, and a pledge to keep the four prohibitions against sexual intercourse, theft, harm to life, and boasting of superhuman perfection. Initiates were bound to observe other practices, including abstinence from intoxicants; not eating after midday; refraining from worldly amusements, use of cosmetics, and other adornments and luxuries, such as thick mattresses or mats; and refusal to accept gold or silver. These commitments did not bind a monk for life but only for the time he remained in the monastery. Daily exercises in the monastery consisted of morning prayers, recitation of primary verses, outdoor begging, a midday meal followed by rest and meditation, and evening service. Buddha also founded an order for nuns as well as a third order for lay people, who were obliged to abstain from killing, stealing, lying, intoxicants, and fornication.

Buddha's original doctrine lapsed into heresy resulting in diverse interpretations of his original teachings. Throughout its long history the religion has been influenced by diverse cultures and geographical locations with the result that Buddhism is no longer defined by strict boundaries and divisions but is characterized by openness and variety among the various schools. There are now organizations that bring the various strains of the religion together for dialogue and sharing.

Islam

Islam is the religion set out in the Qur'an, a religious book looked upon by its adherents to be the very word of the single incomparable God and of the prophet of Islam, Muhammad.[54] The term *islam* simply means "submission to God." One who adheres to this religion is a Muslim, one who submits to

God. Muslims regard their religion as a complete and universal version of the monotheistic faith revealed to the earlier prophets Noah, Abraham, Moses, and Jesus. Their religious practices include the Five Pillars, which are five duties uniting Muslims in community. Islamic law covers almost every aspect of life, including laws about diet, banking, warfare, and welfare. Muslims believe that God's final message to humanity is revealed through the prophet Muhammad, communicating through the archangel Gabriel. They believe that prophets are human, not divine. As a historical religion, Islam originated in Arabia in the early seventh century CE. Today it is the predominant religion in the Middle East, North Africa, and large parts of Asia, but converts and immigrant communities are found in almost every part of the world. Islam is the second largest religion in the world and one of the fastest growing religions worldwide.

Unfortunately, the media often generate a negative stereotype of Islam, due to the acts of violence committed by Muslim extremists in the last few decades. However, in a positive sense Muslims present strong challenges to contemporary Christians and other religions. For Muslims, the God of Abraham and Moses is also the God of Jesus, even though Christians and Muslims differ considerably in their understanding of Jesus. Christians and Muslims also both affirm the oneness of God, even though they experience that God in different ways. Therefore, it is possible for Muslims and Christians to pray together "in the name of the Lord." Above all, Muslims affirm the importance of living a fully human life in harmony with God, all other human beings, and all of creation. This is reflected in their prayer five times a day symbolized by the call to prayer throughout the world. Their basic equality is symbolized by the fact that when they gather together for prayer they all sit in rows without distinctions. Their submission to God is shown in their prostrations when the forehead touches the ground, for the head is the proudest part of the human body. Formal prayer ends with the gesture of looking over one's shoulder to right and to left, as both angels and neighbor are greeted and blessed. This reflects the basic unity of all creation, both the seen and the unseen. In a sense, the Christian greeting of peace is meant to express the same meaning. Muslims are expected to come together for prayer above all on Friday.

A ritual washing is required before all formal prayer, primarily to emphasize purity; if no water is available, then clean sand or earth is acceptable. Cleanliness of the body is symbolic of cleanliness of the mind, thoughts, and intention. Some Muslims maintain that women should pray in their homes rather than in the mosque; hence, women do not regularly take part in community prayers. Annual fasting from sunrise to sunset is required during Ramadan, the ninth month of the Muslim year. It is usually accompanied by a re-commitment to prayer, the reading of sacred texts, and other spiritual practices. In some ways the observance of Ramadan is similar to the Christian observance of Lent. Hajj, a pilgrimage to Makkah (formerly Mecca), has long been a part of Muslim spirituality for those who can afford the trip.

Many Muslims also observe *zakat*, giving a fixed percentage of capital to the poor, who are the special concern of Allah. Mention should also be made of Sufism, the mystical tradition of Islam, which stresses the importance of personal spiritual experience, illumination by God, repentance, purification of conscience, renunciation of the world, simplicity of life, suffering, trust in God, and submission to whatever might happen in one's life. Finally, there is the primary pillar of Islam, the *shahadah*. It is a short creedal statement affirming the oneness of God and belief in Muhammad as his special messenger. This is a regularly repeated statement of Muslim belief. It contrasts markedly with the Christian creeds, which are often quite complicated.

There are obviously a number of basic truths and commitments that are shared by the various world religions that have just been discussed. These include dedication to prayer, discipline, fasting, asceticism, and ritual practices. However, there has been in the past and continues to exist in the present a clash within these traditions between the exoteric and esoteric characteristics. The exoteric focuses on external observances such as keeping divine commandments and performing public rituals. If the emphasis is placed on the exoteric, stress will be on a specific belief system expressed in a common creed and fulfillment of a specific religious law. Such observance is thought to shape a visible society committed to a specific religious system. By contrast, the esoteric emphasizes the importance of inner experience and conversion of heart. It sees an experience of the divine as of primary importance rather than observance of formal laws and rituals. The exoteric and the esoteric strains tend to coexist in tension with one another in various world religions. In practice, history has shown that it is not easy to keep the tension balanced. History has also shown that overemphasis on the exoteric and the neglect of the esoteric usually results in a system of social and political control, a system in which concern for the transcendent gets smothered and personal and social conversion to the divine disappears.[55]

SHIFT IN THE CENTER OF CHRISTIANITY FROM NORTH TO SOUTH

Philip Jenkins, the distinguished professor of history and religious studies at Pennsylvania State University, has written a trilogy on the future of Christianity.[56] His basic thesis in *The Next Christendom* has been widely accepted by other scholars: "Far from being an export of the capitalist West, a vestige of Euro-American imperialism, Christianity is now rooted in the Third World, and the religion's future lies in the global South."[57] Christianity is at the present time enjoying a worldwide increase in numbers, but the majority of believers are not white, European, or Euro-American. A large proportion of the Christian world is located in Africa, Latin America, and to a limited degree in Asia. The era of Western Christianity has passed. The major religion of the world's poorest people is Christianity, not Hinduism or Islam.[58]

European Christians traditionally interpreted their Christian beliefs through their own understanding of social and gender relations and regularly imagined that their own culturally conditioned synthesis was the only correct version of the Christian faith. But as Christianity moves southward, it is inevitable that it will be radically changed by immersion in the native cultures of the host countries. At the present, and probably into the foreseeable future, the southern-dominated church will be made up primarily of poor people, in contrast to the older, western-dominated world. Until recently the voices of liberation theologians coming from developing countries were those of clerics who had been trained either in Europe or in North America, but their voices were given only a limited hearing. Although the people from the South have not rejected political involvement, their concern has been deliverance from their poverty and from supernatural evil.

Obviously there is no such thing as southern Christianity, any more than there is such a phenomenon as European or North American Christianity. Many Christians from the global South are considered more conservative in terms of their beliefs and moral teachings than are the mainstream churches in the global North. This is especially true of Africa. The Christian denominations that are flourishing in the global South are traditional or even reactionary in comparison with those in the economically well-off nations of the North. The denominations that have made the most dramatic increase in the global South are Roman Catholic, radical Protestant, evangelical, and Pentecostal. There are also newer Christian churches that are attracting converts; they preach the need for a deep personal faith, orthodox doctrine, mysticism, and puritanism, all based clearly on the Bible. Western Christians often find their preaching simplistically charismatic, apocalyptic, and prophetic. Faith-healing, exorcism, and visions are all part of their religious belief system.[59]

The types of Christianity that have surfaced in the global South differ considerably from what North Americans and Europeans consider to be mainstream. They are much more enthusiastic and concerned with the immediate presence and power of the supernatural through visions, dreams, ecstatic speech, healing, and prophecy. Illness and other misfortunes are often attributed to evil spirits; often these tragedies are thought to be due to personal sin. Hence, many people are apt to turn to witch doctors to ward off dangers. Keen interest in exorcism and demonic possession are characteristic of non-western Christian cultures. Traditional Christians have usually looked upon Jesus as the redeemer and great high priest set out in the letter to the Hebrews, but contemporary Africans, and to some extent East Asians, think of Jesus as their great Ancestor, one who exercises the same concern and love that the ancestors of a specific tribe or group would manifest for their descendants. Because of the activity of evangelical and Pentecostal missionaries, Christians from the global South often read the Bible in very literal and fundamentalist terms. Catechizing and forming the large numbers of converts to Catholicism are major concerns.[60]

For many Protestants in Africa, membership in the World Council of Churches provides an important focus of unity. The Roman Catholic Church does not belong to the WCC; therefore, it does not affect the majority of Latin Americans. Nevertheless, the Christian churches in Africa, Latin America, and Asia share a number of important common experiences. Growth characterizes all the Christian denominations, and all are independently developing similar theological and social worldviews. All face the serious problems of race, inculturation, and efforts to maintain their distinctive colonial heritages. These important issues distinguish the northern and southern churches. Likewise, they all share a passionate drive toward evangelism and mission within their own regions.[61]

The South is a region of extraordinary diversity, and the terms *conservatism* and *liberalism* are defined quite differently from the way they are in the North. Their conservative theological and moral stands are often accompanied by very progressive economic views. As the churches in the South continue to develop, they will intensify their own distinctive identity and define themselves in ways that are often radically different from the Christian churches in the North. With the shortage of clergy in the North, especially among Roman Catholics, southern Christian missionaries are already being imported, along with their distinctive cultural traits.[62]

In the global South there seems to be a consensus about matters of social justice. There is the general opinion that globalization produces a wide gap between the wealthy and the poor. Liberal economic policies have destroyed the fabric of the family, it is believed, and local ownership of businesses has been stifled, leading to a large gap between the rich few and the poor majority. There is considerable skepticism about the global influence of the United States.[63]

In Latin America, despite Protestant growth in recent decades, the Roman Catholic Church is still the largest single religious denomination. The majority of people define their religious commitment in Roman Catholic terms. In Africa, the leading denomination is Roman Catholic, followed by Anglican and Methodist; the emphasis on healing and visions, however, has made the Pentecostal and other independent churches especially attractive. In general, Protestants tend to be more faithful churchgoers than Catholics.[64] Pentecostalism is attracting many converts in the global South.[65] Protestants rely on the Bible alone as the sole source of religious authority; Roman Catholics rely on both scripture and tradition. Pentecostals rely on direct personal revelations that complement biblical authority. In Latin America mainline Protestantism appeals generally to middle-class people, whereas Pentecostals get their converts primarily from the poor, sometimes the poorest strains in society.[66]

Pentecostals generally espouse a "low church" ecclesiology with little or no stress on a hierarchical priesthood. They maintain that ordinary people can make contact with the divine without any intervening structures such as sacraments and ordained clergy. They have a strong commitment to evangelization, that is, sharing their faith with nonbelievers. They generally subscribe to a conservative moral code in areas of homosexuality, extramarital sex, abortion, divorce, and consumption of alcohol and drugs. They also support a strong role for religion in public life. Because of their faith in God, they believe that God will reward the faithful with both material prosperity and physical health.[67]

Although Roman Catholicism is the dominant religious denomination in Latin America, there is considerable Protestant and Pentecostal expansion. Christian numbers have also been increasing in societies around the Pacific Rim, though it is difficult to tabulate the exact number of converts. This is especially the case with the People's Republic of China, which prior to the Communist takeover in 1949 was a favorite mission site. Public religious life for Christians seriously deteriorated under the Communist government, which is both antireligious and xenophobic. In 1951 all foreign missionaries were expelled. Christians were tolerated, but they were expected to associate themselves with organizations officially registered with the Communist government. Roman Catholics were required to join the Catholic Patriotic Association; Protestants were to accept the Three-Self Principles of self-government, self-support, and self-propagation.

Christianity has made great progress in South Korea. It is estimated that over a quarter of the national population is Christian, predominantly Protestant and Pentecostal. North Korea is fanatically anti-Christian. In Vietnam, which is under Communist control, Christianity is not only surviving but flourishing. Most of the Christians are Roman Catholic. India's Christian roots are deeply planted, but the number of Christians at the present time is hard to tabulate. Although Christianity is certainly marginal to the Hindu cultural tradition, Christianity, especially Roman Catholicism, has produced innovative theologians, including Michael Amaladoss, Felix Wilfrid, and Aloysius Pieris, who have explored the relationships between Christianity and Asian faith. Catholicism is especially respected because of its network of hospitals, schools, and social services agencies.

CHRISTIANITY IN THE TWENTY-FIRST CENTURY

Because of globalization and the extensive migration of peoples throughout the world, various cultures tend to change quite rapidly. Hence, it is very difficult to project accurately how Christianity will fare as we move deeper and deeper into the twenty-first century. Mainline Christian denominations in the northern hemisphere tend to be highly polarized these days due to differences concerning serious doctrinal and moral issues. The ordination of women to the priesthood and episcopacy, the recognition of same-sex unions, the recognition of the rights of active gay and lesbian people, including their right to ordination, and the legitimacy of abortion and other sexual issues have caused and continue to cause major tensions and divisions, perhaps especially among Anglicans and Roman Catholics, but also to some extent among Lutherans, Methodists, and Presbyterians.

Institutional Roman Catholicism tends to think in terms of centuries and is usually very slow to adapt to current trends and developments. Other Christian denominations have more flexible governing structures or simply lack official magisterial structures with binding force, so they are often able to live with compromises; at other times they experience ruptures that result in the formation of what appear to be new churches or denominations. There tends to be considerable movement from one Christian denomination to another because people find the preaching, style of liturgical celebration, or tolerance of diverse political and theological views more accommodating in a new congregation than they did in their former one.

Revelation of the sexual abuse of minors by clergy and religious throughout the northern hemisphere has been a cause of considerable disillusionment among many Roman Catholics. This has been accompanied by a major reinterpretation of the documents of the Second Vatican Council, giving the impression that nothing of major significance really happened at Vatican Council II—it was all a matter simply of continuity and development. It is well known that a number of Roman curial officials who attended the sessions of the Second Vatican Council were adamantly opposed to various liturgical and ecclesial changes included in the documents, which were nonethelss approved by a vast majority of the council fathers. That spirit of opposition has never died in the curia; in fact, it has resurfaced in recent times with a vengeance.[68]

In the years after Vatican Council II a distinguished school of church historians developed in Bologna under the direction of Giuseppe Alberigo. Scholars from around the world contributed to a five-volume history of the Second Vatican Council that was translated into various languages and was highly praised by reviewers. In recent years scholars have noted that there have been three general types of interpretation of Vatican II: (1) that given by the so-called progressives, who have looked on the council as a positive happening that took serious steps to accommodate Roman Catholicism to history and the modern world; (2) that given by the traditionalists, who have tended to see the council as an unfortunate happening involving the capitulation of Catholicism to principles and movements it had rightly resisted since the middle of the nineteenth century; and (3) that given by the so-called reformists, who have played down the eventful character of the council as a rupture or break with the church's authentic tradition. Benedict XVI, who was a theological *peritus* at the council, has maintained that the elements of discontinuity have been exaggerated by those who insist on some vague notion called the "spirit of the council" while ignoring the authentic texts of the council.[69]

In 2005 Editrice Vaticana published a book by Archbishop Agostino Marchetto that attacked Alberigo's Bologna School of interpretation as setting out an incorrect understanding of the council. The book asserted that among the false interpretations were an anti-curial bias, comparisons of Pope Paul VI with Pope John XXIII unfavorable to the former, emphasis on the so-called novelty of the council and its difference from previous councils, an underlying "reformist" ideology, and finally, diminishing the importance of the official final documents of the council in favor of the council as an event.[70]

There is no doubt that the Roman Catholic Church has become highly centralized in recent decades, more centralized than it has ever been in history. Collegiality and the exercise of subsidiarity have certainly been curtailed or at least undeveloped, with the result that local bishops often have been reduced to the role of mere "messenger boys" delivering Vatican mandates to the laity, whose members feel that they have no input into major decisions that significantly affect their lives. Local bishops often feel that they are more vicars of the pope than vicars of the apostles. Women feel intensely marginalized in this age when the rights and responsibilities of women are increasingly recognized and respected, at least in the northern hemisphere. It is a truism that the hopes inspired by the Second Vatican Council for a more collegial church, with active lay participation and a balancing of the power of the papacy and Roman curia with the influence of the local churches have for the most part not been realized. Many in the church feel that it is at the present time a dysfunctional church impregnated with autocratic clericalism.

Another problem is associated with the fact that the present pope is a prolific theologian, frequently writing about a wide range of issues in his own name. However, his theology is often at odds with that of other distinguished theologians. Benedict XVI's theology is quite clearly rooted in Platonist, Augustinian, and Bonaventurian writings.[71] He emerged as a theologian in war-torn Germany, which has inclined him to see the Roman Catholic Church as the only sure and certain hope in the face of the horrors of the modern world. He clearly finds in his reading and understanding of the scriptures, the fathers of the church, and the statements of the magisterium answers to just about every question and to all the hopes and aspirations of every age. He seems to be sure that any other answer is bound to fail. For him, the pressing theological issues of the present time have already been settled by the church. The answers are present in the tradition that has been handed down.

Pope Benedict's encyclicals have won respect, but experience and historical events find little place in his theological work. His "closed hermeneutical circle" allows recourse only to a particular reading of scripture, the texts of the fathers, and the magisterium. It has been noted that though the pope acknowledges that the natural law is not fully understood but rather is something about which we grow in knowledge, he is absolute in his teachings about sexual matters, including premarital sex, remarriage, homosexuality, and mandatory clerical celibacy, as well as the impossibility of ordaining women to the priesthood. The theological themes of Pope Benedict allow little room for change in the teachings of the contemporary church, which means that theologians who are seeking to open new areas of investigation in their understanding of complex doctrinal and moral issues are often given little room for creativity or imagination in their craft. The pope has stated publicly that the current crises in the church can be solved by personal conversion and penitence; he sees no need to change the ecclesial structures.

The tensions within the Roman Catholic Church almost always deal with internal problems, since the church's strong support of progressive movements toward social justice rarely causes overt tension. Although there are major social and political developments in the global South, the global North in the church is not about to disappear. Major cities such as Los Angeles, New York, Chicago, Paris, London, Toronto, Rome, and Barcelona will continue to be important centers of Christian and particularly Roman Catholic thought. Activists and theologians in the North will continue to exert strong influence because they have a disproportionate share of resources. At the same time, Christianity in the South, particularly Roman Catholicism and Anglicanism, will be influenced by what is happening in Africa, Latin America, and Asia. On the pastoral level, where strong political currents often manifest themselves, the Anglican Church and the Roman Catholic Church in the South will continue to develop native leadership that will eventually influence the centers of these two important denominations. Both Roman Catholicism and Anglicanism will become increasingly non-western, non-white, and non-affluent. In increasing numbers immigrants from the South will continue to bring their values and cultural traits to bear on the northern hemisphere. These values will reflect conservative doctrinal and moral positions, liberal positions on social justice issues, and a strong emphasis on the Bible rather than on magisterial statements. Many migrants are also apt to bring with them allegiance to non-Christian religions, especially Islam and Buddhism as well as a commitment to their indigenous spiritual practices, such as divination, reverence for their ancestors, a commitment to faith healings, and robustly incultur-ated forms of liturgical celebration. They are apt to see any imposition of Latin, Gregorian chant, and rigid rubrics concerning liturgical celebrations as examples of European neo-colonialism. Especially in Africa, rather than being concerned about gay marriages, Christians are apt to struggle with the issue of polygamy; they are little concerned about atheism but much concerned about witchcraft.[72]

When traditional doctrinal positions are threatened, the Roman Catholic Church tends to reassert its traditional teachings and seeks to develop new pastoral methods to defend them. Hence, the church is apt to be increasingly assertive about bioethical stands it has taken and even to threaten sanctions against Roman Catholic politicians and others who act against Catholic teach-ings in public life. Distinctive characteristics of church life, such as individual confession, eucharistic adoration, and Marian devotions, are apt to find a more enthusiastic manifestation of what it means to be Catholic, especially among younger Catholics. It should be noted, however, that many Roman Catholics are now well educated and often affluent. In many northern countries lay men and women now have advanced degrees in theology, pastoral ministry, liturgical theology, and even canon law. They are apt to insist that their voices be heard in the institutional church. If not, they will be tempted to walk away and join another denomination. The rise of China and India on the international scene has already created a new situation for modern Catholicism. Though Asians and Africans often feel that their voices are not heard in the Roman curia, it will become increasingly clear that the Roman Catholic Church is no longer domi-nated by its European cultural heritage. The Anglican Communion has already been deeply affected by the extraordinary growth of Anglicanism in Africa.

3

The Bible and Christian Moral Life

Acrimonious debates among and within the various Christian churches are often expressions of the deep-seated moral and doctrinal differences that divide them. Churches these days are often highly polarized; likewise, polarization often characterizes the lives of individuals within the various churches. The dialogue across the divide is frequently hostile and grossly unkind. These Christian churches, however, clearly affirm that they are committed to the Bible as a source of norms for the way they seek to live the Christian life. They affirm that the Bible is a principal source of divine revelation on which they ground their faith; they also view the Bible as an indispensable resource for discerning the moral life they are expected to live as Christians. In recent years complex moral questions have begun to confront and often divide the various Christian churches. What stance should be taken about issues of sexual morality, medical ethics, birth control, euthanasia, marriage, social inequality, war, responsible government, and the rights of individuals and communities?

In light of the moral confusion and tension existing among the Christian churches concerning the proper interpretation of the many complex moral issues that have surfaced in recent years, the Roman Catholic Pontifical Biblical Commission decided that it would be both opportune and helpful to make some statement about the use of the Bible in moral teaching. Consequently, on 11 May 2008, the commission published a major statement, *The Bible and Morality: Biblical Roots of Christian Conduct*.[1] The 235-page text was six years in the making; however, it received little public notice, at least in the English-speaking world, because there was a very limited edition of the text published in English.[2]

The statement does not attempt to solve complex moral issues by using the Bible as a proof text. Rather, it explores how the inspired text of the Bible can shed light on contemporary moral issues and shows that there is often a convergence between biblical morality and the laws and moral stances prevalent in contemporary cultures and peoples. It encourages Christians to dialogue with contemporary cultures and with the various moral and philosophical systems of other religions in a common search for norms of conduct regarding moral problems.

The document recognizes that in an era of globalization and under the impact of extensive migration, social relationships have become increasingly complex because of scientific progress, above all in the fields of psychology, genetics, and communication. This has had a profound influence on the moral consciences of individuals and groups, with the result that a widespread culture has developed based on relativism, tolerance, and an acceptance of new ideas that are based on false or inadequate theological and philosophical foundations. This culture of tolerance has resulted in a mistrust of magisterial moral teaching and a neglect or rejection of any consideration of what the Bible might have to say about moral issues.[3]

The biblical commission decided on two basic objectives. The members sought to situate Christian morality within the broader context of anthropology and biblical theologies and to propose some methodological criteria for making proper use of the Bible in seeking to shed light on moral questions. These objectives, therefore, determined the twofold structure of the document: "A Revealed Morality: Divine Gift and Human Response"; and "Biblical Criteria for Moral Reflection."[4]

Part I of the document reviews the books of the Bible from Genesis to Revelation while searching for consistent traits in its understanding of the human person and the various moral values that should guide human action. It concludes that the human person is one who is open to the transcendent, that human life and creation are both gifts of God, that both are to be reverenced and esteemed, that both human freedom and reason are biblically endorsed, and that God has entered into a covenant with the human community that results in the human need to be responsible, just, and compassionate, especially toward those who are vulnerable.[5] This biblical understanding of the human person gives rise to the articulation of the Decalogue set out in both Exodus and Deuteronomy. It results in a strong emphasis on justice in the writings of the prophets, in the Lord's articulation of the beatitudes and his Sermon on the Mount in the Gospels, in the stress on community in the Acts of the Apostles and in the Apocalypse, which contains a vision of a new earth and a new heaven in the future when justice is restored.[6]

In Part II the statement sets out criteria that can guide the use of the Bible in drawing out moral reflections. First of all, two very general principles are emphasized: the dignity and responsibility of the human person created in the image of God and living in the world, and the responsibility for those persons to imitate Christ, who is the perfect expression of divine presence and action in the world. Then follow six guiding criteria rooted in the biblical tradition and suggesting various ways in which each might facilitate a discovery of biblical foundations for moral actions.[7] The first criterion, convergence, recognizes moral values that are common to both the Bible and various secular human cultures and people of goodwill who confront complex moral issues. For example, the early prescriptions of the Torah closely resemble prescriptions of Near Eastern law codes. But there are also significant differences. For example, the Code of Hammurabi does not show much zeal for the poor or concern for the equal rights of every individual. Likewise, the Pauline list of virtues and vices is similar to those in Stoic morality, but the latter is not concerned with the responsibility of every individual to contribute to the common good.[8]

The second criterion, contrast, acknowledges that in some cases the Bible encourages the church to take a prophetic stance in opposition to false values. In this regard the text connects the biblical condemnation of idolatry and the contemporary imperative to oppose social or political ideologies, such as capitalism, materialism, consumerism, individualism, and hedonism because the latter are in opposition to the dignity of the human person and are in opposition to the biblical affirmation of the transcendent.[9]

The third criterion, advance, has far-reaching implications and illustrates that the Bible allows for development or progression of moral discernment. For example, within the Bible itself there is advance from an early acceptance of polygamy and revenge to a more sensitive treatment of these issues in the teaching of Jesus and Paul. In other words, this criterion leaves open the possibility for further advances, such as the eventual abolition of slavery, the outlawing of war, and ways to affirm the basic equality of women.[10]

The fourth criterion deals with community, which is especially characteristic of the Bible's observations about morality and certainly provides an important challenge to the often exaggerated emphasis on the individual and individual rights in contemporary societies. In the biblical perspective the common good and communal responsibility are rooted in the very nature of the human person. This stress on the community is ratified by the covenant and is foundational for Jesus' command to love, which is at the heart of his teaching. The awareness that Israel has a mission to all people grows stronger as the Old Testament develops. In the New Testament the teaching on the body of Christ, on the church as the people of God, and on the universal mission of the church encouraged people to be responsible for one another and to seek to respond to the needs of all people.[11]

The fifth criterion is finality, which situates moral reflection not only within the transcendent dimensions of the human person but also within the ultimate destiny of the human community and creation itself. This implies ongoing transformation and renewal. This focus on the future informs the human understanding of moral responsibility in the present. The biblical stance places before individuals and communities ecological responsibilities, so that our natural resources are not exploited. We are called to develop an horizon that includes the future and to have hope for a redeemed and renewed creation. Hence, with the development of hope in an afterlife and a new understanding of the meaning of death, the values of this passing world diminish in importance and the call for authentic Christian life becomes more important so that one might play a responsible role in welcoming the kingdom. This development does not negate the values of this world, but it does give them a certain provisional status and may in some cases lead to martyrdom and self-sacrifice in imitation of Jesus.[12]

Finally, there is the criterion of discernment, which seems to be a method of applying the first five criteria rather than a criterion itself. It implies an evaluation of the criteria and their priority in case they seem to be in opposition to one another. The text provides guidelines for resolving such clashes. Certainly attention must be given to the literary genre and the context in which a particular text occurs. For example, is the text an explicit part of the Torah, is it a proverb, part of the Sermon on the Mount, or a casual recommendation? Attention must also be given to a theological foundation for a rule rather than simply its cultural basis, such as a particular ethnic custom or a teaching about simple hygiene. Examples of a clear theological foundation for a text would be its reference to Jesus' fundamental option for the poor or proper familial relationships. Finally, the cultural background of a text is important, so that the food restrictions imposed when eating with Jewish Christians need no longer be imposed. This final criterion highlights the complexity of biblical texts as well as contemporary moral issues. Such discernment is not simply the responsibility of individual consciences but is the responsibility of the whole human community and the church as a whole in its responsible dialogue with contemporary culture.

This important and very helpful text from the Pontifical Biblical Commission makes no claim to solve any problems definitely but is rather meant to stimulate responsible discussion. It was not given approval by the pope; it only has the authority that results from responsible scholarship and lengthy discussions on the part of the members of the commission. It has been offered by the church, but it has not been promulgated by the church. It hopes that those who teach moral theology and engage in pastoral responsibility will avoid mere legalism, casuistry, and fundamentalism. Rather than give clear and precise directives, the commission sought to recommend an approach to morality in a spirit derived from the Bible itself.[13]

THE OLD TESTAMENT AND MORALITY

Creation. In the first two chapters of Genesis God is presented as the creator of all that exists. In the Bible the great vision of salvation history unfolds in light of the two accounts of the origins of creation in the first two chapters of Genesis. In the canonical arrangement of the books of the Pentateuch the divine act of creation stands at the beginning of the narrative. The initial creation includes everything, both heaven and earth; there is a clear affirmation that everything is due to God's free decision to create. The Creator's special gift to humanity consists in the fact that God created human beings in God's own image. Hence, human beings are endowed with the ability and responsibility to know and to understand the created world. They have freedom to make decisions and to be responsible for the decisions that they make. Under God's leadership they have the ability to exercise leadership in creation. In their life in creation they are to imitate the qualities that God has revealed concerning God's own identity. Hence, human beings are relational beings, capable of having personal relationships with God and with other human beings. As God is holy, so human beings are holy.[14]

In the Bible nothing that exists is self-created, nor does anything exist by chance; everything is due to God's creative power. Hence, the world and human beings are radically dependent on God. It follows that we cannot speak of God without speaking of humanity or speak of human beings without speaking of God. However, God is transcendent, not part of creation. Human beings are to govern, administer, and give shape in a creative way to what God has created. Creation is not meant to be preserved simply as it is but to undergo continuous development.[15]

Throughout history the Christian theology of creation has been marked by several characteristics. First of all, from the early post-apostolic period, Christians have affirmed creation from nothing, *creatio ex nihilo*. This means that the world was not created out of some preexisting matter; everything was created by God. Christians sought to affirm the sovereignty of God over all creation and to affirm that all belongs to God, not to some other being. Second, the world that God created is good. Even though there is evil and sin in the world, the world is intrinsically good. Evil entered the world only after God created the world. Consequently, all creation, both that which is living and that which is inanimate, must be treated as good and as a gift of God. Third, Catholic Christians have generally maintained that through creation God can be known by natural reason. In other words, creation is revelatory of God, even without taking into account the special revelation given to Israel and in and through Jesus Christ. God's creation reflects God's own goodness, glory, and beauty. This belief, however, is not accepted by many Protestant Christians because they believe that human reason is limited unless it is aided by God's grace.[16]

Some Christians maintain the literal truth of the Genesis account of creation, holding that God created the world a little over four thousand years ago, a position known as creationism. Most contemporary Christians, however, at least in the northern hemisphere, hold an evolutionary view and look upon the Genesis accounts of creation as theological rather than historical writings. Some commentators have retrieved the patristic view of creation as involving a continuous act of creation so that creation is viewed as a dynamic ongoing process; God's designs are continually unfolding. They also caution against any irresponsible interpretation of the Genesis command that humans dominate the earth; they emphasize ecological responsibility and care for the earth's preservation and development. Closely linked to the ecological concerns is the emphasis on a just distribution of the world's goods; that is, justice is integral to a Christian theology of creation.[17]

Exodus. Biblical scholars are in agreement that the Exodus of the Israelites from their bondage in Egypt was the central phenomenon in the whole Old Testament, for it was in that event that the discouraged and unorganized band of slaves encountered God and became God's chosen people.[18] The Exodus is foundational for all that was written in the Old Testament; even the account of creation and the patriarchal sagas reflect the Exodus, which is Israel's own creation story.

There are three elements in the Exodus event: bondage, liberation, and covenant. Israel's experience of slavery was extremely painful, but it was the occasion for its salvation when the people became aware of their situation and accepted it. Bondage alone leads to nothing but more bondage, whereas bondage that is acknowledged can lead to freedom and salvation. The Israelites lived in slavery for many years, but their situation changed radically when they acknowledged their helplessness and cried out for help. The biblical text does not indicate the one to whom the people cried out; it is unlikely that they would have remembered the patriarchs, who had lived about four hundred years earlier. They cried out to anyone who would hear them. It was God who remembered and had pity on them: "They cried out, and their appeal for rescue from their slavery rose up to God. He heard their groaning and remembered his covenant with Abraham, Isaac, and Jacob; he saw the plight of Israel, and he took heed of it" (Ex 2:23–25).

Demetrius Dumm points out that in a sense all human beings are born in Egyptian bondage. We are called to be free, but we are not born free. For the Israelites bondage was primarily physical because their lives were restricted and they were forced to do hard labor without just recompense. It was also psychological, for they were valued only for their work and productivity. And their bondage was spiritual, because they felt that they had no future, no hope.[19]

Our bondage is more likely to be psychological or spiritual than physical. We may feel that we are not appreciated and that our gifts are not acknowledged; we may be fearful or feel guilty; we may suffer from various addictions; we may feel enslaved and not find rescue in a God who is both powerful and compassionate. As in the case of the Israelites, our way out of bondage begins with an acknowledgment of our need and our decision to cry for help. It is our cry that triggers divine remembrance. The biblical story of Israel's slavery and of God's compassionate response reminds us that such a petition made in time of true need will not be ignored by our God, who is the caring God of the Exodus.[20]

The basic meaning of the Exodus is that God liberated the people who were in bondage. In a biblical sense salvation always implies liberation and freedom. The first step in the process of Israel's liberation was God's call given to Moses: "Come, I will send you to Pharaoh and you shall bring my people Israel out of Egypt" (Ex 3:10). Moses was reluctant to respond to the call, but God assured him of God's provident care. The account shows that the liberation of the Israelites will be God's work and not the work of Moses. The human agent must respond to God's initiative, but it is ultimately God who achieves the victory. It was God's loving kindness, his gracious mercy, that resulted in the Israelites' liberation; it was their experience of this goodness that freed the discouraged slaves and gave them the courage and confidence to defy Pharaoh and to march away from their bondage.[21]

The dramatic account of the ten plagues can be appreciated in this context. Commentators generally agree that there might be some kernel of historical truth in the plagues, but they are basically embellished literary accounts that highlight the miracle that is at the heart of the Exodus, namely, the miracle of transforming and enlivening a group of motley slaves into God's people through their experience of God's love. Perhaps the basic lesson to be learned from the Exodus event is the truth that liberation from slavery to freedom comes from the merciful love of God and not from the exercise of brutal power. This contrasts with the common practice today of amassing power and often using it quite ruthlessly. God's way is to love, to care, and to foster development.[22]

The Exodus resulted in a special bond between God and the Israelites, a bond that was affirmed by the covenant, which was much more than a legal contract. It was the expression of a profound personal relationship that involved the gift of God's love for the people and their response of loving service and loyalty. On God's part there was a pledge of constant fidelity: "I will walk to and fro among you" (Lv 26:12); on Israel's part there was to be a response of love and gratitude befitting God's people: "I will be your God and you will become my people" (Lv 26:12). The remaining parts of the Old Testament are basically an account of the ups and downs that characterized that relationship. Idolatry would often characterize the life of the Israelites, but God was to be loved and adored exclusively because he alone brought the people out of bondage into the freedom of the children of God.[23]

The Ten Commandments. God's communication of the Ten Commandments was the first attempt to spell out the practical implications of the loving response that Israel was expected to give to God. They are not simply standards for proper conduct but are guidelines for how people should live when they have been liberated and have experienced the love of God. Their primary emphasis is on the interior dispositions of each person, which in turn should inspire proper actions. If this is understood, the commandments will not become occasions for pride and complacency when they are obeyed or occasions for guilt and shame when they are disobeyed. They are to be obeyed because they show the people how they are to use their freedom responsibly. They demonstrate clearly that in religious matters, loving people and enhancing their freedom should always precede holding people accountable and imposing commands upon them.[24]

The first commandment, "You shall have no other god to set against me" (Ex 20:3), obliges the Israelites to give exclusive loyalty to the God who delivered them from slavery and who made a covenant with them. The second, "You shall not make a carved image for yourself nor the likeness of anything. . . . You shall not bow down to them or worship them; for I, the Lord your God, am a jealous God" (Ex 20:4–5), forbids the Israelites to acknowledge or worship any rival gods; they are also forbidden to craft any images of the Lord, for such images would possibly violate the mystery of God. The third commandment, "You shall not make wrong use of the name of the Lord your God: the Lord will not leave unpunished the one who misuses his name" (Ex 20:7), is similar to the second in the sense that it forbids turning authentic religion into magic. This practice is forbidden because it reduces God to an impersonal deity and fails to reverence him as a loving, caring God.[25]

The fourth commandment, "Remember to keep the Sabbath day holy" (Ex 20:8), is a transitional commandment, addressing the human tendency to eliminate mystery from life and to control creation by means of work. Hence, the Israelites are to interrupt their work every seventh day as a reminder that work is to enhance the mystery of life rather than destroy it. Work is not an end in itself, but rather it is meant to enhance the environment and reveal it as a mysterious gift of God. Work prepares for the enjoyment of God's gift of creation through the observance of the Sabbath.[26]

The fifth commandment and those that follow are concerned with major areas of human life. The fifth commandment requires the Israelites to honor, respect, and care for aged parents (Ex 20:12). This is significant because in a society ruled by merely human pragmatics, the elderly are apt to be considered a burden and useless; in a society governed by divine wisdom, the elderly are revered and cared for as a source of special beauty and mystery. Worth is determined not by usefulness and productivity but by wisdom and love. The sixth commandment, "You shall not commit murder" (Ex 20:13), concerns not only murder but all forms of violence, psychological as well as physical. Where life is most fragile and vulnerable, it must be most carefully cared for. The seventh commandment, "You shall not commit adultery" (Ex 20:14), explicitly forbids adultery, but it also embraces all attacks on loving relationships perpetrated through any forms of seduction.[27]

The eighth commandment, "You shall not steal" (Ex 20:15), was especially significant for the Israelites. In a clan society stealing was considered especially harmful because it deprived a person of the enjoyment of property and violated the trust that made peaceful life in a community possible. The ninth commandment, "You shall not give false evidence against your neighbor" (Ex 20:16), is of special interest to the Israelites because deceitful and malicious speech destroys the trusting atmosphere that should characterize community life. Finally, the tenth commandment, "You shall not covet your neighbor's house; you shall not covet your neighbor's wife, his slave, his slave-girl, his ox, his ass, or anything that belongs to him" (Ex 20:17), prohibits the envious behavior that destroys enjoyment of a person's legitimate blessings. Thus the Ten Commandments are basically ten ways of exercising that God-given freedom which was conferred upon the Israelites through the covenant.[28]

Prophecy. As Walter Brueggemann has noted, "The task of prophetic ministry is to nurture, nourish, and evoke a consciousness and perception alternative to the consciousness and perception of the dominant culture around us."[29] In the Old Testament the prophets are messengers for God; their function is to convey to the people God's desires for them. This responsibility involves both energizing and criticizing. The prophets criticized the people for abandoning God's covenant, for worshiping other gods, and for relying on their own achievements. They criticized the people for their harsh treatment of the poor and for perverting justice.[30]

The prophets also energized the people so they were able to imagine a different present and a different future. They encouraged the people to observe God's rule by developing virtuous lives inspired by justice, charity, and hope for the future where God will reign in peace. The prophetic message was directed primarily toward the prophet's own time; hence, there is often severe criticism of the political, economic, and religious institutions that are contrary to God's reign. The prophets hoped to energize the creation of a different present. Their message was often supported by appeals to past praiseworthy behavior on the part of the people. However, their message also offered a vision for the future as a motivation for present reforms on the part of the people. Nevertheless, the prophetic message was directed primarily toward the present.[31] It was not so much directed toward the elimination of specific actions as it was to the formation of fidelity to the covenant and to God as the source of all righteousness.

Wisdom. In the Old Testament the Wisdom literature includes aphorisms, poems, reflections, and even diatribes. The books included in this genre are the product of a teaching tradition based on actively encouraging the transmission of the right conduct found in daily life, especially in the relationship of fathers and sons, and teachers and pupils. The tradition is actually part of a much wider tradition in the ancient world, for similar collections of sayings are also found in Egypt, Babylon, and throughout the ancient Near East. Wisdom is an attribute of God, the creator and governor of the universe. The tradition sets out the natural world, rather than history, as the primary source of revelation, for creation inspires a sense of awe through its order and beauty. The wisdom tradition develops its own creation mythology rooted in the personification of Lady Wisdom, who keeps close company with God and is present even at the creation of the world. Folly is the opposite of wisdom. The Book of Proverbs counsels young men to guard themselves against folly that might lead them to fall for loose women. The wise person is promised prosperity, whereas the fool will simply perish. Nevertheless, as Ecclesiastes points out, both the wise and the foolish will end up in the grave.[32]

The Book of Job also is part of the wisdom tradition, but it serves to critique much of the tradition.[33] Job's comforters appeal to the traditional belief that his sufferings are due to the fact that he must have offended God and so is being justly punished. But knowing that he is innocent, Job protests and appeals to God, as the primary guarantor of cosmic and moral order, to set things right in his life. God overwhelms him with a vision of the mysterious character of the cosmos, reduces him to silence, and finally vindicates him before his accusers.[34]

In the Old Testament a moral life is the result of internalizing those virtues that will issue in right conduct. It is the result of fidelity to the covenant that God has made with God's people.

THE NEW TESTAMENT AND MORALITY

The kingdom of God is the horizon for Jesus' ethical teachings. According to the parables in the Synoptic Gospels, that kingdom belongs to God and is both a present and a future reality, but the emphasis is certainly on the future when the fullness of the kingdom will be realized. For the followers of Jesus, the biblical teachings about the kingdom constitute the horizon within which the disciples of Jesus live out their lives as Christians. The reign of God is not something that faithful disciples bring about; it is exclusively the work of God, but it is the goal for all Christian living.[35]

If Christians are to become members of the kingdom of God, they must be faithful disciples of Jesus. Being a disciple of Jesus, made in the image and likeness of God, establishes the primary identity for Christians; hence, they must define themselves not only in relationship to Jesus but also in relation to other Christians, since following Jesus is a communal activity, never a solitary pursuit. Christian disciples want to be in the presence of Jesus and to share in his mission. They are members of a new family, meant to take on a simple lifestyle, and called to subordinate their own wants and needs for the sake of the kingdom. This means that faithful disciples share in Jesus' mission of teaching and healing. Teaching and healing reveal the presence of God's kingdom. A simple lifestyle should exist at the service of mission; it is never an end in itself but is meant to be a useful aid toward proclaiming the kingdom in both word and deed.

The challenge for today's disciples of Jesus is how to translate his instructions to his disciples into terms that are appropriate and helpful for life in the contemporary world. It must be noted that the three writers of the Synoptic Gospels faced the challenge of transfer in bringing the good news of Jesus to the various communities who were their intended recipients. Each writer emphasized certain aspects of Jesus' teaching that seemed relevant to his communities. Mark stressed success and failure along the way; learning from Jesus as the great teacher was emphasized by Matthew; carrying on the work of Jesus was distinctive of Luke's Gospel. The challenge of interpretation illustrated by these writers is also a great challenge for Christian teachers and preachers today. There are, however, core values in the various passages on discipleship, for they all stress the necessity of absolute commitment to God's kingdom, the importance of sharing in Jesus' mission, the need for following a simple lifestyle, and the willingness to suffer opposition and persecution for the sake of the gospel. Those values should give a definite shape to the meaning of being disciples of Jesus in every time and place.[36]

Paul's writings. The significance of the apostle Paul for our understanding of Christian ethics is extremely important. Paul views himself as a model to be imitated as he himself imitates Jesus.[37] Likewise, Christian disciples are to be models for one another. The moral standard, however, is not to be found in particular actions but rather in the identity of Christians as Christ-bearers. Paul frequently stresses the importance of internal dispositions. For example, he proposes certain virtues to be pursued and vices to be avoided; he likewise stresses the role of the Spirit in transforming human hearts. Above all, he insists on the primacy of love in the Christian life, which is expressed in terms of both personal and communal concerns. The church, as a community of disciples, is a living body that is both expressed and nurtured by the celebration of the Lord's Supper. The community is expected to practice hospitality and to respond to needs through its collections. It is clear that Paul never stresses the person at the expense of the community. He has a keen interest in who we will become by the life that we live and the actions that we perform, for actions shape the identity of the person.[38]

Paul's letters are frequently cited in support of various complex ethical questions, including divorce and remarriage, sexual behavior, social responsibilities, and submission to government authority. His letters do contain numerous statements about how to serve God and live as responsible members of the Christian community; however, specific commands about moral behavior constitute only a small part of Paul's overall corpus of writings. He was insistent that observance of the Jewish Law, including its ethical commands, should not constitute the foundation for a person's relations with God. He was very careful not to formulate a new code of law that might be interpreted as an alternative means for achieving moral righteousness.[39]

Furthermore, in his writings Paul usually begins by affirming the great saving event that God has done and is still doing for his people in Christ. It is only after carefully setting out the foundations for our relations with God that Paul moves on to lay out imperatives about how Christian disciples are to live because they have been justified by God in Christ. It follows then that Paul's ethical imperatives should always be situated in their proper theological and historical context.[40]

It should also be noted that Paul wrote his letters for specific communities in the Mediterranean world of the first century. Hence, Paul's assertions about women and slaves must be carefully related to the cultural situation of the communities who were the recipients of the letters. Discussing Paul's ethical teachings must first of all be grounded in the larger theological themes that he sets out and in his overall understanding of the teachings of Jesus.[41]

Confrontation among gospel preaching, Jewish justice, and Greek wisdom. In preaching the Christian gospel Paul encountered two vastly different concepts of morality: the Jewish concept based on the Law and the search for justice, and the Greek concept characterized by the teachings of wisdom and the classical virtues. The confrontation between gospel preaching and these two moral theories is set out primarily in two of Paul's major letters: the First Letter to the Corinthians (57 CE) and the Letter to the Romans (57–58 CE). The gospel that Paul preached with great zeal was rejected by many of the Jews for whom it was first intended; they rejected it because of their commitment to the Law. Then it was rejected by many of the Gentiles; they ridiculed it in Athens because it seemed to reject human wisdom.[42]

Jewish morality was characterized by a search for justice in God's eyes; it was dominated by fidelity to the Law of Moses with its Ten Commandments, countless prescriptions, customs and strict observances, such as circumcision. Grounded in hope for the fulfillment of divine promises on behalf of those who faithfully observed the Law, Jewish morality was rooted in the covenant God made with the chosen people and was sustained by God's fidelity to the promises made. What was expected of the people above all was conformity of their actions to the precepts of the Lord, linked with promises of happiness in return for human fidelity.[43]

Greek moral theory was based on Plato's *Decalogues,* Aristotle's *Ethics,* and to some extent the Stoic teaching on the virtues. Under the heading of wisdom and the natural attraction of the good and the beautiful, and sustained by practice of the virtues, human actions were expected to bring human happiness. It was such a moral theory that dominated the moral life of the people in the Mediterranean world during Paul's life. Roman moral theory, which prized justice, political honesty, order, and courage, did not constitute a moral system in itself but rather found expression in Roman law and so constituted a strong current of thought in Paul's negotiations with the Romans. It might be said that Paul had to confront the secular humanism of his day in order to proclaim the gospel of Jesus Christ, a challenge that also confronts preachers and teachers today.[44]

With brutal realism Paul attacked the wisdom of the Greeks because it led to folly and various forms of corruption that are verified by the Roman historians Tacitus and Suetonius. He was not more lenient with the Jews, because their supposed fidelity to the Law led to blasphemy against God. In contrast, Paul described Christian morality as based primarily on faith in Jesus Christ crucified and risen from the dead, thus becoming for all people the source of God's justice and wisdom. Faith in Jesus was a virtue the Greeks did not know and that the Jews misunderstood. Paul certainly did not deny the rightful place of justice and wisdom in human life, but he gave them a new source—they were rooted not in mere human virtues but what might be called the power of God acting in and through Jesus Christ. Such faith, however, was a scandal to the Jews and folly to the Greeks. Paul, in turn, accused the Jews of causing scandal and the Greeks of using their wisdom to breed folly. Hence, Paul laid out the foundation for all Christian ethics, namely, faith in Jesus Christ.[45]

Paul maintained that it was pride that led the Jews to hypocrisy and the Greeks to shameful practices. Faith presupposes humility in the presence of God's Son, who humbled himself and became obedient even to the cross. Faith enabled people to transcend themselves, to entrust themselves to one so much greater than themselves. As a result the human heart was opened to the power of God's own Spirit coming from the risen Lord. Paul clearly substitutes humility and faith for human wisdom and mere observance of the Law.[46]

At the heart of Christian morality, then, is a person, Jesus Christ. Jesus is not simply the great preacher of a new morality given by God; he is not another Moses; he is not simply a perfect model to be imitated, as the Greeks might admire and try to imitate their great philosophers. Rather, through his death and resurrection and the outpouring of the Spirit on all humanity, Jesus is the source and cause of a new kind of holiness and wisdom that comes only from God. Through baptism, Christians are always "in Christ" in and through the power of the Holy Spirit. This personal union with Christ leads Christians to transcend the limitations of the present world and to move beyond their suffering and death to a new world where the risen Christ is seated at the right hand of the Father. Every action, every virtue of the Christian is empowered within the human heart by the reality of faith and life with the risen Christ through the presence and the power of the Spirit. Faith in Christ transcends the realm of precepts; it models and enables Christians to apply moral theory to the problems of daily life. Slowly yet surely they are transformed so they produce good works and manifest virtue, but the source is not their own moral power but the power and presence of God's Spirit within them.[47]

Faith, the foundation of Pauline morality. For Paul, faith is an active and practical virtue. For centuries dogmatic theology and moral theology were separate disciplines; in the Protestant tradition faith and good works are clearly separated. Paul, however, roots his moral teaching in profound Christian doctrine. Faith joins the believer so intimately to Christ that it gives birth to a new being. Through baptism Christians have a new source of life. As Paul wrote in his Second Letter to the Corinthians, "For anyone who is in Christ there is a new creation; the old creation is gone, and now the new one is here" (2 Cor 5:17). This is not simply an abstract dogmatic statement. For Paul, there has been a profound change in the identity and life of the baptized Christian. Death to the old self and birth to new life have taken place in the Christian. The change is not simply on the ontological or theoretical level but affects both perception and consequent activity.[48]

Christian faith plants in the believer the seed of change in character that Paul describes as a transition from the "old man" to the "new man." It does indeed engender a new character and a new identity in the life of the Christian. In his passion and death Christ took on himself the effects of his condemnation by the Roman and Jewish authority figures and in his resurrection he poured out on us the very life of God's own Spirit. The result of our faith in Christ and intimate union with him is a fundamental transformation that provides Paul with the foundation for his treatment of virtues and vices. He stresses, on the one hand, life according to the flesh when it is isolated from the Spirit; the result is evil desires and actions that lead to death. On the other hand, he writes of life according to the Spirit, which is directed by God's own Spirit and so inclines one to live a life of peace and holiness (Rom 8:5–11).[49]

Paul's understanding of Christian morality always implies a dominant place for the action of the Holy Spirit. Such a morality centers above all on charity, a love that surpasses all charisms and other virtues (1 Cor 13:13). For Paul, charity does not mean a general sort of kindness but is rooted in the gift of faith; Paul looks on charity as a gift that proceeds from faith and is the result of the presence of the Holy Spirit in human hearts. Charity does not spring from human affections, but it certainly transforms human affections. It is at one and the same time both deeply personal and communal. Paul describes it in terms of daily human relations manifest in the routine activities of life in community. His moral teaching, then, is dominated by a call to unity, to the elimination of divisions among Christians but also among those who are not baptized. This is clearly affirmed in his remarkable statement to the Galatians: "All baptized in Christ, you have all clothed yourselves in Christ, and there are no more distinctions between Jew and Greek, slave and free, male and female, but all of you are one in Christ Jesus" (Gal 3:27–28).[50]

It should be noted that the exercise of both faith and charity actually implements the various virtues appreciated by the Greek philosophers and stressed in the sapiential literature in the Bible; however, Paul understands these purely natural virtues as somehow being wonderfully transformed by the presence of the Holy Spirit. This is exemplified in his Letter to the Philippians: "Finally, brothers and sisters, fill your minds with everything that is true, everything that is noble, everything that is good and pure, everything that we love and honor, everything that can be thought virtuous or worthy of praise" (Phil 4:8).

Paul has an organic understanding of the virtues; neither the theological nor the natural virtues have an independent status. The virtues appreciated by the Greeks were inserted into a moral and spiritual organism vastly different from

Greek wisdom. Nevertheless, Paul made it clear that the distinctive virtues and charisms possessed by Christians were the direct result of their relationship with Christ and the Spirit. The organic unity of the virtues was clearly substantiated by Paul's profound teaching on the body of Christ. Paul made all the virtues dependent on the theological virtues of faith, hope, and charity that bound the baptized Christian to Christ. This implied that any transformation in holiness was not due to one's own strength of character but to divine initiative and generosity. This necessitated a deep appreciation of humility in the life of the Christian. This emphasis on humility contrasted with the pride underlying Greek wisdom and the justice stressed by the Jews.[51]

Paul constructed a new moral organism penetrated through and through by the theological virtues of faith, hope, and charity. In this way he assimilated as much as possible the truths and goodness that were found in the Old Law and in the wisdom philosophies of the Greeks. Hence, he maintained that the merely human virtues were transformed from within so that certain important virtues, such as humility and chastity, were given a certain prominence in view of their special relationship with the love of Christ and the transforming action of the Spirit.

Paul's moral theology was profoundly christological. The person of Christ, including his humanity, which suffered death on a cross and which was raised from the dead, was really the center around which all moral life revolved. A vibrant moral life presupposed a vibrant relationship with Christ. As Paul reminded the Philippians, "We preach Christ crucified. . . . In your minds you must be the same as Christ Jesus" (Phil 2:5).[52] Paul's moral theology may also be described as trinitarian, since Christ is the manifestation of the loving kindness of the Father, who, through the gift of the Son in the incarnation, forgave the sins of Jews and Greeks, thus giving them justice and wisdom through faith. It was the gift of the Holy Spirit that actualized the gift of Christ in the lives of the baptized. Paul's moral teaching joined dogma and morality and made no dichotomy between morality and spirituality. Those distinctions and dichotomies have characterized the history of Christian theology for centuries; those categories and those distinctions, however, would be quite foreign to Paul's way of thinking.[53]

The Sermon on the Mount and Christian ethics. The Sermon on the Mount is probably the most important gospel text for Christian ethics. It appears in a longer version in Matthew's Gospel (Matt 5—7) and in a shorter version in Luke's (Luke 6:20–49). Throughout history the interpretation of the sermon has stimulated considerable discussion among both theologians and exegetes because, on the surface, the moral teaching appears to be so sublime and so demanding that no one can possibly follow it perfectly, at least not the great majority of people. Catholic commentators have in the past maintained a distinction between a moral code for all Christians, expressed primarily in the Decalogue, and a more spiritual doctrine to be applied to a specialized group, such as professed members of a religious institute. They maintained that the sermon was not aimed at all Christians because it falls under the classification of counsels rather than commands. They also held that the sermon was not addressed to the crowd but only to a group of disciples and apostles whom Jesus called to be his special followers. Contemporary commentators, however, have rejected that interpretation.[54]

Another interpretation holds that the sermon should be viewed as the expression of an ideal that is not at all practical but is meant to inspire people to pursue their Christian vocation more seriously. Still other commentators hold that the sermon, in contrast to Judaism's obsession with good works, presents a new version of morality that applies primarily to one's interior dispositions. Even Protestant commentators are becoming more and more convinced of the need for effective external actions that are demanded by the sermon. Most commentators today maintain that the sermon simply cannot be turned into a teaching on one's interior life separated from practical experience.[55] What, then, do the majority of contemporary commentators hold concerning the interpretation of this important gospel text?

The Sermon in Matthew's Gospel. A major concern for Matthew in writing his Gospel was to set out large sections of Jesus' teaching; he presents that teaching in five major discourses. They deal with true happiness, the proper interpretation of the Law and the prophets, genuine piety, wise attitudes and behavior in everyday life, and the need to transform wisdom into concrete actions. As a Jewish wisdom text, in many ways Matthew's Gospel summarizes the wisdom of Jesus.[56]

The first and longest discourse is commonly known as the Sermon on the Mount and was addressed to the crowds, to all Israel gathered to hear Jesus. Jesus was setting before Israel his new teachings and was challenging the people to accept and act upon them. The basic theme of the sermon is that Jesus came, not to abolish the Law and the prophets, but to fulfill them (5:17). It is important to recognize that Matthew places Jesus' teaching in an eschatological context but that it also concerns appropriate conduct in the present. The sermon is not designed as a strictly personal ethic or as a plan for the establishment of a social utopia. It is addressed to ordinary people, not to an elite; its primary role is to remind the hearers of their status as sinners in need of conversion. Like Matthew's Gospel as a whole, the sermon is meant to set out a compendium of Jesus' teaching primarily for Jews, since Matthew was writing for a Jewish-Christian community. It aims to show how Jesus fulfills the Law and the prophets rather than to show the superiority of his teaching to the Jewish scriptures. Jesus, in fact, presents for his disciples an authoritative interpretation of the Torah; however, he is more concerned with principles and attitudes than with practical laws.[57]

Before setting out the demanding way of life that constitutes the main part of the sermon, Jesus affirms clearly that those who embrace such a pattern of life are truly blessed. He declares that those who practice certain virtues will be blessed or happy, and he promises them an eternal reward in God's kingdom. The sermon sets out a vision centered on the coming rule of God; although it will be rejected by many, it will in the end triumph. If the people listen to Jesus' teaching, rather than feeling coerced to act in a particular way, they will firmly desire to live according to the vision.[58]

In Matthew's Gospel the beatitudes are not primarily prescriptive in an ethical sense. Jesus is not telling the people that they must do certain things; rather, he is commending certain clear values, virtues, and attitudes. He wants to share with the people a vision that, if implemented, will enable them to internalize the very values and attitudes which Jesus himself espouses and wants others to accept because his vision is God's own vision for the people. Likewise, the beatitudes presuppose an important distinction between the present, in which there is much suffering, and the future, when there will be no persecution or pain. They assert that people who espouse certain values and attitudes are blessed not because of their present situation, which is so often one of suffering, but because of the future that will come about for them because of the power and faithfulness of God.[59]

Certainly the attitudes that Jesus commends are not meant to provide his followers with a comfortable existence in the world here and now. All the beatitudes cohere around the *basic idea of living in a non-grasping way.* To be poor in spirit; to mourn because of an unfortunate situation; to be gentle rather than aggressive; to be passionately committed to justice; to be merciful rather than competitive; to be pure in heart; to be peacemakers; and to endure calumny, detraction, and abuse out of loyalty to Christ all make a person vulnerable and subject to diminishment. But all these attitudes imply that one will be truly blessed, for those who live by such qualities will be comforted, filled, and have mercy shown to them by God. The present may involve loss and sacrifice, but in light of the coming reign of God those who espouse such qualities are truly blessed, even at the present time.[60]

Faithful disciples who espouse the beatitudes will be salt of the earth and light of the world. The implication is that those who are willing to live in the way set out in the beatitudes are the very ones who can really help others. Those who live in a vulnerable, non-materialistic way are the ones who are blessed and who can help to lift humanity's burdens, thereby functioning as salt of the earth and light of the world. Those who put into practice the Law as interpreted by Jesus will make Israel the light to the nations. Their good works function as a lamp bringing light to a world darkened by sin and evil; they try to live a life of righteousness not to attract attention to themselves but to lead others to God so that they too will be salt of the earth and light for the world.[61]

The Sermon on the Mount contains many teachings that contemporary scholars attribute with confidence to the historical Jesus. In fact, the sermon serves as a summary or compendium of Jesus' most important and distinctive teachings, his wise teachings. It is neither a law code nor the new Torah. Rather, Matthew presents Jesus as an authoritative interpreter of the Law of Moses. The sermon is best understood as part of an ethics concerned with Christian character. It tells us how to prepare to enjoy the fullness of life in the future by teaching us how to act in the present. Jesus is not only set out as a master teacher, but he is also the best example of one who has implemented his own teachings.[62]

The Sermon on the Mount sets out three virtues that are distinctively Christian: mercy, a reconciling spirit, and hope. In the sermon, mercy is closely associated with God, who gives the kingdom to those who are poor in spirit; it is God who gives comfort to those who mourn, who provides for our needs, and who is the source of all good gifts. Mercy is also a virtue that character-izes those who follow Christ. Mercy is a dominant virtue in the Bible. God's covenant with us is characterized above all by God's *hesed* or loving mercy.[63]

The spirit of reconciliation is prominent in Matthew's Sermon on the Mount. The spirit of forgiveness is essential to live peacefully in community. Likewise, the Sermon on the Mount is pervaded by a sense of hope for the future. It is hope that is foundational for our understanding of the beatitudes, for it enables us to trust that God will indeed be our salvation.[64]

The Sermon in Luke's Gospel. Luke also presents Jesus in his Galilean ministry delivering an important body of teaching in the form of a sermon. His version of the beatitudes (Lk 6:17–35), however, is much more concise than Matthew's. Luke includes in his account of Jesus' journey to Jerusalem much of the material that Matthew includes in his Sermon on the Mount. In both cases the sermon begins with a discussion of the beatitudes.[65]

Matthew has nine beatitudes, but Luke has only four, which are followed by woes. Luke's language is blunt. He writes, "Blessed are you poor" rather than Matthew's more qualified "blessed are the poor in spirit." Furthermore, in the biblical tradition the term *blessed* does not refer to a moral attitude; it strikes a congratulatory note. The language of Luke's beatitudes is highly provoca-tive, for they contain a series of oxymorons that link together two clashing concepts. Unfortunately, our familiarity with the language has tended to soften their sharpness.[66]

The beatitudes and the woes make sense only in the light of the reversal of human fortune that is so pronounced in Luke's Gospel. There is a clear reversal of situations that, on one hand, appear to be fortunate and, on the other, seem to be disastrous. The reversal of the human situation makes it better to be poor, hungry, weeping, and reviled by others than wealthy, well fed, happy, and well spoken of. The dramatic change that will soon take place is sure to reverse the situation so that the very thought of the change makes it possible to endure the present pain. It is this reversal that makes it possible to hold together both being blessed and being poor as well as the other contradictory terms. It is clear that Jesus is not praising poverty or pain, but he is asserting that what most people consider to be positive or negative situations are relative and actually reversed in light of God's future action.[67]

In Luke's Gospel the beatitudes portray a situation of extreme vulnerability diametrically opposed to the world's accepted values. In God's eyes, however, vulnerability makes sense, because God has promised to act on behalf of the poor, the victimized, and the marginalized. God has made a fundamental option for the poor. There is no doubt that the beatitudes and woes are challenging for both the rich and the poor. However, there is no suggestion that the poor and the marginalized should be content with their situation and passively accept their fate. The poor, however, can only benefit if God acts on their behalf. Their advantage consists in the fact that they have an emptiness that only God can fill because of God's overflowing generosity.[68]

Are the poor who are blessed in Luke's Gospel economically poor or are they spiritually poor? There seems little doubt that, in light of Mary's Magnificat, the poor are economically poor, but in Jesus' time the poor were those who were open to receive fulfillment from God. In that sense the poor were those who waited in hope for God's eventual intervention in their lives. This attitude was found in a special way in the lives of Simeon and Anna. Their hope for salvation included both economic and spiritual salvation. In other words, the poor were those whose emptiness offered scope for God's generosity. In Luke's version of the sermon the disciples of Jesus are vulnerable and so blessed because they offer God scope for the exercise of divine power. They were open to receive the hospitality of God, who wants to make the world a safe place for all.[69]

After setting out the beatitudes and woes, Luke's version of the sermon proceeds to discuss generosity in human relationships. God's people are expected to imitate in their relations with one another the same generosity that God manifests toward them. Luke's chapter 6 begins and ends with the command to love one's enemies (vv. 27–42). Faithful disciples are to return a blessing for a curse; they are to turn the other cheek when they are struck; they are to give their shirt to one who has taken their coat. They are to respond to injury or insult with nothing but generosity and the abandonment of all claims to retribution. In our world, as well as in the world of Jesus' disciples, such actions make no sense. But one must bear in mind that exaggeration often marks the prophetic speech of Jesus. He is not establishing laws that must be kept literally. He is seeking to inculcate an attitude in which one would be willing to be vulnerable to a degree that would seem utterly foolish by the standards of the world. It is imitation of God's generosity that is important, for God is kind even to the ungrateful and the wicked (Lk 6:35).[70]

The disciples of Jesus are to be merciful as God is merciful; they are to refrain from judging others harshly. If they forgive, then God will forgive them; if they are generous, God will be extraordinarily generous with them. It is God's nature to be generous, because God lives for giving. It is possible, however, for human beings to block reception of God's gifts so they are ineffectual in human lives.[71]

The challenge not to judge or condemn others highlights the difficulty that human beings have in understanding others as God understands them. Human relations are often based on retribution or perhaps on strict justice, but our judgments are often wrong because of our difficulty in understanding what is actually going on in the lives of others. It is God who sees clearly the human heart, and yet God always acts generously—with understanding and compassion. God sets a model for us and asks us to anticipate the proper relations that will prevail in God's kingdom.[72]

There should be continuity between our interior dispositions and attitudes and our exterior actions. God's actions in our hearts must flow over into our external actions toward others. If we imitate God's actions toward us, we contribute to the building of the kingdom here and now; we build the foundation for the exercise of God's power and fidelity to all the promises God has made.[73] The virtues and interior dispositions matter most; these, in turn, should manifest themselves in exterior acts of justice and charity.

The Johannine writings. The Gospel of John sets out a different portrayal of Jesus from that we find in the Synoptic Gospels, where the humanity of Jesus is stressed. In fact, John's Gospel fills a lacuna in the Synoptics, for it begins Jesus' public ministry with his call of the first disciples north in Galilee. In John, the author anticipates that moment in the south near the place where the Jordan empties into the Dead Sea. It was there that the Qumran community lived in caves and gathered in a complex network of buildings for their ritual baths, meals, and work. John the Baptist may have lived for a while with the Qumran community; also, some of John's disciples, like Andrew and John, may have followed John the Baptist when he moved away from Qumran to preach and baptize. Commentators note the noticeable influence that the Qumran community had upon the preaching of Jesus and eventually on the author of the Fourth Gospel.[74]

In the Fourth Gospel, Jesus is set out as a majestic, serene figure who is omniscient and in control of his destiny. It is plausible that John represents a parallel but independent tradition, not dependent on the Gospel of Mark, as in the Synoptic tradition. Although the Gospel is ascribed to John as the author, the actual author is unknown, since the text refers to the author simply as the "disciple whom Jesus loved" (13:23; 19:26; 21:7, 20). The text as we have it seems to have gone through at least three stages of development and represents the tradition and teaching of the Johannine community rather than just one author.[75]

The Gospel of John reflects the life and tensions of the time and place where it was written. There is a very black-and-white portrayal of the world, which is either good or evil, light or dark. There is a clear contrast between spirit and flesh. The final compilation seems to date from around 90 CE, when the Christian community was involved in a very acrimonious debate with fellow Jews. Consequently the term "the Jews" *(hoi ioudaioi)* is regularly used in a pejorative sense, usually to describe the enemies of Jesus. We must remember, however, that both Jesus and his disciples were Jews, so we must not conclude that Jesus ever vilified or rejected his own people.[76]

At the beginning of the Gospel of John, Jesus is introduced, not as an infant born in Bethlehem but as the eternal Word of the Father made flesh. He is the Word of God come down from heaven who through his life, death, and resurrection draws all people to himself, thereby opening the way for them to enjoy eternal life. Through the symbols of light, water, bread, and the vine, the Gospel shows Jesus as the response to the deepest hopes of humanity. His saving death is crucial to the work of bringing people to union with God. At his death, blood and water flowed from his side, symbolic of baptism and Eucharist, which are now the channels of life and salvation in the church.[77]

In chapters 14 and 15 we find, at least implicitly, what might be described as the Gospel's teaching on morality, for following Jesus is described as the "way" to eternal life. The term was used earlier in the Acts of the Apostles. Jesus is described as the great manifestation of the truth; knowing him sets one free. Life is a dominant theme in the Gospel, and the bestowal of eternal life is the primary mission of Jesus. Hence the three terms—*way, truth,* and *life*—all refer to the person of Jesus. Knowing him is the same as knowing the Father, since Jesus in his own person is the perfect manifestation of the Father. Fidelity to Jesus is achieved by keeping his commandments. In fact, Jesus gave his disciples only one commandment—to love one another—but it is clear from other references that it is equally important to believe that Jesus is the one sent from God. Love, then, is not only a mode of knowing God, but it is also an empowering principle, for Jesus and his Father will love and reveal themselves to those who love Jesus. All of this is possible through the sending of the Advocate, who will ensure a permanent divine presence in the community of believers. The Johannine community is a Spirit-filled community in which teaching and God's revelation are continuous.[78]

The final gift of Jesus to his disciples is the gift of God's peace, which is vastly different from the earthly peace that implies the absence of violence. God's peace given through the Spirit abolishes fear and any sense of separation from God. Jesus promised the disciples that he would always be present in the community. In describing the nature of the union of the disciples with Jesus and his Father, Jesus uses the metaphor of the vine. Jesus himself is the true vine; his disciples are the branches, intimately connected with the vine. Those who remain linked to the vine are sustained and nourished, but those who distance themselves from the vine wither and die. The branches are judged according to the fruit that they bear, that is, by the good works they perform in obedience to the commandments of Jesus, especially his commandment to love one another. Because of this intimate union with Jesus, the disciples are no longer servants or slaves. They are friends who have personal knowledge of Jesus and his mission. The basic moral teaching in the Gospel of John is that we love one another.[79]

The letters of John were written sometime after the Gospel, possibly between 100 and 115 CE. They were written by an anonymous elder and intended for the various house churches making up the Johannine community.[80] The first letter is not written in the style of a letter; rather, it suggests a homily to be read to the assembled community. The second and third letters are terse and follow the conventions of ancient letter writing. The three texts are examples of moral exhortation or parenesis. The author seeks to ensure that the members of the community continue to believe and act in a manner consistent with the faith they proclaim. The idealized view of the Christian life presented in the Gospel of John has given way to a realistic look at human life, which often involves serious crises. A schism has developed and ecclesial unity has been broken; consequently, those who deny Jesus the Christ are actually anti-Christs, liars, and false prophets. The author of the three letters forcefully reiterates the essential elements of the Gospel, especially the importance of the divine incarnation, the commandment of love, the gift of the Spirit, the nature of sin as a rupture, and eschatological hope for the future. As in the Gospel, the letters set out the stark contrast between light and darkness, truth and falsehood, love and hate. There is no middle ground. A disciple stands in the light or in the darkness.[81]

4

Moral Theology and Ethics:
A Historical Survey

In the history of moral theology each era is characterized either by an emphasis on becoming a faithful disciple of Christ or on avoiding sin and evil. When the first emphasis prevailed, moral theologians tended to rely on the Bible as their primary text; they tried to develop an integrated anthropological profile of Christian disciples and generally pursued a positive agenda that accommodated the concerns of ascetical theology and the development of human holiness. When the emphasis was on sin and the avoidance of evil, moral theologians tended to neglect the teachings of the Bible and often drew conclusions that were more reflections of their own imaginations than expressions of principles grounded in divine revelation. In what follows an attempt will be made to summarize the dominant characteristics of moral theology in the major periods of church history.

PATRISTIC PERIOD

Authors differ in their understanding of the scope of the patristic period. Some maintain that it runs from the end of New Testament times or the end of the Apostolic Age (100 CE) to either the date of the Council of Chalcedon (451 CE) or to the eighth-century Second Council of Nicaea (787 CE).[1] Still others maintain that the period extends, at least in the West, to the middle of the twelfth century when Scholasticism developed as a new method of theological study. It is, however, during this latter period that moral theology developed as a distinct science and an essential part of theology; but it did not receive a systematic form and organization until the thirteenth century.[2]

The patristic writing on moral theology has been derived from numerous homilies and commentaries on scripture, collections of various personal compositions, and treatises dealing with particular moral issues. It was clear to the fathers of the church that the bishops' primary task was to proclaim and explain the scriptures. They accomplished that task through their homilies and catechesis, above all in a liturgical context. These commentaries, whether spoken or written, were the primary sources for their teaching on morality. They related the teaching of the scriptures to the ordinary lives of their people. In the East, especially with Athanasius, Cyril, and the Alexandrians generally, stress was placed on the possibility of human divinization through a response to the power and presence of the Holy Spirit.[3] Basil the Great (330–379) composed a treatise entitled *Moralia*, but it was simply a collection of New Testament extracts with a brief introduction. John Chrysostom (344–407) was a major patristic homilist. He delivered almost one hundred homilies on the Gospel of Matthew, almost ninety on the Gospel of John, about two hundred and fifty on the Pauline letters, as well as homilies on numerous psalms and other books of the Bible. He is probably the most significant moralist among the church fathers because of his oratorical ability, the soundness of his teaching, and his pastoral sensitivity. In the West, Augustine (354–430), because of his personal history, tended to take a pessimistic view of human nature and stressed the opposition between human nature and grace.[4] He produced extensive homilies on the Sermon on the Mount, also 125 homilies on the Gospel of John and ten homilies on the First Letter of John, as well as his much appreciated commentaries on the psalms. Biblical commentaries in various forms are the first and primary source for patristic moral teaching.[5]

Among documents that contain significant moral teaching is the *Didache,* written at the end of the first or beginning of the second century and usually considered the first Christian manual of moral teaching. The document outlined two ways open to the Christian: the way of life and the way of death. The former was inspired by charity, including love of enemies, and encouraged a fight against evil by observing counsels concerning the poor and the proper education of children.[6]

In *The Teacher* Clement of Alexandria (150–211) confronted pagan morality with a treatise on Christian ethics centered on the virtues. For him the true teacher was the incarnate Logos. Origen (185–255) wrote a major work on spiritual exegesis that included a treatment of morality (Book III). He concentrated on freedom and its relationship to the world and the flesh and the final triumph of good over evil. In addition to his commentary on the Sermon on the Mount, Augustine also wrote *The Christian Way of Life,* in which he pointed out that the classical virtues of prudence, justice, courage, and temperance were transformed by the Christian virtue of charity. In *De doctrina Christiana* Augustine carefully distinguished between the ultimate good, which is God, and other goods people may use and enjoy. That distinction dominated his concept of morality and the Christian attachment to what is good. In *Enchiridion ad Lautentium* Augustine discussed the theological virtues and highlighted hope and charity as the goal of all the commandments.[7]

There are other works that deal with particular ethical problems. For example, Tertullian (c.160–c.225) wrote treatises on games, idolatry, feminine practices, prayer, patience, fasting, chastity, and monogamy. Augustine wrote about lying, continence, prayer, and fasting. John Chrysostom wrote on the education of children, virginity, and widowhood. This brief survey shows that the early fathers dealt with various moral issues, but their reflections are scattered throughout their scriptural commentaries and homilies.[8]

In the patristic period a principal characteristic of Christian moral teaching was the acceptance of the Bible as the primary source for the revelation of all Christian teaching. The fathers were largely concerned with clarifying biblical concepts and applying them to the practice of living as a Christian. Even their more speculative commentaries on Christology and trinitarian theology had practical implications for the shaping of a Christian moral life.[9] However, the fathers read and interpreted scripture quite differently than we do today. They believed that all scripture contained a moral dimension and meaning; scripture was meant to be actualized in the life and activities of every Christian. They thought that the principal concern of moral theology was salvation and the various ways leading to eternal happiness. They believed that certain books and sections of the Bible were especially relevant for moral teaching, including the Wisdom literature, the Sermon on the Mount, and the parenetic or moral sections of Paul's letters.

The primary objective in the exegesis of the fathers was to go beyond the words to the reality signified and to encounter the mystery of God, especially God's Son. They realized they could approach that mystery only through faith in the Lord Jesus and attentive listening to his word. Hence, their interpretation of the scripture was aimed at transforming human lives; it was based on faith and meant to be practical, but practice was made possible through the action of the Holy Spirit, who was the primary author of holy scripture. The fathers stressed imitation of Christ and encouraged disciples to espouse a unified anthropology. Just as Christ brought his humanity and divinity into the unity of his person, so Christian disciples were called to bring body and soul together. Integration was a major task for Christian disciples.[10] The fathers hoped that reading the scriptures would stir up faith in the disciples and lead to Christian transformation. In that way their interpretation was keenly related to the moral life.[11] In fact, the Christian moral life was looked upon as a response to the word of God incarnate in Jesus Christ.

Greek wisdom was also an important source in patristic theology. Ancient ethical reflections centered around the cardinal virtues of prudence, justice, fortitude, and temperance. As a result, the fathers paid considerable attention to philosophy. They found Platonic thought especially useful because they felt it was closest to Christianity in its stress on transcendence and the world of ideas. Unfortunately, the Platonic opposition between body and spirit inclined some of the fathers to disparage the material world and an active life, which seemed to be in opposition to a life of contemplation. This resulted in the exaltation of the monastic life over the life of lay people living in the world. The mystical doctrine of Dionysius the Areopagite (fifth century), inspired by Neo-Platonism, played an especially important role in western theology. Augustine, for example, acknowledged in his *Confessions* that reading the Neoplatonists had turned his attention to God and helped him understand the word of God. Stoic influence was also important, especially because of its teaching on the role of the virtues in daily life. Ambrose (c.339–97) used Cicero's *De officiis* as the basis for his reflections on morality. In fact, the philosophical works of Cicero were foundational for the writings of many of the Latin fathers.

Mention should also be made of the influence of Roman law and its understanding of justice, which, especially through the writings of Tertullian and Ambrose, influenced the body of Christian teaching for many years. Roman law, however, never had any essentially Christian character about it. It was the law of the empire, and its governing principle was that the will of the sovereign was always law. Eventually Roman law became the basis for canon law. It was that system of domination that Christ explicitly condemned and rejected for his disciples because it was based on the fundamental flaw that there is neither need nor place for the accountability of those who govern to those whom they govern.[12] This is a major problem in the church today. Nevertheless, the conclusion may be drawn that historically there was a close relationship between Christian faith and the natural philosophy of the early centuries of the church.[13]

The patristic writers did not distinguish between morality and spirituality, a practice that became customary in the later Middle Ages. For them spirituality was simply the result of the full development of a moral life and was manifested in a special way in a life of virginity and in martyrdom. Virginity was extolled by many of the fathers, especially in the fourth century. Gregory of Nyssa, John Chrysostom, Ambrose, and Augustine all wrote treatises on virginity. They based their reflections on the letters of Paul and chapter 13 of Matthew's Gospel concerning the Lord's teaching on eunuchs.[14] The patristic spirituality of martyrdom also had its basis in the New Testament. It proposed to all Christians the ideal of imitating Christ, even to the extent of giving one's life in order to witness to Christ, who sacrificed his life for the life of the world. The letters of Ignatius of Antioch, as well as the accounts of the martyrdom of Polycarp, Cyprian, and others, are evidence of the great value that the fathers placed on martyrdom. After the persecution of Christians gradually ended in the fourth century, it was held that such witness to Christian values was shown above all in the life of the desert fathers and mothers. Every Christian was urged to bear witness to Christ in life and death, a teaching brought out not only in patristic writings but in the lives of numerous martyrs.

The vast collection of patristic writings dealing with moral issues certainly bears witness to the fact that after the scriptures, the works of the fathers constitute a primary source for understanding the development of Christian moral theology and also provide a source for evaluating the development of moral theology in later periods of church history.[15] The fathers were not interested primarily in the observance of external laws but rather on inspiring Christians to internalize Christian values and to develop strong Christian virtues.

THE HIGH MIDDLE AGES

In the period from Gregory the Great (c.540–604) until Bernard of Clairvaux (1090–1153) there was not a single major work issued in moral theology. It was not a particularly creative period; writers simply exploited the doctrines that the fathers had produced in the first six centuries. It was considered adequate, especially in Benedictine monasteries, to read the writings of the fathers as *lectio divina*. Bede the Venerable (c.637–735), monk of Jarrow, wrote commentaries on the Bible that were based on the writings of Augustine, Jerome, Ambrose, and Gregory the Great. Rabanus Maurus (c.780–856) was more interested in ecclesiastical law than in spirituality, although he enriched the liturgy of the Abbey of Fulda by composing new hymns and a revised martyrology. To reconstruct a moral theology during this period, one has to consult the decrees of the popes, the councils, and the bishops, all of whom sought to remedy abuses and thereby to improve the moral life of the Christian people.

Following Gratian and his *Decrees* (1140), canon lawyers gave considerable attention to moral issues, above all laws and contracts, crimes and sins, and various sacraments, especially marriage. The only important development in this period was the diffusion of the *Libri poenitentiales*—manuscripts that originated in Ireland or the British Isles and that were diffused through France, Germany, Switzerland, and northern Italy by Irish missionaries. The practice of confessing one's sins with some regularity originated in the sixth century, especially in a monastic context. In the Celtic lands spiritual leaders, especially abbots and abbesses, cultivated the practice among their disciples and even extended the practice among devout laity. As a result, the penitentials developed. These books were not treatises on moral theology but simply detailed lists of sins and their appropriate penances. They were generally organized around the seven deadly sins—pride, anger, envy, sloth, avarice, gluttony, and lust. With this emphasis on an individual's private moral state, a long period of moral narcissism was inaugurated. Christians became anxious and worried not about the spread of God's reign or the needs of the church and other Christians but rather about the state of their individual souls. Judgment Day was looked upon not as a day of deliverance but rather as a day of damnation for the masses of corrupt humanity. These penitential manuals provided clerics with an important instrument of social control and stability in a period of considerable turmoil and political instability. They felt secure in their ministry of the sacrament of penance.[16]

In various councils the Carolingian reformers denounced these books and their mechanical use. As a result, several efforts were made to provide sound handbooks for confessors, such as Book 19 of the *Decretum* of Burchard of Worms (c.965–1025), which had great influence.[17] The twelfth century was a period of significant awakening. Canon lawyers began to codify personal rights and procedures through ecclesiastical legislation. After the Fourth Lateran Council (1215) they were involved in developing a theology of penance for the use of confessors. The best example would be Raymond of Peñafort's (c.1180–1275) *Summa de poenitentia.* Abelard (1079–1142/3) attempted to put together a synthesis of Christian morality. More spiritual writers, such as Hugh of St. Victor (d.1141), Richard of St. Victor (1173), Bernard of Clairvaux (1090–1153), and Hildegard of Bingen (1098–1179), attempted to compile syntheses of Christian wisdom by relying on the Bible and the traditional fathers of the church. These writers were fascinated with the human person as the image of God. Peter Lombard (c.1100–1160), whose *Liber sententiarum* served for about four centuries as a basic textbook for theological students, attempted to synthesize the results of these efforts at developing a sound moral theology as well as a doctrinal synthesis. Peter did not separate moral theology from doctrine but wrote about moral issues as implied in dogmatic questions. He is to be admired because he was keenly aware of the deep unity that should exist in theology among doctrinal, moral, and spiritual matters. In the East, Maximus the Confessor (580–662) and John Damascene (675–749) wrote treatises on human action that would later be utilized by Thomas Aquinas.[18]

Under the influence of Peter Abelard and Peter Lombard a significant development occurred in theological method, usually described as the Scholastic method. It consisted of the general acceptance of the major works of antiquity as important sources of knowledge and the use of dialectic as the principal tool in reflecting on and teaching theology. The use of the dialectic method consisted in confronting contrary opinions about an issue by the use of questions and articles. Most important, however, was the fruitful link between faith and reason. Theology became the work of faith relying above all on scripture and the fathers of the church but also analyzing the vast material offered by philosophy and the other sciences. Another characteristic of Scholastic theology was its corporate character grounded in a faculty of theology including both professors and students. Theology was not isolated from contemporary issues but sought to reflect on contemporary major problems. It should be noted too that the major shift in the structure of society from a rural environment to more urban and commercial centers brought Christian thought into contact with long-lost sources of Greek philosophy, especially those of Aristotle and the Arabian and Jewish scholars who transmitted the Greek sources.[19]

From the twelfth through the sixteenth century the Scholastics explored ways of expressing Christian thought through reason. Insofar as theology was viewed as a science investigating both God and humanity, moral theology specifically investigated humanity in its efforts to respond to divine initiative. Hence, this area of theology became intensely anthropological and concentrated on the virtues in its efforts to specify moral identity. Natural law was integrated in moral theology and was looked upon as the way to pursue the good and to avoid evil. Theology in general was almost exclusively an academic pursuit.[20]

In the thirteenth century the scientific character of morality was especially advanced by the masters of the faculty of arts at the University of Paris; they also developed a moral philosophy that was already in place, much of which Thomas Aquinas (c.1225–74) incorporated in his major theological synthesis. Albert the Great (d. 1280) was the primary advocate for the introduction of Aristotle's writings into the University of Paris. While teaching in the Dominican Studium in Cologne he gave a commentary on Aristotle's *Ethics* that was taken down by his student Thomas Aquinas. Albert also treated moral issues in other works, including his commentary on the *Sentences* and his *Summa de bono*.[21]

It is impossible to understand Thomas's treatment of moral theology properly without affirming the importance of his religious formation as a Dominican. Likewise, his moral theology must be situated in the context of the other sections of his *Summa theologiae*. The first part studies the triune God, the true happiness of the human person, and the meaning of human happiness, which is essentially a participation in the life of God. The first part also deals with the human person and his or her faculties, above all, intellect and free will, as well as the emotions. Other themes, such as goodness and love, are also discussed as they are found in God, the angels, and Christ. The third part treats true happiness found in Christ through the essential aid of grace which is communicated through the sacraments. It is essential, then, that the second part of the *Summa* on morality be closely related to the first part on the trinitarian God and the third part, which treats the christological and sacramental dimensions of theology.[22]

The virtues were at the center of Thomas's moral teaching. For him, as for the ancient philosophers, the virtues were the noblest of human moral qualities; they are perfected by the gifts of the Holy Spirit and manifest themselves in the fruits of the Holy Spirit. Sins and vices have traditionally preoccupied moral theologians, but Thomas treated them rather briefly under twenty questions (71–89); he regularly discussed them in relation to the positive virtues. He stressed that the Old Law was centered around the Decalogue, whereas the New Law is inscribed in human hearts by the power and presence of the Holy Spirit and finds its primary expression in the Sermon on the Mount. The Christian life is life according to God's Spirit, revealed to us primarily in the gospel and in the sacramental liturgy. Naturally, Thomas studied grace in conjunction with his treatment of the New Law. His moral system was primarily and soundly rooted in the virtues and in God's gifts. For him sin was a negation of virtue; laws and obligations were simply meant to foster development of the virtues.[23]

Thomas's material is grouped around the three theological virtues of faith, hope, and love, as well as those virtues expounded in the philosophical tradition: prudence, justice, fortitude, and temperance. Fifty-three different virtues are discussed in the *Secunda secundae*. Thomas is careful to show that the virtues do not exist in isolation from one another but interact and form a structured organism. It is somewhat surprising that Thomas gives humility, which is such an important virtue in the writings of Paul, Augustine, the desert fathers, and Benedict, only a modest place, probably because it is not emphasized in the classical writers like Cicero. Likewise, Thomas completely excludes the virtue of penitence, so important in the Christian tradition, because it is not treated by the pagan philosophers. That virtue is treated only in his discussion of the sacrament of penance.[24]

Initially Thomas's moral theology was widely accepted and studied because it responded effectively to the pastoral needs of the time, particularly in the ministry of the mendicant friars, but it was often separated from the overall plan of his *Summa.* However, the overall theology of the *Summa* was quickly accepted by the Dominican Order, but the friars had to defend Thomas from severe criticisms, including those of Stephen Tempier, who condemned certain propositions in 1277, and diverse Franciscan attacks, especially those contained in William de la Mare's *Corrections,* which declared that 117 propositions were false. After 1279 the general chapter of the Dominican Order prohibited all attacks on Thomas, and in 1313 the general chapter declared that his doctrine should be adopted and taught throughout the order. As a result, a Thomistic school of theology was gradually developed by numerous commentators, including John Capreolus (c.1380–1444) and Cajetan (1469–1534), who was recognized as the most important interpreter of Thomas's work. In the sixteenth century Spain experienced a remarkable revival at the University of Salamanca where Francisco de Vitoria (1480–1546), Melchior Cano (1509–60), and

Dominic Bañez (1528–1604) were professors. Two centuries later, in France, Charles R. Billuart (1685–1757) produced important work that provided the foundation for later Thomistic manuals.[25]

It is important to note that a contrasting approach to moral theology was taken by the Franciscan School. From Alexander Hales (c.1186–1245) to Bonaventure (1217–74) and Duns Scotus (1265–1308), the Franciscans produced numerous theological *Summas* that commented on the *Sentences* of Peter Lombard. Alexander's work, which was actually compiled by a group of Franciscans working under him, focused primarily on the study of sin and misconduct. Sins were divided into eight categories: venial and mortal sins, and the seven capital sins along with sins against God, neighbor, and self. The second part of the treatise was designed to cover law, grace, and the virtues, but unfortunately the work stopped with the treatment of faith. In the Franciscan School the teaching of moral theology sought not simply to serve contemplation but to make people better, for all moral life is an expression of love drawn from the source of all love, God in Jesus Christ. The school stressed the primacy of charity and also the primacy of will over intellect.

Pope Innocent III (1160–1216) had a rather depraved view of humanity and was convinced that most people would be damned; consequently, he imposed on the church the requirement that those guilty of serious sin must confess their sins once a year. Because he advised the Dominicans to become trained especially as confessors, they, along with the Franciscans, developed sophisticated confessional manuals that were generally based on the seven deadly sins. These manuals became the dominant instruments for forming both the clergy and the laity in their efforts to discern the moral life. Despite the integrated approach to theology taken by the majority of Scholastics, those involved in the moral lives of ordinary Christians were primarily concerned with sins.[26]

The wholesome balance that distinguished Thomistic moral theology and its treatment of nature and grace was broken by nominalistic dialectics. Early in the fourteenth century William of Ockham (c.1295–1347), an English native who early in his life became a Franciscan and studied and taught at Oxford, challenged many aspects of Thomas's teaching. William held that the good is not defined as an ontological reality but is simply determined by the arbitrary will of God. In other words, the good is what is ordered by God and because God orders it, whereas evil is what God forbids and is evil because God forbids it. God, however, is not bound by his own decrees and can change any of them simply by willing the change. Both revealed and natural laws are simply manifestations of the divine will. All Christian morality consists, then, in the human person's absolutely free will to obey the divine law. William's basic teaching came to be identified with nominalism. He asserted that universals, such as goodness and evil, do not exist in reality but only in the human mind. Every substance is radically individual. William's positions were not accepted by the Franciscan Order or the pope, so he was expelled from the order in 1331. His teachings have come down to us as a form of nominalism and have had significant influence on theological methodology, opening the way to moral casuistry, a study of concrete cases of conscience. The academic center of nominalism was the University of Paris, but Prague, Vienna, and the new German universities were also affected by the system. Gabriel Biel (c.1420–95) gave the system the scholarly form that influenced Martin Luther.[27]

Moral theology reached a high point of development with the second part of Thomas's *Summa;* however, the Franciscan School also made an important contribution by its emphasis on the Augustinian tradition. Thomas affirmed the primacy of the intellect and held that the intellect was the essential faculty used in attaining the vision of God, whereas the Franciscans maintained the primacy of the will and made love the foundation of beatitude. In the Thomistic tradition precept and obligation were regularly at the service of virtue; the Franciscans placed greater emphasis on the commandments and precepts. William of Ockham based obligation at the center of his theology and substituted obligation for happiness and virtue. Nominalism made a sharp break with the previous tradition of moral theology and prepared the way not only for casuistry but also for the development of manuals that became standard texts for the instruction of candidates for ordination and priests from the fifteenth century to the middle of the twentieth.[28]

ORIGINS OF MODERN MORAL THEOLOGY

In the late thirteenth and fourteenth centuries theology became more and more sharply distinguished from the literature on spirituality and mysticism, and more and more speculative and divorced from pastoral concerns. These divisions had an impact on theology as a whole but especially on moral theology. During this period theology along Scholastic lines became a major specialization in the universities with a wide use of dialectic and logic, emphasis on speculation, and preoccupation with distinctions, questions, and arguments. A highly scientific and specialized vocabulary developed, along with a tendency to abstract from the concrete issues of daily life in the world. The speculative character was also affected by the rationalism that characterized the modern era. In the Middle Ages theology was centered in the monasteries and in the cathedrals; later it was centered almost exclusively in the universities, where it was studied and practiced by priests and those preparing for ordination. Nevertheless, theology was a vital discipline during these centuries, especially at the Dominican School at Salamanca. Francisco de Victoria (1480–1545) was one of the most distinguished masters at that time. He replaced Peter Lombard's *Sentences* with Thomas's *Summa*, but the treatise on justice assumed an especially important place in the curriculum because of contemporary problems of natural and human rights that had developed with the discovery of the New World and an increase in trade with the East.[29]

In the fourteenth and fifteenth centuries there was a special interest in mystical phenomena. Writers began to discuss the extraordinary experiences that were claimed by various Christians. They maintained that such experiences should be available to all, and so they encouraged a serious approach to living the spiritual life of faith. In the fourteenth century Meister Eckhart (1260–1327), a Dominican who was not only a theologian but also a spiritual writer and a spiritual director, retained a close link between spirituality and Scholastic theology. Later, with the Rhineland and Flemish writers, including John Tauler (1300–1361), Henry Suso (c.1295–1366), and Jan Ruysbroeck (1293–1381), spiritual literature became much more speculative. Some spiritual writers, such as Thomas à Kempis in the *Imitation of Christ,* went so far as to discourage readers from theological speculation because it could lead to pride. Spanish mystics tended to be more theological, but with the emergence of the Inquisition those who claimed to have mystical experience were often suspected of being frauds and of purveying a false doctrine of Christianity.[30]

Francis de Sales (1567–1622), especially in *Introduction to the Devout Life,* achieved a balance among theology, the spiritual experience of God, and pastoral concerns. He made a great effort to show that a deep spiritual life was available to all Christians, not reserved to a chosen few religious. His work was very practical because he showed ordinary people how they might achieve a deep relationship with God.[31]

The profound separation between theology, on the one hand, and spiritual experience and mysticism, on the other, was undoubtedly affected by nominalism, which stressed the idea of law and obligation in morality rather than the development of the virtues and an interior experience of God's love. Moral precepts, which determined obligations, were imposed on everyone, while superogatory actions were left to the individual initiative of a select few who were interested in achieving Christian perfection. This specialized practice of the counsels was the subject of ascetical and mystical writings.[32] As a result, Christian spirituality tended to become intensely individualistic.

A similar situation prevailed in the relationship between theology and pastoral ministry, with its various concerns for effective preaching, catechizing, and the celebration of the sacraments, especially penance. The majority of priests found the theology as taught in the universities quite incomprehensible because of its technical language and complex thought patterns. The speculative character of most theology was not at all helpful in responding to concrete pastoral issues. Priests in pastoral situations needed to be trained to handle the questions that arose in daily life, particularly moral questions. That need gave rise to the development of manuals for confessors, the most important of which was the *Summa theologiae* of Antoninus of Florence (1389–1459), a distinguished Dominican who eventually became the archbishop of Florence. As a typical Dominican, in his *Summa* he gave attention to the virtues and the gifts of the Holy Spirit as well as precepts and obligations, but there was no rootedness in dogmatic theology. His approach was taken over by the Council of Trent in the sixteenth century and affected the development of manuals that were helpful in solving cases of conscience.[33]

The above developments resulted in a new vocation in the church, namely, that of professional theologian, one whose principal work was research and teaching. The professional theologian was clearly distinguished from the pastor, the spiritual leader, and the mystic. In the early church most theologians were bishops responsible for leading Christians in their dioceses; their theology was regularly developed in a liturgical context and was expressed above all in their preaching. They were primarily pastors responsible for the Christian lives of ordinary people. In the sixteenth century the unity of theology was fractured; the result was the development of distinct branches of theology, including doctrinal theology and moral theology, with the latter clearly distinguished from ascetical, mystical, and pastoral theology. In cutting itself off from the concrete pastoral life of the church, theology tended to lose much of its vitality and creativity. It became distant from the Bible, especially the New Testament, which is meant to nourish the life of faith. Spirituality was increasingly concerned with devotional practices, prayer experiences, and asceticism, not deeply rooted in scripture.[34]

The Protestant Reformers, especially Martin Luther and John Calvin, attacked the confessional manuals and their emphasis on the seven deadly sins; they emphasized the Ten Commandments, which enjoyed divine sanction, functioned as a sound pedagogical tool, and offered not simply negative prohibitions but also positive prescriptions. In fact, the Reformers emphasized both the prescriptions and the prohibitions associated with each commandment. Consequently, Protestant moral education tended to be more integrated, balanced, and scripture based than that found in the moral manuals used by Roman Catholic priests.[35]

During and after the Renaissance the study of the Bible and the method employed underwent radical change. Exegesis took the place of sound theological interpretation; this development paved the way for the emergence of the historical-critical method in Protestant biblical circles in the nineteenth century. Scientific study of the Bible also distanced itself from any spiritual or mystical interpretation of the scriptures and so was not interested in pastoral issues. As a result, the study of the Bible became a scientific discipline. This problem continues to trouble the church today: How does one employ historical-critical method in interpreting the Bible and yet at the same time not lose sight of the fact that the Bible is above all a book of divine revelation meant to guide Christians in their loving response to God and their loving response to one another?[36]

One of the major concerns of the fathers at the Council of Trent (1545–63) was to improve the quality of priestly training. Consequently, they directed that seminaries, where future priests would receive proper intellectual and spiritual formation adapted to their ministerial responsibilities, were to be instituted in dioceses. Candidates for ordination were to be especially instructed in the proper way to administer the sacrament of penance. This necessitated the development of appropriate theological courses, especially in the area of moral theology.[37]

This challenge was taken up by the Society of Jesus, which experienced significant growth in the second half of the sixteenth century and sought to implement the directives of the Council of Trent. Because the Society took on extensive pastoral responsibilities, it realized the need to develop effective courses in theology to respond to contemporary issues and practical problems. The Society became increasingly involved in spiritual direction and often had to deal with cases of conscience. In 1586 the Society formed a commission to draw up a syllabus of theological studies with these specific needs in mind. This was the beginning of the production of theological manuals for seminarians.

In compiling its *Ratio studiorum,* the Society adopted the basic approach taken by Thomas Aquinas in his *Summa theologiae,* but a careful distinction was made between a major and a minor course in theology for students. The major course was much more speculative; the minor course was quite practical and was designed to help students deal responsibly with concrete pastoral cases. This distinction certainly led to a significant division in the study of moral theology. In the minor course the general principles of moral theology were taken over from speculative theology, but the more practical material was set out in accord with the Ten Commandments, thus creating a category of specialized moral theology. In this way various cases of conscience were treated together. The commandments of God and the church were studied in detail, as well as the sacraments, but the latter were studied in terms of the priest's responsibility to administer them properly. Naturally, the canonical requirements of the sacrament of penance received detailed treatment. Obligations, proper to the religious life, were also discussed.[38]

It was with all this in mind that the Spanish Jesuit Juan Azor (1536–1603), while teaching in Rome, set about writing his three-volume manual of moral theology. It was divided into four parts: the Ten Commandments of God, the seven sacraments, ecclesiastical censures and penalties, and states of life and final ends. Azor replaced the traditional organization of moral theology according to virtues and stressed obligations above all. Even the sacraments and states of life were to be studied according to obligations. The virtues were carefully related to commandments and were discussed in light of the obligations they imposed. Azor omitted any study of happiness, the beatitudes, the gifts and fruits of the Holy Spirit, and grace. It was thought that these topics were more properly treated in speculative theology. These omissions from the more practical syllabus led to a clear separation of moral theology and mysticism, which was the subject of very important literature, especially by the Spanish mystics, including Ignatius Loyola, John of the Cross, and Teresa of Avila. Mystical experience was increasingly thought to be the concern only of a select few, not of ordinary Christians. This distinction was in keeping with the strongly held view that all Christians were bound by obligations, but only those in the religious state were bound by the counsels, which were discussed in specialized manuals of asceticism and mysticism.[39]

Azor's volumes treated the Mosaic Law in great detail but neglected the New Law with its emphasis on love. Consequently, from his time on, moral theology tended to concentrate only on obligations and neglected any study of scripture, which, as we have seen, subordinated commandments to the love of God and neighbor as an expression of the New Covenant. The omission of grace stimulated the very complex discussions between Protestants and Catholics in the seventeenth century on the primacy of God's initiative in human acts. Completely lacking was any emphasis on the Holy Spirit in Christian life. Western theology until recently has had a very diminished appreciation of pneumatology in the study of theology. By neglecting the study of grace in moral theology, Catholics tended to become increasingly legalistic, even merely humanistic; they risked becoming Pelagian.[40]

In the seventeenth century, manuals of moral theology proliferated; the major topic of discussion tended to be probabilism, an approach to moral theology that held that where there is a reasonable doubt arising from a matter of conscience on the binding force of some law, it is permissible to act as one believes to be best, providing this is "probable," that it, that it has some support from a moral authority or from a theologian of repute. Regardless of their take on this question, authors tended to divide their work into four sections: human acts, conscience, laws, and sins. Occasionally authors added a brief treatise on the virtues, out of deference to Thomas Aquinas. This approach had most unfortunate effects on the ordinary understanding of the sacrament of penance. The administration of the sacrament took place in what might be described as a courtroom, dominated by laws thought to express the very will of God. Conscience played a central role; in practice, the priest executed the role of judge by applying the law and determining what one could and could not do. The sacrament was set in a legal and juridical context. In practice, however, confessors often had a concern for mercy and sought to favor human freedom whenever possible. The result was the development of great fear and often psychological scrupulosity on the part of many penitents.[41]

Among moralists, this stimulated the development of probabalism, which sought to provide solutions to complex issues. The doctrine originated in Salamanca and received special attention from the Jesuit theologians Gabriel Vazquez (1549–1604) and Francisco Suárez (1548–1617). Probabalism resulted in laxist opinions that actually weakened the ordinary demands of Christian morality. A violent reaction in opposition to any form of laxism developed, especially in France among the followers of Abbé de Saint-Cyran (1581–1643), who hoped to reform Catholicism along Augustinian lines. He became closely associated with the influential Arnauld family and with the convent of Port-Royal and is usually described as the founder of Jansenism. Rooted in a heretical understanding of the relationship between nature and grace, Jansenist moral theology fell into rigorism.[42]

The moral theology of the manualists spread widely through preaching and catechetical instruction. Even dogmas were presented from the standpoint of obligation: if one did not accept dogmatic teachings, one was guilty of serious sin.[43] However, devotional and ascetical manuals also began to appear. Desiderius Erasmus (1466–1536) had extensive influence through his popular *Enchiridion militis christiani*, which underwent numerous editions of the Latin original and was translated into various languages. His work emphasized scripture, stressed interior dispositions rather than external devotional practices, and affirmed that learning and prayer together were meant to provide the guiding principles for growth in holiness.[44]

CATHOLIC MORAL THEOLOGY AND PROTESTANT ETHICS:
EARLY DISTINCTIONS

A comparison between Catholic moral theology and Protestant ethics in the seventeenth century and down to recent decades is important for various reasons. We cannot fully understand Catholic moral theology without taking into account the anti-Protestant stance that characterized much of the Catholic Church after the Council of Trent. Both Catholic and Protestant theologians were influenced by the intellectual environment that prevailed at the time. Both had to confront a theological tradition strongly influenced by nominalism and to respond to the Renaissance humanism that prevailed throughout much of Europe, as well as the significant problems that arose because of the explorations of the New World. Both Catholics and Protestants had to respond to the serious debate between Christianity and Greek humanism, which Paul himself had to confront and did so in his letters to the Romans and the Corinthians.[45]

Catholic moral teaching usually maintained an equivalence between the terms *moral* and *ethical*, but in practice Catholic theologians usually employed the term *moral*. Hence, *moral theology* designated the branch of theology that dealt with human actions taken as a whole, and so could be applied to general principles as well as to particular problems. *Ethical* was more often used by philosophers; however, from the Protestant viewpoint and in contemporary philosophy a distinction is often made between ethics, which is concerned with the principles and criteria of moral judgment, and morality, which is concerned with prescriptions about actions permitted in a particular time and place.[46]

Classic Protestantism was dominated by a preoccupation with justification and the assertion that one is justified by faith alone, not by good works.[47] This firm belief was rooted in faith in Jesus Christ. A person could not in any way give glory to God by human actions, even though they were good. The great fear among the Protestant Reformers was that one would be guilty of pride as a result of good works, even those works performed in accord with the law. Justification was simply a gift given by Christ, who alone could justify. According to Luther, human actions were not characterized by either good or evil; actions became good through the gift of faith granted freely by Christ. John Calvin stressed fidelity to the law much more than Luther, but the two reformers agreed on the concept of justification: human beings could be justified only through incorporation in Christ through faith. A moral life developed in human beings as the manifestation of Christ's indwelling through the Holy Spirit. Protestantism consequently set up a clear separation between the order of faith and the order of good works or ethics. This concept differed considerably from the teachings of the patristic writers, for whom faith was the primary virtue of Christian morality.[48]

Luther maintained that good works followed upon Christ's gift of faith; they did not precede it. These works, however, had no theological value for a person's salvation and were in fact directed not to God but to one's neighbor. In contrast, Calvin believed that good works were an expression of the believer's gratitude for the gift of faith and the salvation that faith made possible. The

Protestant position clearly affirmed justification by faith and faith alone, and it refused to admit that human acts had any intrinsic value; hence, Protestants refused to admit that the grace of Christ operated internally within human persons, lest people come to think that they owned it. Grace was always extrinsic, for justice belonged solely to Christ, who attributed it to human beings. Since the human being was simultaneously *justus et peccator* (just and a sinner), the Christian always needed first of all to be justified by Christ. For the Protestant Reformers there were no supernatural virtues informing the inner life of the Christian; in fact, they were suspicious of virtues in general because they could make the Christian proud.[49]

Luther rejected the idea of personal holiness and sanctification and even rejected the Scholastic teaching that charity informed faith because he felt that such teaching tended to downgrade faith. He also had a suspicion of mystical experience because he felt that it was simply the result of human effort, ascetical practices, and the exercise of various prayer techniques. Along the same lines he claimed that monastic life and the religious state seemed to be based on the assumption that one could achieve holiness through human observances and the practice of contemplation. He even rejected theology as a sacred science; it was simply a work of human reason.[50]

In affirming the primacy of faith in Jesus Christ as the absolute and primary source of justification, Protestantism was in accord with the writings of Paul and the fathers of the early church. The Reformers' challenges confronted Renaissance humanism and the legalism that characterized much thought among Christians in the fourteenth and fifteenth centuries. What separated the Protestant position from the foregoing Christian tradition was its refusal to integrate human virtues; the Christian tradition had consistently sought to integrate the human virtues with the Christian virtues. Such integration is clear in Paul's writings and also in the Greek and Latin fathers. Faith was always considered to be a transcendent gift, but that gift became incarnated in the life of the Christian through acceptance and a positive response to the gift. Protestantism created a deep rift between faith and ethics, a rift that contemporary Protestant ethicists are seeking to bridge. Clearly, the original Protestant positions have undergone considerable change since the sixteenth century, especially as the result of the inter-Christian dialogues since the Second Vatican Council.

Roman Catholics responded negatively to the Protestant position from the time of the Council of Trent to the Second Vatican Council. In fact, much of Catholic theology was characterized by an explicit or at least implicit attack on the Protestant positions. In the area of moral theology an emphasis was placed on the value of good works done in conformity with the Decalogue and the commandments of the church and on the importance of faith and charity, both of course being informed by grace. Catholic moral theology stressed natural law as being accessible to right reason. Unfortunately, natural law was often distanced from faith. In the manuals faith was treated mainly in terms of the obligations and sins connected with the virtue. In fact, the virtue of faith was usually treated simply by dogmatic theologians, who also treated grace and justification; it failed to influence much of Catholic moral teaching. One reason faith was sidetracked in the moral manuals was that the manuals concentrated on obligations arising from law. This emphasis often gave rise to legalism, even in regard to sins against faith, such as the denial of a particular magisterial teaching. The manuals also gave little or no place to scripture except for those texts that emphasized commands or could be used to support a moral argument.[51]

In some Catholic circles the Renaissance humanism of the sixteenth and seventeenth centuries gave moral theology a humanistic orientation that emphasized the loving mercy of God. The Jesuits' stress on humanism and the emphasis on the arts and the classics played a major role in their approach to education; likewise, the discovery of the New World posed many new problems and stimulated a broadening of people's horizons as Catholics discovered that the world's population was not simply divided between Catholics and Protestants but included many who belonged to other world religions or who professed no religion at all. This all contributed to the development of a moral theology that paid much attention to the natural law and what it means to be human. This led to efforts to develop a moral theology applicable to all people. Nevertheless, moralists of the seventeenth century were still preoccupied with the dispute over probabilism and tended to concentrate on individual cases of conscience at a time when philosophers and other humanistic thinkers were preoccupied with developing a new understanding of society and with an increasingly complex world.[52]

Following the prescriptions of the Council of Trent, Catholic moralists concentrated on efforts to provide seminarians, priests, and young religious clerics with proper instruction in how to administer the sacraments, especially penance. This need was felt especially by the Society of Jesus, which developed an extensive pastoral ministry involving much spiritual direction and the hearing of confessions. Moral theology dealt with the multiplicity of sinful acts caused by disobedience to clear precepts; careful distinctions were made between mortal and venial sins, and stress was laid on the proper penance to be imposed in each case. These pastoral concerns, however, further distanced speculative and dogmatic theology from the courses in moral theology. There was the danger that what was considered to be soundly pastoral could become rather antitheological. Precepts were to be applied universally, whereas counsels became an appendage to be observed by an elite group in the pursuit of perfection.[53]

MORAL THEOLOGY IN THE SEVENTEENTH AND EIGHTEENTH CENTURIES

Divorced from dogmatic theology, moral theology tended to focus on the judgments made by conscience; moral theologians were primarily concerned with the problem of probabalism. Hence, in the seventeenth and eighteenth centuries the history of moral theology is basically a history of probabalism. As noted above, there was sharp opposition from the Jansenists, who went to the opposite extreme of rigorism. The Carmelites of Salamanca, however, remained aloof from the controversy. In the eighteenth century there were fierce debates about probabalism, especially among the Jesuits and the Dominicans. These controversies resulted in the sterility of the whole moral enterprise and tended to disregard the unique character of the Christian life. Alphonsus Liguori (1696–1789), the holy founder of the Redemptorists, spent much of his adult life trying to find a happy solution to the problem of probabalism. In *Theologia moralis* (1784) he sought to develop a series of rules removed equally from rigorism and from laxism to which he gave the name "equiprobabalism." If two opinions are equally probable, one should be free to choose the one that favors liberty or the one that favors observance of the law. Above all, in the controversial context of his time Alphonsus sought to develop a collection of moral opinions that he felt were truly certain, balanced, and carefully articulated. He tried to take special account of the concrete circumstances of moral actions. It is important not to attend simply to his works dedicated to moral theology in a strict sense but also to his more devotional works, especially *Practica di amor Gesu Cristo*, which sets out a profound account of the Christian life based on chapter 13 of Paul's First Letter to the Corinthians.[54]

MORAL THEOLOGY IN THE NINETEENTH AND TWENTIETH CENTURIES

The disputes concerning the nature of moral theology continued after the death of Alphonsus. There were, however, useful manuals produced by Redemptorists, Dominicans, and Jesuits that attempted to relate moral issues to dogmatic theology. The names Genicot, Noldin, Vermeersch, and Tanqueray come to mind, for they were primarily concerned with the sound pastoral care of Catholics.

After the French Revolution new approaches to moral theology were developed, especially in Austria and Germany. John Michael Sailer (1751–1832) and John Baptist Hirscher (1788–1865) were the most distinguished pioneers in the effort to provide a vital renewal to moral theology. They realized that the casuistic approach in the age of rationalism and enlightenment sought to establish clear limits for precepts and obligations. In contrast, Sailer and Hirscher sought to recover the evangelical foundations of moral theology, not only for the benefit of confessors but also to help ordinary Catholics live truly Christian lives. In many ways Sailer's work resembles that of Francis de Sales, whom he greatly admired. He sought to set out the full life of perfection rooted in Christian virtues and in the Sermon on the Mount. In contrast to the cold and sterile atmosphere of the Enlightenment, Sailer wanted to cultivate a theology of the heart. Nevertheless, it must be remembered that he was also a man of his time—he belonged to the romantic period in Germany and so sought to emphasize the full development of the personal gifts given to each member of the Mystical Body of Christ.[55]

Hirscher's moral theology was deeply rooted in the biblical theology of the kingdom of God. He was a man of deep psychological insights, and in that regard he presented a more complete system of thought than Sailer.[56] In the footsteps of these two great figures came the distinguished faculty from the newly founded School of Tübingen, which emphasized that the primary goal of moral theology was to facilitate the implementation of grace in the efforts of Christians to respond to the Lord's call to lead a perfect life. The writers acknowledged the importance of doctrinal development, and so they placed their theology in a psychological-dynamic context.[57]

Moral manuals, most of which were written by European authors, were regularly used in seminaries throughout the Catholic world until the Second Vatican Council. In English-speaking countries three texts were widely used: Jesuit Thomas Slater's *A Manual of Moral Theology for English-speaking Catholics*, Jesuit Henry Davis's *Moral and Pastoral Theology in Four Volumes*, and Capuchin Heribert Jone's *Moral Theology*.[58]

Thomas Slater (1855–1928), an English priest, studied canon law and ecclesiology at the Gregorian University in Rome. In 1906 his *Manual of Moral Theology* was published, and along with his two-volume work *Cases of Conscience for English-speaking Countries,* became the most consulted works in English. Because of poor eyesight, he retired from teaching in 1911 and then assisted in a Liverpool parish. Slater sought primarily to help priests in the confessional, but he thought Anglicans could also be helped by his writings. He acknowledged that his work was technical and not intended for edification. Those who were looking for help in developing their spirituality should look elsewhere. Moral theology was to define clearly what is right and what is wrong. He held that the primary purpose of the natural law was to guide people so they could avoid evil. *Manual of Moral Theology* was divided into two parts: the first part dealt with fundamental moral issues, and the second part treated the Ten Commandments, contracts, the commandments of the church, and the duties of priests, religious, and certain lay people who had specific secular vocations, such as physicians and jurists. It is interesting that only sixteen pages were dedicated to the sixth and ninth commandments and that his treatment of consummated sins against nature (masturbation, sodomy, and bestiality) was written in Latin so as not to lead the lay reader into sin. He claimed that he was following the teaching of the Catholic Church, but instead of citing magisterial statements, he cited the moral tradition set out by respected authors. Not surprisingly, he embraced probabalism. He treated the subject of a scrupulous conscience sympathetically, stressed the mother's obligation to breastfeed her children if possible, and forbade parents to send their children to non-Catholic schools.[59]

Henry Davis (1866–1952) was an English moralist who entered the Jesuits in 1883. He spent forty years training clergy and laity, at least physicians, in moral theology. His four-volume manual, *Moral and Pastoral Theology,* was widely used, underwent eight revisions, and was eventually summarized in a one-volume edition in 1952.[60] The publication of the 1917 Code of Canon Law had a definite effect on Davis's approach to moral theology. He was clear that the laws in the code dealt with external actions within society, whereas moral theology considered the obligations in conscience which the church imposed through definite rules of conduct. Many of these rules were in fact to be found in the new code. Following the publication of the code, Vatican congregations began issuing various instructions on moral issues that transformed moral theology from a commentary on the moral tradition to an interpretation of moral utterances from the Vatican. This shift was certainly reflected in the fourth edition of Davis's manual, where he treated in some detail the problems of a social tolerance of prostitution and the issue of female dress, both of which had been discussed in recent instructions from the Vatican. Not surprisingly, Davis took an ahistorical approach to natural law as invariable and universally applicable; no natural precepts could be dispensed. For a mortal sin to be committed, he asserted that there must be a grievous matter, sufficient reflection by the intellect, and full consent of the will.[61]

Heribert Jone (1885–1967) was born in Germany, entered the Capuchins at an early age, and was educated in canon law at Rome's Gregorian University. He published *Commentary for the Code of Canon Law* in 1917 and the first edition of *Katholische Moraltheologie* in 1929. The latter volume went through eighteen editions in German and was translated into eight other languages. The work had enormous influence throughout the Catholic world. He insisted that his text was designed for busy priests in need of quick and convenient answers to practical moral questions. He was committed to probabalism, but he warned confessors that although they could encourage penitents to become better Catholics, they should not impose on them their own more restrictive opinions. In his treatment of the commandments, Jone incorporated the three theological virtues of faith, hope, and charity, but he considered them in terms of specific duties and obligations. His language was typically very legalistic. For example, although charity consists primarily in union with God, self, and neighbor, he reduced the duty of fraternal charity to the obligation of almsgiving. There is not a hint of recognition that charity inclines one to deeper union with God, self, and neighbor. He was especially expansive on the sixth commandment in an almost embarrassing way.[62]

At the beginning of the twentieth century manuals of moral theology widely shaped priests' attitude toward pastoral care; priests, in turn, affected lay people's understanding of the moral life as a strict response to commands and obligations. There were very few ambiguities because the principles that were set out were fairly certain, universal, ahistorical, and often quite remote from the real issues of ordinary Catholics. The moral theologians exuded an extraordinary sense of authority and competency. It seems they never had any self-doubts. They were convinced that they were handing on the practical wisdom of the church, though much of what they taught and wrote was the result of their own reasoning. Ordinary lay Catholics, priests engaged in pastoral work, and seminarians were usually very scrupulous in following the manualists' advice. They relied on clear, concise answers to their problems.[63]

As the twentieth century progressed, the congregations in the Vatican defined more and more matters affecting moral theology. Moral theologians, both in the classroom and in their writings, became translators of official teaching and ceased to be scholars offering what were thought to be very sound opinions. The Vatican became more and more authoritarian and attached various penalties to crimes and serious sins, which were outlined in the 1917 Code of Canon Law and were further refined by later official interpretations of texts, as well as new decrees and instructions. Many of the official teachings emanating from the Vatican were concerned with the necessity of Catholic education, the prohibition of certain theological texts, and the clothing of women. These teachings in themselves were often quite rigorous and, in turn, were interpreted rigorously by the moral theologians and professors. It became increasingly evident that the manualists simply abstracted from the very complex problems that were emerging in the world and that were affecting the lives of ordinary Catholics. In spite of the positive developments in psychiatry and psychology, as well as in the other social sciences, the manualists tended to look upon the ordinary Catholic simply as a wounded and ignorant penitent. The priest was taught that he often had to be a psychiatric caregiver to the sinner. There was little or no room for innovation; the manualists were unsympathetic toward those theologians who urged a more effective integration of moral theology with dogmatic, ascetical, and devotional theology. More and more the manualists receded from sound theology into a narrow interpretation of canon law. The metaphysical principles that were at the basis of their trade were simply inadequate to address the critical issues of the modern world.[64]

INITIATING REFORM

The twentieth century underwent a renewal of moral theology unlike anything witnessed since the thirteenth century. Perhaps the most significant influence was the shift in the nineteenth century from emphasis on moral actions to the human person as the norm for morality. Among the manualists it was the action itself that was most important; therefore the responsibility of the priest was to help Catholics avoid wrong actions. In nineteenth-century philosophy the primary consideration was the person; this interest resulted in the turn to the subject that characterized much systematic and moral reflection in the second half of the twentieth century. This emphasis was welcomed first of all by Protestants; its appreciation by Catholics eventually emerged as a result of new developments in biblical scholarship, especially by Protestants who had introduced the historical-critical method for properly understanding the scriptures. Other disciplines, especially psychology, sociology, and cultural anthropology, began to reflect on the human person, not as a philosophical object to be analyzed but as a historical and dynamic subject. Another significant development eventually affecting moral theology was an appreciation of history as the context in which all persons live and interact with one another.

Certainly many events in the twentieth century were deeply disturbing and raised the question of what responsibility human persons and communities had in shaping history. At the same time, urbanization followed the industrial revolution and had enormous effects on the family and its role in society. These challenges began to affect the thinking of moral theologians. In this context the challenge facing Catholic moral theologians was partly to repudiate the Neo-Scholastic manuals, but more important, to develop a positive approach to the moral life of Christians. Three major figures emerged to initiate this renewal process: Odo Lottin, who sought to recover history; Fritz Tillmann, who sought to recover the Bible; and Gérard Gilleman, who sought to recover the primacy of charity.[65]

Odo Lottin (1880–1965) made a significant contribution to the history of moral theology by demonstrating the complexity of the history of ideas, by showing that some ideas come and go, and by emphasizing that development can never be completely understood because the discourse is subject to numerous variables. As a result, moralists often became much less certain of their universal claims and tentative in their positions.[66]

Lottin was educated at Louvain and ordained a priest in 1904; he became a Benedictine at the Abbey of Mont César in 1914. Although he was primarily a historian, his first publication was a three-volume work, *Psychologie et morale*, which was followed by a major moral theological synthesis entitled *Princeps de morale*. One of his primary goals was to integrate moral theology and dogmatic theology. He insisted that moral theology should not be considered according to the Ten Commandments but by both the theological and moral virtues. An inductive rather than a deductive method should be pursued. Following Thomas Aquinas, Lottin affirmed that the acquired virtues were about sound character formation in conformity with right reason. These virtues were different from the infused virtues, which made it possible for human beings to realize their vocation to perfection.[67]

Since the High Middle Ages theologians regularly spoke of God infusing or pouring into the soul various virtues, especially the theological virtues of faith, hope, and charity. These have been described as infused virtues and have been distinguished from those virtues actively acquired through human practice. Likewise, in spiritual theology commentators were accustomed to speak of infused contemplation as a type of passive prayer directly imparted by God, contrasted with acquired contemplative prayer achieved through the disciplined practice of personal prayer. Certainly the Reformation theologians spoke of God always acting on human persons from the outside, as though God were completely separate from human persons; they insisted that God poured his gifts, especially faith, into us as into distinct containers. Contemporary theologians, however, are apt to take the writings of De Lubac and Rahner seriously and to affirm that we are born into a graced condition; they speak of God acting more immediately and intimately, so divine gifts well up from inside the human person like a fountain. The divine presence is immanent in human persons from the beginning of creation.[68]

It is not surprising that Lottin rejected the major role that canon law had come to play in moral theology, forcing the latter to concentrate above all on external actions. He maintained that moral theology should be primarily concerned with internal dispositions, which in turn should issue in right actions. He also challenged the distance that moral theology had maintained from the Bible, patristic teachings, and dogmatic theology, as well as its clear distinction from ascetical and mystical theology. Lottin also contributed to moral theology a positive, developmental, and anthropological understanding of the human person.[69]

Fritz Tillmann (1874–1953) was a German diocesan priest and an accomplished biblical scholar, but his biblical career was brought to an end in 1912 by a decree of the Consistorial Congregation questioning the interest of theologians in the sources of the Gospels, the so-called Synoptic question. Tillmann then turned his attention to moral theology and became a distinguished moral theologian. In 1919 he produced his first moral theological work, *Personality and Community in the Preaching of Jesus*. In 1934 Tillmann wrote a significant volume on what it means to be a disciple of Christ; a more simple version for lay people was published in 1937, *Der Meister Ruft (The Master Calls)*.[70] The book was in fact a handbook of lay morality, not simply a treatment of sins but an inspiring treatment of the virtues, permeated with biblical theology and inviting people to follow Christ. He demonstrated that it was possible to develop a sound moral theology that was directly rooted in sacred scripture. The English translation was divided into five sections: basic principles, love of God, love of self, love of neighbor, and social relationships. Tillmann insisted that baptism provided the basic foundation for discipleship because it brought Christians to rebirth and a new creation. The first gift of this new life is the Holy Spirit; the second is deep union with Christ.[71]

The language of perfection was usually used to speak of those in religious life, but Tillmann broke down the unfortunate distinctions among laity, clerics, and religious by citing Pauline texts and asserting that Christian baptism included a universal call to all Christians to pursue perfection. From that time on, the call to discipleship and perfection for all Christians became a traditional assertion. By using the language of perfection Tillmann moved readily to a discussion of the virtues because the virtues perfect all that is human. At the same time he bridged moral theology and ascetical theology. He focused on inner dispositions and character traits rather than on external acts, as the traditional manuals had done. Unlike Thomas Aquinas, who did not put great emphasis on humility, Tillmann insisted that those who pursued perfection needed the virtue of humility and had to practice self-denial. Humility, he wrote, teaches us our proper relationship to God, the truth about ourselves, and the need to abandon all forms of denigration. It teaches us about proper self-knowledge and finds expression in true gratitude for all God's gifts and the gifts of others. However, in speaking about self-denial he affirmed that each person's personality and gifts must be taken into account in determining the proper exercise of self-denial. His writing was remarkably sensitive to individual differences. He was keenly appreciative of the fact that the virtues manifest themselves in each person differently, but the development of one's personality must not be isolated from the needs of the community. He effectively integrated the personal with the social. Tillmann's work, although readily accessible to lay people, was especially attentive to the pastoral challenges facing the contemporary priest, counselor, confessor, and preacher.[72]

Gérard Gilleman (1910–2002) was a Belgian Jesuit who defended a distinguished dissertation at the Institut Catholique in Paris; the subject was the role of charity in moral theology. Shortly after submitting his work in 1947, he was assigned to teach dogmatic theology in India. The dissertation was actually prepared for publication by his mentor, Jesuit René Carpentier; it was readily acclaimed for its excellence and creativity. It was published in English as *The Primacy of Charity in Moral Theology* in 1959.[73] Gilleman studied the virtue of charity as it was treated in the works of the Jesuit theologian Émile Mersch (1890–1940). Mersch had examined the doctrine of the Mystical Body of Christ in light of history and sought to bring out its relevance for moral theology and ecclesiology.[74] Gilleman discovered in Mersch's work solid grounds for identifying the baptized Christian with the filial understanding of the incarnate Jesus as the Son of God. In that context he found the grounds for affirming the Christian's foundation for the ontological union of the baptized with God in Christ and through the power of the Holy Spirit.[75]

Gilleman was primarily interested in setting out the contours of moral theology rather than its specific content. In stressing the primacy of charity he was also keenly interested in the interior life of the Christian. In light of Mersch's work, he stressed that the development of the interior life is not simply a private matter but also one that affects the health of the whole body of Christ. Charity unites us not only with God but also with ourselves and one another. In union with God and through God's power, we are empowered to act with prudence, justice, temperance, and fortitude. It is clearly God's love for us that precedes the love we have for ourselves. In as much as this divine love abides within us, we are truly divinized, a truth deeply appreciated in the Eastern Christian tradition. Obviously a moral theology that is rooted in and driven by charity radically changes our understanding of law, which should always be at the service of love.[76]

In the 1950s moral theologians were divided between those who relied on the method of the traditional manuals and those who sought to pursue the fresh approach set out by Tillmann and Gilleman. The former taught and wrote with confession, the magisterium, sin, and canon law in mind. The latter stressed the fundamental theological issues: our deep union with Christ, the primacy of charity, the significance of a historical context, and the vocation to discipleship. Bernard Häring epitomized the approach taken by the reform-minded moralists.

Häring was born in Germany in 1912 and entered the Redemptorists in 1934 with the hope of becoming a missionary. His superiors, however, sent him to be trained in moral theology. He attended the University of Tübingen in 1940, but his studies were interrupted by World War II, so his dissertation under Theodore Steinbüchel was not completed until 1947. The war experience had a profound effect on him, especially on his later pastoral focus as a moral theologian. During his time at Tübingen his theology was shaped not only by Steinbüchel but also by Karl Adam and Romano Guardini, as well as by the Protestant theologians Helmut Thielicke and Friedrich Rückert. His dissertation, *Das Heilige und das Gute (The Sacred and the Good: Religion and Morality in Their Mutual Relationships)*, was published in 1950. That same year he joined the faculty at the Academia Alfonsiana in Rome and remained on that faculty until 1988.[77]

In 1984 Häring published the three-volume, sixteen-hundred-page manual *Das Gesetz Christi (The Law of Christ)*, a landmark contribution to moral theology.[78] Throughout his work he insists on the primary responsibility of the Christian to conform his or her life to Christ through a moral life of virtue. However, he always seeks through his moral theology to engage culture and shows a deep sensitivity to the human person's concrete situation in the world. During World War II he had witnessed the absurd blind obedience of Christians to a criminal regime; therefore he stresses not so much obedience as responsibility. As a Redemptorist and from his wide reading of the writings of St. Alphonsus and his preaching in ordinary parishes, he realized that moral theology must be concerned with the care of the whole person; hence, it must be theologically demanding, pastorally inclined, and spiritually enriching. The result was the development of a profound synthesis of fundamental moral theology, deeply rooted in dogmatic theology, biblical in its source, and ascetical in its construction of normative and practical guidelines for right moral conduct.[79]

Throughout Häring's work there are several central characteristics: a positive orientation, an emphasis on history and tradition, stress on human freedom as foundational for Christian morality, the importance of a properly formed conscience, and the major importance of Christian worship for the moral life. The traditional manualists had been preoccupied with the sacrament of penance and the forgiveness of sins, but Häring brought a fresh approach to the whole sacramental system by developing a sacramental Christology and a sacramental anthropology. He would have been familiar with the well-developed liturgical movement in Germany and other western European countries, especially the emphasis that Dom Lambert Beauduin had placed on the essential link between worship and social action in Belgium. Häring brought that link to bear on his moral theology. His link between moral theology and the whole sacramental system was quite innovative among moral theologians of his time.

It was through the virtue of religion that the divine-human relationship found actual shape and content in the Christian life. Häring saw the virtue of religion as a fundamental moral category that concerned both prayer and liturgy; in that sense it was closely related to all other moral virtues, including justice. He articulated a liturgical anthropology by exploring what it means to be a worshiper of God and how that virtue forms other moral virtues. Häring's understanding of virtue was not only interior and personal but also communal and public.[80] Although contemporary moral theologians have moved beyond *The Law of Christ* and have had to discuss many new questions that have surfaced since the Second Vatican Council, they nevertheless have continued to hold Häring's work in the highest esteem.

Perhaps the great challenge today is to espouse a more visionary way of acting morally, which is usually set out in abstract theological statements, and yet at the same time to provide people with clear reflections on the diverse concrete situations that they face. People surely need guidance in their responsibility to make moral decisions. In the last sixty or so years the revisionists have not only sought to provide people with a more theological foundation for their lives and a more human and social approach to the moral life, but also to give at least tentative answers to complex practical questions.[81]

The remarkable interest in biblical studies, inspired and encouraged by Pius XII's 1943 encyclical *Divino afflante Spiritu*, prodded theologians in general and moral theologians in particular to rely on sound biblical exegesis and hermeneutics for a vital interpretation of God's word of salvation. This interest was accompanied by stimulation from the kerygmatic movement in theology, which placed special emphasis on effective preaching and teaching on all levels of Christian education. It tended to move away from abstractions and focus on the life, death, and resurrection of the Lord Jesus and the gift of the Holy Spirit abiding in human hearts and communities. It invited Christians to a generous response of love to the gift of divine love given by the Lord Jesus through the Spirit. In this way it hoped to situate laws and precepts in their proper Christian framework.[82]

An important effect of the kerygmatic movement was an effort to move away from the negative type of presentation that often characterized parish missions and the fiery preaching of visiting priests who warned people about hell and purgatory and the harsh judgment that awaited them if they did not repent, go to confession, and confess their sins.

Although the roots of existentialism were probably in the writings of the nineteenth-century Dane Søren Kierkegaard (1813–55), its positive and negative influences were especially felt after the Second World War. With its emphasis on real-life situations it drew attention to the subjective factors involved in moral decisions and helped academic moralists, priests, and counselors to be more aware of the increasingly complicated lives that people had to live in the twentieth century. Unfortunately, the atheism that characterized the lives and writings of some existentialists gave encouragement on the popular level to the neglect of divine revelation and magisterial teachings, as though they were completely irrelevant.

In the early 1960s there was a definite effort on the part of moral theologians to attend closely to the proper theological and biblical underpinnings for their writings and teachings; they concentrated less on philosophical and abstract truths and instead sought to be more positive than negative and to treat Christian morality as a personal response to God's call to discipleship. They sought to provide truths and values that would offer people a vision of how they should act morally. Four major concerns gradually surfaced with important effects on Catholic morality: the sanctity of life, consistency in life ethics, preferential option for the poor, and solidarity. As a result, Catholic moral theology was both deeply personal and social. It should be noted that dogmatic or systematic theologians, like Karl Rahner, Yves Congar, and Edward Schillebeeckx, provided moral theologians with an important foundation for their work on such subjects as Christology, ecclesiology, magisterial authority, and love. The Canadian Jesuit Bernard Lonergan provided some very important insights in epistemology. Like so many theologians in the twentieth century, the work of these theologians was often characterized by a special concern for the subject. Lonergan's distinction between the classicist and the historicist was especially important.[83]

For classicists, reality is unchanging and the world is in its final form; truth has already been divinely revealed and has been expressed in tradition. It needs to be rediscovered by each new generation. Truth is universal and unchanging; clarity is most important. Reflection must be deductive. The moral law never changes and always applies because it is always true; consequently, any change in moral teaching is highly problematic. Specific context is unimportant and is relativistic. God is eternal, unchanging, and universal; so are God's teachings. Therefore, neither church authorities nor moral theologians can change church teachings. The credibility of the church is distinguished by its constancy; if the church were to change its teaching, such change would undermine the confidence that ordinary people have in the church. The faithful often do not adhere to what is true simply because they are sinful.[84]

By contrast, historicists look at the world and at truth as constantly emerging; they are apt to believe that the world is always undergoing creation. Historicists reject the charge that they are relativists. However, they firmly believe that their grasp of truth is relative to God, who alone is absolute. As time moves on, we are constantly learning more and more about the world and about ourselves. Historicists do not believe that we create or construct truth; rather, we discover truth in history. Truth has its objectivity, but it is only gradually grasped by human beings over time through experience; consequently, situations and circumstances are important in the emergence of truth. Catholic historicists, however, are not situation ethicists in the sense that that category was developed by the Protestant ethicist Joseph Fletcher.[85] Historicists are suspicious of deductive logic; they affirm that real truth is discovered through analogy. They tend to be modest about their judgments and assertions and tentative about any truth-claims. They are comfortable living with doubts. Unlike the classicists, historicists point out the church's changing attitudes on subjects such as usury, capital punishment, religious liberty, and slavery. The historicist is concerned with the knower, whereas the classicist is concerned with what is known. For the historicist the moral agent is very important and is always involved in moral judgment. These distinctions between classicism and historicism were very important throughout the second half of the twentieth century and certainly continue in the present century.[86]

As many Catholic moral theologians turned to the person to find moral truth, the Catholic hierarchy more and more taught according to the classicist model. Popes and many bishops believe that moral truth is found primarily in unchanging norms and principles; they tend to think that truth is contained in propositions. Regardless of their background and training, they frequently speak and write very authoritatively about a wide range of moral questions, such as life support, pain relief, and ectopic pregnancy. They do not hesitate to teach in the complex areas of sexual, medical, and social morality. They usually make a strenuous effort to show that their teachings are in accord with previous official utterances. Continuity is extremely important. As a result, in the second half of the twentieth century and certainly in this century, papal and episcopal utterances constitute unchanging moral truth. In a sense, papal, episcopal, and curial teachings have replaced the content of the traditional moral manuals, which in the past were frequently accepted by professors, confessors, and ordinary people without any questioning.

Many Catholic moral theologians have continued to function as historicists, to do their research, and to discuss their findings and observations among themselves or at meetings of learned societies; they often work in close collaboration with Protestant ethicists, but they are usually very reluctant to put their original findings in print, at least in popular publications, lest they be the subject of curial investigation. They remember that various distinguished theologians were condemned in the decade immediately preceding Vatican Council II but then were exonerated and played a very important role in the proceedings of the council; several were made cardinals. Sadly, the gulf between the official magisterial teaching and the strongly held views of many Catholic moral theologians and ordinary Catholics continues to widen today.[87]

The Second Vatican Council's admonition to moral theologians validated the work of many moral theologians, especially in its decree on the training of priests, *Optatam totius,* which stated: "Special care should be given to the perfecting of moral theology. Its scientific presentation should draw more fully on the teaching of Holy scripture and should throw light upon the exalted vocation of the faithful in Christ and their obligation to bring forth fruit in charity for the life of the world" (no. 16). But shortly after the close of the council, Pope Paul VI issued the encyclical *Humanae vitae,* in which he reasserted the traditional manualists' notion of moral truth and their insistence on avoiding certain actions under the pain of serious sin. Consequently, since that time the papacy and many bishops have expressed their teaching in accord with the method taken by the traditional manualists. This has resulted in serious conflict and opposition to the approach taken by many contemporary moral theologians.[88]

Over the past two thousand years moral theology has tended to swing between a singular concern for external actions and universal claims, on the one hand, and a more inclusive understanding of the natural law, the development of internal dispositions, and an appreciation for specific notions of moral truth, on the other. When the Bible serves as the foundation for moral theology, moralists renew their understanding of the natural law's stress on the importance of doing good and avoiding evil, but they also turn to spiritual and ascetical writings to emphasize human transformation and the importance of the virtues in the lives of all Christians. Consequently, they seek to develop a more integrated understanding of the whole of theology and make serious efforts to develop a more relational anthropology.[89] It is this emphasis on virtues that should have a decided influence on our understanding of church and also on our celebration of the liturgy today.

5

A Virtuous Church

VIRTUE ETHICS

Virtue ethics emphasizes the character of the moral agent rather than rules or consequences of an action. This approach contrasts with consequentialism, which maintains that the results of a particular act form the basis for any proper moral judgment about that action. It also contrasts with deontology, which considers the rightness or wrongness of an action in light of the character of the action itself rather than the consequences. In other words, the difference among these three approaches to morality lies in the way moral issues are approached rather than in the moral conclusions that are reached.[1]

In the West the roots of virtue ethics lie in the works of Plato and Aristotle. This approach to ethical thinking prevailed in the ancient and medieval periods and was dominant until the fourteenth century. It underwent an eclipse during the Renaissance and the early modern period as the Aristotelian and Thomistic synthesis of ethics and metaphysics went out of favor in the West. The approach returned to prominence in the twentieth century and is today one of the three dominant approaches to ethical thinking—the other two being consequentialism and deontology. Virtue ethics is really not in conflict with consequentialism or deontology, however, since virtue ethics is simply concerned with the morally desirable virtues that will aid a person to live a morally good life and will facilitate the proper decisions that are appropriate to a good moral life.

Virtue ethics emphasizes being rather than doing. It holds that morality flows from the identity and character of a person; consequently, it does not reflect primarily on a person's actions or the consequences that flow from those actions. There is much debate today about which specific virtues are praiseworthy, since the meaning of particular virtues is frequently conditioned by the cultural and historical context in which a person lives. There is nevertheless general agreement that morality is the result of intrinsic virtues. Virtue ethicists ask three very basic questions: Who are we? Who should we become? How do we get there?

The contemporary revival of virtue ethics is usually traced to the English philosopher Elizabeth Anscombe's 1958 essay "Modern Moral Philosophy"[2] and to Philippa Foot's collection of essays published in 1978 entitled *Virtues and Vices*.[3] Scottish philosopher Alasdair MacIntyre, above all, stimulated interest in the retrieval of virtue ethics in 1981 by his major publication *After Virtue: A Study in Moral Theory*.[4] He argued that contemporary ethics had disintegrated and that people live in an environment of moral disagreement so that each person assumes a position on the morality of an action, staunchly defends that position, and dismisses the opinions of all others. He believed that this disintegration occurred because ethics had become depersonalized. The ethics of Plato, Aristotle, Augustine, and Thomas Aquinas was an ethics of character, virtue, and being. Action followed being. Without a foundation in being, ethicists were able to reflect and comment only on isolated actions.[5]

Instead of asking whether an action is right, MacIntyre invited ethicists to consider who people should become. Christian ethicists readily acknowledged the importance of this question in light of Jesus' invitation to people to become his disciples, children of God, heirs of the kingdom through Christian initiation. In the New Testament the teaching of Jesus always focuses on the call to discipleship and what that entails in terms of a Christian moral life. The Second Vatican Council in *Optatam totius (Decree on the Training of Priests)* admonished moral theologians to "draw more fully on the teaching of Holy Scripture and throw light upon the exalted vocation of the faithful in Christ and their obligation to bring forth fruit in charity for the life of the world" (no. 16).

As we have seen, following the Council of Trent the work of Catholic moral theologians was usually quite distinct from ascetical theology, but today, following the lead of Bernard Häring, moral theologians seek to reintegrate the two fields. From the end of the fourth to the early years of the twentieth century, Christian lives were usually divided into three stages: the purgative way, or the way of beginners; the illuminative way, or the way of the proficient; and the unitive way, or the way of the perfect. The presumption was that most people were on the purgative way, which consists simply of avoiding sin and keeping in the state of grace. Moral theologians were preoccupied with this first stage; they wrote extensively about sin and gave counsel to priests about how to develop into effective confessors. The second stage was for those who were serious about their baptismal commitments, especially men and women religious; through spiritual reading and various ascetical manuals they sought to deepen their commitment as disciples of the Lord Jesus. They sought to develop the virtues of humility, patience, fidelity, charity, and chastity. The final stage was for the very few who were given extraordinary graces and were able to advance into what was termed the mystical life. In these three categories moral theologians were preoccupied above all with helping people avoid evil. Serious attention recently has turned to the development of virtues and the intention of the moral agent rather than focusing exclusively on the moral act.

Against that background we now turn our attention to the church, the community of the disciples of Jesus, and to the virtues that should characterize their lives so they become effective agents in the world, transforming the church more and more into the dynamic body of Christ and so making way for the establishment of the reign of God.

ECCLESIOLOGY: HISTORICAL BACKGROUND

New Testament. In the New Testament the Pauline literature provides a rich theology of the church, for Paul's vocation and ministry required him to reflect on issues and problems related to the nature of the church and the bearing that identity should have on the life of Christians. Although the Greek word *ekklesia* occurs only three times in the Gospels, the word occurs sixty-times in the letters attributed to Paul. The Pauline letters also employ other concepts, including the community as the body of Christ, the identification of the community as the temple of God, and the use of familial and election terms to describe the Christian community.[6] Paul wrote regularly in response to specific problems, so we do not find in his writings a fully developed ecclesiology.

In secular Greek the word *ekklesia* designated an assembly of free citizens entitled to vote; eventually it attained a religious meaning in the New Testament. Paul used the term in various ways, but in most instances he refers to a local assembly of Christians in a particular city or province. Sometimes, however, he uses the term in a more general sense, but even in those instances he has local communities in mind. The *ekklesia* is, above all, an assembly in which God's Spirit is active, distributing various gifts or charisms for the building up of the church as a local congregation.[7]

The letters to the Colossians and Ephesians were probably written by others in Paul's name. They develop the concept of the church as the body of Christ in light of how the concept appears in Paul's First Letter to the Corinthians and his Letter to the Romans. Body of Christ sometimes refers to the crucified body of Christ (Rom 7:4) or to the eucharistic body of Christ (1 Cor 10:16), but in 1 Corinthians 12:27 the term clearly refers to the Corinthian church. When Paul uses the expression, he is not employing it abstractly but uses the concept in his response to a number of serious problems existing in the Corinthian community. After asserting the need for diversity in the human body (12:14–26), Paul tells the Corinthians that they are indeed the body of Christ and then, using *ekklesia* along with this image, he enumerates the various ministries and gifts God has appointed for the church (12:27–31). In 1 Corinthians 12:12–31 and Romans 12:3–8, Paul has the local community in mind when referring to the body of Christ; he uses the image to stress the different gifts and roles within the local congregation. The church, however, is not simply *like* a body; it *becomes* one body in Christ because the members share in the one eucharistic Body of Christ (10:16–17). As members of Christ's body each individual has a distinctive role to be played for the common good.[8]

Paul speaks of the *body* of Christ, but the authors of the letters to the Colossians and Ephesians speak of Christ as the *head* of the body, which is the church. The authors of Colossians and Ephesians employ the term *ekklesia* in a more general sense than Paul; for them the term refers to the church spread throughout the world.

Conscious that all those who are in Christ have been called, chosen, sanctified, and set apart for worship in the Spirit, Paul also looks upon the Christian community as the temple of God. He clearly affirms the reality of the divine indwelling; because God's Spirit abides within them, all Christians belong to a new family in Christ. Every baptized Christian is *in persona Christi.*

Paul is keenly aware that he has the serious responsibility to exercise authority in the communities he has evangelized. He is not only able to claim the title *apostle* but also apostolic authority (1 Cor 7:10, 12); nevertheless, he prefers to relate to his communities because of the spiritual gifts he has received (1 Cor 7:40). He knows that God has shown him special favor and empowered him to minister effectively. He is even grateful for his weaknesses because he knows that God is pleased to act through them too (2 Cor 11:30). He refrains from asserting the rights he might possess and is primarily concerned with the exercise of his responsibilities. His life is entirely devoted to service and in giving to others rather than receiving from them (1 Cor 15).[9]

The Gospels. Throughout Mark's Gospel, Jesus teaches the Twelve that greatness consists primarily in service to others rather than in dominating others through power or authority (Mk 10:41–44). The church must pattern itself on the Son of Man, who came to serve, not to be served (10:45). Christians therefore must take up the cross (8:34) and respond to the needs of others through service (9:33–37).[10]

The Gospel of Matthew relies on Mark's Gospel as its primary source; consequently, it shares many of Mark's ecclesiological concerns. Composed for a community of both Jewish and Gentile Christians of Syrian provenance about 85 CE, the Gospel contains a more explicit ecclesiology than Mark's Gospel, especially in terms of church discipline and structure. Matthew's Gospel comprises five discourses, addressed to the Matthean community, that function as the risen Lord's moral instructions and so disclose the essentials of Matthean ecclesiology. In the Sermon on the Mount we read that the church is primarily a community of disciples that fulfills the Mosaic Law as that law is interpreted by Jesus. In the missionary discourse Matthew emphasizes the missionary character of the church. Jesus limited his own mission and that of his immediate disciples to the lost sheep of the house of Israel, but the risen Lord commissions the church to make disciples of all peoples. In the parable discourse there is an indication that not all is well in Matthew's community, for it is like a field that contains both weeds and wheat. While some members of the community are inclined to root up the weeds, Matthew's Jesus advises them to wait in patience for the time of judgment, when the Son of Man will separate the bad from the good. Because there are failures in the church, Matthew's Jesus provides a community rule for dealing with those disciples who have sinned or gone astray. Jesus' eschatological discourse instructs the church about how to live in the period between Jesus' resurrection and his return in glory.

In his Gospel, Matthew portrays Jesus as the founder of the *ekklesia,* with Peter as its rock foundation. But Jesus is the one who calls the church into being and is really the foundation; Peter is his vicar. As such, Peter is granted a unique and authoritative role within the church. Matthew is certainly aware that most Israelites have not accepted Jesus as the Messiah, but he is careful to see continuity between Israel and the church. It is in continuity with historic Israel because its founder is the Messiah; nevertheless, the church is distinct because it now embraces all nations, including Israel.[11]

It should not be surprising that the Gospel of Luke is similar to the Gospel of Mark, because it uses Mark's Gospel as one of its sources. Because Luke developed his ecclesiology not only in his Gospel but also in the Acts of the Apostles, he presents the origins of the church within a broad context and he clearly distinguishes between the time of Jesus and the time of the church. The Gospel focuses on the time of Jesus, and the Acts on the time of the developing church. Luke, however, emphasizes the continuity between Israel and the community of those who have faith in Jesus. This is demonstrated in the infancy narrative, where he shows how the God of Israel discloses the fulfillment of his promises to the faithful Israelites, including Zechariah, Elizabeth, Mary, Joseph, Simeon, and Anna. It is in the Acts that Luke shows how and why Gentiles came to embrace the church.[12]

In the Acts of the Apostles the church plays a central role. The text recounts how the Gospel spread after the death and resurrection of Jesus through the preaching of the apostles and the witness of all those who believed in Jesus. Luke sees the church as a creation of the Spirit that comes into existence at Pentecost. It is ruled by the twelve apostles, so it is neither a new Israel nor a community separated from Israel. In the early chapters Luke describes the church as a community of believers who are faithful to the teaching of the apostles, to life in common, to the breaking of the bread and to prayer. They share all things in common so the early church is set out as an ideal example of communal life. The Twelve are central in the community because they witness to the Lord's resurrection. In most instances *ekklesia*, which is used frequently in Acts, refers to a local community, but the community at Jerusalem holds pride of place. The church in Acts is structured but it is also charismatic. In the early stages of development the apostles play an indispensable role, but there are also elders in both the church in Jerusalem and in the communities evangelized by Paul. However, the church is guided above all by the Spirit who gives special charisms to the members of the community.[13]

The Gospel of John is not primarily concerned with ecclesiology but concentrates on Christology. It was composed toward the end of the first century for a community that gathered around a figure identified as the "disciple whom Jesus loved." The Gospel refers to the Twelve, but there is no reference to Jesus calling them; it seems they did not play a major role in John's view of the church. Peter, however, does play a major role. The sheepfold and the vine are the two images that dominate John's ecclesiology. Jesus uses the metaphors of the gate and the good shepherd, as well as the metaphor of the vine and the branches, to describe his intimate relationship to the disciples. In a sense, then, the Johannine church is a community of mystical participation in the life of the risen Lord through the power of the Holy Spirit. The community sees itself as opposed to the world and its hostile forces. It worships in spirit and in truth but displaces the old worship because it no longer serves the community's needs. The risen Christ has become the true temple of the living God.[14]

The authors of the four Gospels insist that rank in the community implies humble and loving service. Authority or power over the community is never put forward as a primary datum. Rather, authority is meant to provide order for the community, a service that derives solely from the presence of God as love and life. God is presented as God for us, in touch with us, close to us. Everything that belongs to an individual comes from God and exists for others. There is no place for domination or possession or any spirit of possessiveness. The basic law of the Christian life is that Christians should consider themselves as stewards of God's gifts, which are always meant for the good of all.[15]

Moral exhortation is given to the Christian community in 1 Peter, Hebrews, Revelation, and 1 Timothy. These works focus on the church as the people of God, a pilgrim community, a persecuted community that will eventually share in the heavenly Jerusalem after it has borne witness to the Lamb who was slain but who is now risen. As the missionary activity of the church expanded and the number of Christians increased, structures became more necessary in the church; however, those who held office in the structures did not dominate the rest of the community; they were given offices in order to serve. Thus, in the Acts of the Apostles and the pastoral epistles we find the titles *episkopos* and *presbyteros,* titles that appear to be interchangeable. They are the titles for the chief leadership position in a local church. Those who held administrative responsibilities also seem to have functioned as preachers and teachers. Leadership is minimally alluded to in both the Acts of the Apostles and the pastoral epistles. The practice of virtues, however, is important, as is noted in 1 Timothy, where he is instructed to practice "righteousness, godliness, faith, love, endurance, and gentleness."[16]

Some conclusions might be drawn from this discussion of the church in the apostolic period. First of all, some form of ministry is clear from the earliest days of what eventually became a well-structured church. The apostles were considered the ministers of highest rank, as is indicated in the Pauline letters, in the Gospels, in the Acts of the Apostles, and in the pastoral letters. However, it seems that the ministry of apostle was not continued beyond the founding leaders. The early church did not employ the sacral title of priest *(hiereus)* for church ministers. It was probably shunned by the early church because of its association with the Jewish temple and with pagan cults. In the New Testament only the Jewish priests, Jesus himself, and all of the baptized are given the title *hiereus.* Certainly in the New Testament, ministry cannot be seen as the "power to preside at the Eucharist."

Christian ministers in the early church were neither self-appointed nor appointed by the community; rather, the ability to minister was considered a gift from the Lord. The model for all ministry was Jesus himself, who clearly came to serve, not to be served.[17]

The church from 90 to 210 CE. First of all, it should be noted that documentation on this period is extremely limited, so one must be careful in drawing broad conclusions. Although it is not a text written by an apostolic father, the *Didache* carries important implications for our understanding of the early developments of the Christian church. The document is actually a compilation of documents and is dated around the year 100 CE; in its present format it seems to have come from a Christian community in Syria. The first section (chaps. 1–6) deals with the two ways of Christian living: the way of virtue and the way of vice. Chapters 7–10 deal with the rituals of baptism and Eucharist. The third section treats itinerant ministers. It is the quality of the minister, not the function, that is discussed. There are no clear indications that would warrant the existence of a monarchical episcopate. The heads of communities are called *episkopoi* (overseers or bishops) and *diakonoi* (envoys), but whether the former were simple *presbyteroi* (priests) or actually bishops is not clear. In the document special attention is given to the prophets, who are to celebrate the Eucharist. It seems that presiding over the community rather than liturgical activity is the primary function of church ministers.[18]

Besides the New Testament and the *Didache*, the earliest Christian writings generally accepted in the church are those of the apostolic fathers, whose writings manifest a concern for the unity of the church in face of the threats of heresy, schism, and persecution. This concern for unity appears in *1 Clement*, a letter written about 96 CE by Clement of Rome to the church in Corinth. Clement views the church as a hierarchical society in which Christ, the apostles, and the bishops and deacons are comparable to the high priest, priests, and Levites in Israel. The office of bishop seems to have been exercised collegially rather than by one man acting alone, so that a monarchical episcopacy (the rule of a church by a single bishop) developed later for both the church at Rome and the church at Corinth. For Clement, ministry is radically christocentric; it is the Lord who appoints church ministers.[19]

Emphasis on authority marked the writings of Ignatius of Antioch, who wrote about 110 CE to various churches in Asia Minor while being taken to Rome for his execution. Concerned about the divisions in the churches, he stressed that church unity must be rooted in the bishop, who functions as a monarch in his own church. The bishop is assisted by presbyters and deacons, so there is a threefold ministry in the church. Although Ignatius insists on the importance of office in the church, he stresses that office is nothing in comparison with faith and love.[20]

As the church spread widely, it was often in conflict with the official religion of the state. Christian apologists, such as Justin Martyr (c.100–c.165), attempted to defend the gospel as an effective answer to humanity's search for truth. In the same century Gnostics, Marcionites, and Montanists constituted heretical movements that needed a response from authentic church leaders. Among the most effective was Irenaeus, the bishop of Lyons. For him, the *episkopos* was the chief leader in the Christian community, not simply in Lyons but, as he maintains, throughout the Christian world. It seems that by 180 CE or so the names for Christian ministry had become stabilized; the *episkopos* was the chief leader, assisted by the *presbyteroi* and the *diakonoi*. However, up to the time of Irenaeus the function of the various ministers was by no means uniform. It seems that emphasis was on leading the community rather than presiding at liturgies. But if one were the leader of the community, he was probably also the leader of the liturgy.[21]

In the writings of Origen and Tertullian as well as the third-century text entitled *Apostolic Tradition*, priestly language tends to be used for both the *episkopos* and the *presbyteros*. It seems that the hierarchy of *episkopos*, *presbyteros*, and *diakonos* had become standard, at least in the East. Origen sets out a strong theology of ministry, which is clearly christocentric and spiritual. It is in the writings of Tertullian that we find the terms *ordinatio* and *ordinare*, so that lay people constituted one group and the ordained another. The *Apostolic*

Tradition gives us the oldest known ordination ritual for the *episkopos*, *presbyteros*, and *diakonos*. Neither prophet nor teacher became part of the special ordo, though both ministries lasted for some time. They never became part of official ecclesial ministry.

The church from 210 to 600 CE. In this period there was increased clericalization as the ordained became more and more separated from the laity. From the beginning of the third century the clericalization process was already strong, so that any suggestions that originally the church was completely democratic cannot be authenticated. The clergy were given special privileges; bishops were ranked with the senators. As a result, church authority ran the risk of becoming increasingly secular and much more juridical in nature. In many ways monastic spirituality, including celibacy, was imposed on the secular clergy. From the early part of the fifth century the ordained began to wear distinctive dress. This clear distinction between the ordained and the laity set up tensions within the church.[22]

Furthermore, increased theologizing on ministry tended to stress the notion of priest. There was increased emphasis on the role of the bishop of Rome, with the result that the monarchical aspect of the episcopacy was highlighted. It was only in relationship to the pope that a bishop was to be understood theologically, either as an individual bishop or as part of a college of bishops. Monasticism developed as a protest against the church, which had become too rich and too powerful. It stressed the importance of charismatic or spiritual authority and the primacy of the spiritual life over worldly success. There were, however, many bishops who were monks or who had been trained in a monastic setting. Included here would be the distinguished names of Basil, John Chrysostom, Augustine, Caesarius of Arles, Martin, and Gregory the Great. In their writings these men stressed the basic responsibility of the church to care for people's souls; they had an essentially moral understanding of authority that was to be exercised in a genuine spirit of service and with a sincere sense of humility. These great church leaders carefully maintained a close relationship to their Christian communities—that was inherent in their understanding of the word *ekklesia*. In his sermons Augustine regularly reminded his community: "I am a bishop for your sake, I am a Christian together with you." One of Gregory the Great's mottos was *Servus servorum Dei* (servant of the servants of God). He took a genuine interest in ordinary people and made an effort to explain the reasons for decisions that he made. For him, the church was not a vast organization but a community of the baptized moving toward the perfection of charity.[23]

The church from 600 to 1300 CE. One of the most important achievements of Gregory the Great as pope at the end of the sixth century was laying the foundations for a new social and political order in Europe, one centered on the papacy rather than on the western empire. After his death it was monks who contributed most to the development of Christendom. Celtic monks carried their own brand of Christendom throughout Europe during the sixth and seventh centuries. They also strengthened Christendom's close link with the papacy; for example, Boniface (680–745) was sent by the pope from England to Germany and helped reform the church there. Charlemagne's coronation by the pope in 800 symbolized the union of the religious and political orders in Europe and the formation of western Christendom. This all blurred the distinction between church and state.[24]

The tenth century witnessed the development of monastic renewal and reform associated above all with the Benedictine Abbey of Cluny founded in 909. A highly centralized network of communities, the monasteries enjoyed considerable freedom from the influence of local lords and also from bishops. They accumulated vast amounts of property and wealth, earning severe criticism from other monastic communities. An overall reform of the church was inaugurated by Pope Leo IX (1049–54) and was continued with intense vigor by Pope Gregory VII (1073–81). This reform resulted in major changes in the understanding of church doctrines, especially in the understanding of church authority. Gregory claimed for the church absolute autonomy and a sovereign system of rights proper to a spiritual society. The foundation of the church was the pope, whose authority came directly from God. Gregory also claimed absolute authority over the kings and their kingdoms. To support these claims he asked churchmen to set out all the juridical texts they could find in support of his claims. These developments began to eclipse the understanding of the church as Mystical Body, which originally had referred to the Eucharist but began to refer primarily to the church as a social body. Likewise, the authority of bishops and priests, which had been looked upon mainly as moral authority derived from the power of their ordination, began to be viewed more and more as jurisdiction.[25]

This all resulted in an amazing development in the study of canon law. Increasingly, legalism began to characterize the life of the church; the church was thought of not primarily as a community of the faithful but as a legal system, an impersonal depositary of rights whose representatives were the hierarchy and ultimately the pope and the Roman curia. Under Gregory, canonists provided support for his goals, but the publication of Gratian's *Decretum* about 1140 provided the papacy with a systematic presentation of its already vast legal tradition. Bishops then thought of themselves as governing their dioceses, priests as governing their parishes, and the pope as sovereign, as vicar of Christ. They were also the judges of the people. A juridical understanding of the church as a visible, hierarchical society gained prominence in the West.[26]

Innocent III reigned as pope from 1198 to 1216. One of the most important popes in the High Middle Ages, he set about reforming the church, especially by convoking the Fourth Lateran Council in 1215. Innocent approved the constitutions of the Franciscans and Dominicans, thus authorizing the ministry of new mendicant orders whose ministry was vastly different from that of the monks and canons.[27] The latter had much in common with monks; they lived in community under a rule, took vows, and were attached to a church where they celebrated the liturgy, including the Divine Office. Examples are the Canons of St. Norbert and the Canons of St. Augustine.

From the eleventh century onward church authority in general and papal authority in particular borrowed many of the features, vocabulary, insignia, ceremony, and style of life from the imperial courts. Even the term *curia*, referring to the papal administration, was borrowed from secular vocabulary.[28]

Protests were made, especially by the anti-ecclesiastical spiritual movements that were frequent during the twelfth century and that continued in the fourteenth century with the Franciscan spiritual movement. They all sought a reform of the church so that there might be less pomp and more gospel. In the thirteenth century Thomas Aquinas and Bonaventure both sought to lay out a profoundly spiritual understanding of the church as a community of God's faithful people. They looked at authority not in juridical terms but as a spiritual gift reflected in a life of charity, personal freedom, and loving service of others. The early church reformers sought to reaffirm the right of conscience and the right to resist tyranny in the political sphere. They asserted the need to protect the poor and the weak, a traditional role of the episcopacy, the right to protest, and the right to disobey unjust laws and procedures. Indeed, the authority of bishops and clergy in general was never insisted on so clearly as in the thirteenth and fourteenth centuries.

In the fourteenth century opposition to the monarchical papacy found expression in the theory of conciliarism, which maintained that authority resided in the Christian community as a whole and not simply in the papacy. As a proponent of conciliarism, the Czech priest Jan Hus (c.1372–1415), following the lead of the Oxford theologian John Wycliffe, drew a distinction between the visible church under the jurisdiction of the pope and the invisible but gospel-based church under the jurisdiction of God. He was excommunicated for his views but decided to appeal to the Council of Constance. When he arrived, he was arrested, tried, and condemned for heresy and then burned at the stake.[29]

The Reformation and the Council of Trent to the Present. The Protestant Reformation challenged authority not only in its historical forms but also as a principle. Martin Luther (1483–1546), inspired by the beliefs of Hus and Wycliffe, sought to restore the church to its true identity, which was obscured by ecclesiastical bureaucracy and a popular piety that bordered on magic. He held that the church had abandoned its conviction that all people are saved not by their good works but by the gift of faith from God. He emphasized the primacy of God's word in the Bible, which was greater than the authority of tradition, the church's magisterium, or the pope. He insisted that the church was instituted by God as a means of grace; hence, its primary responsibility was to preach the gospel and administer the sacraments of baptism and Eucharist. Luther rejected the authority of the hierarchy in mediating salvation and emphasized the priesthood of all the baptized, who are called to be ministers of God's word to one another. Obviously, Luther's understanding of the church has little place for an institution; the church is invisible and its membership is known only to God.[30]

The Protestant Reformation occurred at the same time as the development of the great forces that created the modern world, including the science of observation, the primacy of individual personality, the passion for invention and discovery, and the growth of historical and philosophical criticism. The

Catholic Church's reaction to all this at the Council of Trent (1543–65) was a reassertion of authority and an effort to control diversity by a greater degree of centralization. But the council also revived the concept and practice of authority as rooted in the gospel and in a deeply spiritual life. While stressing the authority of God, of divine revelation, of Christ, of the state, and of parents, the council's assertion of authority in the church set the pattern so that the whole treatise on ecclesiology became a treatise on public law and what Congar has called "hierarchiology." In this context the papacy received the lion's share of attention. The pope became the universal bishop, so individual Catholics had a much more immediate relationship with the pope than with the local bishop. Since Trent, the pope's discourses and writings have instructed people about what they ought to think, the liturgy has become very carefully regulated by universally implemented liturgical books containing numerous detailed rubrics, and training for ordination has been governed by a plan of studies to be implemented in seminaries. In other words, from the time of Trent the exercise of authority in the modern Catholic Church has emanated from its central and supreme seat in Rome.[31]

Since the sixteenth century the Catholic Church has put into practice a "mystique" of authority in which the Society of Jesus, founded by Ignatius of Loyola (1491–1556), undoubtedly played a part. In particular, a distinguished Jesuit theologian, Robert Bellarmine (1542–1621), played a major role in defending the Catholic Church from Protestantism. He is especially remembered because of his clear and concise definition of the Catholic Church as "the community of men brought together by the profession of the same Christian faith and conjoined in the communion of the same sacraments, under the government of the legitimate pastors and especially the one vicar of Christ on earth, the Roman pontiff." In light of that definition the church is an institution whose authority is derived immediately from God and is to be identified with God's will. The pope is the visible Christ and, to some extent, every other authority figure in the church is a visible image of Christ. This is all quite removed from the biblical identification of the whole church as the people of God, the body of Christ, and the temple of God's presence. The church, the *ekklesia,* ceased to be viewed primarily as the Christian community of the faithful.[32]

The priesthood became much less monastic in terms of a life of contemplation. The ordained were no longer committed strongly to *lectio divina* and the study of scripture; consequently, their preaching was not based primarily on the Bible but rather on doctrinal propositions and moral laws. They were often absorbed in administrative and financial concerns. Since Trent, priests in general have been keenly aware of their pastoral and apostolic responsibilities. However, the term *apostolic* has taken on a distinctive meaning in modern times, for it now simply means "zealous" or "having a missionary spirit."[33]

The Roman Catholic Church's stress on the church as a visible society inevitably raised an important question: How does this society relate to the secular kingdoms? The answer took the form of Gallicanism in France and Febronianism and Josephinism in Germany and Austria. There were two strains of Gallicanism: the one royal, which asserted the independence of the monarch from ecclesiastical and especially papal authority; and the other episcopal, which affirmed the rights of individual bishops and national hierarchies over the pope and the Roman curia. The episcopal strand of Gallicanism found expression in German-speaking lands in the eighteenth century in a movement known as Febronianism. The most significant effort to implement the strands of royal Gallicanism in Austria was Josephinism, named for the emperor Joseph II (1741–90), who held that the church and its ministers were subordinate to civil authority in all matters that did not pertain to doctrine. He held that changes in liturgical practices, discipline of the clergy, regulation of church schools, and parish and diocesan boundaries were all matters that should be governed by the state. Most of Joseph's ideas were repudiated by his successor, Leopold II. In 1786 the bishop of Pistoia, Scipione de' Ricci (1741–1810), presided over a synod that formally adopted the various Gallican positions.[34]

In the nineteenth century there were several key issues in ecclesiology: the development of a systematic theology of ecclesiology, an appreciation of a rich understanding of tradition, Ultramontanism, and the centralization of authority in the papacy, culminating in the declaration of papal infallibility at the First Vatican Council.[35] In the Catholic theological faculty at the University of Tübingen, founded in 1812, several distinguished faculty members surfaced who contributed much to the positive development of ecclesiology. These included Johann Sebastian Drey and his student Johann Adam Möhler. Drey taught that the theologian's task was to give systematic form to the church's worship, preaching, and practice. He realized that doctrine itself had a history and a development and maintained that it was the theologian's task to both trace that development and to advance it.

Möhler was what might be described as the creator of ecclesiology as a distinct field within systematic theology.[36] He gave ecclesiology a strong pneumatic component and consequently produced an ecclesiology very different from that of the Catholic Reformation. The inner life of the members of the church was generated by the Spirit through their active participation in the community; hence, Möhler defined the church in terms of its "soul," not its body. As his academic career matured, he developed a different position in which he confirmed the primacy of divine grace but also asserted the necessity of human freedom. Using a christological rather than a pneumatological model, he sought to develop an ecclesiology based on the incarnation, implying that the church is actually a manifestation of the Son of God in human form. Consequently, he stressed the visibility of the church but did not defend the legitimacy of institutional forms and offices; instead, he insisted on the ongoing presence of the incarnate Christ in history through the presence of the church. Thus, his ecclesiology emphasized a Spirit-centered understanding of the church that would bear much influence on the ecclesiology of Yves Congar in the twentieth century; it recovered the image of the church as the Mystical Body of Christ, reflected in the twentieth century in Pope Pius XII's encyclical *Mystici Corporis*; and it deeply affected the way subsequent theologians understood the church because of the way it interacted with both Christology and theological anthropology. After Johann Adam Möhler the church was not simply the bearer of the mystery of faith but was itself an aspect of that mystery. Hence, ecclesiology developed from being primarily concerned with institutional issues to a mature treatment of both the inner nature and external mission of the church, both of which play major roles in the economy of human salvation.[37]

The Tübingen theologians used the model of organic life to describe tradition, an approach that John Henry Newman (1801–90) employed to show that doctrine develops. He also recovered the notion of the *sensus fidelium* as an important element in the preservation and development of a living tradition that involved both the *ecclesia docens* and the *ecclesia discens* (the teaching and the learning church). Newman's ecclesiology sought to restore unity and order in the church by affirming the role of the local community, the theological schools, and the hierarchy, which he believed should be held in a creative tension.[38]

Following the French Revolution in the nineteenth century there were major efforts to reestablish a social and political system that would counteract the excesses of the revolution and the Napoleonic era. Ultramontanism was an attempt to ensure the unity and good order of the church by seeking to establish a highly centralized and omni-competent papacy exercising strong authority through a closely linked chain of command in which the bishops were the basic links. Those who espoused the Ultramontanist desires played an important role in preparations for the First Vatican Council (1869–70), which declared the primacy and infallibility of the pope. Although the council intended to treat both the nature of the church and the role of the bishops in the church, it was recessed before it had an opportunity to discuss either. Although the council affirmed that bishops are divinely appointed successors of the apostles and that actual jurisdiction is assigned to them, presumably by the pope, the council ended by leaving the document on the pope unrelated to any clear statement on episcopal collegiality.[39]

From Vatican I to Vatican II (1870–1960). During the ninety years between Vatican I and Vatican II there were three significant developments that affected the understanding of ecclesiology. First of all, Neo-Scholasticism, which began to emerge prior to Vatican I, characterized most Catholic theology, especially because of encouragement by Pope Leo XIII. It had a major effect on the theological manuals used in seminaries, especially in the first half of the twentieth century. Second, the image of the church as the Mystical Body of Christ, which had been emphasized by Möhler, became a prominent motif in ecclesiology due to Pope Pius XII's encyclical *Mystici Corporis*. Third, in spite of the Modernist controversy, keen interest in biblical, liturgical, patristic, and ecumenical studies flourished and in many ways transformed Roman Catholic reflection on the church's nature and mission. These developments prepared the way for the documents issued at Vatican II.

Developments in modern philosophy were severely criticized in the nineteenth century by Catholic scholars who encouraged a return to the medieval synthesis of Thomas Aquinas. Leo XIII (1810–1903) supported that movement by encouraging a return to Thomistic thought in his encyclical *Aeterni Patris* (1879). As a result, Neo-Scholasticism formed the foundation for most clerical training in the late nineteenth century and up to Vatican II. It focused on an apologetic approach to theology and demonstrated the need to show a continuous authoritative witness to revelation rooted in the human desire for ultimate salvation. As a result, ecclesiology became a tract within fundamental theology, whereas the other tracts in dogmatic theology treated the church as a hierarchically structured visible society. The link between Christ and the church was reduced to that of a founder and an institution. The rich biblical, patristic, and liturgical foundations were either muted or ignored.[40]

A much richer christological ecclesiology, rooted in the work of Matthias Scheeben and Möhler, was set out in Pius XII's encyclical on the Mystical Body, *Mystici Corporis,* in 1943. The letter stresses the corporate unity of all the members of the church with Christ and with one another in a real union that is mystical rather than physical. It identifies the body of Christ with the Roman Catholic Church and with those who are united with that church at least by desire, a position that would be altered by Vatican II.[41]

Although Roman Catholic scholarship was under siege following the condemnation of Modernism by Pope Pius X in 1907, distinguished scholars, such as Lambert Beauduin, Romano Guardini, Odo Casel, and Joseph Jungmann, avoided condemnation by concentrating on patristic and liturgical sources for their thought and writings. Modern biblical scholarship was eventually encouraged by Pius XII's encyclical *Divino afflante Spiritu* (1943), which placed the church within the context of salvation history and carefully distinguished between the church and the kingdom of God. Through their study of both scripture and patristic texts, theologians began to recover the role of the Holy Spirit, thus balancing and complementing the almost exclusive emphasis on Christology in ecclesiology. The important themes of salvation history and the church as a sacrament of salvation were keenly developed in the work of distinguished theologians, such as Marie-Dominique Chenu (1895–1990), Henri de Lubac (1896–1991), Karl Rahner (1904–84), Yves Congar (1904–95), and Edward Schillebeeckx (1914–2009), all of whom made important contributions to the texts issued by Vatican II by their reflections on the nature, mission, and structure of the church.[42]

Religious institutes and the church. Institutes of Religious Life is the technical term used in official Roman Catholic documents for ecclesiastical societies in which members profess the evangelical counsels of perfection: poverty, chastity, and obedience. The traditional distinction between solemn and simple vows and the way in which vows are observed are defined in the constitutions of each group. Institutes are established either by the Holy See or a diocesan bishop. The main distinction is between religious institutes (still popularly known as religious orders) and secular institutes. The members of religious institutes take public vows and are expected to live a common life. The members of secular institutes follow the evangelical counsels and commit themselves to the sanctification of the world; they live alone, in groups, or in families.

The history of religious institutes is rather complicated. Until the thirteenth century monasteries had a dominant effect on the nature and mission of the church, but that was radically changed in the early thirteenth century by the approval of the constitutions of the Dominicans and Franciscans. Along with other mendicant orders they represented a radical departure from the past monastic tradition by adopting a rule of community poverty and setting aside many aspects of institutionalized monastic life. The monastic communities had settled in rural areas where they cultivated the land and to a limited extent ministered to their neighbors. In the late Middle Ages, however, the city, the bourgeoisie, and the merchant classes began to characterize much of European society. The mendicants went where the people were and sought to minister to them in terms of their concrete needs.[43]

The Order of Friars Preachers, founded by St. Dominic (1170–1221), was the first religious order to incorporate as an integral part of its religious life a ministry that shared the bishops' fundamental responsibility to preach the word of God. The friars emphasized community life but not in a specific place. Although the order quickly came to be widely dispersed, unity was preserved because of the carefully structured constitutions that established a firm bond among the friars. In this the order was distinguished from both the monks and the bourgeoisie.[44]

Contemporary with the foundation of the Dominicans was the foundation of the Order of Friars Minor. One of Dominic's great gifts—the gift of organization—was a charism sadly lacking in the founder of the Franciscans; Francis of Assisi (1181/2–1226) failed to establish a stable religious institute. In the beginning Francis and his disciples were an intimate fraternity of nomadic preachers; some were clerics, but most were lay men who moved from town to town preaching in the market squares. They were committed to a life of absolute poverty. In 1210 Francis took his companions to Rome, where he persuaded the pope to authorize their activities. Because of their lack of structure, their early history was extremely turbulent. It was left to St. Bonaventure, who was general of the order from 1257 to 1273, to translate Francis of Assisi's brilliant originality into a permanent institution that could survive.[45]

Like Dominic, Francis provided a rule for women that insisted on strict enclosure based on the Rule of St. Benedict, for mendicancy was unthinkable for women at the time. Hence, the Poor Clares, though strongly committed to evangelical poverty, became an enclosed monastic order of the traditional type.[46]

After the foundation of the Dominicans and Franciscans, the Hermits of St. Augustine, the Carmelites, the Servites, and the Minims all modeled themselves and their way of life on the example of the first orders of friars.[47] Mention should also be made of the Beguines, an anomalous movement of urban women in the Low Countries who did not take vows and who followed no specific rule but lived together in small communities and supported themselves by working in textiles or other crafts. Because they lacked firm clerical supervision and did not live within an enclosure, the Beguines were often held in suspicion, but they survived those who persecuted them and provided a model for later institutes of women religious that would surface in the seventeenth and later centuries. In a real sense the Beguines represented an early movement toward women's liberation.[48] Their male counterparts were the Beghards, who were usually weavers, dyers, or fullers, kept a common purse, and had no private property; they were relatively few in number.

In the period between the High Middle Ages and the Reformation there were newly founded religious orders that demonstrated a strong commitment to an active pastoral or charitable ministry. Among male religious these groups constituted a new type of religious order, namely, the clerks regular. They were modeled after the Dominicans and other mendicant orders, which had become clericalized. As ordained priests they lived in community, generally following the Rule of Augustine with their own constitutions and practicing the evangelical counsels.

The most important new foundation in the sixteenth century was that established by Ignatius of Loyola (1491–1554). Following a deep religious conversion, he and six companions took vows in 1534 committing themselves to a life of poverty and chastity, to make a pilgrimage to Jerusalem, and to work for the salvation of souls. From the beginning their community was a clerical society, even though some of the members were lay brothers. In 1549 Pope Paul III confirmed the community under the title Society of Jesus. Their ministry was divided into preaching, teaching, and works of mercy. A fourth vow was added to the usual three religious vows of poverty, chastity and obedience—the members were to obey without any hesitation all commands of the pope concerning the salvation of souls and the spread of the gospel. A strong bond of obedience bound the individual Jesuit to his superior, and the whole society was committed to fidelity to the pope.[49]

In the sixteenth century a major innovation took place in the history of women's religious orders with the foundation of a new way of religious life by St. Angela Merici (1464–1540). In 1525 she founded a society in Italy for the education of orphaned girls and the care of the sick and named the group after the martyr St. Ursula. Until that time women's religious orders were generally strictly enclosed and had very limited contact with the secular world. In the case of Angela Merici's order, there was no bond with a community of men; she also abandoned common life. In this latter regard her group resembled a modern secular institute. The members were united by a common rule of life, common prayer, worship, regular community meetings, and a common ministry. They were essentially a society of devout women committed to charitable work. Their uniform clothing, however, and their custom of taking private vows moved them in the direction of traditional orders of women religious.[50]

Angela's death in 1540 coincided with preparations for the Council of Trent. On 3 December 1563, at the end of the first session, the council fathers hastily decreed that all nuns were to observe strict enclosure and were forbidden to go out of the monastery without episcopal approval. In 1566 Pope Pius V decreed that the law should be applied to all professed nuns. Consequently, the Ursulines became an order of nuns under strict enclosure.[51]

No less daring than St. Angela's efforts to found a new type of religious life for women was the attempt made by Mary Ward (1585–1645), who came from an old English Catholic family. Inspired to found a new religious community for English women, she sought first to strengthen the Catholic faith in England by providing women with a religious education so that they could take part in the re-conversion of England to Catholicism. Besides the work of education, the sisters were to assist the Catholic priests with their apostolic activities. The sisters were to live in community but without a distinctive habit and with no strict enclosure. In developing her order Mary Ward was obviously inspired by Ignatius of Loyola; she wanted a similarly mobile order of women to work together with the Jesuits. In fact, when she drew up the constitutions for her order, she carefully followed the constitutions of the Society of Jesus. The Jesuits, however, were not at all interested in collaborating with a female branch of the Society, and the papal curia could not tolerate the abandonment of enclosure. Mary Ward was misunderstood; consequently, her plans did not receive approval in Rome. In 1631 Pope Urban VIII suppressed her institute. A number of her foundations, however, survived, especially through support from secular authorities. Eventually the so-called English Ladies were "domesticated" to the extent that they became an order within the traditional framework of religious life, but an order that earned special recognition because of its work in education.[52]

In the same period there were foundations of women's orders devoted specifically to charitable work. Under the direction of St. Vincent de Paul (c.1580–1660) and St. Louise de Marillac (1591–1660), various religious groups of devout women were united into a community and called the Daughters of Charity. In 1654 Pope Innocent X confirmed the congregation; however, its members were not religious in the strict sense. Common life under a superior, in the monastic tradition, was prescribed for these women, but their life was committed to social and charitable ministries outside the convent.[53] After the founding of the Daughters of Charity with their freedom for apostolic work because of their lack of cloister, various societies of women were founded for education, nursing, and missionary work, for example, the Sisters of St. Joseph, Sisters of Divine Providence, and the Sisters of the Immaculate Heart of Mary.

The Jesuits had introduced the practice of simple vows for some of their members, thus breaking the long tradition that solemn vows were the only vows permitted in religious orders. Their lead in this matter was followed by many religious congregations after the Council of Trent. Some communities took only simple vows, while others took no public vows at all; the former were called religious congregations, the latter societies of common life without vows. Many of these groups were clerical groups, such as the Sulpicians, Redemptorists, Passionists, Oblates of Mary Immaculate, Marists, Marianists, and Oratorians.

The nineteenth and twentieth centuries in the history of religious institutes were characterized by a clear process of consolidation and stabilization. A major turning point in the history of religious life occurred in 1917 with the promulgation of the Code of Canon Law. In the years after 1917 all religious orders and congregations had to adapt their particular legislation to the general ecclesiastical laws of the church. The highest authority for all questions about religious life was the Congregation for Religious, which had existed since 1586.[54] Canon 478 of the 1917 code defined religious life as "a stable manner of living in community, by which the faithful, in addition to the common commandments, also undertake to observe the evangelical counsels through vows of obedience, chastity, and poverty." That definition was drawn from history and current practice, but it soon lagged behind further developments in religious life. The change was characterized by the development and approval of secular institutes in 1947 by Pope Pius XII. In his apostolic constitution *Provida mater ecclesia* he defined these new forms of life in the church as "societies, clerical or lay, whose members make profession of the evangelical counsels, living in a secular condition for the purpose of Christian perfection and full apostolate" (Art. 1).

At first glance secular institutes seemed to be new ecclesiastical structures, quite different from the usual structures of traditional religious institutes. Members engage in apostolates involving pastoral, social, charitable, and educational work, but often the secular institute does not own the places where the members minister and work. They profess the evangelical counsels, but they do not necessarily live the common life; many work in secular professions. They often have much in common with the members of the various religious movements, such as the Focalare movement, that have gained popularity in the Roman Catholic Church in recent years.

From this cursory review of the history of various institutes of consecrated life some specific problems and general conclusions may be drawn. First of all, the great majority of the members of religious institutes are lay men and women. Consequently, ecclesiastical legislation has generally held that they may not exercise true jurisdiction in the church. The 1917 Code of Canon Law affirmed that only ordained members of the church could exercise true jurisdiction. It was asserted that lay religious could only exercise dominative power but not true jurisdiction. But the simple fact is that lay men and women, especially religious sisters and brothers, often govern very large international communities, sometimes numbering several thousand members. The 1983 Code of Canon Law in canon 596 failed to address the issue adequately, so in recent years various religious institutes have petitioned the Holy See to elect or appoint major superiors who are not ordained. Occasionally that permission has been granted. The issue, however, has not been satisfactorily resolved. Many women religious still maintain that they are unnecessarily marginalized in the church, are needlessly prevented from exercising true jurisdiction, and are excluded from all the major decision-making processes in the church.[55]

Second, institutes of consecrated life are expressions of the charismatic rather than the hierarchical dimension of the church. But it should be noted that both lay religious and ordained members of the church share a common baptism and so are primarily and basically equal in the eyes of God. Although members of religious institutes have a right to legitimate autonomy provided for institutes of consecrated life in the Code of Canon Law, they also have a responsibility to be in respectful dialogue with diocesan authorities, especially concerning their ministries, and to be faithful to the just directives emanating from the Holy See concerning all institutes of consecrated life. It is no secret that various religious institutes have at times felt unjustly treated by ecclesiastical officials and that their legitimate autonomy has been jeopardized.

Third, the members of institutes of consecrated life normally take public vows in the church, but the various vow patterns have often undergone considerable change over the centuries. Each institute, attentive to its own proper character and purpose, defines in its own constitutions the manner in which the vows are to be observed. The juridical effects of the vows are regularly spelled out in approved constitutions.

Fourth, the members of institutes of consecrated life are expected to live in community. In recent years this has created problems, because many religious feel obliged to find work where they receive a just salary and can contribute to the financial support of the many aged members of their communities. As a result, many do not live in community. Their lifestyle often resembles that of members of secular institutes. This is a serious problem that is not easily resolved.

Finally, the work or ministry of most institutes was originally specified in their constitutions. In recent years, however, many institutes have had to give up their hospitals, orphanages, and schools. While making an effort to maintain some relationship with the original ministry of the institute, communities have had to diversify, due especially to financial exigencies. The challenge in all institutes is to maintain the primacy of each member's union with God through prayer so that all ministry flows out of and is an expression of the institute's primary commitment to God and to the church.

Although some religious institutes are under the jurisdiction of the local bishop, most of them have a canonical status as institutes of pontifical right; hence they have a certain independence from parochial and diocesan structures. Their members' primary responsibility is to make their lives dynamic symbols of the need that all baptized Christians have to strive for holiness. Through their vows they have committed themselves to bear public witness to the Christian values that all Christians should pursue. Because of their public status their failures usually seem more shocking than those of other Christians. In practice, many religious are involved in parochial and diocesan structures; nevertheless, most do not profess any commitment to a locality and are free to move and to respond to needs that are discerned by the institute at large.

The church and Vatican II. When Pope John XXIII entrusted to a theological commission the preparation of documents for Vatican II, it was natural that the members of the commission, who were mainly curial officials and their Roman consultors, should think that their task was simply to repeat and reinforce the traditional teaching of the church, especially as it was articulated by recent popes. They produced a document on the church that summarized the basic theology contained in the Syllabus of Errors (1864), the condemnation of Modernism (1907), and the encyclicals of Pius XII, especially *Humani generis* (1950), which was severely critical of the "new theology" produced especially by the French theologians Marie-Dominique Chenu, Henri de Lubac, and Yves Congar. The document was rejected out of hand once the fathers of Vatican II received the text.[56]

For several decades theologians had been commenting on the church as the pilgrim people of God and had written about the church as a sacrament.

Likewise, the relationship between the church and the Eucharist was a major theme in liturgical theology, especially in the writings of Henri de Lubac. Grass-roots relations with other Christian churches surfaced the important relationship between word and sacrament and between scripture and tradition. The role of lay people in the church, especially in various forms of Catholic Action and the major theological writings of Yves Congar, was a subject that certainly needed official affirmation and clarification. Eventually a new text was produced that emerged from the council as the *Dogmatic Constitution on the Church (Lumen gentium).*[57]

The first chapter of the document treats the church as mystery and contains reflections on the church as sacrament and as communion in the divine life. The second chapter discusses the church as the people of God, while the third turns to differentiations among the members of the church, beginning with the hierarchy. Chapter 4 is concerned with the laity, and chapter 5 with the universal call to holiness. Chapter 6 deals with religious, chapter 7 with the pilgrim church, and chapter 8 with Our Lady. It needs to be emphasized that one cannot find a definitive and systematic treatise on the church in any of the conciliar documents or in the documents combined. Throughout, the *Dogmatic Constitution on the Church* opts for a variety of images derived from scripture, patristic writings, and the liturgy. The document is descriptive rather than synthetic. The church is at once a community of faith, hope, and love, and also a visible society and a spiritual community, existing on earth but endowed with divine gifts. Hence, the church is both human and divine. Certainly the Spirit is found outside the Catholic Church, and therefore the living body of Christ cannot be simply identified with the Catholic Church. Consequently, the council chose to speak of degrees of communion with the church.[58]

The council spoke of the church of Christ *subsisting in* the Catholic Church; this allowed room for the existence of ecclesial elements in other Christian communities. The council's *Decree on Ecumenism (Unitatis redintegratio)* affirms that "it is only in the Catholic Church of Christ, the common help of salvation, that can be found all the fullness of the means of salvation" (no. 3). In other words, the scriptures, the creed, the sacraments, and the ministries are found in their totality only in the Catholic church.[59]

A major issue that has concerned theologians since Vatican II is the relationship between the local and the universal church, between the papacy and the college of bishops. *Lumen gentium* sets out a clear statement that its teaching on the episcopate is to be seen as continuation of the teaching of Vatican I on the governance and teaching authority of the papacy (no. 3). It recalls Christ's gathering of the apostles and the continuation of their proper ministry in their successors, the bishops. Attention is drawn to the important fact that the three offices of the bishops (governing, teaching, and sanctifying) are basically communicated through episcopal ordination; they are not the result simply of papal delegation. Hence, the college of bishops embodies, makes present, and exercises the role of the college of apostles represented by the Twelve. It should be clear that defining the authority of the episcopal college in this way in no way infringes on the primatial role of the papacy. The pope has "full, supreme, and universal power in the church, which he may always exercise freely," but "the order of bishops . . . in union with its head, the Roman Pontiff, and never without this head, is also the subject of full and supreme power of the whole Church, a power which can only be exercised with the consent of the Roman Pontiff" (no. 22). As recent decades have clearly shown, the great challenge has been to reconcile the demands of unity and the requirements of diversity, to reconcile the role of the papacy and the role of the episcopacy.[60] In fact, the bishops throughout the world are scarcely ever consulted on major issues that are put into effect by the present pope, even though he is aware that his directives will seriously affect the pastoral life of local dioceses.[61]

As we have already seen, for centuries ecclesiology had been studied from a universalist perspective, probably because so much attention had been given to the role of the pope and because much of the missionary activity of the church had spread from Europe and had presumed that a Roman, European shape and practice should be normative elsewhere. As a result, both in theory and practice, a highly centralized and uniform vision of the church prevailed. This view, however, gradually changed and continues to change for several reasons.

First of all, missionaries developed an increased respect for the diverse cultures they encountered and sought to develop an indigenous clergy in the countries they served. Second, dialogue with the Orthodox Churches of the East brought a fresh appreciation of the diversity and richness of the spiritual, liturgical, and theological traditions of the one church of Christ. Third, theological scholarship on the relation between the church and the Eucharist and the emphasis on the primacy of the eucharistic assembly helped western theologians understand and appreciate the eucharistic ecclesiologies of the East. As a result of these developments significant attention was drawn to the local manifestations of the church not only in the form of the local worshiping assemblies but also in their broad traditions of church life and practice. New emphasis was placed on the local church in the conciliar documents and has stimulated much theological reflection and writing since Vatican II.[62]

In light of the assertion of the *Constitution on the Sacred Liturgy (Sacrosanctum concilium)* that "the chief manifestation of the church occurs in the full and active participation of the whole People of God in the same liturgical celebrations" (no. 42), *Lumen gentium* went on to affirm that the "Church of Christ is truly present in all legitimate local assemblies of the faithful, which, linked with their pastors, are themselves called Churches in the New Testament" (no. 26). Likewise the whole mystery of the church is realized in each local diocese (no. 23). The universal church, then, is not something distinct from the local churches but exists only in them and out of them. Apart from the individual local churches, the universal church is merely an abstraction. The council both affirmed and praised the diversity of disciples, liturgical usages, and theological and spiritual patrimonies found in the various churches and insisted that this variety of local churches clearly demonstrates the catholicity of the undivided church (no. 23).[63]

As we have seen, the first draft of the *Dogmatic Constitution on the Church* turned almost immediately to the hierarchical structure of the church. In the final text of *Lumen gentium* the chapter on the people of God precedes that on the hierarchy. The treatment of the people of God focuses on the whole body of believers—ordained, religious, and laity. This means in practice that the laity must be given their proper dignity and roles in the church. The *Constitution on the Sacred Liturgy* stresses that "all the faithful should be led to that fully conscious, and active participation in liturgical celebrations that is demanded by the nature of the liturgy itself and for which the Christian people, 'a chosen race, a royal priesthood, a holy nation, a people God has purchased,' have a right and duty to participate in virtue of their baptism" (no. 14). The *Dogmatic Constitution on the Church* says: "There is, therefore, no inequality in Christ and in the Church. . . . Although by Christ's will some are established as teachers, dispensers of the mysteries, and pastors for others, still there is among all an equality in dignity and in the activity common to all the faithful with regard to the building up of the Body of Christ" (no. 32). These affirmations ground the "bill of rights" of the laity that has been set out in the 1983 Code of Canon Law, canons 208–223.[64]

In his 1943 encyclical *Mystici Corporis*, Pius XII asserted that there are people in the church who are endowed with the charismatic gifts of the Spirit but who do not belong to the hierarchy of the church. At Vatican II the fathers took a definite stand against those who claimed that charisms were confined to the early church and that they no longer had a legitimate place in ecclesial life.[65] It is surely the Lord himself who rules and guides his church; however, he not only operates through hierarchical offices but also through charisms that are not linked to offices. The Spirit of the Lord has always been with the church, but that presence has often been manifested in unexpected and creative ways. Official authority and laws have an important place in the church because they derive from the Spirit of the Lord, but time and time again the hierarchy has been brought to recognize that in the last analysis the presence of the Spirit cannot be controlled or confined to offices and laws, nor can the Spirit's ways of operating be clearly foreseen. In fact, the gifts of the Spirit have often been present in the midst of ecclesiastical corruption and weakness.[66]

The hierarchy is bound by the charisms of the church. This close link of fidelity between the episcopacy and charisms parallels the liaison between the bishops and the deposit of faith that abides in the whole of God's people. The hierarchy's authority is not only an instrument of service to the church, but it is also and above all an instrument of submission to the Lord. The hierarchy has authority not by delegation of the people of God but rather in virtue of the Spirit of God, who informs the episcopal office itself; in the exercise of their authority the bishops direct what exists in the deposit of faith, which abides not simply in the episcopacy but in the whole community of God's people. The bishops find the norm for the exercise of their authority in the teachings and person of Christ, who through the power of the Spirit lives and acts in the whole church and manifests that presence through the charismatic gifts that are given to all the people.

It is understandable that some bishops at Vatican II denied the existence of charisms today for fear of the pernicious effects they might have on church order and discipline. They felt that their authority was under attack. Charisms are essential, not alien, to the church, but they do not necessarily arise as a direct result of the insights or leadership of the hierarchy. In fact, they often arise quite independently of the hierarchy. Those who consider the church in exclusively hierarchical terms rather than in terms of the whole community of God's people are apt to regard charisms that arise in Christians other than the hierarchy with a certain fear and suspicion. Furthermore, since charisms are likely to be the cause of change and development in the church, Christians who think of the church as a perfect, sinless society and of the hierarchy as primarily responsible for maintaining the established order in the church and who look upon the rest of the faithful simply as obedient subjects who themselves should not take any initiative, will inevitably see no place or need for charisms in the church. The charismatic character of the church will not be acceptable to the faithful who view the episcopal office in an autocratic context; likewise, only those bishops who see their role in the church as one of selfless service will be at ease with charisms among their people.

The council's vindication of the co-responsibility of all members of the church certainly has had a major effect in the opening of new opportunities for lay people in liturgy, catechetics, faith formation, and, to some extent, governance of the church. Since the council thousands of lay men and women have become lay ecclesial ministers in the church, many of them on a full-time basis.[67] The focus of the conciliar texts on the laity, however, lies rather on their role in the world. What is distinctive about lay people is their "secular character"; this means that their Christian lives are generally lived in the secular world, where they are employed in secular occupations. In that context their role is to redeem and transform society, culture, and history. It is precisely because they are engaged in the world that they have a right and responsibility to bring their experience and wisdom to bear on the pastoral life of the church.

Religious institutes have traditionally borne witness to the charismatic dimension of the church. Living in accord with the spirit of the charism of their founder, the members have regularly manifested a spirituality that is clearly in keeping with their own traditions and their approved constitutions. The creation of their own educational, healthcare, and social service institutions has been one of the most distinctive and enduring characteristics of religious institutes, especially in the United States. Thousands of hospitals, clinics, Catholic schools, colleges, universities, seminaries, and orphanages have borne effective witness to the Catholic Church's concern for the well-being of its own members and its desire to serve others.[68] One of the sad outcomes of the legitimate reforms in institutes of consecrated life after Vatican II is that the strong witness of institutions owned and operated by religious has largely disappeared from the American scene. This is mainly because of declining numbers in membership and financial exigencies. This situation has been prevalent throughout the western hemisphere.

Against this complex background we now turn to what we mean by a "virtuous church." We discuss the elimination of negative structures that tend to institutionalize the church excessively and the creation of positive structures that might facilitate the mature development and responsibility of all Christians and the development of a virtuous church on the diocesan, national, and universal levels.

Some basic principles. We live in a pyramidally structured church in which the people on the top of the pyramid—the pope, the officials of the Roman curia, and other members of the hierarchy—tell the rest of the people what they are to believe, how they are to worship, and what kind of moral lives they are to live. There is rarely any effective consultation of priests, religious, and laity. The subjects that are dealt with in communications are very frequently the reasons why there is so much contention and so many divisions in the Catholic Church today. In secular society there has been much discussion of the principles of communication and specifically about the principles of dialogue. That discussion, in fact, positively affected some of the documents of the Second Vatican Council, but communication with the Vatican dicasteries has deteriorated in recent decades. Priests who have been ordained since Vatican II usually do not know Latin or at least do not know it well; consequently correspondence between chanceries in the United States and Roman dicasteries is usually transmitted in English but often responded to in Latin, even by Roman officials who could easily write in English. Chanceries usually find that practice very burdensome.

Most literary historians hold that Plato (c.437 BCE–c.347 BCE) introduced the systematic use of dialogue as a literary form, with the result that it became a major literary genre in antiquity. It was often used by early Christian writers, such as Justin Martyr, Origen, and Augustine, and was commonly used through the early Scholastic period, including in Peter Abelard's *Dialogue with a Jew, a Christian, and a Philosopher* in the early twelfth century. Somewhat later, due to the powerful influence of Thomas Aquinas and Bonaventure, the Scholastic method superseded dialogue as a philosophical method. In the twentieth century Martin Buber retrieved dialogue as a theological method in his influential work *I and Thou*.[69] He was interested not primarily in reaching specific conclusions but in establishing proper relationships among human beings and between human beings and God. He saw dialogue as a basic prerequisite for authentic relationships. His work resulted eventually in the development of what is known as the philosophy of dialogue. It should not be surprising, then, that the fathers at Vatican II placed major emphasis on dialogue in several of their final documents: *Nostra aetate* (dialogue with other world religions), *Unitatis redintegratio* (dialogue with other Christians), *Gaudium et spes* (dialogue with modern society), and *Dignitatis humanae* (dialogue with political authorities).

The Brazilian educator Paulo Freire advanced dialogue as an important type of pedagogy.[70] He emphasized that communication in this form means that teachers and students learn from one another in an environment characterized by respect and equality. He also stressed the relationship between dialogue and praxis, since honest dialogue should give way to informed actions based on people's authentic values. In other words, dialogue pedagogy is not simply about deepening understanding but also about people's ability to make positive changes in the world so it becomes a more hospitable place in which to live. Today, dialogue is used in education, in marriage counseling, in business and industrial corporations, in religious communities, and sometimes in small groups in parishes. However, there are not many structures that allow for effective dialogue among pastors and the overall members of the parish, among bishops and their people, among Roman curial officials themselves, and among the pope and curial officials and the rest of the church. Sincere dialogue is a difficult and delicate process; as a result, more confrontational communication forms such as lectures and debate are preferred. There is often fear of the process. In its place there is often simple domination and control, neither of which is truly Christian.

Several helpful rules have been set out to govern effective dialogue.[71] First of all, the primary reason individuals choose to dialogue is to give another person or a group an opportunity to understand what they think, how they feel, where they are coming from, where they would like to go, and what matters are especially important. If individuals intend to convince others to see things their way, they are not engaged in dialogue; individuals speak not to convince but to be understood.

Individuals in dialogue also listen in order to understand the other. One must hear others on their own grounds and seek to understand what their words mean to those speaking, not what they might mean to the person listening. If one starts refuting or arguing internally with what is said instead of listening, one is not engaged in true dialogue.

Participants in true dialogue agree that no one will simply walk away from the conversation if strong differences arise. This disposition gives each participant permission to say whatever he or she thinks needs to be said. There is no need to wonder whether speaking will ruin a relationship.

Fourth, if one participant knows something that will strengthen the other's position and weaken his or her own position—and at the same time realizes that the other person does not have this information, the first participant should share that information. This is what it means to live in truth.

Fifth, after sincere efforts have been made to communicate sincerely and respectfully, differences may prevail. Then the parties should discuss the consequences of each position for the lived experience of each position and which consequences better serve the world the participants would sincerely like to create for themselves and for others.

Implementation of the Vatican II documents that have encouraged dialogue, especially those that concern relations with other world religions and with other Christians, have often surfaced a common interest in the ultimate questions that people face. Is there any real meaning in life? Is there a transcendent God? Is there an afterlife? In recent times various books and articles have been published that are rabidly antireligious and aggressively atheistic. Some of the authors have maintained that a religious outlook on life in fact dehumanizes people and does incredible harm to both individuals and societies. Efforts to respond to those charges have resulted in an increased interest in what have traditionally been called the theological virtues: faith, hope, and charity.

Catholics and indeed many other Christians affirm that the so-called theological virtues are gifts from God that simply cannot be self-induced or self-acquired. How the gift is given and how it is received are always most mysterious, but when the gift permeates one's life, many of the mysteries of life fall into place, especially the experience of tragedy and darkness. The temptation, of course, is to cease praying for the gift of faith when darkness seems to prevail in one's life. Faith, in turn, makes room for the gift of hope, which affirms that life here and now does make sense, that there is meaning to be found in even the most painful experiences, and that there is a future to be found in God. We know in faith that nothing can separate us from the love of God, and because of that nothing will ultimately separate us from the love of others—and so we hope. This then leads to love, which is ultimately about union. Although faith leads to hope, and faith and hope together lead to love, the process at times moves in the other direction. Human lives are mysteriously filled with love, which in turn transforms people into people who have hope and consequently are empowered to share in God's gift of faith.[72]

Christians have traditionally believed that how they approach the "big picture" issues has serious implications for the way they live their daily lives and how they approach what moralists have traditionally called the cardinal virtues—prudence, justice, fortitude, and temperance.

Against this background we proceed now to discuss ecclesial life on the various levels of church life, beginning with life in the parish, and to seek to understand some of the virtues that should characterize relationships.

The Parish

The parochialization of the church in the documents of the Second Vatican Council resulted in the parish being viewed as the center of the local church. Juridically, that is so, but there are many people, especially in the United States, who do not have any real sense of commitment to a local parish. Some are occasional Catholics, who celebrate with the local parish only on major feast days, such as Christmas and Easter, and on other important occasions. Others "shop" for liturgies that are to their liking. They do not feel any sense of responsibility to contribute to the financial support of a parish or to contribute their gifts and talents to the growth of the community. Still others center their Christian lives on the churches and chapels of religious communities in their area. Yet others are committed members of new movements in the church, such as the Communion and Liberation movement and the Neocatechumenal movement. These movements and others have attracted many members since Vatican II. In the case of the new movements tensions have often developed between the members of these groups and diocesan and parochial authorities; however, it must be admitted that these movements do seem to fill an important need in the church and are able to respond to the desire for spiritual nourishment, direction, and leadership that people are not finding in traditional church structures, such as the local parish. Nevertheless, it is in their local parish that most Catholics find their faith rooted; it is there that they celebrate the sacraments and find ecclesial community.

Perhaps the primary virtue that should be found in local parishes is the virtue of hospitality, which enables people of every race, nationality, and background to feel welcome. In the United States in the nineteenth and first half of the twentieth centuries parishes were often "national" parishes because their members had migrated from a particular foreign nation. Today, if people are not Native Americans, they are all at root immigrants, but they have generally been in the American melting pot and have long ceased to identify with their country of origin. In recent decades thousands of foreign-born people have migrated to this country, many of them Christians, including many Roman Catholics. They have joined traditional English-speaking parishes but frequently have maintained a distinctive identity even though they live within traditional parish boundaries. Although they struggle to learn English, they seek to have liturgies celebrated and sacraments administered in their native languages.

In many large cities in the United States there are parishes that must minister to intercultural and multicultural communities, that is, parishes that seek to serve several diverse cultures by maintaining important cultural traditions and by engaging in authentic and enriching dialogue with people of different cultural backgrounds with the goal of becoming one community. In this very complex cultural environment it is imperative that seminarians, priests, and other parish ministers develop language skills so that they may minister effectively to these diverse groups. Needless to say, the steadily increasing immigrant population has placed enormous responsibilities on local parish ministers and administrators. Nevertheless, these people must be made to feel welcome, and their complex pastoral needs deserve to be taken care of. Often the newcomers need food, clothing, proper housing, and healthcare as well as assistance in finding employment and just wages.

Other groups also need to find a welcome in Catholic parishes: the divorced, gays and lesbians, and single parents. The aged and infirm, those who are hearing or sight impaired—those who are disabled in any way—should find easy access and accommodation in all the parish buildings. Special care must be taken so that the acoustics in the church are adequate for the space. Worship aids that are clear should be readily available. Catholics who seek baptism for their children, couples who seek to be married, families who need to bury a loved one all desire and deserve to be received by all parish ministers with respect and sincere hospitality. When they are not received graciously, they may become alienated and cease to maintain any interest in the church. Parishes should assign greeters and ministers of hospitality for liturgical celebrations; likewise, volunteer members of the parish should welcome newcomers who move into the parish boundaries. More and more parishes are hiring parish nurses to administer to the sick, whose needs are often neglected because of an inadequate or expensive national healthcare system.

Parishes today should have a website that clearly identifies the mission of the parish, the various ministers who function on the parish staff, the schedule of parish events, and the opportunities for enrichment and help. This same information should be provided in printed form for those who do not have access to computers. The poor in the parish should know where to turn for help with food if the parish itself does not have a food pantry. The parish should welcome various groups to meet in the parish facilities, for example, members of various twelve-step programs. Canon 215 of the Code of Canon Law states clearly that "the Christian faithful are at liberty freely to found and direct associations for purposes of charity or piety or for the promotion of the Christian vocation in the world and to hold meetings for the common pursuit of these purposes." Note that this canon states two fundamental rights of the faithful: to form associations and to hold meetings.[73] As parishioners, people have a right to meet on church property if meeting space is available. Too often groups of the faithful who are deeply concerned about ecclesial structures and call for reform and renewal are denied access to meeting space by pastors or local ordinaries because their legitimate concerns are not in accord with the personal opinions of those in authority. Those who seek reform, for example, concerning financial transparency, elimination of unnecessary secrecy in the church, procedures for the selection and appointment of pastors and bishops in the church, and the elimination of the marginalization of women in the church, are often denied meeting space and are looked upon as unorthodox troublemakers. There are certainly many areas in the structure of the contemporary church that should be subjects for honest dialogue by all the faithful. Legitimate differences of opinion should not only be tolerated but also should be respected and given a hearing at the dialogue table.

A place for legitimate dialogue in each parish should be at meetings of the parish council. Canon 536 states: "If the diocesan bishop judges it opportune after he has heard the presbyteral council, a pastoral council is to be established in each parish, over which the pastor presides and in which the Christian faithful, together with those who share in the pastoral care by virtue of their office in the parish, assist in fostering pastoral activity."[74] The canon further states that "a pastoral council possesses a consultative vote only and is governed by the norms established by the diocesan bishop." If the lay people in a parish are to exercise their legitimate rights and responsibilities as baptized Christians, they should always be represented effectively by a parish council; in other words, local bishops should mandate the establishment of a parish council in every parish. The members of the council should be elected by the parish at large, and every effort should be made to see that the various ministries and groups in the parish are adequately represented. The pastor certainly should play an important leadership role in the council, but ideally the council should elect its own officers. Terms should be limited so that there is adequate turnover of members. The canon asserts that the council plays only a consultative role, but a wise pastor should be very reluctant to implement any decision that has not been thoroughly dialogued about by all the council members. He should always seek consensus in the council before making decisions.

Canon 537 mandates that each parish should have a finance council: "In each parish there is to be a finance council which is governed, in addition to universal law, by norms issued by the diocesan bishop and in which the Christian faithful, selected according to these same norms, are to assist the pastor in the administration of the parish." The finance council should emphasize the importance of each parish operating in accord with a carefully structured annual budget and should require an annual audit of the parish finances. There should be transparency concerning the finances of the parish; the members of the parish who contribute to its various operations have a right to know how their money is being spent. At a minimum an annual report should be given to the whole parish community.

The finance council should direct the investments that a parish chooses to make. In many large parishes the annual budget is large and requires careful planning. Most seminarians receive scarcely any formation concerning parish administration, especially in the area of finance. Pastors, then, almost always are dependent on the wisdom and experience of the finance council, whose members should be carefully chosen based on their financial expertise and ability to make sound judgments.

All ecclesial ministers, both lay and ordained, should engage in ongoing education programs that will enrich their ministry. In fact, the ordained clergy constitute about the only professional group in this country that is not required to engage regularly in serious educational programs. Some priests give the impression that they have not read a serious book since they left the seminary. Ecclesial ministry has undergone major changes since Vatican II, and it continues to do so; hence, ministers must regularly be brought up to date. Parish budgets should set aside funds for such ongoing education for all ministers in the parish.

It should be clear from the present discussion that the Catholic Church would probably be in a healthier state if Catholics did not define themselves in terms of papal or episcopal oversight but rather focused their attention on the quality of their own faith community centered in the parish. It would be better if they ceased describing the parish simply in terms of the pastor. The primary division in the parish should not be between the pastor and his parishioners but between those who exercise a specific ministry within the community and those whose ministry is carried out in the church's mission to the world at large. All of these ministries are priestly, stemming as they do from the baptism of all and common priesthood of the faithful. Jesus Christ is the unique priest; as such he is the primary teacher, sanctifier, and leader. The church as the primary sacrament of Christ is, in turn, teacher, sanctifier, and leader. Bishops, priests, deacons and lay people are in their own right teachers, sanctifiers, and leaders, but the lay people exercise their ministry either within the ecclesial community or in the wider world.[75] The primary purpose and responsibility of lay ministers within the ecclesial community is to build up and strengthen the community of faith; the primary responsibility of lay ministers in the world is to evangelize the world indirectly through their efforts to exercise justice and charity so as to humanize the world and to eliminate all that devalues human persons and communities.[76]

In addition to a legitimately appointed pastor, almost all parishes today have additional ministers, most of whom are lay people ministering in a variety of areas, including liturgy, catechetical instruction, parish business administration, care for the sick and elderly, and youth ministry. The team members should possess adequate theological formation as well as additional formation in their own proper area of expertise and should clearly recognize the legitimacy of accountability not only to the local ordinary, who exercises the episcopal ministry of oversight, but also to the local parish community and to one another. If the lay ministers are full-time or part-time employees of the parish, they should be issued clear contracts and receive just salaries. However, they should seek to think of themselves as ministers rather than as mere employees; they are meant to be servant ministers, and their concerns should be carefully represented on the parish council.[77]

Effective teaching is a primary responsibility of every parish. Much of this teaching takes place in classrooms, in faith formation groups, or in groups meeting to prepare for celebration of the sacraments, but also in the preaching that parishioners hear during the liturgy. One of the most widely expressed criticisms of Roman Catholic liturgy is that homilies are not helpful in educating people to read the signs of the times and to interpret in light of the gospel what is happening in our complex world. Lay men and women who live and work in the world face day in and day out very challenging problems in their efforts to raise families and to implement Christian values in their professions or workplaces. Homilies should provide help and insight into what it means to be a Christian in the world today. This means that preachers must learn to spend quality time preparing their homilies and seek above all to shed light on the concrete lives of the people who sit in their assemblies. It is unfortunate that the ecclesiastical law (canons 763–64) restricting the homily to deacons, presbyters, and bishops is not changed so that competent lay men and women may give the homily on occasion, for there are areas of the Christian life, such as marriage and family relations, where lay men and women have more experience and wisdom than ordained, celibate clergy.[78]

Because of the shortage of ordained ministers today, the ordained often have responsibility for three or four parishes, so they must function primarily as cultic ministers who are really "circuit riders" traveling many miles in order to provide the Eucharist for the people. It is almost impossible for such priests to get to know their people on a personal level. Where lay ministers are responsible for Sunday celebrations without an ordained minister, they must receive proper theological, liturgical, and homiletic training so they are truly able to respond to the needs and lives of the people in the pews.[79]

On the parish level, then, the virtues that should always be exercised are primarily justice, hospitality, accountability, prudence, and love.

The Diocese

The bishop, the local ordinary, is the leader of the church in his diocese. He is responsible for the good order of all the local communities in the diocese, which is not primarily a juridical or a bureaucratic structure. The diocese is rather an association of local communities of faith. The diocesan bishops are normally chosen from the ranks of auxiliary bishops and priests of the country in which the diocese is located; however, much mystery surrounds their selection. In fact, local ordinaries are most often chosen from the pool of auxiliaries in the country or from among the priests who have served in the various Roman dicasteries. As a result, they often have had no association whatsoever with the diocese to which they are appointed. In fact, men from one part of the country are often transported to very distant dioceses as bishops. What is most unfortunate is that the local diocese is rarely consulted about its particular needs and hopes. Then, of course, there is the perpetual problem of careerism, whereby bishops who have been appointed to a small rural diocese aspire to be promoted to a diocese that is larger and more important. One of the major complaints throughout the church in the West concerns the selection and appointment of bishops; obviously, the procedures need to be changed, especially so there is much more effective consultation on the local level.[80]

The diocesan bishop has the right and responsibility to appoint the officials of the diocesan curia, which consists of those institutions and persons who assist the bishop in governing the diocese. Those appointed to such roles should have the proper qualifications. Since Vatican II countless lay men and women have received advanced degrees not only in theology but also in specialized areas such as canon law and liturgical studies. In those cases where ordination to the presbyterate is not a requirement for holding the position, the bishop should seriously consider the appointment of qualified lay persons, especially lay women.

Canon 492 states: "In every diocese a finance council is to be established . . . consisting of at least three members of the Christian faithful truly expert in financial affairs and civil law."[81] Since the term "Christian faithful" is used, the finance council may consist of bishops, presbyters, deacons, and lay men and women, including members of religious institutes. Their responsibility is to prepare a diocesan budget of incomes and expenditures each year. At the end of each year the council carefully reviews the revenues and expenses of the diocese. A complete financial report should be given to the whole diocese at least annually. This is a very important structure in every diocese.

Among the consultative bodies required by the Code of Canon Law are the presbyteral council (canon 495) and the college of consultors (canon 502).[82] Although both are consultative bodies, the bishop should take their advice very seriously and should hesitate to make important decisions without their agreement. The presbyteral council should elect its own officers and truly represent the diocesan presbyterate; in most cases it should include both diocesan and religious priests who minister in the diocese. It should also represent various aspects of ministry in which priests are engaged in the diocese. The minutes of the regular council meetings should be made available to all the presbyters ministering in the diocese. From among the members of the presbyteral council, the bishop must choose at least six and not more than twelve members to constitute the college of consultors. In seeking his primary advisers, the bishop should consider his own strengths and weaknesses and then seek regular advisers who can best serve him and the needs of the diocese.

The diocesan bishop is also the primary liturgist in the diocese. His cathedral church is the mother church of the diocese. Hence, he should regularly preside and preach in the cathedral, if possible every Sunday and solemnity. At other times he should celebrate the Eucharist and other sacraments throughout the diocese. In many dioceses the only time the bishop visits a parish is to celebrate the sacrament of confirmation; hence, his attention is focused on the young people to be confirmed. He should consider delegating pastors and other diocesan officials to celebrate confirmation so he might be free to make regular pastoral visits to each parish and institution in the diocese. Episcopal vicars, likewise, should spend quality time with the special groups whom they serve and not simply intervene in times of crisis.[83]

So he might have a much more vital relationship with all the people in the diocese, the bishop needs to establish regular means of effective communication so the people are aware of what is transpiring, what has been achieved and the key issues that need to be addressed. Some bishops have regular blogs and seek to communicate with their people daily; others write a regular column in the diocesan paper. There is, however, no adequate substitute for personal association with the people of the diocese, who deserve honesty and transparency and should expect the bishop to be accountable.

Unfortunately, there are no established structures of accountability for bishops on the local level; they seem to be accountable only to the pope and the curia. They are required to give an account of their ministry only when they visit Rome on their regular *ad limina* visits, which usually occur once every five years or so (canon 500). All their subjects are held accountable in the diocese, but nobody on the local level holds them accountable.

Unfortunately, many bishops throughout the western world have lost respect and credibility for complex reasons, most of all because of the way they handled or failed to handle cases of sexual abuse of minors by clergy and religious in their dioceses. They are often fearful and defensive, a far cry from the collaborative, pastorally informed hierarchy that emerged during and after Vatican II. It will take considerable time for them to recover their moral authority. In the meantime they must take time to pray regularly, to study, and to read widely so that their homilies and pastoral messages to their people shed gospel light on the complex issues facing the church and the lives of people in the world. They do well to be willing to entertain self-doubts, to question the positions they hold, and to seek counsel from those who have more wisdom and experience than they do. They should seek to encourage rather than condemn and should be very reluctant to employ condemnatory sentences on their people unless absolutely necessary and then only on just grounds. They will not harm their teaching authority if they state honestly the complexity of issues, especially in areas of moral theology, and express themselves tentatively. If they do not have clear answers, they must learn to say, "I do not know, but I will seek advice and wisdom from those who have a clear understanding of the various sides of this issue." In that way their people will see them as men who are prudent, honestly seeking what is best for their people in days when rhetoric from authority figures is often simply condemnatory.

Episcopal Conferences

In the Roman Catholic Church episcopal conferences, consisting of an official assembly of all the bishops of a given territory, were first established as formal bodies by the Second Vatican Council (*Christus Dominus*, no. 38). Although the operation, authority, and responsibilities of these conferences are governed by the 1983 Code of Canon Law, especially canons 447–59, the nature and magisterial authority in particular was subsequently clarified and severely limited by Pope John Paul II's moto proprio *Apostolos suos*, which stated unambiguously that conferences of bishops do not participate in the teaching authority of the college of bishops, although individual bishops do participate because they are members of the college of bishops, which maintains unity with and under the pope as the bishop of Rome.[84] Consequently, a conference of bishops cannot make any doctrinal declarations unless it receives two-thirds approval of the individual voting bishops of the conference and receives the subsequent *recognitio* or approval of the Holy See. A conference of bishops can assist the individual bishops of the conference, but it cannot substitute for the authority they possess as individual bishops. Pope John Paul's moto proprio in fact emasculated the teaching authority of episcopal conferences. Various commentators have been severely critical of the document, since the conference had since Vatican II functioned as a very effective teaching authority for the church in the United States.[85] Especially important and deserving of much praise were the pastoral letters the conference issued on peace and the economy. Much consultation preceded the publication of those documents; the process was highly respected even by those who did not agree with the stands that were taken.

Since 2002 the episcopal conference in the United States has been primarily concerned with issues associated with the sexual abuse of minors by clergy and religious. It has also given much attention to the issue of abortion. Among ordinary lay people there is often the feeling that so much attention is given to the issue of abortion and other sexual matters that various important social issues are not adequately addressed. At least on diocesan and parochial levels serious efforts have been made to respond effectively to the pastoral care of immigrants in the country as well as adequate and affordable healthcare for all. Positions taken by the various leaders of the episcopal conference, however, have not always been well received in this country and have been a further cause of contention and disagreement.

The Universal Church

At present the pope, the bishop of Rome, is elected by the college of cardinals; this is unlikely to change in the immediate future. As pope he may call a general council, which is a deliberative body, not simply consultative. He is assisted by the Roman curia, which aids him in the administration of the universal church. His primary task is to preserve the unity of the church and to safeguard sound teaching. The church on the diocesan and national level has no authority to formulate doctrine; that is the responsibility of the whole church, symbolized above all by a general council of the church led by the pope. Currently the pope is the only elected leader in the church's hierarchy. Cardinals are selected by the pope and are usually in agreement with his personal theological views. Those who are under eighty have a right to take part in the conclave that elects the pope; those over eighty cannot vote. It has often been suggested that the pope should be elected by a different body, such as the leaders of episcopal conferences, so as to assure a more universal representation and a breadth of theological opinions. Since the college of cardinals, as a college, has no connection with apostolicity in the church and is a medieval creation, critics often see the college as an anachronism that should be abolished. Once named to the college of cardinals, local bishops and archbishops usually acquire special prestige and authority in their national conferences.[86]

Some of the fathers at Vatican II hoped that some kind of permanent council might be developed whereby the bishops of the world could exercise their authority over the universal church in union with the pope. Pope Paul VI, however, forestalled the development of such a council by formally establishing the synod of bishops on 15 September 1965.[87] As the synod has developed over the years it is clear that it is not a deliberative body but rather an instrument that the pope may use to assist him in the exercise of his ministry.[88] It meets when the pope calls it to meet, which is usually about once every five years. He assigns a special topic for consideration, such as the laity or institutes of consecrated life in the church, or he might decide to focus on the concerns of a particular country or area, such as the Middle East. Most of the bishop members of the synod are chosen on a national level, but the pope himself appoints other bishops and officials from the various Roman dicasteries. He also usually invites lay men and women to be auditors. The bishops who are chosen are usually absent from their diocese for about a month; they listen to countless speeches that are often repetitive, and they have very limited occasions to engage in serious dialogue. At the end of the synod they agree on a list of propositions they submit to the pope for his consideration. He, in turn, prepares an apostolic exhortation on the topic, but it often takes many months before it is released. By that time general interest in the topic has dissipated. The synod of bishops needs to be seriously reconsidered and restructured so it in fact becomes a deliberative body able to assist the whole church and the pope in governing the universal church.

As the history of the papacy has made clear, the role and influence of the pope have steadily increased over the centuries, especially since the declaration of papal infallibility in the nineteenth century. There have been great popes in the church's history, like Gregory the Great, but the vast majority have been men of lesser stature and talent, often no match for the political and intellectual challenges of their time. In the beginning the popes considered themselves the vicars of Peter, but more and more they think of themselves and are thought of by others as vicars of Christ. Certainly none of the early popes considered themselves to be infallible or thought they had the right to appoint other bishops. For the past 150 years writing encyclicals has been one of the major papal functions. As a result, popes have considerably increased their teaching authority so that the word *magisterium* inevitably means *papal magisterium*. Likewise, travel by train, plane, and auto has made it possible for popes to be present at huge rallies throughout the world where they are publicly acclaimed by thousands of people. Thanks to developments in photography their pictures are recognized by ordinary Catholics throughout the world. As a result, the church today is governed basically by the pope and his curia; it should be governed by the pope and the bishops. Curial officials are always appointed by the pope and regularly share his point of view on theological and canonical issues. In practice, however, the church often seems to be directed by the curia, whose officials teach and strategize for the whole church. This can easily happen if the pope is not deeply concerned about administrative issues but prefers to give his attention to scholarly pursuits or other enterprises. Diocesan bishops often feel they have been reduced to "branch managers" who simply carry out the directives of curial officials.[89]

Modern medicine has also had an effect on the papacy because human beings tend to live much longer than in the past. In the past 150 years popes have often lived to be very old men; consequently, they have had major influence on the shape of the church and its policies. It is clear that the papacy has undergone major changes, not because of what has happened in the church, but because of what has happened as a result of political and cultural developments. There is little doubt that Catholics today live in what might be described as an Ultramontanist church and under what might accurately be called a papal monarchy. Unless there are significant structural changes in the future, that situation is likely to continue for many years to come.

There are certainly serious crises facing the church today. Pope Benedict is aware of the various crises that have plagued the church since Vatican II, but he has emphasized that these crises may be solved primarily by religious conversion and by a spirit of penitence. For example, in writing to the church in Ireland in 2010 he told the people that the Irish crisis, caused, at least on the surface, by the sexual abuse of minors by priests and religious, could be healed by the retrieval of missions and adoration of the Blessed Sacrament.[90] The pope has said publicly that there is no need to change the structures of the church. Many Catholics, however, are convinced that it is precisely the underlying ecclesial structures that need to be changed. Distressed by the church's failure to address any structural changes, thousands of Catholics, especially well-educated and intelligent Catholics in Europe and North America, have walked away from the church. Critics have charged that several very specific structures need to be addressed. First of all, they call for the elimination of secrecy on all levels of the church and the development of a church that is open and transparent. This applies not only to disclosure of financial matters, but also to the procedures in the appointment of bishops and the Vatican investigations of dioceses, theologians, religious institutes, and seminaries.

Critics of the contemporary church also call for the elimination of triumphalism, especially in the celebration of papal and episcopal liturgies. In papal liturgies the dalmatic has reappeared under fiddle-back chasubles, lavishly decorated mitres have been much in evidence, and lace albs and surplices are once again in fashion. These styles are often disconcerting not only to many Catholics but also to many Protestants who have long been committed to simplicity in their worship patterns and vesture. Many people are appalled by the preoccupation of many bishops and presbyters with clerical attire and vesture. This triumphalism is certainly at odds with the enormous amount of poverty and suffering throughout the world. These concerns are closely associated with the clericalism that has dominated the church for centuries and is indeed a sickness in the contemporary church. Critics call for the restoration of true collegiality in the church, not only in the relationship between the pope and the college of bishops, but also on the levels of the national, diocesan, and parish church. They want the church to practice legitimate subsidiarity so that decisions that can be made on lower levels are not usurped by those in higher authority. This is especially the case regarding the celebration of the liturgy in the vernacular. Perhaps they hope above all for the elimination of the marginalization of women in the church. They realize that countless women, especially in Europe and North America, have advanced degrees in the sacred sciences but are hindered from using their talents and training by "glass ceilings" in the church and the insistence that only the ordained may exercise jurisdiction. They see no convincing reason why women cannot legitimately be ordained to the diaconate in the church.[91]

SOME TENTATIVE CONCLUSIONS

A virtuous church needs to face up to the tensions between unity and diversity in the church, and, as St. Paul urged in his First Letter to the Corinthians, truly embrace unity in diversity. The *Pastoral Constitution on the Church in the Modern World* echoes the memorable words of Pope John XIII: "Let there be unity in what is necessary, freedom in what is unsettled, and charity in any case" (no. 92). The bottom line is that a virtuous church must set as a top priority the virtue of love. A virtuous church takes a serious look at the motives behind planning, strategizing, and structural organization with a view to emphasizing the priority of love and service rather than domination and control. A life of virtue must take priority over the security of the church as an institution. When the latter becomes an end in itself and is not driven by love, then something has gone radically wrong. Virtuous authority brings true freedom to persons and communities within the church; the structures that are established do not simply keep people in their proper places, but rather keep them growing in responsibility and freedom. A virtuous church is one that is committed to continuous reform and renewal; it knows that it is not an end in itself but must give way to the establishment of the kingdom of God. It firmly acknowledges that it is the sacrament of Christ, and as such is a great mystery called, like Christ, to a life of kenosis and self-giving.[92]

A virtuous church is aware of its history as one of sinfulness and redemption. It knows that historical consciousness must inculcate a deep sense of humility in the church on both universal and local levels. It is aware that the papacy is situated in Rome and will undoubtedly remain there. It needs to be aware that Italians pride themselves on observing a longstanding approach to change: *Festina lente!* (we hurry along slowly). In the United States change often occurs very rapidly, sometimes without much forethought; hence, people expect the same pace to occur in Rome. Americans need to practice the virtue of patience both with ourselves and with others, perhaps especially with the bureaucratic structures of our church. We all need to entertain the possibility that we might be wrong in the opinions that we strongly hold.

A virtuous church practices prudence. It acknowledges that many aspects of life and many of its issues are ambiguous. People today are often uncomfortable with ambiguity; they want immediate clarity. They need to remember this wise aphorism: The measure of maturity is the ability to live with ambiguity. The virtuous person seeks to make prudent decisions, tries to do the right thing at the right time for the right reasons, but knows that often the things, the times, and the reasons are not clear. Hence the virtuous person is ready to change when sound reasons require change. Until then, he or she is willing to wait until further clarity surfaces and consensus is achieved about an issue.

A virtuous church practices justice both inside and outside the boundaries of the church. The Catholic Church has a rich tradition concerning social justice.[93] It deals specifically with poverty and wealth, poverty and peace, economics, social organization, and the role of the state. Its foundations are generally held to have been laid by Pope Leo XIII's 1891 encyclical *Rerum novarum* and continued by Pope Pius XI in his encyclical *Quadragesimo anno* in 1931. Further developments have taken place in the last eighty years; serious attention has turned to the problems of social and economic development, international relations, and the effects that economic issues have on the establishment of peace. These concerns are addressed in Pope Benedict XVI's recent encyclicals. It is clear that the church has made strenuous efforts to establish the reign of justice and peace in the world. Sometimes, however, the application of the profound principles that are set out in the social encyclicals have gone unheeded on the local level. Lay ecclesial ministers are often asked to work without contracts or just compensation. Ordained ministers always have job security, but lay ministers may be dismissed when a change of pastors takes place in a parish. Their dismissal is often justified on financial grounds when the real reason is that the pastor and the minister disagree about basic policies and procedures. Likewise, it is widely accepted that when employees in Catholic schools and hospitals try to organize or join unions, their efforts are obstructed by diocesan and parochial authorities. In the church we must not only preach justice on the national and international levels but, like charity, we must practice justice at home.

Another virtue, often not considered a virtue at all, is the virtue of longsuffering. There is no doubt that there is much suffering today not only in the world but also in the church. The media have made us aware of the enormous suffering caused by traumatic catastrophes, by financial disasters, by unemployment, and by sickness and old age. Much of the suffering is on an emotional and a spiritual level. In the church Catholics are often depressed by the crises caused by the sexual abuse of minors by clergy; by the decline in the number of religious, priests, and seminarians; and by the closure or merger of numerous parishes, schools, and hospitals under Catholic sponsorship. Perhaps what many Catholics are experiencing is what St. John of the Cross called the "dark night," a painful, purifying passage from a known and comfortable but somewhat limited stage of spiritual development to a radically new and profound experience of God. The rich mystical tradition of the church can be a very helpful resource for understanding the current experience of diminishment at a deeper level and help us find some direction for living it faithfully. The present crises in the church might be looked upon as challenging forms of the cross in our lives. The cross and suffering, however, are never ends in themselves, but if borne patiently, they are doors to the experience of resurrection. The willingness to bear burdens patiently is rooted in the virtue of courage, which is closely related to the virtue of hope.

As we noted in discussing dialogue as a necessary process in the life of our church, we need to develop the virtue of attentive listening, not only to what is currently happening in the world and in the church but also to one another in our differences. Wisdom often comes to us from unexpected places—from the poor, the marginalized, the nobodies in the world, in the words and actions of those who challenge and disagree with us. Karl Rahner wrote of the need for what he called the "nameless virtue," perhaps best described as the practice of following the *via media,* the middle way, from which we attend to both the left and the right in the hope of arriving at the truth for which we were all made.[94]

Finally, a virtuous church is one that regularly practices the virtue of thankfulness. We are often conscious of and anxious about all that we do not yet possess. In fact, we take much for granted, including membership in a church that is blessed with the word of God, with a compassionate sacramental system, with faithful and hardworking ordained ministers, with generous women and men religious, and more recently with thousands of lay ecclesial ministers who supply pastoral programs with energy, vision, fidelity, and courage.

In a world and a church where there tends to be much cynicism and negativity, we need to develop the virtue of thinking and acting positively. We need to direct our time and attention not only to what needs to be eliminated in the structures of the church but, perhaps more important, to the creation of positive structures to replace the negative ones, structures that promote and support Christian freedom, justice, peace, and charity, structures that promote honest communication in place of secrecy, that promote collegiality and subsidiarity in place of centralization, that provide for significant opportunities for lay people, especially women, to use their many gifts and competencies in the church, to establish patterns that promote simplicity and equality and that discourage triumphalism and clericalism. These structures will instill in the church a hopeful sense of identity, will enable people to act in virtuous ways, and will direct them to a future in God's kingdom. In the final analysis we will be saved, not by an institutionalized church, but by a loving, compassionate, and forgiving God acting through Christ and in the power of the Holy Spirit. That God is the source of our Christian faith, our hope, and our love.

6

A Virtuous Liturgy and Sacramental Practice

Although the bishops in various countries of the northern hemisphere do not give much explicit indication that they are concerned or worried about the percentage of Roman Catholics who are leaving the church, the simple fact is that numerous intelligent and well-educated Roman Catholics are quietly walking away from the Catholic Church, some to no religion at all, others to evangelical churches, and others to mainline Protestant churches (though the latter have serious problems of their own).[1] It has been estimated that for every person who joins the Catholic Church in the United States, four leave the institution. They are leaving for various reasons, but mainly because they feel that the Catholic Church has ceased to focus on the teachings of Jesus on nonviolence, mercy, forgiveness, and compassion. They feel that they hear too little about the beatitudes and too much about judgment, excommunication, and admonition, usually with a focus on sexual behavior. Like other Roman Catholics, they have been scandalized by the sexual abuse of minors by clergy and the coverup by bishops. They are often disheartened by the uninspiring quality of the homilies and the dismal liturgies they find in their parish churches. The women are often walking away because they have no say in key decision-making processes in the church and are marginalized in other ways. These people have lost confidence in church leadership; their departure is a cause for sadness and deep mourning. However, for some bishops and members of the Roman curia, their departure is good news; they maintain that the church will be a smaller church but a purer one without them.

It is also well known that many former Catholics have left the church over the years because of unhappy or unjust encounters with priests and their refusal to offer sacramental rites. Some have been refused baptism for their infants because they were not registered in a parish or did not have Sunday-collection envelopes. Others were not allowed to marry in the church because they were cohabitating. Still others were not allowed to have their youngster confirmed because the young person did not attend a sufficient number of confirmation classes. Some have joined Protestant churches because they have been married, divorced, and remarried and so are not permitted to receive communion, even though they are convinced that their first marriage was invalid. Still others have left the Catholic Church because many years ago they were not allowed to enter a Protestant church to attend the funeral of a close relative or friend. Lesbian and gay partners have left the church because they were not allowed to enroll their children in Catholic schools. Others have left because they were treated harshly or angrily in the confessional. At the present time pastoral practice concerning these issues varies considerably from one diocese or parish to another. If one looks for an ecclesial foundation for the behavior of the clerics involved in these sad sacramental encounters, it is apt to be found in their juridical understanding of the church primarily as a legal institution. Such an ecclesiology has important implications for the theology and practice of the church's liturgy.

MODELS OF THE CHURCH AND SACRAMENTAL IMPLICATIONS

Juridical ecclesiology is a radically secular understanding of the church that developed during the second millennium at the same time that national monarchies were developing in Europe.[2] Modeled on a secular constitutional monarchy, a juridical church conceives of itself as a perfect society with universal authority and a hierarchical structure of superiors and subjects. It espouses an Old Testament understanding of ordained ministry and the feudal custom of conferring powers as personal possessions. The ordained presbyter alone has the power of orders and the power of jurisdiction. Since Christ has ascended on high and sits at the right hand of God, he is in a sense absent from the church, but his presence and work are carried out above all by the pope, bishops, and presbyters acting in his place. In sacramental rites they alone are thought to act in the person of Christ *(in persona Christi)*.

Bishops and presbyters who are entrenched in a legalistic understanding of the church are apt to emphasize the observance of liturgical laws, especially those contained in the 1983 Code of Canon Law and in the rubrics set out in the official liturgical books. For over four hundred years, that is, from the Council of Trent until Vatican II, Roman Catholic presbyters scrupulously observed liturgical rubrics. Moral theologians did not hesitate to label violations of rubrics as sinful, sometimes as gravely sinful. For example, the failure of the priest to mix a few drops of water with the wine at the offertory of the mass constituted grave matter and therefore was a mortal sin. Consequently, rubrics gained an extraordinary importance in the liturgy, and moral theologians gave much attention to their correct observance. In Catholic seminaries the course designated as liturgy was basically a course in rubrics.

Certainly a dignified celebration of the liturgy necessitates the observance of proper norms. However, a scrupulous observance of detailed rubrics, a mentality often described as rubricism, results in a servile observance of rubrics. The *Constitution on the Sacred Liturgy* attempted to break that habit by its insistence that "pastors . . . must . . . realize that, when the liturgy is celebrated, their obligation goes further than simply ensuring that the laws governing valid and lawful celebration are observed. They must also ensure that the faithful take part fully aware of what they are doing, engaged in the rite, and enriched by it" (# 11).

The early sacramentaries did not in fact contain rubrics but only prayer texts to be proclaimed by the presider who was usually assisted by deacons and a master of ceremonies. In time, however, books, such as the Ceremonial for Bishops, developed so that the rubrics for a celebration could be set out in detail.[3]

Fortunately the rubrics in the liturgical books published in the decades immediately following Vatican II were less prescriptive and were not characterized by rigidity. They were more indicative in that they set out guidelines for the dignified performance of the liturgical rites. The books provided the minister with choices and in some instances allowed him to compose original texts, as when the rubric read "*in his verbis vel similibus*"—"in these or similar words." The *Constitution on the Sacred Liturgy* was formulated on the principle of personal and communal consciousness and responsibility and the acknowledgment that ritual forms can be controlled, but worship itself cannot be legislated, for it is the free and loving response of human persons and communities to a loving God. When proper values have been internalized in personal and communal consciousness, the written laws of the church do not have to address minute details. When consciences have been well formed and sound theological awareness has been deepened, it is best that church laws emphasize only the basic norms and principles. In this way there is room for the free development and assimilation of wholesome customs and usages. This is the best way of promoting that unity in diversity that should characterize the church of Jesus Christ.

In recent years various documents emanating from the Roman curia have had a significant but negative effect on liturgical celebrations. These would include the instruction *On Certain Questions regarding the Collaboration of the Non-ordained Faithful in the Sacred Ministry of Priests* (15 August 1997), the General Instruction of the *Roman Missal* (2002), and *Redemptionis sacramentum,* the instruction *On Certain Matters to be Observed or to be Avoided regarding the Most Holy Eucharist* (25 March 2004). These documents indicate a return to the old rubrical mentality. Furthermore, "liturgical police" are quick to report ministers who do not observe the prescribed rubrics to proper authorities.

The observance of rubrics must be balanced with the basic agenda of Vatican II's liturgical reform, namely, active and intelligent participation in the liturgy by the entire assembly. The rubrics must not be ranked above sound theology, accurate historical consciousness, and effective pastoral care. The rubrics are not ends in themselves; they are meant to lead the people to an ever more profound experience of the paschal mystery. If an obsessive preoccupation with the rubrics overshadows the primary goal of sound liturgical reform, something has gone wrong. Rubrics should always be interpreted in the context of the worshiping assembly. They exist for the sake of the community and its worship.[4]

CHRISTOLOGY AND LITURGY

Until recently many in the Roman Catholic Church have espoused an exclusively christomonist communion ecclesiology. They have been inspired by Pius XII's 1943 encyclical *Mystici Corporis.* Of course, christological models of theology have significant sacramental and liturgical implications.[5] What we think of Jesus Christ has direct bearing upon our sacramental theology. Because of its central and constitutive role in theology, Christology has in many ways determined the style and content of sacramental theology. In a book written shortly after Vatican II, John McIntyre investigated three christological models: (1) the two-nature or classical-metaphysical model, (2) the psychological model, and (3) the revelation model.[6] These models are still useful today.

In the patristic period two approaches to the mystery of Christ were developed. The Alexandrian approach was rooted in a descending Christology, since its point of departure was the divine Person of the Word, who came down from heaven to appropriate humanity as a vehicle for his manifestation to the world. On the other hand, the Antiochene approach was rooted in an ascending Christology, since its point of departure was the humanity that the divine Word assumed. Overemphasizing either approach, however, leads to the classical christological heresies of Monophysitism, which affirmed only one divine nature in Christ, and Nestorianism, which maintained that there were two separate persons in Christ, one divine and one human. To help solve the problem, the classical-metaphysical model developed. It can be summarized by the statement that Jesus Christ is one divine person with two natures, one human and one divine. This model speaks of Christ within the framework of classical metaphysics, and hence in terms of subsistence, nature, the act of being, causality, and a faculty psychology. Obviously such terms are foreign to the language and thought of the New Testament. However, although the New Testament does not speak of Christ in such ontological terms, it does require an ontology of those scholars who would exercise their minds in probing the meaning of the divine incarnation.[7]

The classical-metaphysical model yields a sacramental theology and practice that is preoccupied with ontological union with Christ through the sacramental rites as instrumental causes of divine grace. With its emphasis on precise determination of the causality involved in the sacraments, the primary intention is to preserve the priority of Christ's action over the liturgical action of the priest or other minister. This model affirms the transcendence of God but tends to denigrate the role of the church, its ministers, and the community. As Eastern Christian theologians are quick to point out, this model tends to overlook the general sacramentality and holiness of creation as a whole, so emphasized by the patristic writers, and also the holiness of the church itself.[8]

The psychological model of Christology is basically a phenomenological model. It emphasizes the category of the self and advocates some form of human self, and not simply a human nature, in Christ. The principal means for interpreting Christ in this model is the notion of inter-subjectivity as it was developed in modern phenomenology and personalism. It is believed that this approach is far more productive when applied to Christology than are the categories of classical metaphysics, since these categories are derived from the philosophy of nature. Certainly Christ is not a "thing"; he is a person, a subject who stands over against the world of objects and consequently must not be interpreted in terms of the physical world. In terms of the psychological model, it is not so much union of God and human persons in Jesus Christ on the ontological level that is of major importance in Christology and the life of Christian faith as the I-Thou relationship between Jesus Christ and the Father, so stressed in the New Testament. Likewise, our union with Jesus Christ is not considered in this model in metaphysical terms but in inter-subjective terms as the union of mind, will, and heart with Christ through faith and charity. It should be noted that in this model, emphasis in also placed on the sacrament of the human brother and sister, who are the bearers of God's call to human beings and who are also the sacrament of the Word of God as it comes to human persons. This model stresses the significance of personal dialogue between Jesus Christ and human persons.[9]

The psychological model of Christology yields a sacramental theology and practice that places emphasis on a sacramental encounter with Jesus Christ through the power of the Spirit. It leads to a better understanding of the medieval axiom *Sacramenta sunt propter homines* (sacraments are for human persons). The sacraments are for us in the sense that they are an instrumental means for our salvation. But in the psychological model the sacraments are expressions of the human person's deepest existential being and longings and are vehicles for personal encounter with Jesus Christ on the level of the human person's most basic human needs. The sacraments of the church then express the human person's fundamental needs and God's response to those needs in Christ and through the power of the Holy Spirit.[10] Since personal encounter cannot be one-sided, there must not only be Christ's encounter with us but also our encounter with Christ. The structure of the sacramental rite must be effective in communicating the meaning that is intended. Also, the community in which the sacramental encounter is intended to take place must be authentic as an expression of the church as the body of Christ.[11]

The revelation model of Christology attempts to interpret Christ in terms of his role as the unique revelation of the Father. Hence, there is a conscious effort to locate Christ within the whole purview of salvation history and indeed of creation itself as a manifestation of the divine Logos. This model is therefore very biblical. It seeks to exploit as much as possible the rich meaning of the biblical notion of God's Word. It seeks to locate the sacraments within a theology of the Word of God. It considers the sacraments as God's saving Word addressed to human persons in Christ and through the power of the Spirit, and looks upon the human response to that Word as an expression of Christian faith. The Word of God is a saving, loving Word. In the sacraments the liturgy recapitulates the peak moments in salvation history and brings those moments to life in the life of the believer.[12]

The most important sacramental implication of the revelation model is the subsumption of the sacraments under the category of word. Karl Rahner developed this idea in his essay on "Priest and Poet."[13] He rightly insists that *word* cannot be defined univocally as addressed simply to an intellect. Some words do fit that definition, but there are other "great words" that address the whole human person on the deepest levels. These words make the reality of their meaning actually present to the believer, so that when the great word is spoken, something important happens. The great word confronts us and summons forth a response. God's word is preeminently a great word, an effective word. So it is when the word of God is proclaimed in the liturgy. That word is proclaimed in both spoken form and in ritual nonverbal form. The spoken form is meant to shed light on the ritual nonverbal form and the ritual nonverbal form is meant to illuminate the spoken form. In the celebration of the liturgy we speak then of the table of the word and the table of the sacrament. The table of the word looks forward to the table of the sacrament and the table of the sacrament looks back to the table of the word. It is for that reason that the liturgical homily should be an essential part of every liturgical celebration. It is meant to be a bridge between the scripture that is proclaimed and the sacramental rite that is carried out. Its task is not simply to provide exegesis of the biblical texts that are proclaimed but also to play a hermeneutical role, an interpretative role, so that the text proclaimed sheds light on the sacramental action and also on the lives of the people in the assembly.[14]

It should be clear that to the extent that variety or pluralism exists within Christology, there will be a pluralism of sacramental theologies. Christomonist communion ecclesiology emphasizes the liturgy as the celebration of the paschal mystery. In the power of the Spirit, Christ has been deemed to be present above all through the ministry of the bishop, Christ's visible representative in each local church united in communion with all other churches. As representatives of the local bishop, ordained presbyters represent Christ and minister in his name in local parishes.[15]

A christomonist ecclesiology understands the church primarily as an extension of the divine incarnation. Christ and the Spirit are operative in the ministry of the church through the ministry of the bishop and his presbyters. The ordained bishops and presbyters function in the person of Christ *(in persona Christi)*, but there is usually no emphasis on their acting in the name of the church *(in nomine ecclesiae)*. Certainly in and through baptism all Christians share in the presence and power of the indwelling Trinity and consequently in the royal priesthood of Christ, but within the exclusively christomonist model of the church there is often little room for lay men and women to exercise their distinctive charisms. Their role is to witness to Christ in the realm of the secular, in the world. In the church itself they may exercise a consultative or advisory role, but they are usually not allowed to exercise any forms of jurisdiction or what has more recently come to be called lay ecclesial ministry. In this model women usually are marginalized.[16] Likewise, the ordained are the primary celebrants of the liturgy and the ministers of the sacraments; lay men and women are the recipients of the sacraments.

TRINITARIAN COMMUNION ECCLESIOLOGY

Trinitarian communion ecclesiology developed especially in the years after Vatican II. Certainly there have been remarkable developments in the theology of the Trinity in recent years.[17] Special efforts have been made by theologians to retrieve the active and powerful role of the Holy Spirit both in the church and in the church's sacramental celebrations. God comes to us in Christ and through the power of the Holy Spirit; we go to God in Christ and through the power of the Holy Spirit. The church takes the Pentecostal gift of the Spirit seriously. This gift is not something given once and for all on Pentecost Sunday but is continually poured out on all of creation, especially on human persons and communities. Through Christian initiation all the baptized become sons and daughters of God the Father and brothers and sisters of Jesus Christ, all through the power of the Holy Spirit.[18]

In this model the ordained ministers function in the name of the church and in the name of Christ, but they should not consider themselves to be mediators between God and the church, since there is only one mediator, and that is Jesus Christ. They are the leaders of the community; as such they not only preside at the liturgy but also facilitate the implementation of the diverse charisms that are to be found in all the baptized. The gift of the Holy Spirit given to them in a special way at ordination empowers them to act in accord with their responsibilities, but they must realize that the same Spirit animates the lives of all the faithful, who also have responsibility to contribute to the reign of God.

A community motivated by trinitarian communion ecclesiology realizes that the liturgy is celebrated not only by the ordained ministers but by all the baptized. In other words the celebrant of the liturgy is the whole baptized assembly. The ordained have the special roles of presiding and preaching as well as leading the community to discern what the celebration of the liturgy means in the everyday lives of all the people. Hence, the ordained, with their special charisms, and the rest of the faithful, with their distinctive charisms, are meant to work together according to the gifts the Spirit has given to each. The ultimate decisions in the community are made by the bishops and other pastors, but they must strive to bring the community to consensus before they makes decisions or issue mandates so that unity prevails in the body of Christ.[19]

WORSHIP IN SPIRIT AND TRUTH

Much has been written in recent decades about gift giving and its diverse ramifications.[20] Christian theologians responding to this research make an effort to show that God's gift giving is radically different from patterns of gift giving among human persons and communities. They assert that human generosity of any kind is always grounded in and made possible by God, who is ultimately the source of all gifts and who at the same time requires that human persons share among themselves and especially with the poor the diverse gifts that they have received. In other words God gives most generously in order to promote more giving so that justice and peace will prevail among persons and communities.[21] Before Vatican II, Henri de Lubac laid the foundation for contemporary reflections on God's gift giving.[22]

De Lubac maintained that there is no such thing as "pure nature." He held that grace is not something extrinsic or added to nature; it belongs intrinsically to creation itself. It is present within the ordinary textures of human life and the rest of creation. In other words the world is possessed from the very beginning by God's gracious presence. In that sense the world is never simply ordinary;

it is extraordinary. Grace draws all of creation, all of life into communion with God. Grace is more original than sin. The universe is not a two-layered form of existence, one natural on the bottom and one supernatural on top. The whole of the universe is saturated through and through with divine grace, divine presence. Karl Rahner developed a similar line of theologizing when he wrote of a "supernatural existential," of grace within all that exists. He emphasized that grace is God's self-communication.[23] This means that all of us are born into a graced situation, an assertion that has significant implications for the meaning of church, of Christian initiation, and especially of baptism within the church.

When God gives existence and life to any being, human or otherwise, there is no recipient to embrace the divine act because the very existence and life of the creature is itself the gift. Hence, God does not create a debt or obligation on the part of the creature. God's gift occupies the space that, in merely human transactions of gift giving, would be filled by the one who receives the gift. Human beings and other creatures are not recipients that are indebted to God; they are simply gifts. As gift, human existence is simply expected to be itself.[24]

God is a community of givers, a communion of persons who are united in giving themselves to one another and to creation. Each person of the Trinity is totally receptive to the other Persons, so human persons who receive the gift of God's presence must respond to God's giving with further giving. In that way they are true to their identity as creatures made in the image of God. God always precedes the act of communicating the gift of God's life to human creatures. The gift of God's presence is meant to induce in us an awareness of our true identity and a profound sense of what it means to be made in God's image. This identity must not issue in an attitude of arrogance but rather in a deep sense of gratitude. This is reflected in Paul's question to the gifted community at Corinth: "What do you possess that was not given you? And if you received it as a gift why take credit to yourself?" (1 Cor 4:7). The very reason we have been given the identity of gift is to induce more giving; all that we are and all that we have, have been given to us in order that we might share with others. Consequently, our relationship with God and with one another is primarily ethical rather than cognitive. It is basically a virtuous relationship.[25]

In various spirituality programs there is often much emphasis on the self and on personal initiative. Growth in spirituality is set out as the result of a faithful pursuit of ascetical practices and methods of prayer. Underlying such emphasis is a semi-Pelagian approach to salvation—if we work hard enough and long enough, we can save ourselves. In fact it is God in Christ and through the power of the Spirit who always saves us. The initiative is always in God; our response is to embrace the gift that we are and the presence and power of God's Spirit within us. Hence, we need to stress the divine presence of God's Spirit as foundational to a Christian understanding of spirituality, for spirituality does not in the first instance concern the experience simply of the human spirit or even the manifestation of religious beliefs in various ritual and devotional practices. It is rather the transforming effect and understanding of God's Spirit working in persons and communities. When Paul wrote of the *pneumatikos,* the spirit, he was referring to the presence, power, and activity of the Holy Spirit in and among God's people. He was concerned with the impact of God's life on human life and therefore as a manifestation of authentic Christian spirituality.[26]

The Spirit is perhaps above all the Spirit of Jesus Christ (Phil 1:19). Sent upon all of creation, then upon the humanity of Jesus, and then sent by the resurrected and ascended Christ, the Spirit continues the saving ministry of Christ in the church, and along with the whole of creation, strains for the fulfillment of salvation in the transformation of both earth and heaven and in the manifestation of the faithful disciples as children of God and co-heirs with Christ. Where the disciples of Jesus Christ share in his values and his virtues and live according to his commandment of love, there the Spirit is to be found. Obviously the Spirit's presence and power are to be found above all in those saints who through faith and baptism strive to live in solidarity with God's people and to continue here and now the mission of Jesus Christ.[27]

Since the Spirit is the Spirit of Christ, the Holy Spirit is also the Spirit of truth (John 16:13). Every Christian person and community searching for the truth and struggling to live in accord with it is empowered by the Spirit of the One who came to bring us to God's truth, which will set us free from bondage. Formation is the great liberator; hence, the Spirit is the great formator who will lead the disciples of Jesus Christ into all truth (2 Cor 2:1–13). The most significant truth about God is manifested in the cross and resurrection of Jesus Christ, whereby God is revealed as a God who is a God of love, a God who lives for giving. The Spirit reveals to the world the meaning of Christ's cross and resurrection and the way Christ's disciples should live in accord with that paschal mystery.[28]

The Spirit builds up the church as the body of Christ and empowers it to carry out the mission of Christ in the world; however, is it especially in the church's worship, through word and sacrament, that the Spirit is most active. In the latter part of the twentieth century the scholarship of Edward Kilmartin shed considerable light on the presence and power of the Spirit in the liturgy.[29] He taught that Jesus expressed the sacrificial character of his life, his willingness to lay down his life both for God and for God's people, in his prayer for his disciples before he died. As he died, he handed over his Spirit, the Spirit of faith that characterized Jesus' whole life while on earth. It is this sacrificial offering that is celebrated in the liturgy. Jesus' death was the channel through which the Father sent the Spirit of faith upon the church, but individual persons always have the responsibility to open their lives to that gift. In this way they enter into the very life of the Trinity. Christ's own life of faith was the result of the gift of the Holy Spirit; throughout his temporal life Christ received the love of his Father and responded with perfect love not only for his Father but also for all of God's people.[30]

Christ's deep faith was the result of the power of the Spirit present and powerful in his humanity. That same Spirit, sent through the intercession of Jesus Christ at the time of his death and resurrection, comes to Christian believers so they are able to believe as Jesus believed. That faith in us is indeed a free gift of the Spirit. Our life as Christians has a dialogical character whereby God freely shares the divine life with us but asks for a dynamic faith response. The dynamic process of God's self-communication and response was always at the heart of life in the Trinity. The various modes of Christ's presence in the liturgy—presence in word proclaimed, in prayer and song, in the ministers, in the Eucharist—are all interdependent, but Christ's presence by faith in the liturgical assembly is the primary mode of presence, for the church, the localized assembly, is the great sacrament of Christ. While the various modes of real presence point to one another and are in a sense dependent on one another as symbolic expressions of the life of the church, they all must find a faith response in individuals if they are in any sense to transform personal lives.

Through the liturgy and through the rest of our life in the world, God breathes the Holy Spirit into our lives so we may be faithful to our vocation and faithfully finish the work entrusted to us by the risen Lord through the power of the Holy Sprit. Both liturgy and life nurture the Spirit within us as we struggle to complete the mission we have been given in baptism.[31]

THE PASCHAL FOUNDATION OF ALL CHRISTIAN LIFE

We read about the theological virtues of faith, hope, and charity, and about the moral virtues of prudence, justice, courage, and temperance, but today we rarely read anything about the virtue of religion, which is really the virtue that underlies our Christian lives of prayer and sacramental worship. It was a very important virtue for Thomas Aquinas, for he wrote a long article on the topic in his *Summa theologiae* (II-II, Q. lxxxi). It is the virtue whose purpose is to render God the worship that is due to God as the source of all being and the principle of all authority. It is a distinct virtue because its object is to offer God the homage demanded by God's singular excellence. It is not a theological virtue because its immediate object is not God but rather the reverence that we owe to God. Theologians who treat religion as a virtue usually relate it to the cardinal virtue of justice, since by religion we give to God what is in fact due to God. Aquinas maintained that it should rank first among the cardinal virtues. Since human persons are not simply pure spirits but are body-persons, the virtue inspires both interior dispositions and external actions. God, of course, does not need our reverence and awe, but the virtue is essential for our own well-being and is in accord with our identity as creatures of God who need to acknowledge our utter dependence and to worship and praise the source of our identity in a spirit of sincere gratitude.

We should not find the practice of religion a burden since Jesus, the Son of God incarnate, has revealed to us in his teaching that our life as disciples is more than the mere following of commandments; he tells us that our life is grounded in the good news of the gospel and that we live in an age when salvation has already been achieved. Even his call to repentance is not a threat of punishment but rather the joyful news of the fulfillment of salvation at the end of time. In fact, the good news is not simply a message but rather a person who is the incarnate Son of God.

In many sectors of the church today there is a renewed interest in the prayer of solitude, the prayer of the mystic, an interest that runs across denominational lines and needs to be subjected to a careful and disciplined critique. It might well be a privatist escape from social and ministerial concerns and might be based on a false understanding of mysticism that precludes concern for people. The yearning for personal religious experience is often a reaction to life in the contemporary world that many find threatening to their human and religious values. Doctrinal statements are often used to validate their personal past and the past history of the church rather than to guide Christians in interpreting and evaluating their own religious experience. They often fail to sense the continuity that should exist among ritual patterns, creedal statements, and ecclesiastical structures not only in articulating the religious experience of individuals and communities but also in relating the institutional church responsibly to the contemporary world and moving it creatively and justly into the future.[32]

Prayer is certainly essential in every Christian life, but in the experience and practice of prayer we must remain faithful to the example given by Jesus and responsible for the gift of the Spirit if our prayer is to be truly Christian. Our Christian life is a process whereby we are led by the Spirit into the paschal mystery of Christ, but that mystery is not a mere chronological sequence in which we first experience the death and then the resurrection of Jesus and then the gift of the Holy Spirit. No, the three interpenetrate all the time. The paschal mystery is a unity: in the dying of Jesus the glory of God is revealed, and the resurrection is resurrection because Jesus consented to die. Likewise, he shared his Spirit with his disciples not only after the resurrection but all during his earthly ministry. It is the gift of the Spirit that makes all dying and rising possible for his disciples.[33] Throughout his life Jesus died to the temptation to isolate himself and to withdraw from the demands of human community. As a man he acknowledged his total dependence on his loving Father, and day by day he worked out in his humanity the implications of what it means to be Son of God the Father. Allowing the life of a creator God into his humanity, Jesus had no other choice but to beget life in others, so he responded to the challenges that confronted him in life and entered deeply into the healing and corrective dimensions of human life. Where there was death, he brought life.

There is a contemporary effort to retrieve a natural theology that makes room for God, seen not as a divine watchmaker or a deterministic law-enforcer but as one who works in order to bring order out of chaos and life out of death. Theologians who are keenly interested in evolution emphasize the dependence of life at every level on surrender, self-limitation, and death as the prelude to new life. This occurs on both the macro scale of evolution, with its dependence and destruction of entire species, and on the micro level of the individual cell, where a determined cycle of death and renewal is necessary for healthy growth and development. For every organism that dies, it seems a new one is born. Life on all levels is dependent on death. Death, then, is not really the opposite of life but is always a prelude to new life. Just as death paves the way for new life in nature, so also in Christian theology death is the port of entry to resurrection.[34]

As Jack Mahoney notes, human mortality and death are normal features of evolutionary life. The great achievement of Jesus was "his confronting his own death and overcoming it, returning to life in an act of cosmic significance and through his resurrection, ushering the human species into the culminating stage of its evolutionary development, in which it is called to live more fully in the eternal happiness of God in association with the risen Christ."[35] This is what resurrection is all about.

It is always difficult to talk about death, because we have never experienced the finality of death; in a sense we know only the limited preludes. Nor is it easy to grasp the meaning of death, since the term can be understood in various ways.[36] In one sense death is simply the negation of existence, a passage from being to nonbeing that renders any further life impossible. But in a Christian sense death is the achievement of a lifetime because one is thereby exalted; it is the passage, not to nonexistence, but rather to existence on a higher level. Paul certainly looked upon the death of Christ in this way (see Rom 5:8; 14:15; 1 Cor 8:11; Gal 2:20). This passage to new life is rendered possible by a basic attitude that one assumes toward life, namely, an attitude of openness, availability, receptivity, and dependence.

The act of dying derives its meaning from the motive that inspires it. For the Christian that motive is meant to be love. It was surely the motive in the life and death of Jesus. As Paul says, "God shows his love for us in that while we were yet sinners, Christ died for us" (Rom 5:8). Paul reminds the Romans that our life has been bought at a great price, at the cost of great pain: the pain of sharing life, of acknowledging dependence, the pain of obedience, of relinquishing self-preoccupation, the pain of entering into the lives of others. Pain is part of the price of discipleship. The great lesson we learn about God in Jesus is that he lives for giving, even if that means dying. If we live with the same readiness to surrender our lives to one another, we are living with the very life of God. But it is painful to open our lives to God and to one another.[37]

Christian obedience is painful too. It implies attentive listening and response to the demands of life. There is a certain deathlike quality about it. It is a daily dying to one's own self-centered will. In that sense it is a daily practicing for the final assent of our lives, when we shall yield our being into the hands of the Lord at the hour of physical death. Although much of human obedience is quite reasonable, in the sense that it is the response to life that any mature, intelligent person would give, there are instances when the response to life and the obedience asked of us are clouded by the mystery of iniquity. There are times when we collide with the effects of sin in ourselves and in those who are in authority over us. These effects take the form of fear, lack of trust, prejudice, and suspicion; they often surface in misunderstanding and narrow-mindedness. On such occasions we are asked to step with Christ and through the power of the Spirit into the mystery of the loving obedience of Jesus, who embraced his Father's will in the midst of a world that was spoiled by the reality of sin. We confront here the folly of the cross and the foolishness of God, which is always wiser than the wisdom of ordinary people. Because Jesus was incarnate in a world and in a community that was tainted by sin, suffering seems to have been necessary for Jesus in order that he might become fully Son in his humanity.

Suffering is likewise a necessary part of our lives, since we too live in a world and in a community tainted by sin.

If we are Christians, we both experience and acknowledge our radical sinfulness and weakness as well as the positive gift of life. We always have a fundamental need for God's mercy because we have a dual experience of sin in our lives. On the one hand, there is the deliberate rejection of God's will in so many areas of our lives. That kind of sin—a refusal to live as God wants us to live—obstructs Christian life and prayer until there is repentance. On the other hand, there is the diffused and poignant experience of alienation and isolation.[38] Frustrations and disappointments should actually be a help in understanding our true relationship with God. Our lives are mysterious combinations of strength and weakness. To the extent that we have embraced God's free gift of his life, we are strong. To the extent that we have rejected it, lived it out irresponsibly, or been unable to accept it, we are weak. In a sense, then, we are like a beggar at the door holding out an empty bowl, but in another sense we are sinners who have an indisputable claim on Jesus because we believe that he came to raise us to new life. We are sinners and yet we are transformed by the death and resurrection of Jesus.[39] That claim on his loving mercy should be the source of great hope, peace, and consolation. We need only allow the Lord to save us by involving ourselves in the offer of his saving gift.

When we experience suffering, Jesus summons us to plunge deeper into a relationship of trust in a gracious and loving God. He tells us to stop trying to run our own lives and to hand over the controls to his Spirit within us.[40] He asks us to abandon our isolation, asks that we broaden our horizons, asks that we open our lives to the experience of new life. These moments of death to our misconceived presumption that we are self-sufficient can certainly be experiences of new life if they are rightly embraced and understood. Likewise, they can be moments in which we are faithful to the image of God in which we have been created, an image revealed to us in and through the life and person of Jesus.

To sin is to refuse to die to our self-preoccupation; it is to affirm our isolation and alienation. It is the alienation of the authentic self. It is a rejection of that humanity for which we were made, a rejection of the image in which we have been created. If we are meant to live as God lives, our lives must be lives of self-giving.[41] If we are made in the image of God, one of the distinctive characteristics of authentic humanity is a creativity that opens new horizons of being to others. Love is certainly one of the profound forms of creativity open to a person. It is likewise one of the great enlargers of the human person because it requires us to take strangers into our lives, to understand them, and to exercise restraint and reverence as well as imagination to make the relationship develop. What is destructive is impatience, haste, and expecting too much too soon.[42]

When we stress the need for people to die to their own self-sufficiency and to put down roots of dependency, we are confronted with the Christian paradox that we must leave all things to follow Christ. Certainly there is a danger that one may idolize persons and places. What is meant to support our response to the Spirit of God may attract to itself the unconditional love and reverence due to God alone. Supports then become idols. Idols, especially human idols, promise what they cannot give, and by deceiving us they enclose us in what is limited and confined. By usurping the place of God, they diminish our purity of heart.

In an effort to assert the primacy of God in human life the Christian tradition has spoken of detachment from creatures and attachment to God alone, but it often seems that detachment, wrongly understood and practiced, results in a loveless sort of life, a life that is in many ways sterile and indifferent to human persons. Christian detachment must not be confused with psychological rootlessness. As a matter of fact, some kind of authentic love and attachment is necessary for authentic detachment. There is, however, the right kind of detachment, the willingness to let others grow more and more into the image that God has created for them.[43]

People we take into our lives should challenge us, and we should challenge them at deep levels. The relationships should summon us to be what we are called to be and should invite us to respond to the gift of life with our own lives. When we close off the response, all that is left is endurance and empty waiting. But there can be no true communion among human persons until people have in fact become human, for to be able to give ourselves we must have taken possession of ourselves in that painful solitude outside of which nothing belongs to us and we have nothing to give.

If we give ourselves over to the great adventure of life, we get caught up in it and are carried along by its force. The deep loneliness that often characterizes life is experienced as a powerful longing that is transformed through the gift of faith into the experience of love. This is the love that is God's life. Since we have but a limited experience of God's life and love here and now, we continue to experience the pain of loneliness. Nevertheless, we do experience inner power that gives us the strength to bear the responsibility for our own life and also the ability to relate to others. Our relationships, however, emerge out of a certain fullness rather than emptiness. That fullness is a share in the risen life of Christ.

If it is difficult to speak about the experience of death, it is even more difficult to speak about the experience of resurrection. But to speak of Jesus rising from the dead is unintelligible unless in our own lives we experience something of that resurrection and its power to transform us from alienated, isolated beings into persons who truly live.[44] As disciples of Jesus we are not simply servants; we are his friends who share in his life. In the Easter mystery he gives us some insight into the meaning of that relationship. In the gospel account of Jesus' appearances to his disciples after the resurrection, there is a curious blend of familiarity and mystery.[45] He is simultaneously tender and remote, near and loving yet not immediately recognized. He is not like Lazarus or the widow's son after they were raised from the dead, because Jesus has risen to a new and perfect life; he has been exalted and has triumphed over all the alienation, limitations, and isolation that characterize so much of life in the world.[46] He is much more alive than we are. The new world, of which his risen body is the germ cell, transcends the boundaries of our world.[47] As we share in his risen life we too come to life on deeper and deeper levels. The experience of resurrection here and now means that we become more and more the human body-persons we are called to be. This self-realization is accomplished, above all, by means of relationships of knowledge and love. To know and to be known, to love and to be loved more and more deeply are what the present experience of resurrection is all about.[48]

Because we are empowered by the Spirit, God's will for us is not something that happens to us but rather something to be accomplished. Jesus says, "Thy will be done." Doing the will of God means sharing God's life and love with others so that they are able to come to life on deeper and deeper levels too. It means being faithful to the image in which we have been made. The formal point of resemblance between God the creator and God's human creatures is the creative power God has shared with his people. That creativity is an empowering love that makes it possible for people to be what God wants them to be. Such creativity necessarily involves other people; it cannot be exercised in a vacuum. Hence, in order to be as God wants us to be we need to know and be known, to love and be loved. Human being, then, is necessarily plural. One cannot be authentic and not relate to others. Authenticity excludes autonomy and necessitates relationships.

In a real sense the Christian community exists before we exist as persons. We are baptized into the body of Christ, and it is within the context of the Christian community that we emerge as members of that community. Just as there is diversity within the body, so there is diversity in the community, but it is rooted in unity and is meant to promote that unity.[49] Hence, every Christian exists to serve others. Our lives are sacrificial in the sense that our whole being is directed toward others, in imitation of Christ who "emptied himself" and took on the form of a slave.[50]

Life with God in Jesus Christ and through the power of the Spirit is certainly not opposed to life with other people; of necessity, true union with God brings with it union with God's people. If in contemplation we come to share in the vision of God, our horizons do not narrow so as to preclude the world and its people; true contemplation broadens our horizons so that social concerns fall within the scope of our vision.[51] The life of Jesus himself showed that it is possible to be deeply involved in love with the Father and also to be deeply involved in love with God's people. It is not only possible but also essential.

If Christian prayer is authentic, it does not lead into narcissism; it leads us to question and critique the fundamental values of society. Christian life is not an escape from the implications of the incarnation and our responsibility to get involved in the ongoing redemption of the world according to our distinctive vocations. It implies deep confrontation with human alienation; its goal is to undermine illusion and falsehood.

The reign of God in human life through Christ and in the Spirit is the standard by which Christians should live, and by that standard we are meant to discern the signs of our times. Christian life, which is centered in hope for the coming of the reign of God, cannot be escapist or individualistic, for it involves hope for both persons and communities.

Both vision and life are the fruits of Christian contemplation, Christian prayer. Union with God enables us not only to live as God lives but also to see as God sees. It is by sharing in God's vision that we can see beneath the surface of events, see through the illusion and the deceitful claims of many human systems, see beyond the immediate and the transient to what is lasting and complete. It is for this reason that the genuine contemplative is more of a threat to injustice than the social activist who merely sees the partial need. In a sense contemplative vision is revolutionary vision.[52]

Christian vision must flow over into active love. To see with the eyes of God is to see truthfully and lovingly. Such love is neither sentimental nor naive; it is, rather, a love that undermines oppression and abolishes illusion and falsehood. Contemplation is a prerequisite to entering into the struggle against evil in the structures of the world and in the depths of human hearts. As Paul points out in his letter to the Philippians, resistance can only grow out of breadth of knowledge and insight (1:9). Radical action begins with radical contemplation. Injustice and social fragmentation are perpetuated through limited perception, through an unwillingness or an inability to see the truth, and therefore a refusal to act. However, we must be quick to acknowledge that prayer and justice do not always go hand in hand. Of itself, increased awareness is no guarantee of transforming action. The mind's vision must become the heart's desire, and the heart's desire must flow over into liberating action. There are many prayerful people who struggle for justice whose faces become worn and whose bodies grow weary. People who are sensitive to the ways of God and to the dreams for the world that were entertained by his Son, Jesus, often experience the pain of frustration and sadness because of the intransigence of the mystery of iniquity, which continues to be rampant in the world. However, authentic Christians continue to hope because they acknowledge that ultimately God is the savior of the world, God alone.

Death and resurrection take place in the life of Christians in many ways, but they are often not conscious of what is taking place. Paul tells us that in an as yet imperfect but real sense we have died and our life is hidden with Christ in God. But when Christ appears—Christ who is our life—we too will be revealed in glory with him (Col 3:3–4). Although Paul is speaking of Christian life as a whole, his words are also an accurate description of the life of prayer. Our Christian life and prayer are hidden not only from other people but also from ourselves. We are like a chrysalis, a dark uncomely object that does not look as though it could contain life at all, yet inside the beautiful moth is being formed.[53] God's life within us is so near, and yet it often seems to be so far away. It is so near, yet we are often not able to see it for what it is.

The experience of suffering and death, either in our own lives or in the lives of those we love, often throws us into consternation and turns our values upside-down. We usually have our own maps on which we plot our journeys; we have our own plans for personal growth and adventure. But the Lord tells us, as he told the disciples on the road to Emmaus, that our plans are too small and niggardly, that our lives are too self-centered and mean.

Jesus Christ is the Lord of our lives. His resurrection was the result of being loved by his Father. God's love is the language of forever. For the Father to say, "This is my beloved Son in whom I am well pleased," is really to say, "You will not die; I will not abandon you to death, for you share in my life, and I live forever." As risen Lord in his humanity, Jesus finds himself permanently liberated from all perverse, death-dealing forces. It is that risen life he shares with us even now. He wants to be *our* Lord—Lord of every situation in our lives, Lord of our failures and bewilderment, Lord of the chaos we call our Christian lives and our prayer. He prays in us through the presence and power of the Spirit; we must trust him and let him do it. He has ascended to his Father and our Father. The Father loves us not primarily because we are good but because of what we are in his Son, Jesus.

Christian life is not an effort to journey from where we are to somewhere else; it is, rather, a breakthrough to the realization of where we already are in Jesus. We are sons and daughters of God our loving Father in his Son, Jesus Christ, through the power of the Holy Spirit. What we are is pure gift from God, and that is a matter for deep peace and quiet hope.

Christian prayer does not take place in a vacuum but in the real world where we spend our lives. To a great extent the way we pray is determined by the way we live. But the world in which we live soon becomes vacuous if it is not seen and experienced in the light of prayer. The more complex our world becomes and the more extensively human power over the world grows, the more we need the vision and experience of wholeness that Christian prayer brings. But the more we come to see as God sees and the more we experience the life of God within us, the greater is our responsibility to share that life and vision and to engage in the Christian transformation of the world according to our distinctive vocations. To be a prayerful person is to stand in the power and presence of God, but it is also to have a presence that should be powerful in the presence of other people.

As the discussion of the paschal mystery of Jesus Christ has shown, it is a complex theological and ritual phenomenon. In the history of the church the primary aspects of that mystery have been celebrated in the sacraments of the church. In what follows those rituals will be discussed and emphasis put on the positive virtues they presuppose or hope to communicate to those who celebrate them.

A VIRTUOUS LIFE AND THE SACRAMENTS

The Christian sacraments are gifts given by God out of God's own loving generosity. Strictly speaking, we have no right to the gifts. Our proper response is simply gratitude. We are like a beggar standing at the door with an empty bowl in our hands. Our receptivity is shown, for example, by the open hands with which we reach out to receive the Eucharist, symbols of our open, receptive hearts.[54] Gratitude should be our most basic response to all the sacramental rites of the church.

Christian Initiation[55]

The source for the custom of baptizing new Christians is not clear. It seems to have been derived from the practice of John the Baptist, which perhaps arose out of the tradition of prophetic symbolism in the Old Testament, where there is reference to God's people being cleansed with water in preparation for the coming Messianic Age (see Ez 36:25–27). The Synoptic Gospels record Jesus' baptism by John, but they do not say anything about Jesus baptizing his disciples. John's Gospel, however, does speak of Jesus baptizing others (Jn 3:22, 26; 4:1) and Matthew's Gospel contains the Lord's command to baptize all nations. In the New Testament there are several images concerning baptismal practice: in John's Gospel emphasis is on new birth through water and the Holy Spirit (Jn 3:5); in Paul's Letter to the Romans, baptism is interpreted as a rite uniting one with Christ in his death, burial, and resurrection (Rom 6:3–11). The experience is also described as enlightenment (Heb 6:4), as having put off the old nature and put on the new (Col 3:9–10), and as being marked or sealed as God's people (2 Cor 1:22). Whatever the origins of the rite, it seems to have become the ordinary practice to initiate new converts into the church through a process that included baptism in a river or pool.

In the post-apostolic period the process of becoming a Christian involved not only a liturgical rite but also a period of spiritual formation. The *Apostolic Tradition* describes the process as it existed prior to the fourth century. It involved entrance into a catechumenate, which might last for three years. Candidates were required to have sponsors to attest to their ability to lead the Christian life, especially with regard to works of charity. During this time there were regular exorcisms to accomplish their purification from the evil of the world. When the trial period was complete, the actual baptism took place; it seems to have been celebrated at the Easter vigil. The rites began with the bishop's blessing of two oils to be used, the oil of exorcism and the oil of thanksgiving. After the candidates had removed their clothing, they made a renunciation of Satan and were then anointed with the oil of exorcism. Then they descended into the water and were asked to affirm their belief in God the Father, in Jesus Christ, and in the Holy Spirit. As the candidates made their response to each question, they were immersed in the water. After coming out of the water, they were anointed with the oil of thanksgiving; then they put on their clothes. The newly baptized then joined the congregation. The bishop laid his hands upon them, recited a prayer, and anointed them a second time with the oil of thanksgiving, this time pouring it on their head. Then the newly baptized participated in the rest of the eucharistic celebration: the prayers of the faithful, the exchange of the kiss of peace, and the celebration of the eucharistic meal. This ritual continued to be followed in Rome for some time, but there was increasing emphasis on the gift of the Holy Spirit with the post-baptismal prayer and anointing by the bishop.[56]

In Syria a somewhat different pattern of initiation prevailed prior to the fourth century. There does not seem to have been a formal catechumenate or any exorcism of the candidate. The actual initiation seems to have consisted simply of an anointing with oil and an immersion in water. The immersion was accompanied by the minister's recitation of an indicative formula asserting that the person was being baptized in the name of the Father, and of the Son, and of the Holy Spirit. The focus was not on identification with the death and resurrection of Christ but rather on adoption, rebirth, and divinization.[57] Nor was the practice of baptism especially associated with Easter.[58]

When Christianity became the established religion, in the fourth century, there was an increased standardization of both the theology and practice of initiation in both the West and the East. The formal catechumenate gradually declined as large numbers of candidates sought baptism, so there was not a conscientious examination of their readiness for baptism. Nor did candidates always proceed hastily to baptism, since it was believed that only baptism could forgive sins; they wanted to be sure of gaining ultimate salvation at the moment of death. As time went on there was a tendency to emphasize the transformation that automatically took place on the spiritual level; the transformation of personal character was neglected.

Children were being baptized as early as the end of the second century. Nevertheless, most candidates were adults; no adaptations were made to the rites when infants were included, except that parents or sponsors made the appropriate responses on behalf of the children. From the fifth century on, the baptism of infants became more common, and the baptism of adults declined. The high infant mortality rate along with Augustine's teaching on original sin prompted the baptism of infants as quickly as possible after birth so they would not die in the state of original sin. As a result of these developments, the catechumenate disappeared. The role of the bishop was taken over by the presbyter, as had already happened with the celebration of the Eucharist. The bishop, however, continued to consecrate the oils. In Rome the bishop's role was stressed, especially his role in the second anointing. This practice was eventually imposed upon the whole western church with the result that the time between the actual baptism and the anointing by the bishop—which eventually came to be called confirmation—increased. This resulted in efforts to establish a specific age for confirmation with penalties for those parents who did not bring their children for the episcopal anointing. By the end of the medieval period, seven years of age or even later was generally thought to be an appropriate age for confirmation.[59]

This separation of baptism and confirmation in the West resulted in the development of a new theological interpretation of the theology of confirmation as the sacrament that conferred an additional gift of God's grace to strengthen, fortify, and equip the Christian for battle against evil in the world. It was maintained that it was more appropriate for the gift to be given after the person had matured somewhat rather than during infancy. As a result, confirmation became detached from the initiation process; nevertheless, infants were still given communion at their baptism, as was the traditional practice in those areas in the West where chrismation remained part of a unified rite. In the twelfth century in the West, however, with the development of great stress on the real bodily presence of Christ in the Eucharist, infants were increasingly denied communion because they could not properly appreciate the gift that they received. Initially they were given communion under the species of wine, but when communion under the form of wine was withdrawn from the laity, it was likewise withdrawn from infants. It became the general practice that children should not be admitted to communion until they reached the age of discretion. This practice was confirmed by the Council of Trent in 1552.[60]

Clearly, Christian initiation ceased to be a sacramental process and became the celebration of three or more frequently four distinct rites: baptism, first penance, first communion, and confirmation. The rites were more associated with biological maturity than spiritual development. Instead of being a celebration involving the whole Christian community, baptism became a more or less private rite involving sponsors and perhaps the father of the child, since the mother was usually still confined to bed. Instead of descent into a pool of water, the person being baptized was sprinkled with a few drops of water. The Council of Trent, the *Pontificale Romanum* (1595), and the *Rituale Romanum* (1614) did nothing to change the customary practices but simply imposed uniformity of practice concerning baptism and confirmation. In 1910, Pope Pius X lowered the age for first communion but not confirmation. So the customary practice was to celebrate baptism, then first penance, then first communion, then confirmation.

The Second Vatican Council mandated the revision of the sacramental rites. The rites of Christian initiation were issued in three stages: the rite for the baptism of children in 1969, the rite of confirmation in 1971, and the Rite of Christian Initiation of Adults (RCIA) in 1972. The final English translation of the RCIA appeared in 1985 and was made mandatory in the United States in 1988. The RCIA is also used with appropriate adaptations for the initiation of those children who have reached catechetical age, that is, the age of discretion. The text takes a very positive approach to initiation, emphasizing blessings rather than responsibilities or burdens. It stresses that Christian initiation brings the faithful close to Christ. Baptism empowers us to share in the paschal mystery of Christ and frees us from the power of darkness while joining us to Christ's death, burial, and resurrection (no. 1). We pass from the death of sin to new life (no. 6). Furthermore the rite asserts that we are adopted and called children of God, for baptism makes us sharers in God's own life. Furthermore, baptism involves a cleansing water of rebirth (no. 5). The community aspect is also stressed, for baptism incorporates us into the church so that the baptized are built up together in the Spirit, become a house where God abides, and become part of a holy nation and a royal priesthood (no. 4).

The general introduction to the RCIA affirms that the Holy Spirit is truly given in baptism; it asserts that confirmation somehow completes baptism and brings a special gift of the Spirit. The gift is described as a participation in the mission of Christ, "so that we may bear witness to him before all the world and work to bring the Body of Christ to its fullness as soon as possible." It is only in the separate rite of confirmation and in the apostolic constitution that accompanies it that the medieval emphasis on strengthening is explicitly noted.

The general introduction to the RCIA also stresses the unity of the three sacraments of baptism, confirmation, and Eucharist. Likewise, it emphasizes the ecclesiological and missionary themes so that "we may have eternal life and show forth the unity of God's people . . . and we pray for a greater outpouring of the Holy Sprit, so that the whole human family may be brought into the unity of God's family."

Before Vatican II conversion to the Roman Catholic Church was usually a rather private affair. One decided to become a Catholic and approached a priest, who usually met the person in the parish rectory; the priest gave the candidate a basic catechism or a book such as *Father Smith Instructs Jackson,* and then made sure that the candidate had sufficient knowledge of Catholic doctrine. Only then was the person baptized, usually in the presence of his or her sponsor, immediate family, and good friends. Christian conversion was primarily an intellectual conversion; one journeyed from one set of doctrinal truths and accepted another. In the RCIA, however, the experience is envisioned as intellectual, religious, moral, and ecclesial. The larger community is involved throughout the whole process of conversion. As Aidan Kavanagh argues forcefully in *The Shape of Baptism,* the RCIA is especially important because of the strategic vision of the local and universal church that it sets out. The image is that of a people brought together by a common experience of conversion and faith in the Lord Jesus and empowered to live a new life through the presence and activity of the Spirit.[61] The church is set out not primarily as an institution but as the people of God committed to the mission of the Lord Jesus through evangelization, catechesis, and liturgical celebration. It is very important that the whole process involve not only the ordained as minister but all of the baptized, who are expected to give effective witness to the Christian faith and to participate actively in the various ministries that are part of the rite.

The theology and practice of infant baptism has been seriously influenced by the theology of original sin. The traditional teaching, based on an interpretation of Romans 5:12, has described the state from which humanity is saved by Jesus Christ. The belief that all have sinned in Adam and that baptism is intended above all to take away original sin certainly influenced the practice whereby infants were baptized shortly after birth. The theology of original sin was first formulated by the church fathers, especially Augustine during his controversy with the Pelagians. The Council of Trent made the distinction that baptism takes away the guilt of original sin although the tendency toward evil (concupiscence) remains. In recent times there has been a rethinking of the doctrine in light of biblical study and developments in our understanding of the relationship between nature and grace. Authors generally agree, however, that humanity has a dark side that cries out for redemption by Jesus Christ. As we have seen, Henri de Lubac maintained that we are all born into a graced situation because Christ has already redeemed us; hence, there is no such thing as pure nature. But that does not deny that we are also born into a world where the mystery of iniquity is still operative. We need only observe the behavior of a hungry infant to see that the child is indeed very self-centered and not at all altruistic.

The rite of baptism for children contains this formula in the prayer of exorcism and anointing preceding the actual baptism: "We pray for these children: set them free from original sin, make them temples of your glory and send your Holy Spirit to dwell within them" (no. 49). However, an alternate formula reads: "By (Jesus') victory over sin and death, bring these children out of the power of darkness" (no. 221). The alternate prayer is taken from the 1969 *editio typica* of the rite, but Pope Paul VI and the Congregation for the Doctrine of the Faith insisted that a clear reference to original sin be inserted in a new edition of the rite published in 1973. The Rite of Christian Initiation of Adults, however, makes no explicit reference to original sin. Its prayers and exorcisms ask for deliverance from the power of darkness and from personal sin. The *Catechism of the Catholic Church* affirms the reality of sin in human history and shies away from speaking simply of the dark side of reality.[62] It was traditionally believed by many Catholics that infants who died without baptism went to limbo, an abode in which souls were excluded from the full blessedness of the beatific vision but not condemned to any other form of punishment. The doctrine was regularly taught by traditional Catholic writers, including Augustine and Thomas Aquinas; however, the church never pronounced on the doctrine of limbo. At the present time the doctrine of limbo seems to have itself gone into limbo.[63] In fact, the Catholic rite of funerals contains a set of texts that may be used for the burial of a child who dies before baptism.

Christian baptism is a wonderful gift that God gives to an individual in Christ and through the power of the Holy Spirit. It is closely identified with the gift of faith. God takes possession of the baptized person through the saving event of Jesus' death and resurrection. In baptism the person is delivered from the dominion of darkness and is initiated into the reign of God's beloved Son. The rite makes the person a member of the church; it opens the gate that gives one access to the other sacraments. Strictly speaking we do not have a right to baptism; the initiative for our redemption always resides in God. Therefore, our primary response to the gift should first of all be a readiness to acknowledge our total dependence on God and gratitude for the gift of life on all levels. Together with our special relationship with God comes our special incorporation into the priestly, prophetic, and kingly roles of the risen Christ. As members of a priestly people, the baptized share in the worship, thanksgiving, and praise that the church offers God in Christ and through the Spirit; as members of a prophetic people, the baptized receive the word of God in their hearts with the power and responsibility to proclaim that word to others, especially by the witness of their lives; members of a kingly people, the baptized have a dignity and value that they should cherish, perhaps especially these days when human life is so often threatened by abortion, euthanasia, capital punishment, torture, and abuse.

Through baptism, Christians are bound to share in the missionary activity of the church. According to their distinctive vocations they are called to work for justice and peace. Above all, however, they are to live lives of Christian charity. Their whole life is meant to be a response to the love that God shares with them because God is love. God has initiated a special friendship with each one of the baptized, a friendship rooted in the covenant God has made with each of them. God's love that is given is meant to be shared. The baptized are meant to love what God loves; that means loving our neighbor and loving ourselves.

The life of the baptized consists not only of observing the commandments and avoiding sin, but above all, it involves the practice of Christian virtues, "those good moral habits, affections, attitudes and beliefs that lead to genuine human fulfillment, even perfection, on both personal and social levels."[64] Virtues, of course, derive their meaning from different understandings of life. As Christians we believe that our lives are perfected in love and communion with God in Jesus Christ and through the power of the Spirit.[65] Our final destiny transcends our unaided human abilities. In the Christian life we are empowered to live as God wants us to live through the gifts of the infused virtues of faith, hope, and charity, and through the cardinal virtues of prudence, justice, courage, and temperance.[66]

Above all, the network of relationships that is created through baptism must be marked by justice, by the virtue that acknowledges our basic interdependence and empowers us to give to others what is their due. Since we are made in the image of God, who has been revealed as both persons and community, we too are persons and community. The virtue of justice promotes and defends that deep interdependence that is rooted in our very nature as brothers and sisters to one another and sons and daughters of God. The life of the baptized, therefore, must be ordered toward the common good, that well-being we seek to achieve by living in solidarity with and for one another. It ultimately holds the good of the whole to be more important than the good of one individual. It seeks to promote the well-being not only of the human family but also of the church as a community of Christian faith and of the earth in its biodiversity. It holds that the well-being of the individual will flourish to the extent that the whole flourishes.[67]

The network of relationships established by baptism is preserved and strengthened by the virtue of fidelity. The relationships must also be rooted in the virtue of self-esteem, by which one accepts oneself as a mysterious combination of strengths and weaknesses. We come to know the love that God has for us through the human love of others. We must learn to receive from others freely so that in the process we can come to know ourselves as fully accepted by a love that makes no conditions. When we accept the great blessing of being loved by God, then we can love others freely without manipulation or control.[68] Self-esteem is based on self-acceptance. Sometimes people are aware not only of their strengths but also their weaknesses; however, they are often reluctant to admit and accept their weaknesses and so do not seek help when help is needed. It is significant that Jesus asks those who need to be cured: "Do you want to be healed?" Healing is never forced upon us. Sometimes we do not want our weaknesses to be healed because we know or at least sense that weakness can be a very manipulative force and empower us to dominate others.

The life of the baptized must also be characterized by the virtue of prudence, which puts the various virtues into practice in the right way, at the proper time, and for the right reasons. It involves sound judgment about what is appropriate and the ability to discern what is the best way to act in a particular situation.[69]

Human beings have strong appetites, desires, and tendencies. We often have powerful emotions and seek those things we think are good. However, those desires can become so strong that they dominate our lives in excessive ways; we can become obsessed with them—food, drink, sex, money, material things, power, and prestige. Instead of directing us to what is good for us, they can rule over us. Temperance, however, does not mean that we live in squalor or in a puritanical abstemiousness. It means we enjoy those things that are legitimate and good for us but live with a proper sense of detachment and freedom.[70]

There is no doubt that for many people life today is very hard. But with courage and perseverance it can be lived productively. Courage is the virtue that characterizes a brave heart. It gives people the energy, the imagination, the creativity, and strength to face whatever threatens human dignity, integrity, and the rights of a well informed and formed conscience. Much of human life today is characterized by fear—fear of the future, fear of losing employment, fear of disability due to illness, and fear of death. Without courage, we are in danger of succumbing to those fears and becoming inactive cowards. A courageous person does not deny the presence of his or her fears but insists on confronting them so that life does not simply disintegrate. There are really two aspects of courage: perseverance, or patient endurance, and frontal attack. Perseverance empowers us to stand firm in our convictions. However, there are times when sorrows cannot be avoided; patient endurance enables us to enter into the sorrow yet empowers us to believe firmly that life has meaning, that there is still reason to hope. Frontal attack enables us to respond to sorrow or tragedy not simply by resigning ourselves to it but by seeking ways to make the very best of a bad situation.[71] As Christians, we pray in times of such difficulties "Thy will be done," convinced that God knows what is truly good for us. Since we live life forward but understand it backward, we often come to see that sorrows and other difficulties have drawn out the very best in us and in others.

Certainly not all the baptized possess the various virtues outlined above to the same degree; each one has distinctive gifts, distinctive strengths, distinctive weaknesses. But as these virtues work together in the church as the body of Christ, they indeed establish a firm foundation on which the reign of God in the world will be firmly established.

Confirmation

As already noted in our discussion of Christian initiation, confirmation has undergone a complex historical development involving numerous changes in both its ritual forms and its theological meaning. Most scholars have maintained that in light of the New Testament data, no clear distinction between baptism and confirmation can be made. Nevertheless, from an early date in the history of the church certain elements of the baptismal rite were given special attention and distinctive meaning was attached to them. In Tertullian's *De baptismo* the baptismal rite consists of two parts: the water bath and its anointing, and the imposition of hands, with the gift of the Holy Spirit attributed to the imposition of hands. In the *Apostolic Tradition* the presbyteral postbaptismal anointing is completed by a rite in which the bishop imposes his hand, anoints, and seals the forehead of the candidate. In the fifth century Pope Innocent clearly stated that presbyters may anoint the baptized with chrism but they are not to anoint the forehead with oil; the latter anointing is reserved to the bishop. Hence, it became traditional in the West that the anointing of the forehead was reserved to the bishop. By contrast, the East preserved the traditional order of the sacraments: baptism, confirmation, and Eucharist, and saw the bishop's presence simply in the chrism, which he had consecrated.[72]

The history of confirmation as a distinct sacrament was especially influenced by a homily delivered by Faustus of Riez in 458. He maintained that in baptism the candidate is washed and made innocent, but grace is increased through confirmation. In baptism we are regenerated for life; in confirmation we are strengthened for battle. Baptism is passively received, but confirmation involves human effort, an emphasis that appears to be semi-Pelagian. During the Middle Ages confirmation gradually became separated from baptism, emphasis was placed on the gift of fortitude, and the bishop's kiss of peace to the candidate was changed into a strike on the cheek as a symbol of spiritual combat.

The Council of Trent defended confirmation as a special sacrament conferring a distinctive character. The 1917 Code of Canon Law prescribed that confirmation be administered by the bishop imposing his hand while anointing the forehead. The Second Vatican Council said very little about the sacrament; the *Constitution on the Sacred Liturgy*, however, did state that the rite should be revised in order that the intimate link between confirmation and the initiation process should be stressed. A new rite was promulgated by Pope Paul VI in 1971 when he issued *Divinae consortium naturae*. There he stated: "The sharing in the divine nature, which is granted to men and women through the grace of Christ, has a certain likeness to the origin, development, and nourishing of natural life. The faithful are born anew by baptism, strengthened by the sacrament of confirmation, and finally are sustained by the food of eternal life in the Eucharist." The actual rite includes two laying on of hands, a general one over all the candidates as the bishop prays for the sevenfold gifts of the Spirit, and an individual imposition on each candidate as the anointing takes place. The rite affirms that the bishop is the ordinary minister of the sacrament.[73]

The age at which the sacrament is celebrated has varied considerably in the West. The 1917 Code of Canon Law stated: "Although the administration of the sacrament of confirmation should preferably be postponed in the Latin Church until the seventh year of age, nevertheless it can be conferred before that age if the infant is in danger of death or its administration seems to the minister justified for good and serious reasons" (canon 788). Both the Rite for Confirmation (1971) and the Rite of Christian Initiation of Adults (1972) prefer that all three sacraments of initiation be given to adults in the same celebration. Concerning the conferral of confirmation on children, the Rite of Confirmation repeated the legislation of the 1917 code, stipulating the postponement of confirmation until the seventh year of age. However, it added a fresh option: "For pastoral reasons, especially to strengthen in the life of the faithful complete obedience to Christ the Lord in loyal testimony to him, episcopal conferences may choose an age which appears more appropriate, so that the sacrament is conferred after appropriate formation at a more mature age" (no. 11). This reference to appropriate formation at a more mature age is not mentioned in the 1983 Code of Canon Law, which simply states: "The sacrament of confirmation is to be conferred on the faithful at about the age of discretion unless the conference of bishops determines another age or there is danger of death or in the judgment of the minister a grave cause urges otherwise" (canon 891). It is a general opinion that an earlier as well as a later age may be chosen, and that an episcopal conference might decide to opt for the practice of infant confirmation; however, the thrust of the canon is for the celebration of the sacrament at the age of discretion. The end result is that there is considerable variation in the age at which the sacrament is celebrated.[74]

At the present time there are seven models of confirmation that are derived from the liturgical books and pastoral practices of various Christian churches.[75] First, there is the Rite for the Christian Initiation of Adults. The age of adulthood is that of catechetical age or the age at which persons attain the use of reason.[76]

The second longstanding model is that of chrismation. The various Eastern Rites, including those that are in union with Rome, chrismate (confirm) all new members, including infants, immediately after they are baptized.[77]

The third model is that which is customary in many Protestant and Anglican churches. Confirmation is a rite marking a child's achievement of a level of catechesis. It is a maturity rite or a rite of passage, but it is not considered a true sacrament.[78]

The fourth model is that celebrated when validly baptized non-Catholics are received into full communion in the Catholic Church. They are confirmed provided they have received valid baptism in another church.[79]

The fifth model is that celebrated for children baptized as infants. The rite is celebrated at a later age, which varies considerably from diocese to diocese in the Catholic Church.[80]

The sixth model is that celebrated for adolescents. A prevalent model in various parts of the world, it is based on the belief that the teenage years are more appropriate than childhood years for the confirmation of those baptized as infants.[81]

The seventh model is an abbreviated rite of confirmation provided for the dying who were never confirmed.[82]

Certainly one should expect that those who are confirmed as adults and at least to some extent those who have reached the catechetical age should practice the same virtues that were discussed above when treating the virtuous life of the baptized. In many dioceses where confirmation is administered to teenagers, the preparatory program involves the young people in various service programs in the diocese, for example, visiting the sick and the elderly or working in soup kitchens. These experiences often enlarge the candidates' horizons and inspire them to be more effective as Christian witnesses. They usually become more aware of their responsibility to be committed to social justice. A danger, however, is that the young people see their fulfillment of these service hours simply as conditions for their reception of confirmation and fail to internalize a responsibility to live a life of witness to social justice in the world.

Unfortunately, those who are confirmed as adolescents often discontinue the practice of religion, so the rite becomes in a sense a graduation rite. Some of them return to the church when they marry and have children. Special pastoral efforts need to be directed toward the retention of those young people in the church. If they have developed a commitment to social justice, that commitment needs to be deeply rooted in a commitment to Jesus Christ and to the liturgy as the celebration of the paschal mystery. They need help to develop a personal and communal prayer life. Many parishes have programs devoted to youth ministry, but too often the program is primarily social or athletic. Strong community support must accompany teenagers as they leave their teenage years, and that support must continue as they move through young adulthood.

Eucharist

God is essentially other-related and ecstatic. God in Godself is God for us in creation and history. The extravagant life of the Trinity overflows and breaks all boundaries of self-interest and self-preoccupation, since God's goodness is self-diffusive, not self-contained. The Trinity is a community of Persons who are both free and interconnected through self-giving; giving is how God is. In other words, giving is the way in which God should be conceived as well as named. God is a community of givers, a community of Persons who are united in giving themselves to each other and to creation, especially to human persons and communities. God's giving and giving away are basic to the meaning of divine sacrifice, for God is the sacrificing one, the one who alone makes holy, as the term *sacrifice* implies. Sacrifice is at the heart of the Trinity itself and is expressed in the divine decision to create the universe and preserve it in existence. This coming into existence of the world is the work of our self-effacing God, who has been at work through all the stages of the world's evolution. The greatest act of God's self-giving is the gift of the incarnation, the very Word of God incarnate in human flesh and united with all of creation but especially with human persons and communities. The incarnation of the Son of God carried out in time and in our world what God has been doing from all eternity; Jesus followed the example of his Father and gave us an example of the way we should live (Jn 13:15). The risen Lord Jesus, in turn, shares the Spirit with us so we might give as God gives. That gift is not meant to induce in us a sense of arrogance or smug generosity but rather a profound sense of receptivity and gratitude, of thanksgiving. The purpose of the gift is to induce more giving, but we do not have the right to be proud of what we give because all has been given to us precisely in order that we might share it with others.[83]

God's greatest gift, of course, is the gift of the Son. It shows that the gift of creation, which the Logos takes on in the incarnation, is very good in spite of the evil in the world. The death of the Son on the cross signifies the ultimate act of giving, revealing that all giving is an act of sacrifice. It is a holy action initiated by the all-holy God. The Pauline writings, while echoing a theme that many scholars find also in the Johannine writings, provide the most complex yet illuminating treatment of sacrifice in the New Testament, especially in support of God as a sacrificing God.[84] However, in the Pauline writings there is no hint that God or Christ is being sacrificed by humans so that they may be restored to life. The emphasis is on God's activity, on God's costly self-giving, and on God's self-emptying in the Son. As he descended to the bottom of the social scale and into the depths of human suffering, Jesus stands as a strong challenge to our human aspirations toward upward mobility and success in worldly terms.[85]

Central to Paul's thought is the notion that the sacrifice of Jesus is not substitutionary but rather representative. The paschal mystery is not an event that merely happens on our behalf; it is something in which we are intimately involved; the theme of life through death and resurrection is meant to be realized throughout our own lives. In baptism we are initiated into a process whereby we die with Christ and rise with him to new life. Through the Eucharist we are nourished by the body and blood of Christ and rise with him to new life; at the same time we join ourselves to him by remembering his death and resurrection while we seek, through the power of the Holy Spirit, to remember the body of humanity, which is still torn apart by sin and selfishness. Hence, our Christian lives always involve us in participation in the dying and rising of Christ, which means that they must be grounded in the fundamental principles of sacrificial love and self-giving.[86] The way of God is the way of sacrifice; our way to God is the way of self-sacrifice. Hence, salvation comes to us by partaking in the paschal mystery of Jesus Christ through the power of the Spirit, who comes to us through the sacraments, through faith, and through sacrificial living. Paul stresses the mystical participation of Christians in the death and resurrection of Jesus.

It is a share in God's own life that is offered to us in Christ Jesus, the one who offers us his very body and blood, his very life, in the Eucharist. It should be clear, however, that Jesus was not offering his life to placate an angry God who was offended by the sin of Adam and Eve. God the Father was not a child abuser. This assertion has important implications for our understanding of the mass as a sacrifice.[87]

Although the eucharistic liturgy is a meal, the meal characteristic is essentially bound up with the sacrificial character of the celebration. As Edward Kilmartin notes: "Insofar as Jesus instituted the memorial of his symbolic actions of the Last Supper, the sacrificial and meal aspects are inseparable from one another. A sacrificial event is constituted in the form of a ritual meal process. . . . The meal has to do with the *modus quo,* not the *id quod* of the celebration."[88] Our goal in celebrating the Eucharist is communion with Christ in the power of the Holy Spirit and through Christ with the Father, but also communion with the body of Christ that is the church. This latter communion is also achieved through the Holy Spirit. There is then a katabatic or descending self-gift of the Father through Christ and in the power of the Holy Spirit, but there must also be an anabatic or faith response consisting of the self-gift of human beings through Christ and in the power of the Holy Spirit.[89]

In a sense salvation history is realized in the lives of those who share faithfully in the Eucharist. It is a history first of all of the divine offer of personal communion with God extended to human beings, but it also involves the free response of acceptance by those same human beings. The human response is described as an offering of self in the sense that one freely opens oneself to the gift and embraces the gift, so that one ultimately receives the meaning of one's life from God. In other words, one freely chooses to be open to the divine gift that alone gives true and final meaning to human existence. Initially salvation history takes place in the special mission of the Word occurring in the incarnation, life, death, and glorification of Jesus Christ, the Word incarnate. This Christ-event is an expression of the Father's fidelity to the covenant made with his people, an expression that the Father is always faithful to the promises he has made. There is then the incarnation of the Word, the sending of God's only Son. There also is the faithful response of the Son of Man in his humanity to the Father's work in him, namely, the embodiment of the fidelity of humanity to the covenant relation with the Father. In the special mission of the Word, the Holy Spirit is the divine source of the sanctification of the humanity of Jesus of Nazareth; by the power of the Spirit that humanity has been elevated to unity of person with the Word.[90]

It is important to emphasize that the Word and the Holy Spirit are at work in all the actions that God performs in the world, from the very beginning of creation. There is no temporal sequence to these two missions; they are simultaneous and complementary. The gift that comes through the twofold mission of the Word and the Spirit is dependent on the divine initiative, for the gift comes from God as the gift of divine, self-sacrificing, self-giving love.[91]

The response of faith by Jesus was carried out through his whole life; in a sense it consisted in a progressive upward transformation of his humanity into the most perfect embodiment of the acceptable response to his Father's covenant initiative. That goal was finally attained in the death of Jesus on the cross and his triumph over death in his resurrection from the dead. So also in the rest of humanity, the response of faith is the result of a gift, the gift of the Holy Spirit working within each human heart to conform each individual to Christ so that each one has the same interior dispositions as Christ.[92]

The celebration of the Eucharist is, first of all, an expression of the sacrificial gift giving on the part of God in Christ and through the power of the Spirit, but it is also constitutive of that divine gift for God's people. The celebrating community intentionally offers itself; it offers its willingness to embrace the gift, but it also gives back the gift to the giver, not because human beings have no need of the divine gift, but rather because they need to acknowledge that the gift is a gift of God and that each and every human being is in constant need of the divine gift. In a sense the gift is given back, not because human beings have anything of themselves to offer to God but in order to be received back once again from God.

In the celebration of the Eucharist we submit our lives to the paschal rhythms of the church as the body of Christ and we surrender our own natural tendencies to see everything in life as a commodity that we can control. We open our lives to a divine gift that comes to us in Christ by the power of the Spirit, a gift that invites us to offer our human thanksgiving, thus opening our hearts so we receive the gift that allows God to be God in our lives. It is God's presence in our hearts that transforms us so we are glorified by God's initiative. As Irenaeus says so powerfully, "The glory of God is the human person fully alive"—alive with God's own gift of life. As a result, we are empowered to act in relation to others as God relates to us—with self-sacrificing love. It is only in that sense that we can speak of praising God. The basic Christian disposition in life, then, should be one of Eucharist, thanksgiving, which implies a willingness to embrace the gift of God's life and, on an even deeper level, to embrace God as the giver of the gift. It necessitates an acknowledgment of our utter dependence on God.[93]

The Eucharist always calls for a disposition of thanksgiving, of receptivity, for without such a response there can be no true communion between God and us. The response certainly places us in a distinctive relationship with God, one of total dependency, but we in a sense offer our return gifts not because our gifts of openness and thanksgiving can in any way balance the divine gift, but because the giving of a gift in return actually becomes a constitutive part of the reception and makes possible true community. We might say that the ethical practices of justice, love, and mercy are the essential dimensions of our return gift.[94]

The power to be receptive people comes to us from the Holy Spirit; therefore, it is imperative that the role of the Spirit in the Eucharist be clearly expressed in the rite, especially in the Eucharistic Prayer. The Spirit not only transforms the gifts of bread and wine, but also and above all transforms those who gather around the altar to receive the gifts. In other words, the Lord Jesus is not only present on the altar under the symbols of bread and wine, but he is also present in those who come with open hands and hearts to receive the transformed bread and wine. Unfortunately, many Christians, perhaps especially Roman Catholics, give the impression that the Eucharist is simply a commodity to be consumed, one that is readily available in communion services or perhaps in the tabernacle. They fail to see the responsibility for involvement in the whole eucharistic action and consequently in living out the demands of the Eucharist in daily life.

Our celebration of the Eucharist requires that we acknowledge our dependence on God and also on one another. That disposition is often difficult to achieve in our contemporary culture, for people want to be independent, to be self-sufficient, to be self-centered. In that way they think they have power and prestige. In Luke's Gospel, however, the narrative of the Last Supper and the institution of the Eucharist is followed immediately by the account of the disciples' dispute about power and prestige. Jesus condemns their concern for greatness and instructs them, "Let the greatest among you become as the younger, and the leader as one who serves" (Lk 22:26). The implications of Jesus' teaching are brought out in John's Gospel (13:1–11) where we find the account of Jesus' washing the disciples' feet where we would expect to find the text describing the institution of the Eucharist. This is surely John's vivid way of showing the connection between the Eucharist and service, between Eucharist and daily Christian life.

Walter Brueggemann points out that the tools Jesus left his disciples to carry out their mission of service were a towel and basin. Tools determine and define one's trade. If we disciples of Jesus are left the tools of a servant, we can only do the work of a servant. Certainly a towel and basin are used to carry out the work no master would do. They are used to make contact with the soiled dimensions of humanity that call for personal attention. The towel and the basin place heavy demands on us. We are commissioned to make contact with the soiled, sometimes unattractive dimensions of humanity and to carry out our service with loving attention. Such a mission can be fulfilled only by people who are not self-preoccupied, who can take their minds off themselves to focus on their ministry.[95]

Brueggemann further highlights what a servant does in washing another's feet. The servant takes on a subordinate position while positioning the one whose feet are being washed in the place of a master. This is significant if the one who is set in the master's place is precisely the one who has been put down and excluded by society. In our contemporary world there are many who are pushed down by society. Those who are thought to be unworthy or inferior are often denigrated in the community until their own sense of dignity and worth is decimated too. People can be rejected or excluded so long and so vigorously or perhaps so subtly that they perceive themselves as unworthy, inferior, or excommunicated. Our Christian response to these people must be ministry and service after the manner of Jesus. That means that the very ones who are pushed down are the ones to be raised up so they achieve that sense of dignity and worth essential to the redeemed human condition, essential for every member of the body of Christ. Likewise, those who are excluded by society are the ones who must be included by the church. But the only church that can practice such a selfless ministry is one so secure in its salvation by Jesus Christ that it can confidently be a servant. The only church that can take on such a ministry is one that refuses to define itself in terms of secular competence and worldly achievements.[96]

The Johannine text about the washing of the disciples' feet must be complemented by the incident recounted earlier in John's Gospel where Jesus is shown having his feet anointed as a prelude to his self-giving service (Jn 12:18). In receiving that act of generosity from Mary, he rebukes those who want to stop her with a stern, "Leave her alone." Jesus models how to receive as well as how to give. At the Last Supper it is Peter's inability to receive that Jesus firmly challenges: "Unless I wash you, you have no share with me." Peter's image of God is so clearly defined that he cannot negotiate Jesus' movement from an all-powerful deity to a humble servant. His refusal reminds us of how powerful our God images can be. Once they are ingrained, they are capable of alienating us from the very God we are trying to imagine. It is in the reciprocity and mutuality of giving and receiving, so well exemplified by the life of Jesus, that true humanity and Christian community are born. Ministers today are sometimes tempted to think they must always be giving, and so they suffer from burnout because they never take time out to receive, to be rejuvenated, to be refreshed. Because they are not refreshed and refueled, they often end up having little to give to others. It is by both receiving and giving that we become eucharistic people.

It should be clear that the virtues that God seeks to instill in us through the celebration of the Eucharist are a willingness to acknowledge our utter dependence on God, a profound spirit of thanksgiving and praise for God's many gifts, and a willingness to share those gifts with others, especially the needy, the poor, and the marginalized.

Ordained Priesthood[97]

The language of priesthood is prominent in the Old Testament, but that language is radically transformed in the New Testament. In the latter Jesus is the only one who is actually identified as a priest—he is the great high priest who once and for all entered into the heavenly temple bringing not the blood of animals but his own precious blood, thus accomplishing forgiveness, sanctification, and transformation for all of God's people (Heb 9:11–14; 10:1–18). To be a disciple of Jesus Christ implies that one has been incorporated into his body through baptism; hence 1 Peter describes all believers as belonging to a "royal priesthood, a holy nation" (1 Pt 2:4–10). The existence of certain disciples as specially called followers of Jesus who exercised distinctive ministries is clearly attested to in the New Testament. There is no single pattern of church structure described in the New Testament, nor is there any common terminology to describe what exists. It is only with Ignatius of Antioch that the traditional threefold division of church office into the episcopate, the presbyterate, and the diaconate is laid out clearly.

Complex developments in the thought and practice of the medieval western church led to a situation whereby the priestly character of all the baptized in the church gave way to priestly character being restricted to those who were ordained. Originally, though there were various ministries in the church and a variety of charisms, all the baptized were basically equal in the eyes of God. The ordained were special servants of the community with the responsibility of leading the community, preaching the word of God, and presumably presiding at the celebration of the Eucharist. However, an emphasis on the cultic role of the ordained eventually came to distinguish their ministry. In the Middle Ages large numbers of men were ordained, especially in monastic communities, but their role was primarily to celebrate mass. Hence, there was a widespread loss of the centrality of preaching in the ministerial office. This sacral model of the priesthood should be linked to the strongly christological understanding involved in the phrase *in persona Christi,* which eventually led to the common perception of the ordained presbyter as *alter Christus.* In fact, all baptized Christians are *in persona Christi,* not only the ordained. This christological point of reference was almost exclusively liturgical and therefore much narrower than the understanding of the ordained in the early church and patristic period.

The medieval developments provoked strong reactions at the time of the Protestant Reformation. Martin Luther, for example, rejected a priestly or cultic interpretation of Christian ministry and gave priority to preaching. He strongly affirmed the priesthood of all the baptized. In 1563 the Council of Trent, primarily concerned with correcting abuses in the church, simply reiterated the traditional doctrinal positions of the Middle Ages and emphasized the priest's "power of consecrating and offering the true body and blood of the Lord and of forgiving and retaining sins."[98]

Vatican II took an original approach to the structure of the church by affirming the dignity of all the people of God through baptism. The distinctive identity and ministry of ordained priests and bishops should grow out of their basic baptismal dignity. The *Dogmatic Constitution on the Church* affirms the universal call to holiness (chap. 5), but it also clearly affirms the hierarchical constitution of the church (chap. 3). Unfortunately, the term *hierarchical* has regularly been identified with the image of the pyramid, with the ordained bishops and priests at the top of the pyramid and the lay people at the bottom. Of key significance here is that following the first chapter, "The Mystery of the Church," the second chapter deals explicitly with the dignity of all the people of God, including both the ordained and the laity. It is only in chapter 3 that the nature of the hierarchical dimension of the church is delineated.

Vatican II's decree on the ministry and life of presbyters, *Presbyterorum ordinis,* affirms that presbyters, like bishops, participate, although at a subordinate level, in the threefold office of Christ—priest, prophet, and king (or shepherd). Hence, their task is primarily pastoral, one of exercising leadership in the community. Special emphasis has been placed on preaching in all of its forms. The text stresses the necessity of effective collaboration between presbyters and bishops and also between presbyters and the people they serve. Parish and diocesan councils, as well as senates or councils of presbyters, are meant to facilitate a fresh understanding of ordained ministry.[99]

In the First Letter to the Corinthians (chaps. 12, 15), Paul emphasizes the giftedness of all the baptized, but in the letters to the Ephesians (1:22–23) and Colossians (1:18), the Pauline author distinguishes between the members of the body of Christ and Christ as Head of the body. Through ordination some of the baptized are related especially to Christ as Head of the Body. Hence Vatican II's *Decree on the Ministry and Life of Priests* speaks of the ordained as being *"in persona Christi capitis"* (in the person of Christ the Head) (no. 2). In 1938, Pope Pius XI remarked wryly, when speaking to a group of young priests from Canada, that "the church, the Mystical Body of Christ, has become a monstrosity. The head is very large, but the body is shrunken." He went on to say: "The only way that you can rebuild it [the body of Christ] is to mobilize the lay people. You must call upon the lay people to become, along with you, the witnesses of Christ."[100]

Certainly the ordained are especially related to Christ as Head of his body, the church, but we do well to remember that the head of the body is not the heart, the hand, or the foot. One of the primary functions of the head is to coordinate the activities of the body, to facilitate the implementation of the various gifts and charisms that are to be found throughout the body. It is in that sense that we ought to speak of the hierarchical dimension of the church.

The word *hierarchy* comes from two Greek words, *hieros* and *arche,* together meaning "holy order." Ordained ministers are responsible for dynamic order in the Christian community; they are to facilitate the implementation of the diverse gifts existing not only among the bishops and priests but also among lay men and women. In that way the body of the church will no longer be "shrunken" for all will function as witnesses of Christ. The ordained are meant to promote and facilitate good order and unity through their teaching, sanctifying, and governing roles. They are to be leaders of the community. Certainly in the early church it was men who showed that they had the gift of leadership who were ordained, and because they were leaders of the community, they presided at the community Eucharist.[101] It is a major responsibility of the ordained members of the church to lead God's people into the future, not simply into the past.

It is significant that, in discussing the ministry of the ordained, the *Decree on the Ministry and Life of Priests* asserts that "it is the first task [of presbyters] as co-workers of the bishops to preach the gospel of God to all" (chap. II, no. 4). This stands in marked contrast to the teaching of the Council of Trent, which emphasized the presbyter's power to consecrate the Eucharist and to forgive sins. The ordained have the responsibility to hear the word of God in their own hearts through prayer and holy reading and then to break that word open for others so that what they share might shed light on the complex lives of people today and lead them into deeper union not only with God but also with one another. One of the major complaints heard today about the preaching that people hear in their churches is that it is irrelevant and uninspiring; it has nothing to do with the complicated lives they are struggling to lead as Christians. It is felt that the ordained are often out of touch with the reality of ordinary people's lives.

One of the major stumbling blocks to effective presbyteral ministry in the church today is the presence of clericalism, which has been a sickness in the church for centuries.[102] The term *clericalism* designates a constellation of relationships, behavioral patterns, status symbols, and ideas in which bishops and priests live and function as ministers in the church. It is closely associated with a triumphal lifestyle. During the pontificates of John XXIII and Paul VI there was much talk about triumphalism in the church and the need for the church to adopt a simple but honest lifestyle in face of the growing awareness of the widespread poverty and destitution throughout the world. The triumphalism was and still is reflected in the very terms of address that people use in talking with clergy, especially the hierarchy: "Your Eminence," "Your Excellency," "Your Grace," "Your Lordship." People instinctively internalize the identity with which they are addressed.

The triumphalism existed among both bishops and priests, who often saw themselves as accountable to no one but the pope and God. It flourished among the ordained, especially among bishops who lived in palaces, but it was supported by the passive acquiescence and encouragement of lay people, who not only placed the clergy on a pedestal but also adulated their presence there. From their elevated status the ordained were able to load on lay men and women heavy moral burdens that they themselves did not at times carry with integrity.

Even though the various documents of the Second Vatican Council set out a theology whose intent was to dismantle a pyramidal understanding of the church with the ordained at the top and the lay people at the bottom, there are still very influential clerics in the Roman curia and in dioceses who long for the retrieval of a pre-conciliar church where there is little experience of collegiality and no accountability apart from that due to the papacy and ultimately to an unseen God.

In the years before Vatican II a clear identity was deeply ingrained in the ordained. They understood their clearly defined functions, enjoyed respect, and usually found great satisfaction in their ministry. Most Catholics relied on the strong authority of their priests because it gave them a sense of identity, cohesion, and clarity. But after the Second World War that began to change as more and more Catholics gained advanced academic degrees in universities and achieved positions of influence and a certain degree of affluence in society. A variety of social and cultural factors began to affect the cultic model of the priesthood. Today's large parishes in many cities and the shortage of clergy have forced some pastors into a more collaborative style of ministry. Furthermore, many Catholics no longer consider the parish the center of their social and spiritual lives but attach themselves to the new movements in the church or frequent monasteries and religious houses for their spiritual and liturgical nourishment. In increasing numbers lay people are coming to understand that they are invested with serious baptismal rights and responsibilities and so are co-responsible for the life of the church. As a result, they have begun to expect new ways of interacting with the ordained clergy. In large numbers they are receiving advanced degrees in theology, liturgical studies, and pastoral theology, even in canon law, and they are taking up important academic positions in prestigious universities. They often have better theological educations than their priests.

Fortunately, the cultic model of the ordained priesthood does not adequately represent the experience of many priests today. Many older priests have struggled very hard to assimilate both theologically and practically the teachings of Vatican II. Although conditions vary considerably from country to country, especially in the northern hemisphere, many seminarians and younger priests favor the cultic model of the priesthood and have adopted the traditional clerical lifestyle. They are often preoccupied with clerical dress—with cassocks, birettas, capes, lace surplices, amices, and clerical vests. They see themselves as part of a separate clerical caste and often resist the more collaborative approaches associated with the reforms of Vatican II. They generally espouse a very traditional classical theology, have few self-doubts, and see themselves quite separated from older priests who are more attuned to the pluralism of contemporary theology. Naturally, older priests who have struggled to work their way through the profound changes of the council often find it unsettling to be confronted with a new version of the style and approach to priesthood that they left behind. Younger traditionalists are not comfortable with priests who have tried to adapt their ministry to the needs of the modern world. In fact, they sometimes accuse older priests of being the cause of all the serious problems in the church, including the sexual abuse of minors.

There are major pastoral issues in the church today that often seem to be intractable. They are the cause of serious tensions and constitute a significant source of the morale problem among priests today. Priests, while continuing to engage in prayer, responsible study, and reading, should not withdraw into the isolation of their own ministries; they need an experience of community. They need to abstract themselves at least to some degree from those complex issues about which they can do nothing and concentrate on the many good things they are able to do. Reform and renewal flourish in many institutions of the church today. Never before in the history of the church have so many competent lay men and women been so actively involved in the life of the church. Priests, both young and old, who are committed to the teachings of Vatican II might well find that the tensions in the church will become more manageable if they strive to lead lives of deep prayer; celebrate well-prepared liturgies in which they preach homilies that relate to the concrete lives of their people; continue to visit the sick, feed the hungry, comfort the dying and their families; and share the joys and sorrows of their people. It is in that kind of ministry that the ordained are apt to find an existential identity and also experience deep personal satisfaction.

Perhaps the principal virtue that should characterize the life of ordained presbyters today is humility. They are called to participate in the humility of Christ, who "emptied himself, taking on the form of a servant" (Phil 2:7). Christ's life was one of service; he did not seek his own glory (Jn 8:50); he "came not to be served but to serve" (Mt 20:28).[103] Humility implies that the priest quietly acknowledges both his strengths and his weaknesses. He knows that his strengths are gifts from God for which he must be grateful. Acknowledging his weaknesses and his limitations, he knows that he cannot be independent and self-sufficient but needs to rely on the gifts of others. He confesses that some of his weaknesses are due to sin and sincerely seeks forgiveness both from God and from others whom he may have offended. If he is basically humble, other virtues are apt to follow. He will be open and available, approachable and friendly. He will have a vibrant faith, a buoyant hope, and compassionate love, especially for the sick, the elderly, children, the poor, the emotionally struggling and grieving. He will celebrate the Eucharist and other sacraments with reverence and joy because he is clearly a man of prayer, deeply rooted in the life of the Spirit.

Marriage

It is sad that many powerful forces today attempt to interpret marriage and family life as purely secular realities.[104] The Christian view is vastly different. The 1917 Code of Canon Law defines marriage as a contract and as a sacrament between a baptized man and a baptized woman (canon 1012). Vatican II's *Pastorial Constitution on the Church in the Modern World,* however, describes

Christian marriage as a conjugal covenant whereby spouses mutually give themselves and accept each other (no. 48). The word *covenant* is chosen because it is a strong biblical image rooted in the great covenant between God and God's people and the new covenant between Jesus and his people. In the 1983 Code of Canon Law, the legal word *contract* is replaced by *covenant* (canon 1055). Contracts are made for a period of time; covenants cannot be broken. In the Catholic approach marriage is thoroughly personalist. The imaging of marriage as covenant has been a traditionally Protestant approach, whereas the Catholic tradition has imaged it much more as a sacrament. The covenant emphasis stresses an abiding interpersonal relationship grounded in the abiding consent of the spouses, while the sacramental emphasis stresses a sacred bond that is initiated by the spouses but continues to exist until the death of one of the parties. When a man and woman marry in a Catholic celebration, they commit themselves to create and sustain a relationship of personal openness, mutual acceptance, honesty, and love. They also commit themselves to explore together the religious meaning of their life and to respond to their life together in Christian faith. In marriage a man and woman enter into a profound union in which their physical bodies are made one, but above all they enter into a personal union in which their whole persons are made one. The union of their bodies in sexual intercourse is meant to be a symbol of their deep personal union.

The Epistle to the Ephesians provides the scriptural foundation for living out the marriage covenant (Eph 5:21–25). The husband is head of the wife in the sense that he is to be like Christ, who gave his life for the church. The Christian way to exercise authority is to serve. Hence, a husband who wishes to be head of his wife in the way that Christ is head of the church will serve, giving himself. Christlike headship is not control, domination, or manipulation of another. The Christian husband is meant to be the servant of his wife.[105] The primary way in which the marriage covenant is sustained and nurtured is by mutual service.

The 1917 Code of Canon Law describes the primary purpose of marriage as the procreation and education of children. It does not stress emotional closeness, friendship, or the importance of a shared life. It is significant that before the twentieth century one rarely finds Christian love valued and stressed as a major component of marriage. Current theology and Roman Catholic teaching affirm the value of marital sexuality because it is an essential part of each spouse's identity; hence, couples will ordinarily be open to the procreation of new life. When new life appears, it is always the result of a cooperative act of God as creator and the human spouses as cooperators. What needs to be stressed is that marriage is personal, not simply biological. It is the personal union of the spouses that is procreative, not merely physical intercourse.

A spirituality of Christian marriage seeks to help couples understand how the power and presence of God in their relationship fosters community life and holiness. The God of Christians has been revealed as both personal and communal; hence, marital spirituality seeks to promote both the personal and communal aspects of the spouses and any family they might have. This spirituality is profoundly relational; it implies an openness and availability on the part of each party. Married couples manifest the existential possibility of community in diversity. The couples worship God whom they find in one another as well as in the children they might beget; they also find God in those outside the family, especially in those in need. Christian marriage is an important building block of the church and also secular society.

At a time when so many marriages end in separation and divorce, probably the primary virtue that married couples must practice is fidelity. It goes without saying that Christian spouses need to develop the various virtues that should characterize the life of adult Christians. It is usually romantic love that initially attracts a man and a woman to each other, but after marriage and intimate life together, they inevitably become aware of one another's weaknesses, including anger, jealousy, resentment, and impatience. These limitations need to be acknowledged but also forgiven. Common courtesies, like kindness, open communication, and mutual assistance, are essential in any successful marriage. Often these positive requirements for a successful relationship are simply taken for granted and so ignored. A successful marriage is hard work; so is the responsibility of rearing children, especially those who might suffer from developmental limitations. One of the goals of a Christian marriage is to facilitate what might be called psychic health so the spouses have the strength and the bravery to face day in and day out the challenges of family life as well as the crises that happen regularly in the world. Adults cannot help but inflict wounds on one another. Marriage can bring out the worst in individuals; however, it can also facilitate mature growth and responsible adulthood.

At a time when marriage celebrations are often extraordinarily expensive and when there is so much poverty and need in the world, Christian couples approaching marriage might strive for simplicity in their wedding and commit themselves to ongoing generosity to those in the larger community who suffer deprivation of any kind.

Reconciliation[106]

Reconciliation is a biblical expression involving God's invitation and our human response to continual conversion within the context of a community of faith. *Confession* and *sacrament of penance* have served at various periods in history as synonyms but have usually carried more restrictive meanings. The sacraments of Christian initiation celebrate the initial reconciliation of new Christians as they receive forgiveness for their sins and become members of the church and responsible for its mission. It is in that context that Vatican II's *Decree on the Life and Ministry of Priests* describes penance: "By baptism men and women are brought into the People of God. By the sacrament of penance sinners are reconciled to God and the church" (no. 5). In response to the Protestant Reformers, the Council of Trent describes the state of sinners after baptism in juridical language (DS 1671), but Vatican II's *Dogmatic Constitution on the Church* expresses Christian pardon and reconciliation in biblical terms: "Those who approach the sacrament of penance obtain pardon from the mercy of God for offences committed against him. They are at the same time reconciled with the church, which they have wounded by their sins, and which by charity, example, and prayer seeks their conversion" (no. 11).

Vatican II's *Constitution on the Sacred Liturgy* called for a renewal of the sacrament of penance (no. 71); consequently, a new rite was promulgated in 1973. It insists on the personal nature of sin but also acknowledges the ecclesial and social dimensions of both sin and conversion (Rite of Penance, no. 5). The rite includes provision for the proclamation of a biblical pericope, for prayerful communication between the priest and the penitent, for communal celebrations with individual confession and absolution, and, in certain restricted situations, celebration with general confession and general absolution. Since the rite has been implemented individual confession has declined steadily, but the celebration of communal penance and general absolution has grown in various places, despite episcopal and papal prohibition. The 1983 Code of Canon Law (canons 961–63) clearly restricted the situations in which general absolution can be given.

The sacrament of reconciliation has a long and noble history in the lives of many saints, but it has died in the lives of many people today. A sense of sin seems to have died in their lives. Often the blame for all that is wrong in the world is put on others—parents, teachers, pastors, government leaders, or society at large. Karl Menninger, the distinguished psychiatrist, was perceptive when he titled his book *Whatever Became of Sin?* Perhaps that is one of the reasons general absolution is popular in many places; it can take the focus off individual penitents and put it on the whole group. However, it must be noted that it is not easy to account for the demise of the sacrament of reconciliation in the lives of many people; there are undoubtedly many reasons.

Perhaps people feel that they have matured in many areas of their lives, but in regard to this sacrament they often experience their own immaturity. As they approached the sacrament at the age of six or seven, they probably had a "grocery list" of sins, with three of this, four of that, and six of the other thing. And at twenty-seven, forty-eight, perhaps seventy-five they are still thinking of a grocery list. They never seem to get at the roots of the evil in their lives; they sense to some extent the ill effects but have little insights into the causes and basic motives behind their actions.

Nevertheless, reconciliation is a sacrament that has brought much peace and consolation to many people, often because they have been blessed with confessors who were not only wise but were able to sacramentalize the love and forgiveness of the Lord for them. When they have taken time to look into their own hearts, they have discovered that they are a mysterious combination of strengths and weaknesses. When most people approach the sacrament, they seem to have negative self-images, and so they experience shame. It is curious how many people readily identify with the line in "Amazing Grace": "Who can save a wretch like me?" It might be helpful, then, for people to mention, first of all for their own hearing, the many gifts that God has graciously given them since their last celebration of the sacrament of reconciliation, gifts that they have been able to receive and use responsibly and for which they are deeply grateful. They need to express that gratitude and focus their lives in Jesus Christ, who is meant to be the center of every sacrament, including the sacrament of reconciliation. It is significant that the root meaning of the word *confession,* which comes from the Latin *confiteor,* means "to praise." The penitent offers praise for God's great goodness and then, against that positive background, articulates the many gifts that God has offered but which he or she has either refused or lived out irresponsibly. That articulation will not be depressing provided the penitents acknowledge that they cannot save themselves from all their alienation and self-centeredness, but that God in Jesus Christ and through the power of the Spirit can and does want to save them.

That assurance, that wonderful fact, should be mediated into the lives of penitents through the confessor. If they are fortunate, they will have a regular confessor who is a true soul friend—one who understands them, who serves as a memory bank for them over the years, and who loves them with a deep Christlike love. A true soul friend loves his penitents, supports them, challenges them, and holds them accountable; he knows how to raise their consciousness about the working of good and evil in their lives.

When we pray the Lord's Prayer, we pray that God will forgive us as we forgive one another. But forgiveness of others does not come easily. Many people tend to be judgmental, self-serving, and unforgiving, often trying to settle all serious grievances and differences through litigation and claims for monetary rewards. But unfortunately, when lawyers are involved, there is usually little chance for true reconciliation and consequently often little forgiveness. It is an eye for an eye and a tooth for a tooth. But forgiveness is the only door to true peace and happiness. It is a small, narrow door, one that cannot be entered unless one becomes humble. Forgiveness has little to do with human fairness, for life is often quite unfair and full of failures that often cannot be excused. When we forgive someone for a deliberate hurt, we recognize the hurt as such, but instead of striking back, we attempt to see beyond the hurt and make an effort to restore our relationship with the person responsible for the pain. Our forgiveness usually does not take away our pain; perhaps our forgiveness is not even acknowledged or accepted. However, our forgiveness prevents us from being sucked into the downward spiral of bitterness and resentment. It is ultimately the presence and power of a forgiving God in our hearts that makes sincere forgiveness possible.

The power of evil is a reality in the lives of all of us. We all need to be conscious of that, for we are never confirmed in righteousness. We do well to reflect often on the Last Supper discourse and the exchange between Jesus and Judas. Jesus knew that Judas was seeking to betray him, yet he invited Judas to dine with him. He continued to offer the gift of his forgiveness, his life, even in the face of refusal and rejection. The gospel reminds us that left to our own resources, we too are capable of betrayal. At the same time it reminds us that our God is always a God who lives for giving.

The primary virtues that should characterize the lives of those who celebrate the sacrament of reconciliation are humility and forgiveness on the part of the penitent, and wisdom and compassion on the part of the confessor.

Pastoral Care of the Sick: Rites of Anointing and Viaticum[107]

Suffering is a dominant theme running through the Gospels. Our faith is indeed tried and tested when serious pain or tragedy befalls us, when evil somehow seems to take over in our lives. In chapter 13 of Luke's Gospel, Jesus cites two tragic events: one an example of Pilate's cruelty as a representative of the Roman authorities (he mixed some of the Galileans' own blood with the blood of their animal sacrifices), and the other a construction accident in Jerusalem in which eighteen people were killed. In both instances bad things happened to good people. Even in Luke's Gospel the mystery of human suffering and tragedy remains very much a mystery. Jesus does not explain suffering, but he does shift the focus from others, whom we might blame, to ourselves. He rejects the notion that calamities come to people as payment for their sins, but he clearly affirms that we are all sinners and will perish if we do not repent. Jesus implies that we must not think that we are ever standing on firm ground. Life for Jesus' disciples is lived by faith, without any comfortable guarantees—except God's promises. Placing our faith in false securities is an attempt to live beyond faith in the Lord Jesus, who is our only ultimate security. With our faith in the Lord as our security, our question is then changed from "Where does suffering or tragedy come from?" to "Where does it lead?" Does it lead us to deeper faith in God, or does it lead us to a loss of hope and despair? Does it lead to a deeper personal prayer life?

Following the teaching in Matthew 25:34–40 the church has had the practice of visiting the sick as a corporal work of mercy. It has traditionally assisted, encouraged, and prayed with the sick and their families and friends, in fact, with all those who suffer. The sacrament of the anointing of the sick was recommended to the faithful in the Letter of James (5:13–15). In the Middle Ages the anointing became a sacrament primarily for the dying; hence, it came to be known as extreme unction. The Council of Trent, however, enlarged the understanding so that the anointing could be given to all who were sick. Vatican II's *Constitution on the Sacred Liturgy* emphasizes that the rite should more properly be called an anointing of the sick and stresses that it is not meant only for those who are at the point of death (no. 73). The council mandated specific reforms with regard to the sacrament of anointing and the order of the sacraments for the dying: penance, anointing, and Eucharist (no. 74). A new rite was promulgated in 1972 and was provisionally translated into English in 1974. In 1982, following extensive consultation, a final text was prepared by the International Commission on English in the Liturgy (ICEL). *Pastoral Care of the Sick: Rites of Anointing and Viaticum* was approved by Rome in 1983. The text makes a clear distinction between pastoral care of the sick and pastoral care of the dying. Prayer texts are provided for visiting the sick, sick children as well as adults. Adaptations are made when the rite takes place in a hospital and when a communal anointing is celebrated in a church. This latter practice was endorsed by the 1983 Code of Canon Law (canon 1002). The Eastern Orthodox and the Anglican communion, as well as various Protestant churches, also provide services for anointing the sick.

The evangelists frequently depict Jesus healing the sick as a sign of the presence of the reign of God. In the new Jerusalem there will be no more sickness or suffering. The ministry of healing, therefore, is an expression of the paschal mystery. Sickness disrupts the harmony that should exist in the human person; it fragments the integrity of the individual and disturbs relationships within the community. It is a manifestation of that evil from which the Word incarnate came to save us. Christian healing addresses all the dimensions of sickness. The church has a long history of sponsoring hospitals and hospices for both the physical and the spiritual care of the sick. Like the ministry of Jesus himself, pastoral care of the sick and dying is an invitation to conversion and to embrace the presence and power of God in one's life through Jesus Christ and in the Holy Spirit. Hence, there should be a desire not simply for physical healing but for healing on a deeper spiritual level. Consequently, Christian healing consists less in cure and more in conversion. It is a corporal work of mercy, embracing the whole human person, who is not only a person but also a member of a community.

Pastoral Care of the Sick states that the sacrament is reserved for the baptized whose health is seriously impaired by sickness or old age (no. 8). Then it clarifies that a sick person may be anointed before surgery whenever a serious illness is the reason for the surgery; that elderly people may be anointed if they have become notably weakened, even if they have no serious illness; that seriously ill children may be anointed if they have sufficient use of reason to be strengthened by the sacrament; and that seriously ill persons who have lost consciousness may be anointed if they probably would have asked for it were they in control of their faculties (nos. 10–12, 14).

Since the rites are primarily acts of public worship, a communal celebration is preferred over the semi-private forms that prevailed in the church for many years. Family members, caregivers, and friends are usually invited to take part in the celebration because they provide a community of support for the seriously ill person. The rites should normally include a proclamation of the word. The sacrament may be administered to seriously ill baptized non-Catholics as provided for by the 1983 Code of Canon Law (canon 844); the anointing may not be administered to persons who are not baptized. Only a priest may administer the sacrament.[108]

There are indeed cultural impediments to and opportunities for promoting the implementation of post–Vatican II healing rites at this time. The impediments arise from the contemporary outlook on illness and medicine, where people often perceive illness strictly in terms of biological causes and desires for instant cures, sometimes attributing almost magical powers and authority to the medical profession and medical technology. But opportunities emerge at a time when biomedicine has often left the issue of suffering to those who are responsible for pastoral care. Consequently, the liturgical rites are often an underutilized, if not in many places an ignored pastoral resource not only for the sick and dying people themselves but also for their loved ones and the professionals who care for and accompany them in their suffering.[109]

In addition to the celebration of the sacrament, sick persons may be blessed by oil that has been blessed by a priest or deacon using a special formula of blessing; this oil has not been blessed by the bishop at the chrism mass. In some religious institutes oil is blessed in honor of a particular saint and is used with prayer or devotions asking the intercession of the saint for persons who are ill. For example, the Servants of Mary make available oil blessed in honor of the thirteenth-century Servite friar St. Peregrine, the patron saint of those who suffer from cancer. Some Benedictine communities make available oil blessed in honor of St. Walburga.

The sacramental rites for the sick and the dying are meant, above all, to strengthen the faith of the recipient. The special virtues that are also strengthened by the rites are the virtue of longsuffering, hope, prayerfulness, and patience. On the part of caregivers, family, and friends of the sick or dying person, the special virtues that are needed are compassion and hope rooted in the conviction that God's will is often not our will and that God often brings good out of what seems to be evil.

OTHER LITURGICAL AND WORSHIP ISSUES

Since the Second Vatican Council numerous liturgical rites and documents have been issued by the Holy See. The rites have concerned the Liturgy of the Hours, religious profession, the blessing of an abbot and an abbess, the consecration of virgins, the dedication of a church and an altar, and the blessing of oils. Special documents have concerned the worship of the Eucharist, the veneration of Mary, liturgy and seminaries, and sacred music and the liturgy. However, it has probably been the Order of Christian Funerals, issued in 1989 as a revision, reorganization, and English translation of the *Ordo exsequiarium* that was promulgated in 1969, that has touched the lives of most English-speaking Catholics.[110] The rites, which contain a cohesive theology of death and Christian burial, have been of great pastoral benefit to ministers, both in preaching and in presiding. There are excellent pastoral notes as well as newly composed prayers to provide for situations not addressed in the Latin edition, such as prayer for the victims of suicide and on the occasion of the death of children. The rites are usually a great consolation to the bereaved relatives and friends of the deceased and inspire Christian hope and confidence in the future.

Undoubtedly, the most divisiveness among Roman Catholics has been created in this country by the English translation of the third edition of the Roman Missal. The issue has been further complicated by the depressing dismantling of ICEL and the Vatican takeover by the Congregation for Divine Worship of the rights and responsibilities originally granted to the national hierarchies associated with ICEL. Following Vatican II, ICEL proceeded very quickly to produce a translation of the Roman Missal, a task completed in 1972. All the eleven bishops' conferences who were full members of ICEL approved it, and the Holy See gave it the required confirmation *(recognitio)*. The translation was put together in haste, so over the years there was a growing awareness that a fresh and improved translation was needed. ICEL undertook the complicated and laborious task of preparing a revised translation of the Roman Missal in 1981 and continued that work until the translation was completed in 1993. The work was done in accord with an excellent document on the art of translation, generally known by its French title, *Comme le prévoit*, that had been approved by Pope Paul VI in 1969 and that encouraged a dynamic equivalence approach to translation rather than a literal approach. The new translation paid careful attention to a substantive fidelity to the Latin original, but attention was also paid to a fuller vocabulary with a more extensive use of adjectives and strong verbs as well as to speech stresses and the rhythm and cadence of the prayers. Careful attention was given to the requirements of proclamation—facility for those who would proclaim the texts and for those who would hear them.

ICEL issued regular progress reports to both the bishops associated with ICEL and the Roman congregation. Beginning in 1992 the episcopal conferences were requested to give their definitive canonical vote on each of the eight completed segments of the missal. Every one of the conferences voted to approve the ICEL version, usually by unanimous or near-unanimous votes. The English-speaking conferences of bishops therefore submitted their request to Rome for the congregation's confirmation in 1998 or 1999. After many years of hard work and the expenditure of much money on the part of ICEL and the various bishops' conferences, the Congregation for Divine Worship and the Discipline of the Sacraments refused to give the revised translation its confirmation. In a letter to the episcopal chair of ICEL the prefect of the congregation bitterly criticized the work of the ICEL staff and advisory committee. He forbade ICEL to provide any more original texts and ordered ICEL to cease all contacts "with bodies pertaining to non-Catholic ecclesial communities," demanded a reconfiguration of the office of the executive secretary, and required all ICEL employees to be on fixed-term contracts with any extensions being reserved to the congregation. All employees had to receive clearance from the congregation. As a result, ICEL was no longer subject to the bishops' conferences but directly to the Roman congregation.[111]

A new document on vernacular translation of liturgical texts, *Liturgiam Authenticam,* went into effect on 25 April 2001. The Latin edition of the Roman Missal (third edition) was promulgated on 20 April 2000; the literal translation was officially published in English and went into effect in the dioceses of the United States on 27 November 2011. Those who have praised the new translation claim that it is poetic, close to the Latin, and prayerful. Others have wondered how recognized poets in this country would evaluate the poetic quality of the text. There is no doubt that it is close to the Latin original, but a slavish following of Latin syntax and word order and the inclusion of Latinisms like *consubstantial* and *incarnate* certainly do not yield an American English text of high quality. The theology is very convoluted, so that the text is difficult to proclaim intelligently, and it is often hard for ordinary Catholics in the pews to comprehend the meaning. Already Latinists have pointed out mistranslations that yield a faulty theology. Consequently, an official list of corrections will eventually have to be made. The use of noninclusive language is simply incomprehensible for most Americans in the twenty-first century. Pastors worked very hard to help their parishioners master the new responses. When confronted with incomprehensible language, the parishioners are apt simply to abstract from the rite. Unfortunately, that will result in a further distance between the ordained clergy and lay men and women in the liturgical assembly. In time, I suspect that some presiders will begin to make appropriate changes in the text, but unfortunately some presiders who do not have adequate proficiency in creating poetic language or in effective proclamation will simply "tinker" with the text, thus substituting one troublesome text with another. At the basis of this sad saga is the apparent need for the Roman curia to exercise power and control over the bishops and dioceses of the world.

In spite of the liturgical divisions in the Roman Catholic Church, many parish communities continue to flourish. Pastors and ecclesial ministers concentrate on the pastoral responses they are able to make; they do not waste time and energy trying to change what cannot be changed at the present time. The situation has quite accurately been described as one of ecclesial and liturgical impasse.

ECCLESIAL AND LITURGICAL IMPASSE
AND THE RESPONSE OF LAMENT

There are many people in the church these days who sometimes wonder whether the Lord Jesus, as the master of the church, has gone on a very long journey and left the church as an orphan in charge of rascals. There are even days when they are tempted to think that the Lord might not ever return from his journey. Indeed, as we have noted, there is polarization, suspicion, investigations, silencing, anger, alienation, and cynicism, not only in the Roman Catholic Church but also in the various mainline Protestant churches, where divisions are often over sexual matters, the ordination of women to the priesthood and episcopacy, and gay marriages and ordinations.

Many western countries are rocked by economic meltdown caused by years of wrongdoing and greed; the earth itself is menaced with global warming and ecological distress; the major religions of the world are plagued with extremism and distrust that ignite wars and terrorism; and many people throughout the world are abused by violence, slavery, and serious deprivation. In secular societies people throughout the world register their strong antipathies toward governments, the economy, and politicians. Often the dialogue across the divisions in our world is hostile; among Christians it is un-Christian. The sad fact is that many of the baptized have left the Catholic Church and are searching for ultimate meaning elsewhere, often in no religion at all. Hence there is much serious reflection these days on what has been called ecclesial and liturgical impasse.[112]

In his communications with different countries Pope Benedict regularly asserts that there is no need to reform the structures of the church; there is need only for personal conversion. He has made extraordinary efforts to reconcile the disciples of Archbishop Lefebvre with the Catholic Church, even though they have rejected important teachings of Vatican II and the *Ordo missae* approved by Pope Paul VI. Pope Benedict has made an amazing effort to promote the reconciliation with the Roman Catholic Church of those Anglicans and Episcopalians who have disagreed with their churches' policies on ordaining women to the priesthood and episcopacy. He has been a very strong advocate for the regular celebration of the 1962 rite for the Tridentine mass.

Of course, all of us as Christians are called through baptism to ongoing conversion all life long, but there is the strong conviction among many Roman Catholics that various church structures are currently obstructing justice in our church—in some dioceses obstructing the right of lay people to receive communion from the cup whenever the Eucharist is celebrated, the right of women and young girls to minister as acolytes in the celebration of the Eucharist, the right to assemble on church property to discuss policies and practices in the church. They highlight the failure of the Roman curia and local bishops to implement the lay bill of rights so carefully set out in the current Code of Canon Law (canons 208–231). Authority figures often claim that they are simply following approved church laws, but we all know that what is legal is not necessarily moral or ethical.

In the post–Vatican II church various groups, often dominated by lay men and women, have drawn attention to the church's failure to implement policies and practices of collegiality, subsidiarity, and collaboration that could readily be implemented by parish and diocesan pastoral councils, episcopal conferences, diocesan synods, and synods of bishops. Groups, such as Voice of the Faithful, Call to Action, and We Are Church, have developed both in Europe and North American countries. But often their voices have been ignored by church authority figures. Consequently, priests have taken over the initiative for reform in recent years, especially in Austria, Ireland, and Belgium. The parties involved are not revolutionaries; they are deeply committed Christians who love the church and God's people. They are concerned about the future of the church and the church's refusal to even discuss major pastoral issues, such as the diminishing number of priests, priestly celibacy, the ordination of married men to the priesthood, the ordination of women to the diaconate, the ministry to divorced and remarried Catholics, the place of gay and lesbian Catholics in the church, and the appointment of bishops and the role of the lay community in that process.

Luke's Gospel gives the impression that Jesus must have experienced impasse during his life. We read of Jesus traveling to Jerusalem, quite clearly aware that suffering and death awaited him there. On his way he regularly encountered the Pharisees and the lawyers whom he rightly accused of hypocrisy and of laying unjust burdens on the people, burdens that they themselves did not carry. He certainly thought that the religious leaders of his time had lost their way. The laments of the people of God inspired Jesus to teach in order to reveal a new vision of life, to touch so as to heal, to cast out demonic powers in order to free captives, to share table fellowship with outcasts and sinners, and by doing so to manifest God's loving compassion. Jesus' whole life was a response to the laments of those who were overwhelmed by destructive powers.

In our own time we might do well to recover the lament psalms in the Bible, which can forcefully express our grief, even our anger; however, they address that pain to the very ears of God, trusting that God always hears our prayers but answers us in God's good time and in God's good ways. It is only when we entrust the future to God that we find peace.

Walter Brueggemann, the prolific biblical scholar, has written very movingly and pastorally about the lament psalms in several widely read publications.[113] He describes our life of Christian faith as a movement with God from the state of being serenely and comfortably oriented to a situation where we are painfully disoriented, and finally to a state where we are surprisingly reoriented. However, that final state might not be realized as we would wish or even in our own lifetime. Brueggemann's categories allow us to speak of passages in our lives, stages of growth and transformation, even of identity crises. They can also be readily applied to whole communities of faith, even to the church at large.

Being securely oriented is a situation in which we experience equilibrium. We all yearn for that state, but we must admit that it usually does not inspire great prayer and passionate song. It consists in being well settled, convinced that life makes sense and that God abides in the heavens but fortunately is not intervening dramatically in our own lives and communities here and now. In the Bible this mood is infrequent in the psalms; it is reflected in Psalms 37 and 145. In order to pray them sincerely, it seems we must locate them either in our own lives or in the lives of others. Clearly, most of the psalms do not emerge out of situations of equilibrium; rather, people are often driven to poignant prayer during experiences of dislocation, of being overwhelmed and nearly destroyed. At such times they hope that God will radically change the situation so that peace and tranquility will return.

There is much murmuring, complaint, and anger expressed on television and the Internet, in personal conversations and newspapers and magazines, but those sentiments are usually not addressed to God. That is precisely what happens in the lament psalms. It is important that when we pray these psalms, we attend to the simple eloquence, the strong passion, and the bold ways in which the voice of the psalmist turns to God. Numerous psalms fit into this category, including Psalms 22, 25, 31, 40, and 90. They describe situations that drive people to the edge of their humanness, that seem beyond their capacity to cope. The speech of these psalms is abrasive; it stresses that life is not one of well-being but rather is a churning, disruptive experience of dislocation.

Most of us know about chaos, disorder, and disorientation in our personal life. It may be the result of a failed marriage, loss of a job, a financial reversal, a medical diagnosis. Frequently, it is the result of loneliness or the sense of being unloved or rejected. Or it may be anxiety over what is happening on the national and international levels—over which we have little or no control. As we have seen, these days it is often the result of frustration over developments in our church, perhaps especially over what is happening in the liturgy. We discover that there is a direct link between our own experience of dislocation and the laments of the Israelites. It is our work in praying the lament psalms to bring our disorientation into dialogue with the biblical texts. In surprising ways we discover that the psalms come to life because of our personal experience and even more surprising that our experience is somehow dealt with by the psalms. Just as we often feel relief when we are able to talk about our problems with a friend, so we are relieved when we address our grief and anxiety to God. And God responds in God's good time and in God's good way.

We might not experience immediate reorientation, but in mysterious ways our hope is sustained and strengthened. Hope is a mysterious virtue, often difficult to explain. In the Epistle to the Romans, Paul affirms that "hope is not hope if its object is seen. . . . And hoping for what we cannot see means awaiting it with patient endurance" (Rom 8:24–25). We probably know from experience that very large institutions, like the church, change very slowly. Nevertheless, God empowers us to trust that we will not lose our baptismal heritage; we will indeed continue to rise from the dead.

It is inspiring to see that so many people who are deeply committed to the reform and renewal of the church, including its liturgy, communicate a sense of confidence in life. Though they are critical of church authority figures who fail to lead the church into the future but attempt to lead it into the dead past, they nevertheless work very hard to achieve clear goals that are in the realm of the possible. They work to eliminate racism and sexism in their families, workplaces, and parishes; they defend the rights of the aged and unborn, the homeless, and immigrants. They seek to elect political leaders who will enforce laws that seek to eradicate injustice and that promote peace. They are admirable Christians. They are not about to leave the church.

Nevertheless, in the midst of the depressing experience of impasse in our church today, many Catholics ask why they should keep coming back to celebrate the Eucharist each week. Sadly, many have quietly drifted away from the Eucharist and away from the church. But others keep coming back because our faith is not simply in the human structures of an often sinful institution; our faith is in God and in God's Son Jesus Christ and in the power of God's Holy Spirit present in our hearts and our communities of faith. We keep coming back to the Eucharist because it is there that we are embraced and loved in an intimate way by God in Jesus Christ and through the Holy Spirit. Deep in our hearts we know that it is through the experience of being loved that we are healed, that we are transformed, that we in turn continue to be strengthened so we struggle to become just, peaceful, and loving people in our often turbulent world and in our often troubled church.

Conclusion

The disciples called by the Lord Jesus were meant to live in union with one another under the sign of mutual love and forgiveness. In a world where solidarity and love seem to be not only difficult but often unattainable, the church of Jesus Christ is meant to demonstrate the possibility of both unity and love. Beyond all national boundaries, as well as cultural, racial, ethnic, religious, and social distinctions, in face of mutual distrust, contempt, and hostile antagonisms, the church is meant to be a positive force building up relationships manifested by trust, concord, collaboration, and readiness to serve others. The church is meant to be a symbol of God's reign, God's kingdom, where the love of God flows freely so that divisions can be healed and peace prevails.

But the simple fact is that the church of Jesus Christ is a divided church—divided since the Reformation but divided today by major differences concerning doctrines and moral behavior, especially in the areas of human sexuality and worship. It is not only the Roman Catholic Church that is highly polarized; the various mainline Protestant denominations are also seriously divided. Instead of being positive manifestations of God's love for all people, the various Christian churches are manifestations of internecine warfare.

When Pope John XXIII announced in 1958 that he was calling an ecumenical council, he made it quite clear that he wanted the forthcoming council to be different from those that had preceded it. He wanted a council that promoted the Christian faith in a positive light, a council that would be deeply pastoral in the sense that it would seek to proclaim the Christian gospel in terms that would not seek to correct what were thought to be doctrinal errors but would bring the church into dialogue with contemporary cultures and would constitute a new Pentecost. Above all, he wanted a council that would promote the mercy that characterized the life and ministry of the Lord Jesus. He hoped that the council would communicate a vision of a new beginning, one that would highlight the active role of the Holy Spirit in the church and in the world. He clearly saw the church as the body of Christ, not simply concerned with legalities and doctrines, but a force that would play an important role in ending colonialism and affirming the rights of workers, one that would engage in serious discussions with other Christian groups and even with other world religions. His hopes were reflected in his creation of the Secretariat for Christian Unity in 1960. He hoped that the council would develop in the disciples of Jesus Christ a new mindset, one that would be open to fresh insights derived from the Bible and from the rich tradition of the church. He did not want a new statement of the old orthodoxies. His hopes were also reflected in the invitation extended to contemporary theologians to play an important role in the council deliberations by functioning as expert advisers to the council fathers. He included Yves Congar, Karl Rahner, Henri de Lubac, and others who had come under a dark cloud because their theology had been attacked by Pope Pius XII's encyclical *Humani generis* in 1951.

Although the various documents of Vatican II were approved, usually by overwhelming majority votes, there was a strong vocal minority among the council fathers deeply disturbed by the developments in the council; they never ceased to maintain their serious reservations. In fact, in order to maintain peace, their minority views were often included in various compromises and obliquely indicated in footnotes to the approved texts. It is well known that this minority view has been kept alive up to the present, especially by members of the various Roman dicasteries. In recent years two polarized views have developed concerning the proper interpretation of the council. One view maintains that the council was a new event, a new experience; hence the texts should be interpreted in that light. The other view holds that the council must be interpreted not in terms of discontinuity but in terms of its continuity with preceding councils; therefore, it is the texts themselves that are important, not the cultural and ecclesial context in which they were formulated.

The ongoing debate over the interpretation of Vatican II was reflected in the very sharp criticisms of and attacks aimed at the Alberigo School of Church History at Bologna and its five-volume history of the council produced by distinguished theologians. The polarization was also expressed in the mean-spirited attacks against the distinguished liturgical scholars who worked tirelessly on behalf of ICEL during the 1970s, 1980s, and 1990s, until ICEL was reorganized and the former consultants and administrators dismissed in the closing years of the twentieth century.[1]

When John XXIII called the council, the Roman Catholic Church was monolithic; its sure identity was expressed in its commitment to Latin, to Gregorian chant and European polyphony, to a strong hierarchical structure, and to a clear statement of its orthodox theology. In the years since the council, however, the church has become a multicultural church. The numerical center of Christianity has shifted from the northern hemisphere to the southern, with the majority of Christians now living in Latin America, Africa, and Asia. The identity of the church has been deeply affected by the migration of peoples, major changes in the modes of communication, the effects of globalization, and the relations of the Christian churches with other world religions, especially with Islam. These developments have affected not only the Roman Catholic Church but also the mainline Protestant churches.

Problems in all the Christian churches are frequently discussed and judged on the Internet. Commentators on various blogs and on television networks often seek to persuade others of the correctness of their own convictions and the wrongness or heresy implied in the positions of others. These discussions are frequently uncivilized, vitriolic, and unchristian. It is for that reason that this book has proposed a serious retrieval of virtue morality. All Christians presume that they are disciples of Jesus Christ, but in practice they often forget that they are responsible for observing the basic commandment of Jesus, namely, to love one another and to manifest that love in forgiveness, tolerance, understanding, patience, and the other virtues that are implied in the teaching of Jesus, who was the Good Samaritan, the Good Shepherd, the forgiving Father of the prodigal son, the one who welcomed sinners and lived to lay down his life for others.

As this book has shown, virtue morality dominated the New Testament and the Christian tradition down to and including the writings of Thomas Aquinas. Moral teaching turned toward a preoccupation with moral laws with William of Ockham and the development of nominalism. Serious literature concerning virtue morality has reappeared in recent decades. It is not meant to substitute for consequentialism or ontologism but to form the Christian foundation on which all doctrinal and moral decisions are made either by individual Christians or by the various institutionalized Christian churches. We desperately need to manifest to the world that disciples of Jesus Christ belong to a church that is, above all, characterized by the practice of virtue. If the celebration of the Christian liturgy is in a special way the primary cultural expression of the church, then we need a sacramental theology and practice that demonstrate to the world that Christian ministers are not the "owners" of the sacraments but stewards of Jesus Christ. The sacraments are gifts that Christ has given to his church; they are meant to manifest forgiveness and compassion for all Christians who are indeed sinners in need of God's loving mercy.

A major concern of the churches that call themselves Christian is the attainment of union, which is not the result of human effort but is the work of the Spirit of God. Christians nevertheless must labor in every way possible to consolidate this union by promoting justice, freedom, and peace. Paul's letter to the Ephesians makes this point especially clear. The Christian experience of God's love for all people in Christ and through the power of the Spirit must be translated into clear witness to unity. The letter enumerates the grounds on which this unity must be based: "There is one body and one Spirit, just as there is one hope held out in God's call to you; one Lord, one faith, one baptism, one God and Father of all, who is over all and through all and in all" (4:4–5). The letter further enumerates the characteristics that should permeate the lives of Christians: humility, simplicity, patience, bearing one another's burdens, love, and peace (Eph 4:2–3). Christ's friendship with his apostles provides a pattern for our dealing with one another, namely, interest in one another shown in limitless service and trust that opens up the channels of communication. These are the virtues that all Christians and all Christian churches should practice in their relations with one another.

Notes

INTRODUCTION

1. Letter of His Holiness John Paul II to Rev. George V. Coyne, director of the Vatican Observatory, 1 June 1988, as cited by Jack Mahoney in *Christianity in Evolution: An Exploration* (Washington DC: Georgetown University Press, 2011), 1.

2. See, for example, Gabriel Daly, "Creation and Original Sin," in *Commentary on the Catechism of the Catholic Church,* ed. Michael J. Walsh (London: Geoffrey Chapman, 1994), 82–111; Ilia Delio, *Christ in Evolution* (Maryknoll, NY: Orbis Books, 2008); John Haught, *God after Darwin: A Theology of Evolution,* 2nd ed. (Boulder, CO: Westview Press, 2008); idem, *Making Sense of Evolution: Darwin, God, and the Drama of Life* (Louisville, KY: Westminster John Knox Press, 2010); R. Kevin Seasoltz, *God's Gift Giving: In Christ and through the Spirit* (New York: Continuum, 2007).

1. CULTURES AND THE CONTEMPORARY WORLD

1. Gerald Arbuckle, *Culture, Inculturation, and Theologians* (Collegeville, MN: Liturgical Press, 2010), xxii.

2. Bernard Lonergan, *Method in Theology* (New York: Herder and Herder, 1972), xi.

3. Clifford Geertz, *The Interpretation of Cultures* (New York: Basic Books, 1973), 89.

4. Roger M. Keesing, "Anthropology as Interpretive Quest," *Current Anthropology* 28:2 (1987): 161–62.

5. Roger M. Keesing, "Theories of Culture Revisited," *Assessing Cultural Anthropology*, ed. Robert Borofsky (New York: McGraw-Hill, 1994), 309–10.

6. See Robert J. Schreiter, *The New Catholicity: Theology between the Global and the Local* (Maryknoll, NY: Orbis Books, 1997), 26–27; Margaret Mary Kelleher, "Liturgy, Culture, and the Challenge of Catholicity," *Worship* 84 (March 2010): 98–120.

7. Kathryn Tanner, *Theories of Culture: A New Agenda for Theology* (Minneapolis: Fortress Press, 1997).

8. Arbuckle, *Culture, Inculturation, and Theologians*, 22.

9. Ibid., 30.

10. Ibid., 64.

11. Ibid., 35.

12. Catherine Bell, *Ritual Theory, Ritual Practice* (New York: Oxford University Press, 1992), esp. 94–117.

13. See Nathan Mitchell, "Culture," *Liturgy Digest* 3:2 (1996): 94–107.

14. See Michael Paul Gallagher, *Clashing Symbols: An Introduction to Faith and Culture,* new and rev. ed. (New York: Paulist Press, 2003), 9–26.

15. See Aidan Kavanagh, *On Liturgical Theology* (Collegeville, MN: Liturgical Press, 1992); David Fagerberg, *Theologia Prima: What Is Liturgical Theology* (Collegeville, MN: Liturgical Press, 2003).

16. Ansgar Chupungco, *What, Then, Is Liturgy?* (Collegeville, MN: Liturgical Press, 2010), 179.

17. See Christopher Dawson, *Religion and Culture* (London: Sheed and Ward, 1948); idem, *Religion and the Rise of Western Culture* (New York: Sheed and Ward, 1950).

18. R. Kevin Seasoltz, "Anthropology and Liturgical Theology: Searching for a Compatible Methodology," in *Liturgy and Human Passage*, Concilium 112, ed. David Power and Luis Maldonado (New York: Seabury Press/A Crossroad Book, 1979), 3–13.

19. Christopher Dawson, *Progress and Religion: An Historical Enquiry* (New York: Sheed and Ward, 1933); idem, *The Making of Europe: An Introduction to the History of European Unity* (New York: Sheed and Ward, 1937); idem, *The Historic Reality of Christian Culture* (New York: Harper, 1960).

20. See Peter C. Phan, "Contemporary Theology and Inculturation in the United States," in *The Multicultural Church: A New Landscape in U.S. Theologies*, ed. William Cenkner (New York: Paulist Press, 1996), 109–30.

21. The material in this section of the chapter is a revised version of material that was originally published in R. Kevin Seasoltz, *A Sense of the Sacred: Theological Foundations of Christian Architecture and Art* (New York: Continuum, 2005), 4–34.

22. Monica Sjoo and Barbara Mor, *The Great Cosmic Mother: Rediscovering the Religion of the Earth* (San Francisco: Harper and Row, 1987).

23. See John O'Donohue, *Anam Cara: A Book of Celtic Wisdom* (New York: HarperCollins Publishers, 1997).

24. See Thomas Kane, *The Dancing Church in Africa* (New York: Paulist Press, 1992). This filmmaker has also created films about dancing in Polynesia and Melanesia as well as dances coming out of the Mexican, Spanish, and Native American traditions.

25. For an account of Pope Gregory the Great and his relations with the English, especially through Augustine of Canterbury, see Bede, *A History of the English Church and People*, trans. Leo Sherley-Price (Baltimore: Penguin, 1955); see also Jeffery Richards, *Consul of God: The Life and Times of Gregory the Great* (London: Routlege and Kegan Paul, 1980).

26. Ian Bradley, *Celtic Christianity: Making Myths and Chasing Dreams* (New York: St. Martin's Press, 1999), 9; see also Mary Condren, *The Serpent and the Goddess: Women, Religion, and Power in Celtic Ireland* (San Francisco: Harper and Row, 1989).

27. Virgil Elizondo, *Guadalupe: Mother of the New Creation* (Maryknoll, NY: Orbis Books, 1997).

28. See Rosemary Crumlin, ed., *Aboriginal Art and Spirituality* (North Blackburn, Australia: Collins and Dove, 1991).

29. See M. Shawn Copeland, "African American Catholics and Black Theology: Interpretation," in *African-American Catholics and Black Theology: An Interpretation*, ed. Gayraud Wilmore (Durham, NC: Duke University Press, 1989), 228–48.

30. John S. Mbiti, *African Religions and Philosophy* (New York: Praeger Press, 1969), 228–49; Aylward Shorter, *African Christian Spirituality* (Maryknoll, NY: Orbis Books, 1980); Cyprian Davis, "Black Spirituality," *U.S. Catholic Historian* 8 (1989): 39–46.

31. See Andrew Wilson-Dickson, *The Story of Christian Music from Gregorian Chant to Black Gospel* (Minneapolis: Fortress Press, 1992), 191–206.

32. See Vincent L. Wimbush, "Reading Texts through Worlds, Worlds through Texts," in *Black and Catholic: The Challenge and Gift of Black Folk: Contributions of African American Experience and Thought to Catholic Theology*, ed. Jamie T. Phelps, 2nd ed. (Milwaukee, WI: Marquette University Press, 2002), 59–73.

33. Anton Wessels, *Images of Jesus: How Jesus Is Perceived and Portrayed in Non-European Cultures* (Grand Rapids, MI: Eerdmans, 1990), 110–11. See also Robert Brain, "African Art," in *A History of Art*, ed. Lawrence Gowing (Ann Arbor, MI: Borders Press, 2002), 504–20.

34. See Robert Brancatelli, "*Religiosidad Popular* as a Form of Liturgical Catechesis," *Worship* 77 (May 2003), 210–24.

35. See Timothy Matovina, "Liturgy, Popular Rites and Popular Spirituality," in *Mestizo Worship: A Pastoral Approach to Liturgical Ministry*, ed. Virgil Elizondo and Timothy Matovina (Collegeville, MN: Liturgical Press, 1998), 81–91.

36. Donna Pierce, "Portraits of Faith," in *Mexican Churches,* ed. Eliot Porter and Ellen Auerback (Albuquerque: University of New Mexico Press, 1987), 13–20. See also Jonathan Yorba, *Arte Latino: Treasures from the Smithsonian American Art Museum* (New York: Watson-Guptill Publications, 2001).

37. Richard E. Nisbett, *The Geography of Thought: How Asians and Westerners Think Differently . . . and Why* (New York: Free Press, 2003), xiii.

38. See *Images of Asia*, special issue, *The Way* 39 (April 1999).

39. See for example, *Journeys at the Margin: Toward an Autobiographical Theology in American-Asian Perspective,* ed. Peter C. Phan and Jung Young Lee (Collegeville, MN: Liturgical Press, 1999), xvi–xvii.

40. See, for example, Chung Hyun Kyung, *Struggle to Be the Sun Again: Introducing Asian Women's Theology* (Maryknoll, NY: Orbis Books, 1979).

41. See, for example, Jung Young Lee, *A Theology of Change: A Christian Concept of God in Eastern Perspective* (Maryknoll, NY: Orbis Books, 1979).

42. See Aloysius Pieris, *An Asian Theology of Liberation* (Maryknoll, NY: Orbis Books, 1988), 51–58.

43. See, for example, *Christ for All People: Celebrating a World of Art*, ed. Ron O'Grady (Maryknoll, NY: Orbis Books, 2001), 74–75.

44. See Stephen Happel, "Classical Culture and the Nature of Worship," *Heythrop Journal* 21 (July 1980): 294. Happel's treatment of classical versus empirical culture is derived from Bernard Lonergan's works, especially *Method in Theology*, xi–xiii, 301–2, 305–19, and *Doctrinal Pluralism* (Milwaukee, WI: Marquette University Press, 1971), 1–91.

45. See Robert Marks, *The Origin of the Modern World* (Lanham, MD: Rowman and Littlefield, 2002).

46. See Nathan D. Mitchell, "The Amen Corner: 'Liturgical Language: Building a Better Mousetrap,'" *Worship* 77 (May 2003): 250–63; Keith Pecklers, *Dynamic Equivalence* (Collegeville, MN: Liturgical Press, 2003); idem, *The Ethos of the Roman Rite: On the Reception and Implementation of the New Missal* (Collegeville, MN: Liturgical Press, 2009), 1–22.

47. Walter J. Ong has explored at length the complex question of orality and literacy. See, for example, *Interface of the Word: Studies on the Evolution of Consciousness and Culture* (Ithaca, NY: Cornell University Press, 1977); *Orality and Literacy* (New York: Methuen, 1982); *The Presence of the Word: Some Prolegomena for Cultural and Religious History* (New Haven, CT: Yale University Press, 1967). See also Dennis L. Weeks and Jane Hoogestraat, eds., *Time, Memory, and the Verbal Arts: Essays on the Thought of Walter Ong* (Selingrove, PA: Susquehanna University Press, 1989).

48. Philip A. Egan, *Philosophy and Catholic Theology: A Primer* (Collegeville, MN: Liturgical Press, 2009), 129–32.

49. See *Romanesque Architecture, Sculpture, Painting*, ed. Rolf Toman, photographs by Achim Bednorz (Cologne: Könemann, 1997); Bernhard Schütz, *Great Cathedrals* (New York: Harry N. Abrams, 2002); Michael Camille, *Gothic Art: Glorious Visions* (New York: Harry N. Abrams, 1996).

50. Gerald A. Arbuckle, *Violence, Society, and the Church: A Cultural Approach* (Collegeville, MN: Liturgical Press, 2004), 57–58.

51. Yves Congar, "Christianity as Faith and as Culture," *East Asian Pastoral Review* 18 (1981): 310.

52. Richard W. Southern, *Western Society and the Church in the Middle Ages* (Harmondsworth, UK: Penguin, 1970), 212.

53. Theodor Klauser, *A Short History of the Western Liturgy* (Oxford: Oxford University Press, 1979), 95.

54. Ibid., 118–19.

55. Thomas Bokenkotter, *A Concise History of the Catholic Church* (New York: Doubleday, 1990), 231.

56. Arbuckle, *Violence, Society, and the Church*, 73.

57. See Louis Dupré, *Passage to Modernity: An Essay in the Hermeneutics of Nature and Culture* (New Haven, CT: Yale University Press, 1993).

58. Paul Vignaux, *Nominalism au XIVe Siècle* (Montreal: Inst. d'études médiévales, 1948); Marilyn McCord Adams, *William Ockham*, Publications in Medieval Studies 26, 2 vols. (Notre Dame, IN: University of Notre Dame Press, 1987). Ockham asserted that the universal is not found at all in reality but only in the human mind. His form of nominalism withdrew all the data of faith from the realm of reason and thus paved the way for the disintegration of Scholasticism.

59. See Donald K. McKim, *The Cambridge Companion to Martin Luther* (New York: Cambridge University Press, 2003).

60. Galileo Galilei, *The Achievement of Galileo*, ed. with notes by James Brophy and Henry Paolucci (Smyrna: Bagehot Council, 2003); *The Cambridge*

Companion to Galileo, ed. Peter Machamer (New York: Cambridge University Press, 1998).

61. Peter Matheson, *The Imaginative World of the Reformation* (Edinburgh: T and T Clark, 2000), 26–27.

62. See Alister McGrath, *In the Beginning: The Story of the King James Bible and How It Changed a Nation, a Language, and a Culture* (New York: Doubleday, 2001), 5–23.

63. See Colin Gunton, *Enlightenment and Alienation: An Essay toward a Trinitarian Theology* (Eugene, OR: Wipf and Stock, 2006).

64. Herbert Marcuse, *One-dimensional Man* (Boston: Beacon Press, 1966).

65. Arbuckle, *Violence, Society, and the Church*, 120.

66. See Frank C. Senn, "'Worship Alive': An Analysis and Critique of 'Alternative Worship Services,'" *Worship* 69 (1995): 194–224.

67. Arbuckle, *Violence, Society, and the Church*, 123–24.

68. John M. Huels, *The Pastoral Companion: A Canon Law Handbook for Catholic Ministry*, 4th ed. (Montreal: Wilson and Lafleur, 2009), 2.

69. See, for example, Richard Dawkins, *The God Delusion* (New York: Bantam Books, 2006); Sam Harris, *The End of Religion: Religion, Terror, and the Future of Reason* (New York: W. W. Norton and Company, 2004). For Christian responses to recent atheism, see Tina Beattie, *The New Atheists: The Twilight of Reason and the Wars on Religion* (Maryknoll, NY: Orbis Books, 2008); Michael Novak, *No One Sees God: The Dark Night of Atheists and Believers* (New York: Random House, 2008).

70. See Stanley Grenz, *A Primer on Postmodernism* (Grand Rapids, MI: Eerdmans, 1996); Perry Anderson, *The Origins of Postmodernity* (London: Verso, 1998); Paul Lakeland, *Postmodernity: Christian Identity in a Fragmented Age* (Minneapolis: Fortress Press, 1997).

71. See Peter Phan, "Liturgy in a Postmodern World: Unity in Diversity in the Postmodern Age," in *Liturgy in a Postmodern World*, ed. Keith Pecklers (New York: Continuum, 2003), 56.

72. James L. Heft, "Distinctively Catholic: Keeping the Faith in Higher Education," *Commonweal* (26 March 2010), 9.

73. Graham Ward, "Postmodernism," *The Oxford Companion to Christian Thought* (New York: Oxford University Press, 2000), 551.

74. Robert Venturi, *Complexity and Contradiction in Architecture* (New York: Museum of Modern Art, 1966). See also idem, *Learning from Las Vagas: The Forgotten Symbolism of Architectural Form* (Cambridge: MIT Press, 1977).

75. Eleanor Heartney, *Postmodernism* (London: Tate, 2001).

76. Charles A. Jencks, *The Language of Post-Modern Architecture* (London: Academy Editions, 1984).

77. Patrick Nuttgens, *Architecture* (London: Mitchell Beazley International Ltd., 1992), 183–90; Heinrich Klotz, *History of Post-Modern Architecture* (Cambridge: MIT Press, 1998).

78. Phan, "Liturgy in a Postmodern World," 57.

79. Christopher Butler, *Postmodernism* (New York: Oxford University Press, 2002), 62–66.

80. Artists working in this mode include Roger Brown, Charles Burns, Leonard Koscianski, and Ed Pashke.

81. See David Boje, "What Is Critical Postmodern Theory," available online; Leonard Koscianski, "What Is Critical Postmodern Art?" available online.

82. See Antonin Artaud, "The Theater of Cruelty: Second Manifesto," in *The Theater and Its Double*, trans. Victor Dorti (London: Calder and Boyers, 1970), 81–87.

83. Phan, "Liturgy in a Postmodern World," 58–59.

84. Grenz, *A Primer on Postmodernism*, 15.

85. See Jean-François Lyotard, *The Postmodern Condition*, trans. Geoff Bennington and Brian Massumi (Manchester, UK: Manchester University Press, 1986).

86. Egan, *Philosophy and Catholic Theology*, 119. See also Walter Lowe, "Postmodern Theology," in *The Oxford Handbook of Systematic Theology*, ed. John Webster, Kathryn Tanner, and Iain Torrance (New York: Oxford University Press, 2007), 622–28.

87. Ibid., 120.

88. Philip Sheldrake, "Postmodernity," in *The New Westminster Dictionary of Christian Spirituality,* ed. Philip Sheldrake (Louisville, KY: Westminster John Knox Press, 2005), 498.

89. Arbuckle, *Violence, Society, and the Church*, 100–104.

90. See Will Kymlcka, *Multicultural Citizenship: A Liberal Theory of Minority Rights* (Oxford: Clarendon, 1995).

91. Arbuckle, *Violence, Society, and the Church*, 188.

92. Ibid.

93. See Hannah Arendt, *Crises of the Republic* (New York: Harcourt, Brace, 1972), 177.

2. CURRENT TRENDS AND THE CHURCH

1. Manfried B. Steger, *Globalization* (New York: Oxford University Press, 2009), 8. For an introduction to the topic see also James H. Mittelman, *The Globalization Syndrome* (Princeton, NJ: Princeton University Press, 2000); Malcolm Waters, *Globalization*, 2nd ed. (London: Routledge, 2001); Jan Aart Scholte, *Globalization*, 2nd ed. (London: Palgrave Macmillan, 2005); David Held and Anthony McGrew, *Globalization/Anti-Globalization*, 2nd ed. (Cambridge, UK: Polity, 2007).

2. Steger, *Globalization*, 10–12.

3. Ibid., 15.

4. Ibid., 43.

5. See, for example, Jonathan Perraton, *Global Transformation* (Berkeley: Stanford University Press, 1999); Martin Wolf, *Why Globalization Works* (New Haven, CT: Yale University Press, 2005); Heikki Patomaki, *The Political Economy of Global Security* (London: Routledge, 2007).

6. Steger, *Globalization*, 58–65.

7. Ibid., 67–70.

8. Ibid., 73–75.

9. Ibid., 75–77.

10. Abigail Frymann, "Mobile Continent," *The Tablet* (16 January 2010), 4.

11. Steger, *Globalization*, 79–80.

12. Ibid., 81.

13. Ibid., 98–113.

14. Ibid., 113.

15. Robert J. C. Young, *Postcolonialism* (New York: Oxford University Press, 2003), 129–30, 133.

16. Ibid., 134.

17. Steger, *Globalization*, 115–21.

18. Young, *Postcolonialism*, 134–35.

19. Ibid.

20. Ibid., 136.

21. See Olivier Roy, *Globalized Islam: The Search for the New Ummah* (New York: Columbia University Press, 2006); Fawaz A. Gerges, *The Far Enemy: Why Jihad Went Global* (New York: Cambridge University Press, 2005).

22. Steger, *Globalization*, 121–28.

23. Ibid.

24. Luke Timothy Johnson, "Dry Bones: Why Religion Can't Live without Mysticism," *Commonweal* (26 February 2010), 13.

25. John A. Coleman and William F. Ryan, eds., *Globalization and Catholic Social Thought* (Maryknoll, NY: Orbis Books, 2005). See also Pontifical Council for Justice and Peace, *Compendium of the Social Doctrine of the Church* (Washington DC: United States Conference of Catholic Bishops, 2004); Eoin G. Cassidy, ed., *The Common Good in an Unequal World: Reflections on the Compendium of the Social Doctrine of the Church* (Dublin: Veritas, 2007); Kenneth R. Himes, "Globalization with a Human Face: Catholic Social Teaching and Globalization," *Theological Studies* 69 (June 2008): 269–89; Daniel McDonald, ed., *Catholic Social Teaching in Global Perspective* (Maryknoll, NY: Orbis Books, 2010).

26. John L. Allen, *The Future Church: How Ten Trends Are Revolutionizing the Catholic Church* (New York: Doubleday,♥ 2009), 262.

27. Ibid.

28. Ibid., 262–63.

29. Gustavo Gutiérrez, *A Theology of Liberation* (Maryknoll, NY: Orbis Books, 1973).

30. Allen, *The Future Church*, 264–65.

31. Ibid., 265.

32. Ibid., 266.

33. Ibid., 269–97.

34. See William T. Cavanaugh, "Migrant, Tourist, Pilgrim, Monk: Mobility and Identity in a Global Age," *Theological Studies* 69 (June 2009): 340–56.

35. See, for example, Stephen Castles and Mark Miller, *The Age of Migration: International Population Movements in the Modern World*, 3rd ed. (New York: Macmillan, 2003); Robin Cohen, *The Cambridge Survey of World Migration* (New York: Cambridge University Press, 1995).

36. Khalid Koser, *International Migration* (New York: Oxford University Press, 2007), 10–11.

37. Ibid., 11.

38. Ibid., 12.

39. See Bill Jordan and Frank Duvell, *Irregular Migration: The Dilemmas of Transnational Mobility* (London: Edward Elgar, 2003).

40. Koser, *International Migration*, 70–89.

41. Ibid., 97–104.

42. See, for example, S. George Philander, *Encyclopedia of Global Warming and Climate Change*, 3 vols. (Los Angeles: Sage, 2008); Mark Lynes, *Six Degrees: Our Future on a Hotter Planet* (Washington DC: National Geographic, 2008); Jared Diamond, *Collapse: How Societies Choose to Fail or Succeed* (New York: Penguin, 2005); Franz Broswimmer, *Ecocide* (London: Pluto Press, 2002); Richard W. Miller, ed., *God, Creation, and Climate Change* (Maryknoll, NY: Orbis Books, 2010).

43. Steger, *Globalization*, 86–87.

44. Ibid., 87–88.

45. Ibid.

46. Ibid., 91.

47. Ibid., 93.

48. Lynn White Jr., "The Historical Roots of Our Ecological Crisis," *Science* 155 (10 March 1967): 1203–7.

49. See, for example, Woodene Koenig-Bricker, *Ten Commandments for the Environment* (Notre Dame, IN: Ave Maria Press, 2009).

50. Allen, *The Future Church*, 309–10.

51. See Robert Cummings Neville, "Confucianism and Christianity," in *The New Westminster Dictionary of Christian Spirituality*, ed. Philip Sheldrake (Louisville, KY: Westminster John Knox Press, 2005), 206–8; John H. Berthrong, *Transformation of the Confucian Way* (Boulder, CO: Westview Press, 1998); Herbert Fingarette, *Confucius: The Secular as Sacred* (New York: Harper and Row, 1972); Tu Weiming, *Humanity and Self-Cultivation: Essays in Confucian Thought* (Berkeley, CA: Asian Humanities Press, 1979); Yao Xinzhong, *An Introduction to Confucianism* (New York: Cambridge University Press, 2000); Xinzhong Yao and Yanxia Zhao, *Chinese Religion: A Contextual Approach* (New York: Continuum, 2010).

52. See Francis X. Clooney, "Hinduism and Christianity," in Sheldrake, *The New Westminster Dictionary of Christian Spirituality*, 336–38; A. L. Basham, *A Cultural History of India* (New York: Oxford University Press, 1999); Swami Bhaskarananda, *The Essentials of Hinduism: A Comprehensive Overview of the World's Oldest Religion* (Seattle: Viveka Press, 1994); Gavin Flood, ed., *Blackwell Companion to Hinduism* (Oxford: Blackwell Publishing, 2003); K. Klostermaier, *A Survey of Hinduism*, 3rd ed. (New York: State University of New York, 2007); A. Michaels, *Hinduism: Past and Present*, 5th ed. (Princeton, NJ: Princeton University Press, 2004); Stephen Jacobs, *Hinduism Today* (New York: Continuum, 2010).

53. See John P. Keenan, "Buddhism and Christianity," and Michael Barnes, "Zen and Christianity," in Sheldrake, *The New Westminster Dictionary of Christian Spirituality,* 158–60 and 655–57; Ruben L. Habito and John P. Keenan, *Living Zen, Loving God* (Boston: Wisdom, 2004); Donald W. Mitchell and James Wiseman, *The Gethsemane Encounter: A Dialogue on the Spiritual Life by Buddhist and Christian*

Monastics (New York: Continuum, 1999); Anil Goonewardene, *Buddhayana: Living Buddhism* (New York: Continuum, 2010).

54. See Andrew Wingate, "Islam and Christianity," in Sheldrake, *The New Westminster Dictionary of Christian Spirituality*, 376–79; John Esposito, *Oxford History of Islam* (New York: Oxford University Press, 2006); F. E. Peters, *Islam: A Guide for Jews and Christians* (Princeton, NJ: Princeton University Press, 2003).

55. See Johnson, "Dry Bones: Why Religion Can't Live without Mysticism," 11–14.

56. Philip Jenkins, *The Next Christendom: The Coming of Global Christianity*, rev. and exp. ed. (New York: Oxford University Press, 2007); *The New Faces of Christianity: Believing the Bible in the Global South* (New York: Oxford University Press, 2006); *God's Continent: Christianity, Islam, and Europe's Religious Crisis* (New York: Oxford University Press, 2007). Lamin Sanneh, a naturalized U.S. citizen from Gambia, a convert to Roman Catholicism, and currently professor of history and world Christianity at Yale University, has also published a number of highly respected books that concentrate on the Christianity in the southern hemisphere. They include *Whose Religion Is Christianity?* (Grand Rapids, MI: Eerdmans, 2003); *The Changing Face of Christianity: Africa, the West, and the Word*, co-edited with Joel A. Carpenter (New York: Oxford University Press, 2005); and *Disciples of All Nations: Pillars of World Christianity* (New York: Oxford University Press, 2008).

57. Jenkins, "Preface," *The Next Christendom*, xii.

58. Jenkins, *The Next Christendom*, 1–6.

59. Ibid., 7–8.

60. Ibid., 28–29.

61. Ibid., 12–14.

62. Ibid., 16–17.

63. Ibid., 25.

64. Ibid., 69–71.

65. See Allan Anderson, *An Introduction to Pentecostalism* (New York: Cambridge University Press, 2004); Harvey Cox, *Fire from Heaven: The Rise of Pentecostal Spirituality and the Reshaping of Religion in the Twenty-first Century* (New York: Addison-Wesley/Perseus Books, 1994).

66. Jenkins, *The Next Christendom*, 73.

67. Allen, *The Future Church*, 382–83.

68. John W. O'Malley et al., *Vatican II: Did Anything Happen?* (New York: Continuum, 2007); John W. O'Malley et al., *What Happened at Vatican II* (Cambridge: Harvard University Press, 2008).

69. See Joseph Komonchak, "Vatican II as an Event," in O'Malley et al., *Vatican II: Did Anything Happen?* 29.

70. John O'Malley, "Vatican II: Did Anything Happen?" in O'Malley et al., *Vatican II: Did Anything Happen?*, 53.

71. See James Corkery, *Joseph Ratzinger's Theological Ideas: Wise Cautions and Legitimate Hopes* (Dublin: Dominican Publications, 2009); Thomas P. Rausch, *Pope Benedict XVI: An Introduction to His Theological Vision* (New York: Paulist Press, 2009).

72. Allen, *The Future Church*, 433–35.

3. THE BIBLE AND CHRISTIAN MORAL LIFE

1. Pontifical Biblical Commission, *The Bible and Morality: Biblical Roots of Christian Conduct* (Vatican City: Libreria Editrice Vaticana, 2008).

2. Donald Senior, "A Guide for the Perplexed: The Bible as Moral Teacher," *Commonweal* (26 February 2010), 9.

3. Pontifical Biblical Commission, *The Bible and Morality*, 11–12. See Henry Wansbrough, "The Bible and Morality: Biblical Roots of Christian Conduct," *Scripture Bulletin* 40 (January 2010): 91; James T. Bretzke, "How Can Ethics Be Christian?: What the Pontifical Biblical Commission Might Offer in Response," *The Bible Today* 48 (July/August 2010): 209–14.

4. Ibid., 12–13.

5. Ibid., 14–15.

6. Ibid., 17–127. See also Wansbrough, "The Bible and Morality," 92–95; Senior, "A Guide for the Perplexed," 9.

7. Wansbrough maintains that there are actually five criteria, followed by a method of applying the criteria (Wansbrough, "The Bible and Morality," 95).

8. Pontifical Biblical Commission, *The Bible and Morality*, 145–52; Wansbrough, "The Bible and Morality," 95; Senior, "A Guide for the Perplexed," 10.

9. Pontifical Biblical Commission, *The Bible and Morality,* 152–62; Wansbrough, "The Bible and Morality, 95; Senior, "A Guide for the Perplexed," 10.

10. Pontifical Biblical Commission, *The Bible and Morality,* 162–73; Wansbrough, "The Bible and Morality, 95; Senior, "A Guide for the Perplexed," 10.

11. Pontifical Biblical Commission, *The Bible and Morality,* 174–89; Wansbrough, "The Bible and Morality, 96; Senior, "A Guide for the Perplexed," 10.

12. Pontifical Biblical Commission, *The Bible and Morality,* 190–207; Wansbrough, "The Bible and Morality, 96; Senior, "A Guide for the Perplexed," 10.

13. Pontifical Biblical Commission, *The Bible and Morality,* 222–27; Wansbrough, "The Bible and Morality, 97; Senior, "A Guide for the Perplexed," 10.

14. Pontifical Biblical Commission, *The Bible and Morality,* 18–19. See Bruce C. Birch et al., *Theological Introduction to the Old Testament*, 2nd ed. (Nashville, TN: Abingdon, 2005), 35–46; Claus Westermann, *Elements of Old Testament Theology*, trans. Douglas W. Scott (Atlanta: John Knox Press, 1982), 85–102.

15. Pontifical Biblical Commission, *The Bible and Morality,* 22–23.

16. Robert J. Schreiter, "Creation: Pastoral-Liturgical Tradition," in *The Collegeville Pastoral Dictionary of Biblical Theology*, ed. Carroll Stuhlmueller (Collegeville, MN: Liturgical Press, 1996), 191.

17. Ibid., 192.

18. Demetrius Dumm, *Flowers in the Desert: A Spirituality of the Bible* (New York: Paulist Press, 1987), 5; Kyle D. Fedler, *Exploring Christian Ethics: Biblical Foundations for Morality* (Louisville, KY: Westminster John Knox Press, 2006), 89–94.

19. Dumm, *Flowers in the Desert*, 6.

20. Ibid., 6–7.

21. Ibid., 8–9.

22. Ibid., 9–10.

23. Ibid., 10–12.

24. Ibid., 12–13; see also Fedler, *Exploring Christian Ethics*, 94–116. The Ten Commandments are given in two books of the Bible: Exodus 20:1–17 and Deuteronomy 6:4–21. In this discussion the listing in Exodus is followed.

25. Dumm, *Flowers in the Desert,* 12–14.

26. Ibid., 14–16.

27. Ibid., 16–17.

28. Ibid., 18.

29. Walter Brueggemann, *The Prophetic Imagination* (Philadelphia: Fortress Press, 1978), 13. See also Douglas Hall, *Lighten Our Darkness* (Philadelphia: Westminster Press, 1976).

30. Irene Nowell, "Prophet/Prophecy," in *The Collegeville Pastoral Dictionary of Biblical Theology*, ed. Carroll Stuhlmueller (Collegeville, MN: Liturgical Press, 1996), 784–85. See also Adrian Hastings, "Prophecy," in *The Oxford Companion to Christian Thought*, ed. Adrian Hastings et al. (Oxford: Oxford University Press, 2000), 568–70.

31. Nowell, "Prophet/Prophecy," 785.

32. Hugh S. Pyper, "Wisdom," in *The Oxford Companion to Christian Thought*, ed. Adrian Hastings et al. (Oxford: Oxford University Press, 2000), 752.

33. See Mary E. Mills, *Biblical Morality: Moral Perspectives in Old Testament Narratives* (Burlington, VT: Ashgate, 2001), 217–39.

34. Ibid. See also Roland E. Murphy, "Wisdom," in Stuhlmueller et al., *The Collegeville Pastoral Dictionary of Biblical Theology*, 1081–82.

35. Daniel J. Harrington and James F. Keenan, *Jesus and Virtue Ethics: Building Bridges between New Testament Studies and Moral Theology* (Lanham, MD: Rowman and Littlefield Publishers, 2002), 35–45. See also Bruce Chilton, *The Kingdom of God in the Teaching of Jesus* (Philadelphia: Fortress Press, 1984); John Fuellenbach, *The Kingdom of God: The Message of Jesus Today* (Maryknoll, NY: Orbis Books, 1995).

36. Harrington and Keenan, *Jesus and Virtue Ethics*, 49–58. See also Dietrich Bonhoeffer, *The Cost of Discipleship* (New York: Macmillan, 1958); Klaus Demmer, *Shaping the Moral Life: An Introduction to Moral Theology* (Washington DC: Georgetown University Press, 2000); Georg Fischer and Martin Hasitschka, *The Call of the Disciple: The Bible on Following Christ* (New York: Paulist Press, 1999); Richard Longenecker, ed., *Patterns of Discipleship in the New Testament* (Grand Rapids, MI: Eerdmans, 1996).

37. See 1 Cor 4:15–16; Phil 3:17. See also Daniel Harrington and James Keenan, *Paul and Virtue Ethics: Building Bridges between the New Testament Studies and Moral Theology* (Lanham, MD: Rowman and Littlefield, 2010).

38. Harrington and Keenan, *Jesus and Virtue Ethics*, 69–71.

39. Fedler, *Exploring Christian Ethics*, 191–92. See also Rudolf Schnackenburg, *The Moral Teaching of the New Testament* (New York: Herder and Herder, 1965), 261–306; Russell Pregeant, *Knowing Truth, Doing Good: Engaging New Testament Ethics* (Minneapolis: Fortress Press, 2008), 216–99.

40. Ibid., 192.

41. Ibid., 192–93.

42. Servais Pinckaers, *The Sources of Christian Ethics*, trans. Sr. Mary Thomas Noble (Washington DC: Catholic University Press, 1995), 110.

43. Ibid., 111.

44. Ibid.

45. Ibid., 114.

46. Ibid., 115.

47. Ibid., 115–16.

48. Ibid., 117.

49. Ibid., 122–23.

50. Ibid., 127.

51. Ibid., 130.

52. Ibid., 132–33.

53. Ibid., 133.

54. Ibid., 137–38. See also Simon Tugwell, *The Beatitudes: Soundings in Christian Tradition* (Springfield, IL: Templegate Publications, 1980); Dale Allison, *The Sermon on the Mount: Inspiring the Moral Imagination* (Minneapolis: Fortress Press, 1999); Hans Betz, *The Sermon on the Mount* (Minneapolis: Fortress Press, 1995); Jan Lambrecht, *The Sermon on the Mount: Proclamation and Exhortation* (Wilmington, DE: Michael Glazier, 1985).

55. Ibid., 137–38.

56. Harrington and Keenan, *Jesus and Virtue Ethics*, 61.

57. Daniel J. Harrington, *The Gospel of Matthew,* Sacra Pagina 1 (Collegeville, MN: Liturgical Press, 1991). See also C. Bauman, *The Sermon on the Mount: The Modern Quest for Its Meaning* (Macon, GA: Mercer University Press, 1985); Pinches Lapide, *The Sermon on the Mount: Utopia or Program for Action?* (Maryknoll, NY: Orbis Books, 1986); G. Strecker, *The Sermon on the Mount: An Exegetical Commentary* (Nashville, TN: Abingdon, 1988); W. F. Albright and C. S. Mann, *Matthew*, The Anchor Bible (Garden City, NY: Doubleday, 1971).

58. Brendan Byrne, *Lifting the Burden: Reading Matthew's Gospel in the Church Today* (Collegeville, MN: Liturgical Press, 2004), 55.

59. Ibid.

60. Ibid., 55–56.

61. Ibid., 56–57.

62. Harrington and Keenan, *Jesus and Virtue Ethics*, 61–66.

63. Ibid., 72.

64. Ibid., 73.

65. Brendan Byrne, *The Hospitality of God: A Reading of Luke's Gospel* (Collegeville, MN: Liturgical Press, 2000), 64–65. See also Joseph Fitzmyer, *The Gospel according to Luke,* The Anchor Bible (Garden City: Doubleday, 1981); C. H. Talbert, *Reading Luke: A Literary and Theological Commentary on the Third Gospel* (New York: Crossroad, 1989); Luke Timothy Johnson, *The Gospel of Luke,* Sacra Pagina (Collegeville, MN: Liturgical Press, 1991), 105–12.

66. Byrne, *The Hospitality of God*, 65.

67. Ibid.

68. Ibid., 65–66.

69. Ibid., 66.

70. Ibid., 66–67.

71. Ibid., 67.

72. Ibid., 68.

73. Ibid.

74. Carroll Stuhlmueller, *Biblical Meditations for Advent and the Christmas Season* (New York: Paulist Press, 1980), 110.

75. See Francis J. Moloney, *The Gospel of John*, Sacra Pagina 4 (Collegeville, MN: Liturgical Press, 1998), 1–23; Scott M. Lewis, *The Gospel according to John and the Johannine Letters*, New Collegeville Bible Commentary 4 (Collegeville, MN: Liturgical Press, 2005), 5–6; Raymond E. Brown, *The Gospel according to John I–XII*, Anchor Bible 29 (New York: Doubleday, 1966); idem, *The Gospel according to John XIII–XXI*, Anchor Bible 29A (New York: Doubleday, 1970).

76. Lewis, *The Gospel according to John and the Johannine Letters*, 6.

77. Jerome Kodell, *The Eucharist in the New Testament* (Collegeville, MN: Liturgical Press, 1988), 118–19; Eugene LaVerdiere, *The Eucharist in the New Testament and the Early Church* (Collegeville, MN: Liturgical Press, 1996), 112–13.

78. Lewis, *The Gospel according to John and the Johannine Letters*, 74–75.

79. Ibid., 77–78.

80. See Raymond E. Brown, *The Community of the Beloved Disciple: The Life, Loves, and Hates of an Individual Church in New Testament Times* (New York: Paulist Press, 1979).

81. Lewis, *The Gospel according to John and the Johannine Letters*, 108–9.

4. MORAL THEOLOGY AND ETHICS: A HISTORICAL SURVEY

1. Three important texts on the history of moral theology are (1) Giuseppe Angelini and Ambrogio Valsecchi, *Disegno storico della teologia morale* (Bologna: Edizione Dehoniane, 1972); (2) John Mahoney, *The Making of Moral Theology: A Study of the Roman Catholic Tradition* (New York: Oxford University Press, 1987); and (3) Renzo Gerardi, *Storia della morale: Interpretazioni teologiche del'esperienza Cristiana* (Bologna: Edizione Dehoniane, 2003). Mahoney's book begins with a treatment of Augustine and the penitentials.

2. Servais Pinckaers, *The Sources of Christian Ethics*, trans. Mary Thomas Noble, 3rd ed. (Washington DC: Catholic University of America Press, 1995), 195–96. See also idem, *Morality: The Catholic View* (South Bend, IN: St. Augustine's Press, 2001); Bernard Häring, *The Law of Christ*, vol. 1, trans. Edwin Kaiser (Westminster, MD: The Newman Press, 1961), 3–5.

3. F. X. Murphy, "Moral Theology, History of to 700," in *The New Catholic Encyclopedia*, 2nd ed., vol. 9 (Farmington Hills, MI: The Gale Group, 2003), 859.

4. Ibid., 860.

5. Pinckaers, *The Sources of Christian Ethics*, 196.

6. Hubertus van de Sandt and David Flusser, *The Didache: Its Jewish Sources and Its Place in Early Judaism and Christianity* (Assen, Netherlands: Royal van Gorcum, 2002).

7. Pinckaers, *The Sources of Christian Ethics*, 197–98.

8. Ibid., 198.

9. Daniel J. Harrington and James F. Keenan, *Jesus and Virtue Ethics: Building Bridges between New Testament Studies and Moral Theology* (Lanham, MD: Rowman and Littlefield Publishers, 2002), 2.

10. Ibid.

11. Pinckaers, *The Sources of Christian Ethics*, 202.

12. Raymond G. Helmich, *Living Catholic Faith in a Contentious Age* (New York: Continuum, 2010), 94.

13. Pinckaers, *The Sources of Christian Ethics*, 203–4.

14. Contemporary exegesis of that pericope has moved far beyond the patristic interpretation. See Francis Moloney, *A Life of Promise: Poverty, Chastity, Obedience* (Wilmington, DE: Michael Glazier, 1984), 103–8.

15. Pinckaers, *The Sources of Christian Ethics*, 206–7.

16. Harrington and Keenan, *Jesus and Virtue Ethics*, 3.

17. Louis Vereecke, "Moral Theology, History of (700 to Vatican Council I)," in *The New Catholic Encyclopedia,* 861. See also idem, *Guillaume d'Ockham a Saint Alphonse de Liguori* (Rome: Collegium S. Alfonsi de Urbe, 1986).

18. Ibid. See also Harrington and Keenan, *Jesus and Virtue Ethics*, 4.

19. Pinckaers, *The Sources of Christian Ethics*, 217–18.

20. Harrington and Keenan, *Jesus and Virtue Ethics*, 4.

21. Pinckaers, *The Sources of Christian Ethics*, 219.

22. Ibid., 221–22.

23. Ibid., 226–27.

24. Ibid., 228.

25. Ibid., 236.

26. Harrington and Keenan, *Jesus and Virtue Ethics*, 4–5.

27. Vereecke, "Moral Theology, History of (700 to Vatican Council I)," 862. See also M. H. Carr, *Realists and Nominalists* (Oxford: Oxford University Press, 1946).

28. Pinckaers, *The Sources of Christian Ethics*, 251, 254.

29. Ibid., 254–55.

30. Ibid., 256.

31. Francis de Sales, *Introduction to the Devout Life* (New York: Harper, 1960).

32. Pinckaers, *The Sources of Christian Ethics*, 256.

33. Ibid., 257.

34. Ibid.

35. Harrington and Keenan, *Jesus and Virtue Ethics*, 5.

36. Pinckaers, *The Sources of Christian Ethics*, 258–59.

37. Ibid., 259.

38. Ibid., 260.

39. Ibid., 261–62.

40. Ibid., 264.

41. Ibid., 273.

42. Vereeke, "Moral Theology, History of (700 to Vatican Council I)," 863.

43. Pinckaers, *The Sources of Christian Ethics*, 279.

44. Harrington and Keenan, *Jesus and Virtue Ethics*, 6.

45. Pinckaers, *The Sources of Christian Ethics*, 280.

46. Ibid., 282.

47. See Louis Bouyer, *The Spirit and Forms of Protestantism* (Cleveland: World, 1964).

48. Pinckaers, *The Sources of Christian Ethics*, 282–83.

49. Ibid., 283–84.

50. Ibid., 284.

51. Ibid., 288.

52. Ibid., 289.

53. Ibid., 290.

54. Bernard Häring, *The Law of Christ*, vol. 1, trans. Edwin G. Kaiser (Westminster, MD: The Newman Press, 1961), 20–21.

55. Ibid., 23–24.

56. Ibid., 25.

57. Ibid., 26.

58. James F. Keenan, *A History of Catholic Moral Theology in the Twentieth Century: From Confessing Sins to Liberating Consciences* (New York: Continuum, 2010), 9.

59. Ibid., 10–18.

60. Henry Davis, *Moral and Pastoral Theology: A Summary* (New York: Sheed and Ward, 1952).

61. Keenan, *A History of Catholic Moral Theology in the Twentieth Century*, 18–25.

62. Ibid., 25–29.

63. Ibid.

64. Ibid., 30.

65. Ibid., 35.

66. Ibid., 37.

67. Ibid., 36–41.

68. Jack Mahoney, *Christianity in Evolution: An Exploration* (Washington DC: Georgetown University Press, 2011), 117.

69. Ibid., 41.

70. Fritz Tillmann, *The Master Calls: A Handbook of Morals for the Layman*, trans. Gregory J. Roetger (Baltimore: Helicon Press, 1960).

71. Keenan, *A History of Catholic Moral Theology in the Twentieth Century*, 61–62.

72. Ibid., 60–69.

73. Gerard Gilleman, *The Primacy of Charity in Moral Theology* (Westminster, MD: Newman Press, 1964).

74. Émile Mersch, *Le Corps mystique du Christ: Études de théologie historique* (Brussels: Desclée de Brouwer, 1936); idem, *Morale corps mystique* (Paris: Desclée de Brouwer, 1937); idem, *La Théologie du corps mystique,* 2 vols. (Paris: Desclée de Brouwer, 1944).

75. Keenan, *A History of Catholic Moral Theology in the Twentieth Century*, 70.

76. Ibid., 73–74.

77. See Kathleen A. Cahalan, *Formed in the Image of Christ: The Sacramental-Moral Theology of Bernard Häring, C.Ss.R.* (Collegeville, MN: Liturgical Press, 2004), 4–6.

78. Bernard Häring, *Das Gesetz Christi*, 3 vols. (Freiburg: Verlag Wewel, 1954); in English, *The Law of Christ* (Westminster, MD: The Newman Press, 1961, 1963, 1966).

79. Keenan, *A History of Catholic Moral Theology in the Twentieth Century*, 90–91.

80. Ibid., 93–94. See also Cahalan, *Formed in the Image of Christ*, 93–203.

81. Keenan, *A History of Catholic Moral Theology in the Twentieth Century*, 93–94. See also Vincent J. Miller, *Consuming Religion: Christian Faith and Practice in a Consumer Culture* (New York: Continuum, 2008); William C. Mattison III, *Introducing Moral Theology: True Happiness and the Virtues* (Grand Rapids, MI: Brazos Press, 2008); Richard M. Gula, *Just Ministry: Professional Ethics for Pastoral Ministers* (New York: Paulist Press, 2010); Raymond G. Helmick, *Living Catholic Faith in a Contentious Age* (New York: Continuum, 2010).

82. Keenan, *A History of Catholic Moral Theology in the Twentieth Century*, 173–90.

83. Bernard Lonergan, *Insight: A Study of Human Understanding* (New York: Philosophical Library, 1957); idem, "Dehellenization of Dogma," *Theological Studies* 28 (1967): 336–51. See also Keenan, *A History of Catholic Moral Theology in the Twentieth Century*, 111.

84. Keenan, *A History of Catholic Moral Theology in the Twentieth Century*, 112–13.

85. Joseph Fletcher, *Situation Ethics: The New Morality* (Louisville, KY: Westminster John Knox Press, 1966).

86. Ibid., 113–14.

87. Ibid., 119–20.

88. Harrington and Keenan, *Jesus and Virtue Ethics*, 7.

89. Ibid., 8.

5. A VIRTUOUS CHURCH

1. Rosalind Hursthouse, *On Virtue Ethics* (Oxford: Oxford University Press, 2001), 1–24. See also Christine Swanton, *Virtue Ethics: A Pluralistic View* (Oxford: Oxford University Press, 2003); Richard Taylor, *An Introduction to Virtue Ethics* (Amherst, MA: Prometheus Books, 2002); Joseph J. Kotva, *The Christian Case for Virtue Ethics* (Washington DC: Georgetown University Press, 1996); James Keenan, "Virtue Ethics," in *Christian Ethics: An Introduction*, ed. Bernard Hoose (London: Cassell, 1998), 84–94; Raymond Devettere, *Introduction to Virtue Ethics* (Washington DC: Georgetown University Press, 2002); Charles E. Curran and Lisa A. Fullam, eds., *Virtue*, Readings in Moral Theology 16 (New York: Paulist Press, 2011).

2. G. E. M. Anscombe, "Modern Moral Philosophy," *Philosophy* 33 (January 1958).

3. Philippa Foot, *Virtues and Vices* (Oxford: Oxford University Press, 2002).

4. Alasdair MacIntyre, *After Virtue*, 3rd ed. (Notre Dame, IN: University of Notre Dame Press, 2007). See also Thomas D. D'Andrea, *Tradition, Rationality, and Virtue: The Thought of Alasdair MacIntyre* (Burlington, VT: Ashgate, 2006); Mark C. Murphy, ed., *Alasdair MacIntyre* (New York: Cambridge University Press, 2003).

5. James F. Keenan, "What Is Virtue Ethics?" *Priests and People* (November 1999): 401.

6. Frank J. Matera, "Theologies of the Church in the New Testament," in *The Gift of the Church*, ed. Peter C. Phan, A Michael Glazier Book (Collegeville, MN: Liturgical Press, 2000), 12. See also Robert Banks, *Paul's Idea of Community* (Peabody, MA: Hendrickson, 1984); Lucien Cerfaux, *The Church in the Theology of St. Paul*, trans. Geoffrey Webb and Adrian Walker (New York: Herder & Herder, 1959); Helen Doohan, *Paul's Vision of the Church*, Good News Studies 31 (Wilmington, DE: Michael Glazier, 1989); Rudolph Schnackenburg, *The Church in the New Testament* (New York: Herder & Herder, 1965).

7. Matera, "Theologies of the Church in the New Testament," 14.

8. Ibid., 14–15.

9. Yves Congar, "The Historical Development of Authority in the Church: Points for Christian Reflection," in *Problems of Authority*, ed. John M. Todd, 119–56 (Baltimore: Helicon Press, 1962), 121.

10. Matera, "Theologies of the Church in the New Testament," 4.

11. Ibid., 5–6.

12. Ibid., 7.

13. Ibid., 9–11.

14. Ibid., 7–8.

15. Congar, "The Historical Development of Authority in the Church," 121–23.

16. Matera, "Theologies of the Church in the New Testament," 17–19.

17. Kenan B. Osborne, *Priesthood: A History of the Ordained Ministry in the Roman Catholic Church* (New York: Paulist Press, 1988), 40–85. See also Paul Bernier, *Ministry in the Church: A Historical and Pastoral Approach* (Mystic, CT: Twenty-third Publications, 1992), 11–49.

18. Osborne, *Priesthood*, 91–93; Bernier, *Ministry in the Church*, 56–57.

19. Eric Plummer, "The Development of Ecclesiology: Early Church to the Reformation," in *The Gift of the Church*, ed. Peter C. Phan, 23–31 (Collegeville, MN: Liturgical Press, 2000), 24; Osborne, *Priesthood*, 95–97.

20. Plummer, "The Development of Ecclesiology," 25–26.

21. Osborne, *Priesthood*, 107–10; Plummer, "The Development of Ecclesiology," 27.

22. Congar, "The Historical Development of Authority in the Church," 132–35.

23. Ibid., 128–36.

24. Plummer, "The Development of Ecclesiology," 35.

25. Ibid., 36.

26. Ibid., 36–37.

27. Ibid., 37.

28. Congar, "The Historical Development of Authority in the Church," 140–42.

29. Plummer, "The Development of Ecclesiology," 40.

30. Ibid., 40–41.

31. Congar, "The Historical Development of Authority in the Church," 144–45.

32. Ibid.

33. Ibid., 147–48.

34. Michael J. Himes, "The Development of Ecclesiology: Modernity to the Twentieth Century," in Phan, *The Gift of the Church*, 53–54.

35. See Roger Aubert, "Le géographie ecclésiologique au XIXe siècle," *L'Ecclésiologie au XIXe siècle,* ed. Maurice Nédoncelle (Paris: Éditions du Cerf, 1960), 11–55.

36. See Michael J. Himes, *Ongoing Incarnation: Johann Adam Möhler and the Beginning of Modern Ecclesiology* (New York: Crossroad, 1997).

37. Ibid., 57–59.

38. Ibid., 60.

39. Ibid., 61–62.

40. Ibid., 63–64.

41. Ibid., 64.

42. Ibid., 64–66.

43. C. H. Lawrence, *Medieval Monasticism: Forms of Religious Life in Western Europe in the Middle Ages* (London: Longman, 1984), 142–45.

44. Simon Tugwell, *The Way of the Preacher* (Springfield, IL: Templegate Publishers, 1979), 1–96; William A. Hinnebusch, *The Dominicans: A Short History* (New York: Alba House, 1975), 3–18.

45. William J. Short, *The Franciscans* (Collegeville, MN: Liturgical Press, 1989).

46. Lawrence, *Medieval Monasticism*, 214–15.

47. Ibid., 216–18.

48. Saskia Murk-Jansen, *Brides in the Desert: The Spirituality of the Beguines* (Maryknoll, NY: Orbis Books, 1998).

49. Karl Suso Frank, *With Greater Liberty: A Short History of Christian Monasticism and Religious Orders*, trans. Joseph Lienhard (Kalamazoo, MI: Cistercian Publications, 1993), 153–56; John W. O'Malley, *The First Jesuits* (Cambridge, MA: Harvard University Press, 1993).

50. Frank, *With Greater Liberty*, 158.

51. Ibid.

52. Mary Wright, *Mary Ward's Institute: The Struggle for Identity* (Sydney: Crossing Press, 1997).

53. Frank, *With Greater Liberty*, 156–60.

54. The congregation is now known as the Congregation for Institutes of Consecrated Life and Societies of Apostolic Life.

55. For a further discussion of this complex issue, see R. Kevin Seasoltz, "Institutes of Consecrated Life and Ordained Ministry," in *A Concert of Charisms: Ordained Ministry in Religious Life*, ed. Paul Hennessy (New York: Paulist Press, 1997), 151–53; Sharon Holland, "Laity and the Power of Governance: A Statement of the Question," in *Selected Issues in Religious Law*, ed. Patrick J. Cogan (Washington DC: Canon Law Society of America, 1997), 26–32.

56. See Giuseppe Alberigo and Joseph A. Komonchak, eds., *History of Vatican II*, vol. 2 (Maryknoll, NY: Orbis Books, 1998), 281–357.

57. For a history of the development of *Lumen gentium,* see Antonia Acerbi, *Due ecclesiologie: Ecclesiologia giuridica ed ecclesiologia di communione nelle "Lumen Gentium"* (Bologna: Dehoniane, 1975).

58. Joseph A. Komonchak, "The Significance of Vatican Council II for Ecclesiology," in Phan, *The Gift of the Church*, 76–77. See also Richard R. Gaillardetz, "What Can We Learn from Vatican II?" in *The Catholic Church in the Twenty-first Century*, ed. Michael J. Himes (St. Louis: Liguori, 2004), 80–95.

59. Ibid., 78–79.

60. Komonchak, "The Significance of Vatican Council II for Ecclesiology," 87.

61. John W. O'Malley, *What Happened at Vatican II* (Cambridge, MA: Harvard University Press, 2008), 302–5, 311.

62. Ibid., 80.

63. See Joseph A. Komonchak, "The Local Church and the Church Catholic: The Contemporary Theological Problematic," *The Jurist* 52 (1992): 416–45.

64. Komonchak, "The Significance of Vatican II for Ecclesiology," 83–84.

65. Cardinal Ruffini led those who opposed the view that charisms exist in the church today. Opposition to this view was led by Cardinal Suenens and Archbishop Florit of Florence.

66. See John O'Malley, *A History of the Popes: From Peter to the Present* (Lanham, MD: Rowman and Littlefield, 2010), 109–68; Yves Congar, *True and False Reform in the Church*, trans. Paul Philibert (Collegeville, MN: Liturgical Press, 2010).

67. See *Co-Workers in the Vineyard of the Lord* (Washington DC: United States Conference of Catholic Bishops, 2005).

68. Doris Gottemoeller, "History of Catholic Institutions in the United States," *New Theology Review* 14 (May 2001): 16.

69. Martin Buber, *I and Thou*, trans. Ronald Gregor Smith (New York: Charles Scribner's Sons, 1958).

70. Paulo Freire, *Pedagogy of the Oppressed*, 30th anniv. ed. (New York: Continuum, 2000).

71. See Bernard Lee and Michael Cowan, *Gathered and Sent: The Mission of Small Church Communities Today* (New York: Paulist Press, 2003).

72. James F. Keenan, *Ethics of the Word: Voices in the Catholic Church Today* (Lanham, MD: Rowman and Littlefield, 2010), 157–73. See also William C. Mattison III, *Introducing Moral Theology: True Happiness and the Virtues* (Grand Rapids, MI: Brazos Press, 2008), 213–28, 251–71, 290–309.

73. See James A. Coriden, *The Rights of Catholics in the Church* (New York: Paulist Press, 2007), 69–87; Sharon Holland, "Equality, Dignity, and the Rights of the Laity," *The Jurist* 47 (1987): 103–28; James H. Provost, "Protecting and Promoting the Rights of Christians: Some Implications for Church Structure," *The Jurist* 46 (1986): 289–342; R. B. Douglas and D. Hollenbach, eds., *Catholicism and Liberalism: Contributions to American Public Philosophy* (Cambridge: Cambridge University Press, 1994), esp. 296–322.

74. J. Renken, "Pastoral Councils: Pastoral Planning and Dialogue among the People of God," *The Jurist* 53 (1993): 132–54.

75. Kenan B. Osborne, *Orders and Ministry* (Maryknoll, NY: Orbis Books, 2006), 172–91.

76. Paul Lakeland, *The Liberation of the Laity: In Search of an Accountable Church* (New York: Continuum, 2004), 267–68.

77. Ibid., 268–69.

78. Nadine Foley, ed., *Preaching and the Non-ordained: An Interdisciplinary Study* (Collegeville, MN: Liturgical Press, 1983).

79. See Barbara Anne Cusack and Therese Guerin Sullivan, *Pastoral Care in Parishes without a Pastor: Applications of Canon 517, par. 2* (Washington DC: Canon Law Society of America, 1995).

80. Lakeland, *The Liberation of the Laity*, 272.

81. See A. Farrelly, "The Diocesan Finance Council," *Studia Canonica* (1989): 149–66.

82. See James Provost, "Prebyteral Councils and Colleges of Consultors," *Canon Law Society of America Proceedings* (1987): 194–211.

83. See Secretariat, Bishops' Committee on the Liturgy, *The Bishops and the Liturgy: Highlights of the New Ceremonial of Bishops* (Washington DC: National Conference of Catholic Bishops, 1986); idem, *Shepherds and Teachers: The Bishop and Liturgical Renewal* (Washington DC: National Conference of Catholic Bishops, 1980); idem, *The Cathedral: A Reader* (Washington DC: National Conference of Catholic Bishops, 1979).

84. John Paul II, Apostolic Letter *Apostolos suos,* "On the Theological and Juridical Nature of Episcopal Conferences," 21 May 1998; English translation in *Origins* (30 July 1998): 152–58.

85. See Francis Sullivan, "The Teaching Authority of Episcopal Conferences," *Theological Studies* 63 (2002): 472–93.

86. Lakeland, *The Liberation of the Laity*, 274–76.

87. Pope Paul VI, motu proprio *Apostolica sollicitudo, Acta Apostolicae Sedis* 57 (1965): 794–804.

88. The synod of bishops is treated in seven canons in the Code of Canon Law, canons 342–348, although there are additional norms contained in the *Ordo synodi episcoporum celebrandae, Acta Apostolicae Sedis* 61 (1969): 525–39.

89. O'Malley, *A History of the Popes*, 325–29.

90. *Pastoral Letter of the Holy Father Pope Benedict XVI to the Catholics of Ireland* (19 March 2010).

91. See *The Canonical Implications of Ordaining Women to the Permanent Diaconate: Report of an Ad hoc Committee of the Canon Law Society of America* (Washington DC: Canon Law Society of America, 1995).

92. See Gerard Mannion, *Ecclesiology and Postmodernity: Questions for the Church in Our Time* (Collegeville, MN: Liturgical Press, 2007), 223–27.

93. See Charles E. Curran, *Catholic Social Teaching: 1891–Present* (Washington DC: Georgetown University Press, 2002).

94. Karl Rahner, "Plea for a Nameless Virtue," *Theological Investigations* 23 (London: Darton and Todd, 1992), 34.

6. A VIRTUOUS LITURGY AND SACRAMENTAL PRACTICE

1. See Peter Steinfels, "Further Adrift: The American Church's Crisis of Attrition," *Commonweal* (22 October 2010), 16–20.

2. See John W. O'Malley, *A History of the Popes: From Peter to the Present* (Lanham, MD: Rowman & Littlefield, 2010).

3. Ansgar Chupungco, *What, Then, Is Liturgy? Musings and Memoir* (Collegeville, MN: Liturgical Press, 2010), 168.

4. Ibid., 169–70. See also R. Kevin Seasoltz, "Liturgy and Ecclesiastical Law: Some Canonical and Pastoral Challenges," *The Jurist* 70 (2010): 114–30; John M. Huels, *Liturgy and Law: Liturgical Law in the System of Roman Catholic Canon Law* (Montreal: Wilson and Lafleur, 2006).

5. See Richard N. Berube, "Christological Models and Their Sacramental Implications," *The Living Light* 11 (Summer 1974): 181–93.

6. John McIntyre, *The Shape of Christology* (Philadelphia: Westminster Press, 1966), 8.

7. Berube, "Christological Models and Their Sacramental Implications," 182–83.

8. Ibid., 184–85. See also Alexander Schmemann, "Sacrament: An Orthodox Presentation," *Oecumenica 1970: Gospel and Sacrament*, ed. G. Gassmann and V. Vajta (Minneapolis: Augsburg, 1970), 97.

9. Bernard Cooke, "The 'Presence' of Jesus," *Commonweal* 87 (1967), 267. See Paul Janowiak, *Standing Together in the Community of God: Liturgical Spirituality and the Presence of Christ* (Collegeville, MN: Liturgical Press, 2011).

10. Edward Schillebeeckx, *Christ the Sacrament of the Encounter with God* (New York: Sheed and Ward, 1963), 3.

11. Berube, "Christological Models and Their Sacramental Implications," 183–84, 186–87.

12. Ibid., 184–85.

13. Karl Rahner, "Priest and Poet," *The Word: Readings in Theology* (New York: P. J. Kenedy, 1964), 4–5.

14. See *Preaching in the Sunday Assembly: A Pastoral Commentary on Fulfilled in Your Hearing*, ed. James A. Wallace (Collegeville, MN: Liturgical Press, 2010); Paul Janowiak, *The Holy Preaching: The Sacramentality of the Word in the Liturgical Assembly* (Collegeville, MN: Liturgical Press, 2000).

15. Mary M. Schaefer, "Presence of the Trinity: Relationship or Idea?" *Liturgical Ministry* 19 (Fall 2010): 152.

16. Ibid.

17. See Catherine Mowry LaCugna, *God for Us: The Trinity and Christian Life* (San Francisco: HarperCollins, 1993); Walter Kasper, *The God of Jesus Christ* (New York: Crossroad, 1986); David M. Coffey, *Deus Trinitas: The Doctrine of the Triune God* (Oxford: Oxford University Press, 1999); Colin Gunther, *The One, the Three, and the Many* (New York: Cambridge University Press, 1999); Karl Rahner, *Trinity* (New York: Continuum, 1970).

18. R. Kevin Seasoltz, *God's Gift Giving: In Christ and through the Spirit* (New York: Continuum, 2007). See also Edward J. Kilmartin, "Theology of the

Sacraments: Toward a New Understanding of the Chief Rites of the Church of Jesus Christ," *Alternative Futures for Worship*, vol. 1, ed. Regis Duffy (Collegeville, MN: Liturgical Press, 1987), 123.

19. Schaefer, "Presence of the Trinity," 152.

20. See Stephen H. Webb, *The Gifting God: A Trinitarian Ethics of Excess* (New York: Oxford University Press, 1996); Alan D. Schrift, ed., *The Logic of the Gift: Toward an Ethic of Generosity* (New York: Routledge, 1997).

21. Seasoltz, *God's Gift Giving*, 1; see also Webb, *The Gifting God*, 9.

22. See Henri de Lubac's *Catholicism*, trans. Lancelot C. Sheppard (New York: New American Library, 1964); idem, *Corpus Mysticum: L'Eucharistie et l'église au moyen âge* (Paris: Aubier, 1949). His work has been summarized by Nathan D. Mitchell in two columns in *Worship*: "Contextualizing Henri de Lubac's Work," *Worship* 84 (May 2010): 275–84; "*Ecclesiae Dei Sociari; Ecclesiae Incorporari; in Corpus Ecclesiae Transire*," *Worship* 84 (July 2010): 345–54.

23. Karl Rahner, "Nature and Grace," *Theological Investigations* 4 (Baltimore: Helicon, 1966), 165–88.

24. Mitchell, "Contextualizing Henri de Lubac's Work," 277–78.

25. Webb, *The Gifting God*, 130.

26. Christopher Cocksworth, "Spirit, Holy," in *The New Westminster Dictionary of Christian Spirituality,* ed. Philip Sheldrake (Louisville, KY: Westminster John Knox Press, 2005), 594–95.

27. Ibid., 595.

28. Seasoltz, *God's Gift Giving,* 178.

29. See Edward Kilmartin, *The Eucharist in the West*, ed. Robert J. Daly (Collegeville, MN: Liturgical Press, 1999); see also the commentary on Kilmartin's work by Jerome M. Hall, *We Have the Mind of Christ: The Holy Spirit and Liturgical Memory in the Thought of Edward J. Kilmartin* (Collegeville, MN: Liturgical Press, 2000).

30. Hall, *We Have the Mind of Christ*, 154–55.

31. Seasoltz, *God's Gift Giving*, 190.

32. R. Kevin Seasoltz, "Christian Prayer: Experience of the Experience of Jesus' Dying and Rising," *Worship* 53 (March 1979): 100.

33. See Karl Rahner, "The Spirit That Is over All Life," *Theological Investigations* 7 (New York: Herder and Herder, 1971), 193–201.

34. Seasoltz, *God's Gift Giving*, 50–51.

35. Jack Mahoney, *Christianity in Evolution: An Exploration* (Washington DC: Georgetown University Press, 2011), x.

36. Ibid.; see also Seasoltz, "Christian Prayer," 98–119.

37. Ladislaus Boros, *Pain and Providence* (Baltimore: Helicon, 1966), 72. See also Karl Rahner, "Reflections on a Theology of Renunciation," *Theological Investigations* 3 (Baltimore: Helicon, 1967), 47–57.

38. Maria Boulding, "Prayer and the Paschal Mystery according to Saint Benedict," *The Downside Review* 94 (October 1976): 278. See also Alan W. Jones, *Journey into Christ* (New York: Seabury Press, 1977), 60–67.

39. Karl Rahner, "Justified and Sinner at the Same Time," *Theological Investigations* 6 (Baltimore: Helicon, 1969), 218–30.

40. Boulding, "Prayer and the Paschal Mystery according to Saint Benedict," 282.

41. Jerome Murphy-O'Connor, *Becoming Human Together* (Wilmington, DE: Michael Glazier, 1977), 31.

42. See May Sarton, *Journal of a Solitude* (New York: W. W. Norton, 1973), 92–93.

43. Karl Rahner, "Self-Realization and Taking Up One's Cross," *Theological Investigations* 9 (New York: Herder and Herder, 1972), 253–57.

44. Gerald O'Collins, *The Resurrection of Jesus Christ* (Valley Forge, PA: Judson Press, 1973), 101–3.

45. Boulding, "Prayer and the Paschal Mystery according to Saint Benedict," 283.

46. Raymond E. Brown, *The Virginal Conception and Bodily Resurrection of Jesus* (New York: Paulist Press, 1973), 111–13.

47. O'Collins, *The Resurrection of Jesus Christ*, 111–15.

48. See Peter Selby, *Look for the Living: The Corporate Nature of Resurrection Faith* (Philadelphia: Fortress Press, 1976).

49. Murphy-O'Connor, *Becoming Human Together*, 195.

50. See Robert J. Daley, *Sacrifice Unveiled: The True Meaning of Christian Sacrifice* (New York: T&T Clark, 2009).

51. See Jean Leclercq, "The Relevance of the Contemplative Life," *Contemplative Life*, trans. Elizabeth Funder (Kalamazoo, MI: Cistercian Publications, 1978), 92–107; Kenneth Leech, *Soul Friend: A Study of Spirituality* (London: Sheldon Press, 1977), 191.

52. Leech, *Soul Friend*, 192.

53. Boulding, "Prayer and the Paschal Mystery according to Saint Benedict," 284.

54. See Margaret Visser, *The Gift of Thanks: The Roots and Rituals of Gratitude* (Boston: Houghton Mifflin Harcourt, 2009); Terrance McConnell, *Gratitude* (Philadelphia: Temple University Press, 1993).

55. There is an extensive literature on Christian initiation: Gerard Austin, *Anointing with the Spirit* (New York: Pueblo, 1985); Michel Dujarier, *A History of the Catechumenate: The First Six Centuries* (New York: Sadlier, 1979); Thomas F. Best, *Baptism Today: Understanding, Practice, Ecumenical Implications* (Collegeville, MN: Liturgical Press, 2008); Susan K. Wood, *One Baptism: Ecumenical Dimensions of the Doctrine of Baptism* (Collegeville, MN: Liturgical Press, 2009); Aidan Kavanagh, *The Shape of Baptism* (New York: Pueblo, 1978); Aidan Kavanagh, *Confirmation: Origins and Reform* (New York: Pueblo, 1988); Edward Yarnold, *The Awe-Inspiring Rites of Initiation: Baptismal Homilies of the Fourth Century* (Slough, UK: St. Paul Publications, 1971); Maxwell Johnson, *The Rites of Christian Initiation: Their Evolution and Interpretation* (Collegeville, MN: Liturgical Press, 1999); Paul Turner, *Confirmation: The Baby in Solomon's Court* (Chicago: Hillenbrand Books, 2006); Michael G. Witczak, *The Sacrament of Baptism* (Collegeville, MN: Liturgical Press, 2011).

56. Paul F. Bradshaw, "Initiation, Christian," in *The New Dictionary of Sacramental Worship*, ed. Peter E. Fink (Collegeville, MN: Liturgical Press, 1990),

601–7; Maxwell Johnson, "Baptism," in *The New Westminster Dictionary of Liturgy and Worship*, ed. Paul Bradshaw (Louisville, KY: Westminster John Knox Press, 2002), 35–37.

57. Sebastian Brock, "Studies in the Early History of the Syrian Orthodox Baptismal Liturgy," *Journal of Theological Studies* 23 (1972): 16–64.

58. See Gabriele Winkler, "Baptism, Eastern Churches," in Bradshaw, *The New Westminster Dictionary of Liturgy and Worship*, 37–39.

59. Bradshaw, "Initiation, Christian," 605–6.

60. Ibid., 606.

61. Kavanagh, *Confirmation*, 127.

62. *Catechism of the Catholic Church* (Collegeville, MN: Liturgical Press, 1994), 97.

63. See Paul Turner, "Baptism and Original Sin," in Fink, *The New Dictionary of Sacramental Worship*, 81–82.

64. Russell B. Connors and Patrick T. McCormick, *Character, Choices and Community: The Three Faces of Christian Ethics* (New York: Paulist Press, 1998), 25.

65. Patricia Lamoureux and Paul J. Wadell, *The Christian Moral Life: Faithful Discipleship for a Global Society* (Maryknoll, NY: Orbis Books, 2010), 137. See also Richard M. Gula, *The Way of Goodness and Holiness: A Spirituality for Pastoral Ministers* (Collegeville, MN: Liturgical Press, 2011).

66. William Mattison III, *Introducing Moral Theology: True Happiness and the Virtues* (Grand Rapids, MI: Brazos, 2008), 207.

67. Richard M. Gula, *Just Ministry* (New York: Paulist Press, 2010), 84–87.

68. Ibid., 89–92.

69. Lamoureux and Wadell, *The Christian Moral Life*, 124–27; see also Gula, *Just Ministry*, 97–105.

70. Lamoureux and Wadell, *The Christian Moral Life*, 130–32.

71. Gula, *Just Ministry*, 111–15; Lamoureux and Wadell, *The Christian Moral Life*, 132–34; Mattison, *Introducing Moral Theology*, 180–93.

72. See Austin, *Anointing with the Spirit;* Johnson, "Confirmation," 126–30; Turner, *Confirmation*.

73. Austin, "Confirmation," 221–24.

74. Ibid., 224–25.

75. Turner, *Confirmation*, xi.

76. Ibid., 1–21.

77. Ibid., 22–37.

78. Ibid., 38–60.

79. Ibid., 61–74.

80. Ibid., 75–96.

81. Ibid., 97–139.

82. Ibid., 140–44.

83. Stephen H. Webb, *The Gifting God: A Trinitarian Ethics of Excess* (New York: Oxford University Press, 1996), 130.

84. J. D. G. Dunn, "Paul's Understanding of the Death of Jesus as Sacrifice," in *Sacrifice and Redemption: Durham Essays in Theology*, ed. S. W. Sykes, 35–56

(New York: Cambridge University Press, 1991). See also Mark Heim, *Saved from Sacrifice: A Theology of the Cross* (Grand Rapids, MI: Eerdmans, 2006).

85. See David N. Power, *Love without Calculation: A Reflection on Divine Kenosis* (New York: Crossroad, 2005), 123.

86. Ibid., 125–26.

87. Mahoney, *Christianity in Evolution*, 121–37.

88. Edward Kilmartin, *The Eucharist in the West* (Collegeville, MN: Liturgical Press, 1998), 340.

89. Ibid., 341.

90. Ibid., 356.

91. David N. Power, "Sacrament: An Economy of God," *Louvain Studies* 23 (1990): 150. See also Rowan Williams, "Word and Spirit," in *On Christian Theology* (Oxford: Blackwells 2000), 107–27.

92. Kilmartin, *The Eucharist in the West*, 363.

93. See R. Kevin Seasoltz, "God's Gift Giving: Constitutive of Christian Persons and Communities," in *The Echo Within*, ed. Mary Collins and Catherine Dooley (Allen, TX: Thomas More, 1997), 45–49.

94. Louis-Marie Chauvet, *Symbol and Sacrament* (Collegeville, MN: Liturgical Press, 1995), 99–109. See also Gula, *The Way of Goodness and Holiness*, 37–44.

95. Walter Brueggemann, *Living toward a Vision: Biblical Reflections on Shalom* (Philadelphia: United Church Press, 1976), 134.

96. Ibid., 135.

97. There is an extensive literature on the identity and history of ordained priesthood. For examples, see Kenan B. Osborne, *Priesthood: A History of the Ordained Ministry in the Roman Catholic Church* (New York: Paulist Press, 1988); idem, *Orders and Ministry* (Maryknoll, NY: Orbis Books, 2006); Paul Bernier, *Ministry in the Church: A Historical and Pastoral Approach* (Mystic, CT: Twenty-third Publications, 1992); David N. Power, *Ministers of Christ and His Church: The Theology of the Priesthood* (London: Geoffrey Chapman, 1969); Bernard Cooke, *Ministry to Word and Sacrament* (Philadelphia: Fortress Press, 1976); Thomas O'Meara, *Theology of Ministry* (New York: Paulist Press, 1983); Gisbert Greshake, *The Meaning of Christian Priesthood* (Blackrock, Co. Dublin: Four Courts Press, 1988).

98. Trent, Session 23, *Decretum de sacramento ordinis,* canon 1 (DS 1771).

99. Daniel Donovan, "Priest," in *The New Dictionary of Theology*, ed. Joseph A. Komonchak, Mary Collins, and Dermot Lane (Wilmington, DE: Michael Glazier, 1987), 798–801; Patrick McGoldrick, "Orders, Sacrament of," in Fink, *The New Dictionary of Sacramental Worship*, 896–908.

100. Pius XI, quoted in Ladislas M. Örsy, *Receiving the Council: Theological and Canonical Insights and Debates* (Collegeville, MN: Liturgical Press, 2009), 36.

101. Hervé-Marie Legrand, "The Presidency of the Eucharist according to the Ancient Tradition," *Living Bread, Saving Cup*, ed. R. Kevin Seasoltz (Collegeville, MN: Liturgical Press, 1987), 196–221.

102. R. Kevin Seasoltz, "Clericalism: A Sickness in the Church," *The Furrow* (March 2010): 135–42.

103. See Bernard Häring, *A Sacramental Spirituality* (New York: Sheed and Ward, 1965), 183–93.

104. Ibid., 194–216. There is an extensive literature on sacramental marriage. See, for examples, Walter Kasper, *Theology of Christian Marriage* (New York: Crossroad, 1981); Michael G. Lawler, *Secular Marriage, Christian Sacrament* (Mystic, CT: Twenty-third Publications, 1985); Theodore Mackin, *What Is Marriage?* (New York: Paulist Press, 1982); Edward Schillebeeckx, *Marriage: Secular Reality and Saving Mystery* (New York: Sheed and Ward, 1965); Richard Malone and John Connery, eds., *Contemporary Perspectives on Christian Marriage* (Chicago: Loyola University Press, 1984); David M. Thomas, *Christian Marriage: A Journey Together* (Wilmington, DE: Michael Glazier, 1983); Markus Barth, *Ephesians: Translation and Commentary on Chapters 4—6* (New York: Doubleday, 1974); David Cloutier, *Love, Reason, and God's Story* (Winona, MN: St. Mary's Press, 2008); Richard Gaillardetz, *A Daring Promise: A Spirituality of Marriage* (New York: Crossroad, 2002); Kieran Scott and Michael Warren, eds., *Perspectives on Marriage: A Reader* (New York: Oxford University Press, 2001).

105. See Barth, *Ephesians*, 618.

106. See Regis Duffy, "Reconciliation," in Komonchak et al., *The New Dictionary of Theology*, 830–36; Ladislas M. Örsy, *The Evolving Church and the Sacrament of Penance* (Denville, NJ: Dimension, 1978); James Dallen, *The Reconciling Community: The Rite of Penance* (New York: Pueblo, 1986).

107. See Jennifer Glen, "Rites of Healing: A Reflection in Pastoral Theology," in *Alternative Futures for Worship*, vol. 7, *Anointing of the Sick*, ed. Peter Fink, 33–63 (Collegeville, MN: Liturgical Press, 1987); Genevieve Glen, ed., *Recovering the Riches of Anointing: A Study of the Sacrament of the Sick* (Collegeville, MN: Liturgical Press, 2002); Charles Gusmer, *And You Visited Me: Sacramental Ministry to the Sick and Dying* (New York: Pueblo, 1984); John J. Ziegler, *Let Them Anoint the Sick* (Collegeville, MN: Liturgical Press, 1987); Lizette Larson-Miller, *The Sacrament of the Anointing of the Sick* (Collegeville, MN: Liturgical Press, 2005).

108. John M. Huels, "Ministers and Rites for the Sick and Dying: Canon Law and Pastoral Options," in *Recovering the Riches of Anointing: A Study of the Sacrament of the Sick* (Collegeville, MN: Liturgical Press, 2002), 83–112.

109. See Bruce T. Morrill, *Divine Worship and Human Healing: Liturgical Theology at the Margins of Life and Death* (Collegeville, MN: Liturgical Press, 2009).

110. See Richard Rutherford, *The Death of a Christian: The Order of Christian Funerals*, rev. ed. (Collegeville, MN: Liturgical Press, 1990).

111. See Maurice Taylor, *Being a Bishop in Scotland* (Blackrock, Co. Dublin: Columba Press, 2006); idem, *It's the Eucharist, Thank God* (Brandon, Suffolk: Decani Books, 2009), 35–74; Ansgar J. Chupungco, *What, Then, Is Liturgy: Musings and Memoir* (Collegeville, MN: Liturgical Press, 2010), 173–216.

112. See Bradford E. Hinze, *Practices of Dialogue in the Roman Catholic Church: Aims and Obstacles, Lessons and Laments* (New York: Continuum, 2006); Constance FitzGerald, "From Impasse to Prophetic Hope: Crisis of Memory," *Catholic Theological Society of America Proceedings* 64 (2009): 21–42.

113. For example, Walter Brueggemann, *The Message of the Psalms: A Theological Commentary* (Minneapolis: Augsburg, 1984); idem, *Spirituality of the Psalms* (Minneapolis: Fortress Press, 2002).

CONCLUSION

1. For an account of that sad history, see Maurice Taylor, *Being a Bishop in Scotland* (Blackrock, Co. Dublin: Columba Press, 2006), 131–38; idem, *It's the Eucharist, Thank God* (Brandon, Suffolk: Decani Books, 2009), 35–74.

Reference List

Adams, Marilyn McCord, *William Ockham* (Notre Dame, IN: University of Notre Dame Press, 1987).

Alberigo, Giuseppe, and Joseph Komanchak, eds., *History of Vatican II* (Maryknoll, NY: Orbis Books, 1997-2003).

Allen, John L., *The Future Church: How Ten Trends Are Revolutionizing the Catholic Church* (New York: Doubleday, 2009).

Allison, Dale, *The Sermon on the Mount: Inspiring the Moral Imagination* (Minneapolis: Fortress Press, 1999).

Anderson, Allan, *An Introduction to Pentecostalism* (New York: Cambridge University Press, 2004).

Anderson, Perry, *The Origins of Postmodernism* (London: Verso, 1998).

Angelini, Giuseppe, and Ambrogio Valsecchi, *Disegno storico della teologia morale* (Bologna: Edizione Dehoniane, 1972).

Arbuckle, Gerald A., *Culture, Inculturation, and Theologians* (Collegeville, MN: Liturgical Press, 2010).

————. *Violence, Society, and the Church: A Cultural Approach* (Collegeville, MN: Liturgical Press, 2004).

Arendt, Hannah, *Crisis of the Republic* (New York: Harcourt, Brace, 1972).

Artaud, Antonin, "The Theater of Cruelty: Second Manifesto," in *The Theater and Its Double* (London: Calder and Boyers, 1970), 81-87.

Austin, Gerard, *Anointing with the Spirit* (New York: Pueblo, 1985).

Basham, A. L., *A Cultural History of India* (New York: Oxford University Press, 1999).

Beattie, Tina, *The New Atheists: The Twilight of Reason and the Wars of Religion* (Maryknoll, NY: Orbis Books, 2008).

Bede, *A History of the English Church and People,* trans. Leo Sherley-Price (Baltimore: Penguin, 1955).

Bell, Catherine, *Ritual Theory, Ritual Practice* (New York: Oxford University Press, 1992).

Bernier, Paul, *Ministry in the Church: A Historical and Pastoral Approach* (Mystic, CT: Twenty-third Publications, 1992).

Berube, Richard N., "Christological Models and their Sacramental Implications," *The Living Light* 11 (Summer 1974): 181-93.

Birch, Bruce, *Theological Introduction to the Old Testament* (Nashville, TN: Abingdon, 2005).

Bokenkotter, Thomas, *A Concise History of the Catholic Church* (New York: Doubleday, 1990).

Bonhoeffer, Dietrich, *The Cost of Discipleship* (New York: Macmillan, 1958).

Boros, Ladislaus, *Pain and Providence* (Baltimore: Helicon, 1966).

Boulding, Maria, *Marked for Life: Prayer in the Easter Christ* (London: SPCK, 1979).

Bouyer, Louis, *The Spirit and Forms of Protestantism* (Cleveland: World, 1964).

Bradley, Ian, *Celtic Christianity: Making Myths and Chasing Dreams* (New York: St. Martin's Press, 1999).

Brain, Robert, "African Art," in *A History of Art*, ed. Lawrence Gowing (Ann Arbor, MI: Borders Press, 2002), 504-20.

Brancatelli, Robert, "*Religiosidad Popular* as a Form of Liturgical Catechesis," *Worship* 77 (May 2003): 210-24.

Brown, Raymond E. *The Community of the Beloved Disciple: The Life, Loves, and Hates of an Individual Church in New Testament Times* (New York: Paulist Press, 1979).

Brueggemann, Walter, *The Prophetic Imagination* (Philadelphia: Fortress Press, 1978).

———, *Spirituality of the Psalms* (Minneapolis: Fortress Press, 2002).

———, *The Message of the Psalms: A Theological Commentary* (Minneapolis: Augsburg, 1984).

———, *Living toward a Vision: Biblical Reflections on Shalom* (Philadelphia: United Church Press, 1976).

———, *The Virginal Conception and Bodily Resurrection of Jesus* (New York: Paulist Press, 1973).

Buber, Martin, *I and Thou* (New York: Charles Scribner's Sons, 1958).

Butler, Christopher, *Postmodernism* (New York: Oxford University Press, 2002).

Byrne, Brendan, *Lifting the Burden: Reading Matthew's Gospel in the Church Today* (Collegeville, MN: Liturgical Press, 2004).

———, *The Hospitality of God: A Reading of Luke's Gospel* (Collegeville, MN: Liturgical Press, 2000).

Cahalan, Kathleen, *Formed in the Image of Christ: The Sacramental-Moral Theology of Bernard Häring* (Collegeville, MN: Liturgical Press, 2004).

Camille, Michael, *Gothic Art: Glorious Visions* (New York: Harry N. Abrams, 1996).

Carr, M. H., *Realists and Nominalists* (Oxford: Oxford University Press, 1946).

Cavanaugh, William T., "Migrant, Tourist, Pilgrim, Monk: Mobility and Identity in a Global Age," *Theological Studies* 69 (June 2009): 340-56.

Cerfaux, Lucien, *The Church in the Theology of St. Paul* (New York: Herder and Herder, 1959).

Chauvet, Louis-Marie, *Symbol and Sacrament* (Collegeville, MN: Liturgical Press, 1995).

Chilton, Bruce, *The Kingdom of God in the Teaching of Jesus* (Philadelphia: Fortress Press, 1984).

Chung Hyun Kyung, *Struggle to Be the Sun Again: Introducing Asian Women's Theology* (Maryknoll, NY: Orbis Books, 1979).

Chupungco, Ansgar, *What, Then, Is Liturgy?* (Collegeville, MN: Liturgical Press, 2010).

Cloutier, David, *Love, Reason, and God's Story: An Introduction to Catholic Sexual Ethics* (Winona, MN: St. Mary's Press, 2008).

Coffey, David M., Deus Trinitas: *The Doctrine of the Triune God* (Oxford: Oxford University Press, 1999).

Coleman, John, and William Ryan, eds., *Globalization and Catholic Social Thought* (Ottawa: Novalis, 2005).

Condren, Mary, *The Serpent and the Goddess: Women, Religion and Power in Celtic Ireland* (San Francisco: Harper and Row, 1989).

Congar, Yves, *True and False Reform in the Church* (Collegeville, MN: Liturgical Press, 2010).

———, "The Historical Development of Authority in the Church: Points for Christian Reflection," in *Problems of Authority,* ed. John M. Todd (Baltimore: Helicon Press, 1962), 119-56.

Connors, Russell B., and Patrick T. McCormick, *Character, Choices, and Community: The Three Faces of Christian Ethics* (New York: Paulist Press, 1998).

Copeland, M. Shawn, "African American Catholics and Black Theology: Interpretation," in *African-American Catholics and Black Theology: An Interpretation* (Durham, NC: Duke University Press, 1989), 228-48.

Coriden, James A., *The Rights of Catholics in the Church* (New York: Paulist Press, 2007).

Corkery, James, *Joseph Ratzinger's Theological Ideas: Wise Cautions and Legitimate Hopes* (Dublin: Dominican Publications, 2009).

Cox, Harvey, *Fire from Heaven: The Rise of Pentecostal Spirituality and the Reshaping of Religion in the Twenty-first Century* (New York: Addison-Wesley/Perseus Books, 1994).

Crumlin, Rosemary, ed., *Aboriginal Art and Spirituality* (North Blackburn, AUS: Collins and Dove, 1991).

Curran, Charles E., *Catholic Social Teaching: 1891-Present* (Washington DC: Georgetown University Press, 2002).

Curran, Charles, E., and Lisa A. Fullam, eds., *Virtue: Readings in Moral Theology* 6 (New York: Paulist Press, 2011).

Cusack, Barbara Anne, and Therese Guerin Sullivan, *Pastoral Care in Parishes without a Pastor* (Washington DC: Canon Law Society of America, 1995).

Daley, Robert J., *Sacrifice Unveiled: The True Meaning of Christian Sacrifice* (New York: T and T Clark, 2009).

Dallen, James, *The Reconciling Community: The Rite of Penance* (New York: Pueblo, 1986).

Davis, Cyprian, "Black Spirituality," *U.S. Catholic Historian* 8 (1989): 39-46.

Davis, Henry, *Moral and Pastoral Theology: A Summary* (New York: Sheed and Ward, 1952).

Dawkins, Richard, *The God Delusion* (New York: Bantam Books, 2006).

Dawson, Christopher, *Religion and the Rise of Western Culture* (New York: Sheed and Ward, 1950).

———, *Religion and Culture* (London: Sheed and Ward, 1948).

———, *The Making of Europe: An Introduction to the History of European Unity* (New York: Sheed and Ward, 1937).

———, *Progress and Religion: An Historical Enquiry* (New York: Sheed and Ward, 1933).

De Lubac, Henri, *Catholicism* (New York: American Library, 1964).

Demmer, Klaus, *Shaping the Moral Life: An Introduction to Moral Theology* (Washington DC: Georgetown University Press, 2000).

De Sales, Francis, *Introduction to the Devout Life* (New York: Harper, 1960).

Deveterre, Raymond, *Introduction to Virtue Ethics* (Washington DC: Georgetown University Press, 2002).

Dumm, Demetius, *Flowers in the Desert: A Spirituality of the Bible* (New York: Paulist Press, 1987).

Dupré, Louis, *Passage to Modernity: An Essay in the Hermeneutics of Nature and Culture* (New Haven, CT: Yale University Press, 1993).

Egan, Philip A., *Philosophy and Catholic Theology: A Primer* (Collegeville, MN: Liturgical Press, 2009).

Elizondo, Virgil, *Guadalupe: Mother of the New Creation* (Maryknoll, NY: Orbis Books, 1997).

Esposito, John, *Oxford History of Islam* (New York: Oxford University Press, 2006).

Fagerberg, David, *Theologia Prima: What Is Liturgical Theology* (Collegeville, MN: Liturgical Press, 2003).

Fedler, Kyle D., *Exploring Christian Ethics: Biblical Foundations for Morality* (Louisville, KY: Westminster/John Knox Press, 2006).

Fitzmyer, Joseph, *The Gospel according to Luke* (Garden City, NY: Doubleday, 1981).

Flood, Gavin, ed., *Blackwell Companion to Hinduism* (Oxford: Blackwell Publishing, 2003).

Foley, Nadine, ed., *Preaching and the Non-Ordained: An Interdisciplinary Study* (Collegeville, MN: Liturgical Press, 1983).

Foot, Philippa, *Virtues and Vices* (Oxford: Oxford University Press, 2002).

Frank, Karl Suso, *With Greater Liberty: A Short History of Christian Monasticism and Religious Orders* (Kalamazoo, MI: Cistercian Publications, 1993).

Freire, Paulo, *Pedagogy of the Oppressed* (New York: Continuum, 2000).

Frymann, Abigail, "Mobile Continent," *The Tablet* (16 January 2010), 4.

Fuellenbach, John, *The Kingdom of God: The Message of Jesus Today* (Maryknoll, NY: Orbis Books, 1995).

Gaillardetz, Richard, *A Daring Promise: A Spirituality of Marriage* (New York: Crossroad, 2002).

Gallagher, Michael Paul, *Clashing Symbols: An Introduction to Faith and Culture* (New York: Paulist Press, 2003).

Geertz, Clifford, *The Interpretation of Cultures* (New York: Basic Books, 1973).

Gerardi, Renzo, *Storia della morale: Interpretazioni teologiche del'esperienza Cristiana* (Bologna: Editione Dehoniane, 2003).

Gerges, Fawaz, *The Far Enemy: Why Jihad Went Global* (New York: Cambridge University Press, 2005).

Gilleman, Gérard, *The Primacy of Charity in Moral Theology* (Westminster, MD: The Newman Press, 1964).

Goonewardene, Anil, *Buddhayana: Living Buddhism* (New York: Continuum, 2010).

Grenz, Stanley, *A Primer on Postmodernism* (Grand Rapids, MI: Eerdmans, 1996).

Gula, Richard M., *The Way of Goodness and Holiness: A Spirituality for Pastoral Ministers* (Collegeville, MN: Liturgical Press, 2011).

———, *Just Ministry* (New York: Paulist Press, 2010).

Gunton, Colin, *Enlightenment and Alienation* (London: Wipf and Stock, 2006).

Gutiérrez, Gustavo, *A Theology of Liberation* (Maryknoll, NY: Orbis Books, 1973).

Habito, Ruben L. F., and John Keenan, *Living Zen, Loving God* (Boston: Wisdom, 2004).

Hall, Jerome M., *We Have the Mind of Christ: The Holy Spirit and Liturgical Memory in the Thought of Edward J. Kilmartin* (Collegeville, MN: Liturgical Press, 2000).

Happel, Stephen, "Classical Culture and the Nature of Worship," *Heythrop Journal* 21 (July 1980): 87-101.

Häring, Bernard, *A Sacramental Spirituality* (New York: Sheed and Ward, 1965).

———, *The Law of Christ* (Westminster, NJ: The Newman Press, 1961, 1963, 1966).

Harrington, Daniel J., *The Gospel of Matthew* (Collegeville, MN: Liturgical Press, 1991).

Harrington, Daniel J., and James F. Keenan, *Paul and Virtue Morality* (Lanham, MD: Rowman and Littlefield Publishers, 2010).

———, *Jesus and Virtue Ethics: Building Bridges between New Testament Studies and Moral Theology* (Lanham, MD: Rowman and Littlefield Publishers, 2002).

Harris, Sam, *The End of Religion: Religion, Terror, and the Future of Reason* (New York: W. W. Norton and Company, 2004).

Hastings, Adrian, ed., *The Oxford Companion to Christian Thought* (Oxford: Oxford University Press, 2000).

Heartney, Eleanor, *Postmodernism* (London: Tate, 2001).

Heft, James, L., "Distinctively Catholic: Keeping the Faith in Higher Education," *Commonweal* (26 March 2010), 9-10.

Heim, Mark, *Saved from Sacrifice: A Theology of the Cross* (Grand Rapids, MI: Eerdmans, 2006).

Helmich, Raymond G., *Living Catholic Faith in a Contentious Age* (New York: Continuum, 2010).

Hinze, Bradford E., *Practices of Dialogue in the Roman Catholic Church: Aims and Obstacles, Lessons and Laments* (New York: Continuum, 2006).

Huels, John, *The Pastoral Companion: A Canon Law Handbook for Catholic Ministry* (Montreal: Wilson and Lafleur, 2009).

———, *Liturgy and Law: Liturgical Law in the System of Roman Catholic Canon Law* (Montreal: Wilson and Lafleur, 2006).

Hursthouse, Rosalind, *On Virtue Ethics* (Oxford: Oxford University Press, 2001).

Jacobs, Stephen, *Hinduism Today* (New York: Continuum, 2010).

Jencks, Charles A., *The Language of Post-Modern Architecture* (London: Academy Editions, 1984).

Jenkins, Philip, *The Coming of Global Christianity* (New York: Oxford University Press, 2007).

———, *God's Continent: Christianity, Islam, and Europe's Religious Crisis* (New York: Oxford University Press, 2007).

———, *The New Faces of Christianity: Believing the Bible in the Global South* (New York: Oxford University Press, 2007).

Johnson, Luke Timothy, "Dry Bones: Why Religion Can't Live without Mysticism," *Commonweal* (26 February 2010), 13-14.

Johnson, Maxwell, *The Rites of Christian Initiation: Their Evolution and Interpretation* (Collegeville, MN: Liturgical Press, 1999).

Jordan, Bill, and Frank Duvell, *Irregular Migration: The Dilemmas of Transnational Mobility* (London: Edward Elgar, 2003).

Kane, Thomas, *The Dancing Church in Africa* (New York: Paulist Press, 1992).

Kasper, Walter, *The God of Jesus Christ* (New York: Crossroad, 1986).

———, *Theology of Christian Marriage* (New York: Crossroad, 1981).

Kavanagh, Aidan, *On Liturgical Theology* (Collegeville, MN: Liturgical Press, 1992).

———, *Confirmation: Origins and Reform* (New York: Pueblo, 1988).

———, *The Shape of Baptism* (New York: Pueblo, 1978).

Keenan, James F. *Ethics of the Word: Voices in the Catholic Church Today* (Lanham, MD: Rowman and Littlefield, 2010).

———, *A History of Catholic Moral Theology in the Twentieth Century: From Confessing Sins to Liberating Consciences* (New York: Continuum, 2010).

Keesing, Roger M., "Theories of Culture Revisited," *Assessing Cultural Anthropology*, ed. Robert Borofsky (New York: McGraw-Hill, 1994), 74-83.

———, "Anthropology as Interpretive Quest," *Current Anthropology* 28 (1987): 29-43.

Kelleher, Margaret Mary, "Liturgy, Culture, and the Challenge of Catholicity," *Worship* (March 2010): 98-120.

Kilmartin, Edward, *The Eucharist in the West* (Collegeville, MN: Liturgical Press, 1999).

Klauser, Theodor, *A Short History of the Western Liturgy* (Oxford: Oxford University Press, 1979).

Klotz, Heinrich, *History of Post-Modern Architecture* (Cambridge, MA: MIT Press, 1998).

Kodell, Jerome, *The Eucharist in the New Testament* (Collegeville, MN: Liturgical Press, 1988).

Koenig-Bricker, Woodene, *Ten Commandments for the Environment* (Notre Dame, IN: Ave Maria Press, 2009).

Komonchak, Joseph, "Vatican II as an Event," in *Vatican II: Did Anything Happen?*, ed. David Schultenover (New York: Continuum, 2007).

Koser, Khalid, *International Migration* (New York: Oxford University Press, 2007).

Kotva, Joseph, *The Christian Case for Virtue Ethics* (Washington DC: Georgetown University Press, 1996).

Kymlcka, Will, *Multicultural Citizenship: A Liberal Theology of Minority Rights* (Oxford: Clarendon, 1995).

LaCugna, Catherine Mowry, *God for Us: The Trinity and Christian Life* (San Francisco: HarperCollins, 1993).

Lakeland, Paul, *The Liberation of the Laity* (New York: Continuum, 2004).

————, *Postmodernity: Christian Identity in a Fragmented Age* (Minneapolis: Fortress Press, 1997).

Lamoureux, Patricia, and Paul J. Wadell, *The Christian Moral Life: Faithful Discipleship for a Global Society* (Maryknoll, NY: Orbis Books, 2010).

Larson-Miller, Lizette, *The Sacrament of the Anointing of the Sick* (Collegeville, MN: Liturgical Press, 2005).

LaVerdiere, Eugene, *The Eucharist in the New Testament and the Early Church* (Collegeville, MN: Liturgical Press, 1996).

Lawrence, C. H., *Medieval Monasticism: Forms of Religious Life in Western Europe in the Middle Ages* (London: Longman, 1984).

Lee, Bernard, and Michael Cowan, *Gathered and Sent: The Mission of Small Church Communities Today* (New York: Paulist Press, 2003).

Lonergan, Bernard, *Method in Theology* (New York: Herder and Herder, 1972).

————, *Insight: A Study in Human Understanding* (New York: Philosophical Library, 1957).

Longenecker, Richard, ed., *Patterns of Discipleship in the New Testament* (Grand Rapids, MI: Eerdmans, 1996).

Lowe, Walter, "Postmodern Theology," *The Oxford Handbook of Systematic Theology* (New York: Oxford University Press, 2007), 622-28.

Lyotard, Jean-François, *The Postmodern Condition* (Manchester, UK: Manchester University Press, 1986).

Machamer, Peter, ed., *The Cambridge Companion to Galileo* (New York: Cambridge University Press, 1998).

MacIntyre, Alasdair, *After Virtue* (Notre Dame, IN: University of Notre Dame Press, 2007).

Mahoney, Jack, *Christianity in Evolution: An Exploration* (Washington DC: Georgetown University Press, 2011).

————, *The Making of Moral Theology: A Study of the Roman Catholic Tradition* (Oxford: Oxford University Press, 1987).

Mannion, Gerard, *Ecclesiology and Postmodernity: Questions for the Church in our Time* (Collegeville, MN: Liturgical Press, 2007).

Marcuse, Herbert, *One-dimensional Man* (Boston: Beacon Press, 1966).

Marks, Robert, *The Origin of the Modern World* (Lanham: Rowman and Littlefield, 2002).

Matheson, Peter, *The Imaginative World of the Reformation* (Edinburgh: T and T Clark, 2000).

Matovina, Timothy, "Liturgy, Popular Rites and Popular Spirituality," in *Mestizo Worship: A Pastoral Approach to Liturgical Ministry,* ed. Virgil Elizondo and Timothy Matovina (Collegeville, MN: Liturgical Press, 1998), 25-37.

Mattison, William C., *Introducing Moral Theology: True Happiness and the Virtues* (Grand Rapids, MI: Brazo Press, 2008).

Mbiti, John S., *African Religions and Philosophy* (New York: Praeger Press, 1969).

McDonald, Daniel, ed., *Catholic Social Teaching in Global Perspective* (Maryknoll, NY: Orbis Books, 2010).

McGrath, Alister, *In the Beginning: The Story of the King James Bible and How It Changed a Nation, a Language, and a Culture* (New York: Doubleday, 2001).

McKim, Donald, ed., *The Cambridge Companion to Martin Luther* (New York: Cambridge University Press, 2003).

Mersch, Emile, *La Théologie du corps mystique* (Paris: Desclée de Brouwer, 1944).

———, *Morale corps mystique* (Paris: Desclée de Brouwer, 1937).

———, *Le Corps mystique de Christ* (Brussels: Desclée de Brouwer, 1936).

Michaels, A., *Hinduism: Past and Present* (Princeton, NJ: Princeton University Press, 2004).

Miller, Richard, ed., *God, Creation, and Climate Change* (Maryknoll, NY: Orbis Books, 2010).

Miller, Vincent J., *Consuming Religion: Christian Faith and Practice in a Consumer Culture* (New York: Continuum, 2008).

Mills, Mary E., *Biblical Morality: Moral Perspectives in Old Testament Narratives* (Burlington: Ashgate, 2001).

Mittelman, *The Globalization Syndrome* (Princeton, NJ: Princeton University Press, 2000).

Moloney, Francis J., *The Gospel of John* (Collegeville, MN: Liturgical Press, 1998).

———, *A Life of Promise: Poverty, Chastity, Obedience* (Wilmington, DE: Michael Glazier, 1984).

Morrill, Bruce T., *Divine Worship and Human Healing: Liturgical Theology at the Margins of Life and Death* (Collegeville, MN: Liturgical Press, 2009).

Murk-Jansen, Saskia, *Brides in the Desert: The Spirituality of the Beguines* (Maryknoll, NY: Orbis Books, 1998).

Murphy-O'Connor, Jerome, *Becoming Human Together* (Wilmington, DE: Michael Glazier, 1977).

Nisbett, Richard E., *The Geography of Thought: How Asians and Westerners Think Differently . . . and Why* (New York: Free Press, 2003).

Novak, Michael, *No One Sees God: The Dark Night of Atheists and Believers* (New York: Random House, 2008).

Nuttgens, Patrick, *Architecture* (London: Mitchell Beazley International, 1992).

O'Collins, Gerald, *The Resurrection of Jesus Christ* (Valley Forge, PA: Judson Press, 1973).

O'Donohue, John, *Anam Cara: A Book of Celtic Wisdom* (New York: HarperCollins Publishers, 1997).

O'Grady, Ron, ed., *Christ for All People: Celebrating a World of Art* (Maryknoll, NY: Orbis Books, 2001).

O'Malley, John, *A History of the Popes: From Peter to the Present* (Lanham, MD: Rowman and Littlefield, 2010).

———, *What Happened at Vatican II?* (Cambridge: Harvard University Press, 2008).

———, *Vatican II: Did Anything Happen?* (New York: Continuum, 2007).

———, *The First Jesuits* (Cambridge: Harvard University Press, 1993).

Ong, Walter J., *Interface of the Word: Studies on the Evolution of Consciousness and Culture* (Ithaca, NY: Cornell University Press, 1977).

————, *The Presence of the Word: Some Prolegomena for Cultural and Religious History* (New Haven, CT: Yale University Press, 1967).

Örsy, Ladislas M., *The Evolving Church and the Sacrament of Penance* (Denville, NJ: Dimensions, 1978).

Osborne, Kenan B., *Orders and Ministry* (Maryknoll, NY: Orbis Books, 2006).

————, *Priesthood: A History of the Ordained Ministry in the Roman Catholic Church* (New York: Paulist Press, 1988).

Pecklers, Keith, *The Ethos of the Roman Rite: On the Reception and Implementation of the New Missal* (Collegeville, MN: Liturgical Press, 2009).

————, *Dynamic Equivalence* (Collegeville, MN: Liturgical Press, 2003).

————, ed., *Liturgy in a Postmodern World* (New York: Continuum, 2003).

Perraton, Jonathan, *Global Transformation* (Berkeley, CA: Stanford University Press, 1999).

Peters. F. E., *Islam: A Guide for Jews and Christians* (Princeton, NJ: Princeton University Press, 2003).

Phan, Peter C., "Liturgical Inculturation: Unity in Diversity in the Postmodern Age," in *Liturgy in a Postmodern World*, ed. Keith Pecklers (New York: Continuum, 2003), 55-86.

————, ed., *The Gift of the Church* (Collegeville, MN: Liturgical Press, 2000).

————, "Contemporary Theology and Inculturation in the United States," in *The Multicultural Church: A New Landscape in U.S. Theologies*, ed. William Cenkner (New York: Paulist Press, 1996), 109-30.

Phan, Peter C., and Jung Young Lee, *Journeys at the Margin: Toward an Autobiographical Theology in American-Asian Perspective* (Collegeville, MN: Liturgical Press, 1999).

Philander, S. George, *Encyclopedia of Global Warming and Climate Change* (Los Angeles: Sage, 2008).

Pierce, Donna, "Portraits of Faith," in *Mexican Churches,* ed. Eliot Porter and Ellen Auerback (Albuquerque: University of New Mexico Press, 1987), 13-20.

Pieris, Aloysius, *An Asian Theology of Liberation* (Maryknoll, NY: Orbis Books, 1988).

Pinckaers, Servais, *Morality: The Catholic View* (South Bend, IN: St. Augustine's Press, 2001).

————, *The Sources of Christian Ethics* (Washington DC: Catholic University of America Press, 1995).

Pontifical Biblical Commission, *The Bible and Morality: Biblical Roots of Christian Conduct* (Vatican City: Libreria Editrice Vaticana, 2008).

Power, David N., *Love without Calculation: A Reflection on Divine Kenosis* (New York: Crossroad, 2005).

Pregeant, Russell, *Knowing Truth, Doing Good: Engaging New Testament Ethics* (Minneapolis: Fortress Press, 2008).

Rausch, Thomas P., *Pope Benedict XVI: An Introduction to His Theological Vision* (New York: Paulist Press, 2009).

Richards, Jeffery, *Consul of God: The Life and Times of Gregory the Great* (London: Routlege and Kegan, 1980).

Roy, Olivier, *Globalized Islam: The Search for the New Ummah* (New York: Columbia University Press, 2006).

Sanneh, Lamin, *Disciples of All Nations: Pillars of World Christianity* (New York: Oxford University Press, 2008).

————, *The Changing Face of Christianity: Africa, the West, and the Word* (New York: Oxford University Press, 2005).

————, *Whose Religion Is Christianity?* (Grand Rapids, MI: Eerdmans, 2003).

Schaefer, Mary M., "Presence of the Trinity: Relationship or Idea?" *Liturgical Ministry* 19 (Fall 2010): 151-54.

Schillebeeckx, Edward, *Christ the Sacrament of the Encounter with God* (New York: Sheed and Ward, 1963).

Schnackenburg, Rudolf, *The Church in the New Testament* (New York: Herder and Herder, 1965).

————, *The Moral Teaching of the New Testament* (New York: Herder and Herder, 1965).

Scholte, Jan Aart, *Globalization* (London: Palgrave Macmillan, 2005).

Schreiter, Robert J., *The New Catholicity: Theology between the Global and the Local* (Maryknoll, NY: Orbis Books, 1972).

Schütz, Bernhard, *Great Cathedrals* (New York: Harry N. Abrams, 2002).

Seasoltz, R. Kevin, "Liturgy and Ecclesiastical Law: Some Canonical and Pastoral Challenges," *The Jurist* 70 (2010): 114-30.

————, *God's Gift Giving: In Christ and through the Spirit* (New York: Continuum, 2007).

————, *A Sense of the Sacred: Theological Foundations for Christian Architecture and Art* (New York: Continuum, 2005).

————, "Anthropology and Liturgical Theology: Searching for a Compatible Methodology," in *Liturgy and Human Passage*, Concilium 112, ed. David Power and Luis Maldonado (New York: Seabury Press, 1997), 3-13.

————, "Christian Prayer: Experience of the Experience of Jesus' Dying and Rising," *Worship* 53 (March 1979): 98-119.

Senior, Donald, "A Guide for the Perplexed: The Bible as Moral Teacher," *Commonweal* (26 February 2010), 9-10.

Senn, Frank C., "'Worship Alive': An Analysis and Critique of 'Alternative Worship Services,'" *Worship* 69 (1995): 194-224.

Sheldrake, Philip, "Postmodernity," in *The New Westminster Dictionary of Christian Spirituality*, ed. Philip Sheldrake (Louisville, KY: Westminster John Knox Press, 2005), 498-99.

Shift, Alan D., *The Logic of the Gift: Toward an Ethic of Generosity* (New York: Routledge, 1997).

Short, William J., *The Franciscans* (Collegeville, MN: Liturgical Press, 1989).

Shorter, Aylward, *African Christian Spirituality* (Maryknoll, NY: Orbis Books, 1980).

Sjoo, Monica, and Barbara Mor, *The Great Cosmic Mother: Rediscovering the Religion of the Earth* (San Francisco: Harper and Row), 1987).

Southern, Richard W., *Western Society and the Church in the Middle Ages* (Hammondsworth, UK: Penguin, 1970).

Steger, Manfried B., *Globalization* (New York: Oxford University Press, 2009).

Steinfels, Peter, "Further Adrift: The American Church's Crisis of Attrition," *Commonweal* (22 October 2010), 16-20.

Stuhlmueller, Carroll, ed., *The Collegeville Pastoral Dictionary of Biblical Theology* (Collegeville, MN: Liturgical Press, 1996).

Tanner, Kathryn, *Theories of Culture: A New Agenda for Theology* (Minneapolis: Fortress Press, 1997).

Taylor, Maurice, *It's the Eucharist, Thank God* (Brandon, Suffolk: Decani Books, 2009).

———, *Being a Bishop in Scotland* (Blackrock, Co. Dublin: Columba Press, 2006).

Tillmann, Fritz, *The Master Calls: A Handbook of Morals for Laymen* (Baltimore: Helicon Press, 1960).

Toman, Rolf, ed., *Romanesque Architecture, Sculpture, Painting* (Cologne: Könemann, 1997).

Tugwell, Simon, *The Beatitudes: Soundings in Christian Tradition* (Springfield, IL: Templegate Publishers, 1980).

———, *The Way of the Preacher* (Springfield, IL: Templegate Publishers, 1979).

Turner, Paul, *Confirmation: The Baby in Solomon's Court* (Chicago: Hillenbrand Books, 2006).

Van de Sandt, Hubertus, and David Flusser, *The Didache: Its Jewish Sources and Its Place in Early Judaism and Christianity* (Assen: Royal van Gorcum, 2002).

Venturi, Robert, *Learning from Las Vagas: The Forgotten Symbolism of Architectural Form* (Cambridge: MIT Press, 1977).

———, *Complexity and Contradiction in Architecture* (New York: Museum of Modern Art, 1966).

Vignaux, Paul, *Nominalism au XIVe Siècle* (Montreal: Inst. d'Études Médiévales, 1948).

Visser, Margaret, *The Gift of Thanks: The Roots and Rituals of Gratitude* (Boston: Houghton Mifflin Harcourt, 2009).

Wallace, James A., ed., *Preaching in the Sunday Assembly: A Pastoral Commentary on* Fulfilled in Your Hearing (Collegeville, MN: Liturgical Press, 2010).

Wansbrough, Henry, "The Bible and Morality: Biblical Roots of Christian Conduct," *Scripture Bulletin* 40 (January 2010): 91-92.

Ward, Graham, "Postmodernism," in *The Oxford Companion to Christian Thought*, ed. Adrian Hastings, Alistair Mason, and Hugh Pyper (New York: Oxford University Press, 2000), 551-52.

Waters, Malcolm, *Globalization* (London: Routlege, 2001).

Webb, Stephen H., *The Gifting God: A Trinitarian Ethics of Excess* (New York: Oxford University Press, 1996).

Weeks, Dennis L., and Jane Hoogestraat, eds., *Time, Memory, and the Verbal Arts: Essays on the Thought of Walter Ong* (Selingrove, PA: Susquehanna University Press, 1989).

Wessels, Anton, *Images of Jesus: How Jesus Is Perceived and Portrayed in Non-European Cultures* (Grand Rapids, MI: Eerdmans, 1990).

Westermann, Claus, *Elements of Old Testament Theology* (Atlanta: John Knox Press, 1982).

White, Lynn, "The Historical Roots of Our Ecological Crisis," *Science* 155 (10 March 1967): 1203-7.

Wilson-Dickson, Andrew, *The Story of Christian Music from Gregorian Chant to Black Gospel* (Minneapolis: Fortress Press, 1992).

Wimbush, Vincent L., "Reading Texts through Worlds, Worlds through Texts," in *Black and Catholic: The Challenge and Gift of Black Folk: Contributions of African American Experience and Thought to Catholic Theology*, 2nd ed., ed. Jamie T. Phelps (Milwaukee: Marquette University Press, 2002), 59-73.

Witczak, Michael, *The Sacrament of Baptism* (Collegeville, MN: Liturgical Press, 2011).

Wolf, Martin, *Why Globalization Works* (New Haven, CT: Yale University Press, 2005).

Wright, Mary, *Mary Ward's Institute: The Struggle for Identity* (Sydney, AUS: Crossing Press, 1997).

Yao Xinzhong, *An Introduction to Confucianism* (New York: Cambridge University Press, 2000).

Yao Xinzhong, and Zhao Yanxia, *Chinese Religion: A Contextual Approach* (New York: Continuum, 2010).

Yorba, Jonathan, *Arte Latino: Treasures from the Smithsonian American Art Museum* (New York: Watson-Guptill Publications, 2001).

Young, Robert J. C., *Postcolonialism* (New York: Oxford University Press, 2003).

Index

1 Clement, 119
1 Corinthians, 73, 75, 115
2 Corinthians, 75

Abelard, Peter, 89, 136
Acts of the Apostles, church in,
   116–17, 118
Aeterni patris (Leo XIII), 125–26
African American culture, 11–14
After Virtue (MacIntyre), 113–14
Alberigo, Giuseppe, 60, 200
Albert the Great, 90
Ambrose, 87, 88
Analects (Confucius), 52
Anscombe, Elizabeth, 113
Antoninus of Florence, 94
Apostolic Tradition, 119–20, 168, 174
Aquinas, Thomas, 90–93, 122,
   125–26, 136
Arbuckle, Gerald, 6, 33
Aristotle, 18, 73, 90, 113
Arrupe, Pedro, 42
Artaud, Antonin, 29
Asian American culture, 15–16
asylum seekers, 47
atheism, 26–27
Augustine, 19, 86, 87, 88, 120, 136,
   171
authority, church: in Gospels, 117–18;
   as hierarchy, 20–21, 60–61,
   134–35, 136; and liturgy, 152–53;
   in Middle Ages, 121–22; in modern
   period, 123–24, 125–26; in patristic
   period, 118–20; in Pauline writings,
   115–16; Vatican II on, 133–35
Azor, Juan, 96–97

Bañez, Dominic, 92
baptism, 168–74; and confirmation,
   169–70, 174–75; Paul on, 74–75,
   168, 183; virtues and, 173–74

Basil the Great, 85
Bataille, Georges, 30
beatitudes, 77–78, 79–80
Beauduin, Lambert, 108
Bede the Venerable, 88
Beguines, 127
Bell, Catherine, 7
Bellarmine, Robert, 123
Benedict XVI, 5, 31, 41, 42–43, 50,
   60, 61, 147, 195–96
Bernard of Clairvaux, 19, 21–22, 88
Bible and Morality, The (Pontifical
   Biblical Commission), 63–66
Biel, Gabriel, 93
Billuart, Charles, 92
bishops: conferences of, 145; develop-
   ment of, 118, 119–20; and papacy,
   21, 25–26, 123, 125, 132–33,
   146–47; synod of, 146; virtuous,
   142–44
body of Christ: church as, 76, 115,
   124, 125, 126, 183
Bonaventure, 92, 122, 127, 136
Brigit of Kildare, 10
Brueggemann, Walter, 70, 181, 197
Buber, Martin, 136
Buddhism, 16, 53–54
Burchard of Worms, 89

Cajetan, 91
Calvin, John, 95, 98–99
Cano, Melchior, 91
canon law, 87–88, 89, 105, 121; dio-
   cese in, 143–44; episcopal confer-
   ences in, 145; parish in, 140–41.
   See also Code of Canon Law
Capreolus, John, 91
Caritas in veritate (Benedict XVI), 42–43
Catholic Church: on ecology, 50–51;
   on globalization, 41–44; sexual
   abuse in, 59–60, 145, 147

charity, 166–67; Aquinas on, 91; Gilleman on, 106–7; Paul on, 75–76
Chenu, Marie-Dominique, 126, 131
China, Christianity in, 58–59
Christianity: and classical culture, 16–22; and global South, 56–59; Pentecostal, 58–59; and primal culture, 10–11
Christology, 153–57. *See also* Jesus
Chupungco, Ansgar, 8
church: as body of Christ, 76, 115, 124, 125, 126, 183; as diocese, 142–44; and episcopal conferences, 145; in Gospels, 116–18; and hierarchy, 20–21, 60–61, 134–35, 136, 183; in modern period, 123–26; in New Testament, 114–18; as parish, 138–42; in patristic period, 118–20; and religious institutes, 126–31; triumphalism in, 147–48, 184–86; Tübingen School on, 124–25; as universal, 145–48; Vatican II on, 131–35, 183, 186–89; virtuous, 138–50
classical culture, 16–22
Clement of Alexandria, 86
Clement of Rome, 119
clergy, and lay people, 20, 106, 120, 134, 183–84. *See also* bishops; presbyters; priesthood
clericalism, 184
Cluny, Abbey of, 121
Code of Canon Law (1917), 102–3, 104, 129–30, 175, 186–87
Code of Canon Law (1983), 130, 134, 176, 187, 189, 193; diocese in, 143–44; episcopal conferences in, 145; parish in, 140–41
Coleman, John A., 41–43
collegiality, 60–61
Colossians, 115
Comme le prévoit, 194
common good, 41
Complexity and Contradiction in Architecture (Venturi), 28
conciliarism, 122

confession. *See* reconciliation
confirmation, 174–77; and baptism, 169–70, 174–75
Confucianism, 52–53
Congar, Yves, 21, 109, 124, 126, 131, 132
Constitution on the Sacred Liturgy (Vatican II), 5, 133, 134, 152, 153, 175, 189, 191
courage, 174
covenant, 68–69, 73, 187
creation, 66–67
culture: African American, 11–14; Asian American, 15–16; classical, 16–22; definitions of, 5–9; and globalization, 6, 37–38; Hispanic American, 14–15; modern, 22–26; postmodern, 26–33; primal, 9–16

Darwin, Charles, 24
Daughters of Charity, 129
Davis, Henry, 102–3
Dawson, Christopher, 8–9
death, 161–62, 191–93
Decalogue, 64, 69–70, 96
Decree on Ecumenism (Vatican II), 132, 136
Decree on the Ministry and Life of Priests (Vatican II), 183, 184, 188
Decree on Priestly Training (Vatican II), 111, 114
Decretum (Gratian), 89, 121
de Lubac, Henri, 105, 126, 131, 132, 157–58, 171
Derrida, Jacques, 30
de Saint-Cyran, Abbé, 97
de Sales, Francis, 94, 101
Deus caritas est (Benedict XVI), 41
de Vitoria, Francisco, 91, 93
dialogue, 136–38; in parish, 140–41
Didache, 86, 118–19
diocese, virtuous, 142–44
Dionysius the Areopagite, 87
Divino afflante Spiritu (Pius XII), 109, 126
Dogmatic Constitution on the Church (Vatican II), 132–34, 183, 188–89

Dominicans, 90–92, 121, 127
Drey, Johann Sebastian, 124
Dumm, Demetrius, 68
Duns Scotus, 92

Eastern Catholic Churches, 26. *See also* Catholic Church
ecclesiology, 124–25; and Christology, 153–57; juridical, 152–53; Tübingen School on, 124–25. *See also* church
ecology, 48–51; Catholic Church on, 50–51; and globalization, 48–49
Enlightenment, 23–24
Ephesians, 115, 187
episcopal conferences, 145
episcopate. *See* bishops
Erasmus, 97
ethics, definition of, 98. *See also* morality; moral theology
Eucharist, 177–82; and virtue, 180–82
Evangelium vitae (John Paul II), 43
Exodus, 67–69

faith: Aquinas on, 91; Paul on, 74–76; Protestant Reformers on, 98–100
Faustus of Riez, 175
Febronianism, 124
fidelity, 173, 188
Fletcher, Joseph, 110
Focolare, 130
Foot, Philippa, 113
Franciscans, 92, 121, 122, 127
Francis of Assisi, 22, 50, 127
Freire, Paulo, 136–37

Galilei, Galileo, 22
Gallicanism, 123–24
Gaudium et spes. See *Pastoral Constitution on the Church in the Modern World*
Gautama, 53–54
Gehry, Frank, 28
Genesis, 66–67
Geertz, Clifford, 6
Gilleman, Gérard, 106–7

globalization, 35–44; Catholic Church on, 41–44; and culture, 6, 37–38; and ecology, 48–49; and migration, 36, 45
Globalization and Catholic Social Thought (Coleman), 41–43
global South, Christianity and, 56–57
God: in Exodus, 68–69; in Genesis, 66–67; grace of, 157–60; in Luke, 79–80; in Matthew, 78
grace, 157–60
Gratian, 89, 121
Gregory the Great, 88, 120
Gregory VII, 21, 121
Grenz, Stanley, 29
Guadalupe, Our Lady of, 10–11
Gutiérrez, Gustavo, 42

Habermas, Jürgen, 31
Hales, Alexander, 92
Häring, Bernard, 107–8, 114
Hauerwas, Stanley, 30
hierarchy, ecclesial, 20–21, 60–61, 134–35, 136, 183
Hinduism, 53
Hirscher, John Baptist, 101–2
Hispanic American culture, 14–15
Holy Spirit, 158–60; Paul on, 75, 158–59; in Western theology, 97
hope, 79; Aquinas on, 91
hospitality: and Hispanic American culture, 14; and parish, 139–40
Humanae vitae (Paul VI), 111
human being, as image of God, 66
humanism, 100
human rights, 41
human trafficking, 43
humility, 106, 186, 190
Hus, Jan, 122
hybridity, 6, 37

I and Thou (Buber), 136
Ignatius of Antioch, 88, 119, 182
Ignatius of Loyola, 123, 128
Imitation of Christ (à Kempis), 94
immigration. *See* migration

initiation, Christian, 168–77. *See also* baptism; confirmation
Innocent III, 92, 121
Introduction to the Devout Life (de Sales), 94
Irenaeus of Lyons, 119, 180
Islam, 40, 54–56

Jansenism, 97, 100–101
Jenkins, Philip, 56
Jesuits. *See* Society of Jesus
Jesus, 153–57; Holy Spirit and, 157–59; paschal mystery of, 165–67. *See also* Christology
jihadist globalism, 40
Job, Book of, 71
Johannine writings, 81–83
John, Gospel of: church in, 117; morality in, 81–82
John XIII, 148
John XXIII, 60, 131, 199, 200
John Chrysostom, 85–86
John Damascene, 90
John Paul II, 1, 41, 43, 50, 145
Jone, Heribert, 102, 103
Josephinism, 123, 124
justice, 42, 149, 173. *See also* social justice
justice globalism, 38–40
justification, 98–100
Justin Martyr, 119, 136

Kavanagh, Aidan, 171
Keesing, Roger, 6
Kierkegaard, Søren, 24, 109
Kilmartin, Edward, 178
kinship, 13

Laborem exercens (John Paul II), 41
Lacan, Jacques, 30
laity: and clergy, 20, 106, 120, 134, 183–84; and ministry, 141–42, 186
lament, liturgy and, 195–98
Lateran Council IV, 89
law: canon, 87–88, 89, 105, 121; Mosaic, 64, 69–70, 72–73, 96; natural,

99–100; Roman, 73–74, 87; and Sermon on the Mount, 77–78
Law of Christ, The (Häring), 107–8
Leo IX, 121
Leo XIII, 25, 125–26
Liguori, Alphonsus, 101
listening, 150. *See also* dialogue
Liturgiam authenticam, 194
liturgy, 167–98; and Christology, 153–57; in classical culture, 18; and ecclesial authority, 152–53; and lament, 195–98; moral theology and, 108; translation of, 193–95. *See also* sacraments
Lombard, Peter, 89, 92
Lonergan, Bernard, 5, 109–10
longsuffering, 149–50
Lottin, Odo, 105
love. *See* charity
Luke, Gospel of: church in, 116–17; Sermon on the Mount in, 79–81. *See also* Acts of the Apostles
Lumen gentium. See *Dogmatic Constitution on the Church*
Luther, Martin, 22, 93, 95, 98–99, 122, 182–83
Lyotard, Jean-François, 28, 30

MacIntyre, Alasdair, 30, 113–14
Mahoney, Jack, 161–62
Manual of Moral Theology (Slater), 102
Marchetto, Agostino, 60
Marcuse, Herbert, 24
Mark, Gospel of, church in, 116
marriage, sacrament of, 186–88; virtues of, 188
Mary, in Hispanic American culture, 14–15
Matthew, Gospel of: church in, 116; Sermon on the Mount in, 77–79, 116
Maximus the Confessor, 89–90
McIntyre, John, 154
mercy, 78–79, 80
Merici, Angela, 128

Merleau-Ponty, Maurice, 7
Mersch, Émile, 107
Middle Ages: church in, 120–22;
 moral theology in, 88–93
migration, 6, 44–48; and globalization, 36, 45; and human trafficking,
 45–46
ministry, pastoral: lay people and,
 141–42, 186; in New Testament,
 115–16, 17–18; in parish, 141–42;
 and theology, 94–95; Trent and, 95,
 122–23, 183; and virtue, 181–82.
 See also authority
modern culture, 22–26; church in,
 122–26; and moral theology,
 93–101
Möhler, Johann Adam, 124–25, 126
monasticism: Asian, 16, 54; Buddhist,
 54; Christian, 120, 121; in classical
 culture, 18
Moral and Pastoral Theology (Davis),
 102–3
morality: biblical, 63–83; in Exodus,
 67–69; in Genesis, 66–67; Greek,
 73–74; in Johannine writings,
 81–83; in Pauline writings, 72–76;
 prophets and, 70; Roman, 73–74;
 Sermon on the Mount and, 64,
 76–81; in Ten Commandments, 64,
 69–70, 96; Wisdom literature and,
 71
moral theology: history of, 85–111;
 in Middle Ages, 88–93; in modern
 period, 93–101; in patristic period,
 85–88; Tübingen School and,
 101–2; twentieth-century, 104–11;
 and virtues, 75–76, 91, 96, 99, 105,
 106
Moral Theology (Jone), 102, 103
Muhammad, 54–55
multiculturalism, 31
Mystical Body, church as, 124, 125,
 126
Mystici corporis (Pius XII), 124, 125,
 126, 134
myth, 6–7

natural law, 99–100
Neoplatonism, 87
Neoscholasticism, 125–26
Newman, John Henry, 125
new religious movements, 130,
 138–39
New Testament: church in, 114–18;
 morality and, 71–83; priesthood in,
 182, 183
nominalism, 22, 92–93, 94

obedience, 162–63
Old Testament: morality and, 66–71;
 priesthood in, 182
Optatam totius. See *Decree on Priestly
 Training*
Origen, 86, 119–20, 136

papacy: and bishops, 21, 25–26,
 60–61, 123, 125, 132–33, 146–47;
 development of, 20–21, 25–26,
 120–22, 123–24, 125, 132–33;
 virtuous, 145–48
parish, virtuous, 138–42
paschal mystery, 160–67, 178, 179
Pastoral Care of the Sick, 191–93
*Pastoral Constitution on the Church in
 the Modern World* (Vatican II), 5,
 148, 186–87
pastoral ministry. See ministry
patristic period: church in, 118–20;
 moral theology in, 85–88; virtues
 in, 86
Pauline writings, 72–76; church in,
 114–16, 183; faith in, 74–76; Holy
 Spirit in, 75, 158–59; virtues in,
 75–76
Paul VI, 41, 60, 111, 146
penance, sacrament of. See reconciliation
penitential manuals, 89
Pentecostalism, 58–59
Peter Lombard. See Lombard
Philippians, 75
philosophy, Greek, 73–74, 87, 113
Pius XI, 25

Pius XII, 109, 124, 125, 126, 130, 134
Plato, 73, 113, 136
Pontifical Biblical Commission, 63–66
poor, preferential option for the, 42,
    79–80
popes. *See* papacy
Populorum progressio (Paul VI), 41
postmodern culture, 26–33
preferential option for the poor, 42,
    79–80
Presbyterorum ordinis. See *Decree on
    the Ministry and Life of Priests*
presbyters, development of, 118, 119–
    20, 123, 182. *See also* priesthood
priesthood, sacrament of, 182–86; vir-
    tues of, 186. *See also* presbyters
primal culture, 9–16; and religion,
    10–11
probabilism, 97, 100–101, 103
prophets, 70
Protestant Reformation, 22, 23,
    98–100; church in, 122–23; and
    sin, 95
Proverbs, Book of, 71
prudence, 149, 173
Psychologie et morale (Lottin), 105

Rabanus Maurus, 88
Rahner, Karl, 105, 109, 126, 155, 158
Raymond of Peñafort, 89
reconciliation, 79
reconciliation, sacrament of, 89, 97,
    188–90
refugees, 46–47
religion: and African American
    culture, 12–13; and Asian Ameri-
    can culture, 15–16; and classical
    culture, 16–18; and culture, 8; and
    Hispanic American culture, 14–15;
    and postmodern culture, 31; and
    primal culture, 10–11; virtue of,
    108, 160–61; world, 51–56
religious institutes, 126–31, 135
resurrection, 164–65
Ricoeur, Paul, 31

Rite of Christian Initiation for Adults,
    170–71, 172, 176
Roman law, 73–74, 87
Romans, Letter to the, 73, 75, 115
rubrics, 152–53
Rumi, Julaladdin, 40

sacraments, 167–93; and Vatican
    II, 170, 175, 183, 184, 186–87,
    188–89, 191; and virtue, 173–74,
    180–82, 186, 188. *See also* liturgy
sacrifice, 177–78
Sacrosanctum concilium. See *Consti-
    tution on the Sacred Liturgy*
Sailer, John Michael, 101–2
Scheeben, Matthias, 126
Schillebeeckx, Edward, 109, 126
Scholasticism, 18, 19–20, 90–93
scientific culture, 22–26
scientific revolution, 23–24
self-esteem, 173
Sentences (Lombard), 89, 92
Sermon on the Mount, 64, 76–81; in
    Matthew, 77–79, 116
sexual abuse of minors, in Catholic
    Church, 59–60, 145, 147
Sheldrake, Philip, 32–33
Shinto, 16
sin, 163–64; and baptism, 171–72;
    Franciscans on, 92; penitentials
    and, 89; Protestant Reformation
    and, 95; and sacrament of reconcili-
    ation, 189–90
Slater, Thomas, 102
social justice, 58. *See also* justice
Society of Jesus, 95–96, 100, 123, 128
solidarity, 41
Sollicitudo rei socialis (John Paul II),
    41
spirituality, theology and, 93–94, 96
Steger, Manfred, 36
stewardship, 50
Stoicism, 73
Suárez, Francisco, 97
subsidiarity, 42, 60

Sufism, 40, 55–56
Summa theologiae (Antoninus), 94
Summa theologiae (Aquinas), 90–91, 93
synod of bishops, 146

Tanner, Kathryn, 6
temperance, 173–74
Ten Commandments, 64, 69–70, 96
Tertullian, 86, 119–20, 174
thankgiving, 150, 180
Theologia moralis (Liguori), 101
theological virtues, 75–76, 91, 99, 105, 106, 137–38
theology: and ministry, 94–95; professionalization of, 94–95; Scholastic, 18, 19–20, 90–93; and spirituality, 93–94, 96; and universities, 19
Theology of Liberation, A (Gutiérrez), 42
Thomas à Kempis, 94
Thomas Aquinas. *See* Aquinas
Tillman, Fritz, 106
Toynbee, Arnold, 27
trafficking, human, 43
translation, and liturgy, 193–95
Trent, Council of: and church, 122–23; and liturgy, 21; and ministry, 95, 122–23, 183
Trinitarian theology, 156–57, 158
triumphalism, 147–48, 184–86
Tübingen School: and ecclesiology, 124–25; and moral theology, 101–2

Ultramontanism, 124, 125, 147
Unitatis redintegratio. See *Decree on Ecumenism*
universal church, virtuous, 145–48
university, development of, 18–19
Ursulines, 128

Vatican Council I, 124, 125
Vatican Council II: on church, 131–35, 183, 186–89; interpretation of, 60, 200; and moral theology, 111; and

sacraments, 170, 175, 183, 184, 186–87, 188–89, 191; *Constitution on the Sacred Liturgy*, 5, 133, 134, 152, 153, 175, 189, 191; *Decree on Ecumenism*, 132, 136; *Decree on the Ministry and Life of Priests*, 183, 184, 188; *Decree on Priestly Training*, 111, 114; *Dogmatic Constitution on the Church*, 132–34, 183, 188–89; *Pastoral Constitution on the Church in the Modern World*, 5, 148, 186–87
Vazquez, Gabriel, 97
Venturi, Robert, 28
virtue: Aquinas on, 91; Azor on, 96; and baptism, 173–74; church and, 138–50; diocese and, 142–44; ethics, 113–14; and Eucharist, 180–82; Lottin on, 105; and marriage, 188; natural, 75–76, 99; papacy and, 145–48; parish and, 138–42; in patristic thought, 86; Paul on, 75–76; of priesthood, 186; Protestant Reformers on, 99; and sacraments, 173–74, 180–82, 186, 188; theological, 75–76, 91, 99, 105, 106, 137–38; Tillman on, 106; and universal church, 145–48

Ward, Mary, 128–29
White, Lynn, 50
William of Ockham, 92–93
Wisdom literature, 71
women: in Asian American culture, 15–16
world religions, 51–56
Wycliffe, John, 122